A New Megasport Legacy

A New Megasport Legacy

Host-Country Human Rights and Anti-Corruption Reforms

ANDREW BRADY SPALDING

OXFORD
UNIVERSITY PRESS

OXFORD
UNIVERSITY PRESS

Oxford University Press is a department of the University of Oxford. It furthers the University's objective of excellence in research, scholarship, and education by publishing worldwide. Oxford is a registered trade mark of Oxford University Press in the UK and certain other countries.

Published in the United States of America by Oxford University Press
198 Madison Avenue, New York, NY 10016, United States of America.

Library of Congress Control Number: 2021054388
ISBN 978–0–19–750361–4

DOI: 10.1093/oso/9780197503614.001.0001

1 3 5 7 9 8 6 4 2

Printed by Integrated Books International, United States of America

Note to Readers

This publication is designed to provide accurate and authoritative information in regard to the subject matter covered. It is based upon sources believed to be accurate and reliable and is intended to be current as of the time it was written. It is sold with the understanding that the publisher is not engaged in rendering legal, accounting, or other professional services. If legal advice or other expert assistance is required, the services of a competent professional person should be sought. Also, to confirm that the information has not been affected or changed by recent developments, traditional legal research techniques should be used, including checking primary sources where appropriate.

(Based on the Declaration of Principles jointly adopted by a Committee of the American Bar Association and a Committee of Publishers and Associations.)

Contents

Preface vii
List of Abbreviations xi

PART I: ORIGINS OF THE NEW LEGACY

1. The Founding through Globalization 3
2. Globalized Standards 43

PART II: EARLY INTIMATIONS

3. An Awakening: Brazil 85
4. A Pattern Emerges: South Korea 119

PART III: APPROACHING A MODEL

5. The First Intentional Legacy: Qatar 167
6. A Latent Legacy: France 229
7. Future Legacy Opportunities 249

PART IV: BUILDING A FRAMEWORK

8. The Legal Foundation 271
9. From Reforms To Legacies 315
10. A How-To Guide 331

Index 343

Preface

Reims, France, June 2019. I am on sabbatical with my wife and three young daughters, passing through this city to catch the first 2019 FIFA Women's World Cup game of the US Women's National Team (USWNT). While on a pre-game stroll through the historic downtown, we spy a small crowd gathered outside a hotel. The USWNT's team bus is parked in front. Making the connection, we join the crowd and wait for what seems like hours. And then they come. One by one these women process, bearing themselves with the dignity of gods. They wear headphones and game faces. They are dialed in. They look different, their walk is different, as is often true of elite athletes. Overhead a helicopter hovers, waiting to escort the bus to the stadium. In the crowd are dozens of young kids, girls and boys, their eyes aglow with reverence. Alongside them stand their parents, for whose generation female soccer role models of this stature were quite rare. Norms, dreams, and institutions, indeed the character or even souls of these young soccer fans, are changing in real time. It is plain for anyone to see.

Weeks later I sit with my daughter at a Paris pub. Brazil's national women's team is playing on TV, featuring Marta, the greatest female player of all time. I start up a conversation with a lonely, middle-aged, unshaven patron. As the camera zooms in on Marta, I ask, "Do you know that player?" "I don't think so," he replies. I then ask, "Do you know Pelé?" He exclaims, "Of course! The king!" I answer, "Well, Marta is the Pelé of women's football." His aspect visibly changes, as if his mind had suddenly realized something new, and important. With light in his eyes and gravitas in his voice he says, "Ah. The queen." Again, norms are changing, in real time.

Yet a couple weeks later we're in Lyon for the finals, which the USWNT would win. The stadium erupts with fireworks and cheers. FIFA President Gianni Infantino walks onto the field for the trophy ceremony, and the crowd—including this author—spontaneously begins to chant in unison, "Equal pay! Equal pay!" As this book goes to press, these norms too are changing.

This book is about the social impact of megasports. We've seen the capacity of megasports to stretch our thinking since at least Jesse Owens' tacit repudiation of Aryan supremacy at the 1936 Berlin Olympics. But something new is happening. The long latent power of megasports to positively shape our values and our practices is now being harnessed with an intentionality and impact unseen in history. It's worth studying, and it's worth supporting. Or so I now argue.

For this author, far more impactful than megasports themselves has been the study thereof. Whether as an academic, or a player, or a coach, sports are essentially about people, about relationships. I could not have written this book with a great many of them, and the list of persons to whom I owe debts of gratitude is far too long to mention. But I'll try.

First and foremost are the students in successive iterations of my research seminar on megasports, corruption, and human rights at the University of Richmond School of Law in Virginia. Through the extraordinary support of my dean, Wendy Perdue, the law school enabled eight students to spend a year conducting research on the anti-corruption and human rights reforms of a particular host country and take research trips to the host country: Brazil in 2014–2015; South Korea in 2016–2017; France in 2018–2019; and the COVID-grounded 2020–2021 group. These students helped me research issues, interview stakeholders, and brainstorm the ideas that became this book. Numerous research assistants helped along the way. This book would not exist without them.

Second are my colleagues at the University of Richmond School of Law, particularly Dean Perdue, Associate Deans Jessica Erickson and Jim Gibson, and countless others who, in workshops, hallway conversations, and one particular brainstorming session at the whiteboard in my office, helped me craft promising but ill-formed ideas into the present book. So too have I known the great privilege of working with numerous academics, advocates, and practitioners of good faith and expansive intellect, particularly the members of the Olympics Compliance Task Force. The book does not exist without them either.

I will further thank the Olympic Studies Centre at the International Olympic Committee (IOC) for a research grant that enabled empirical research and, even more importantly, several in-person group sessions with IOC personnel where so many of these ideas were refined. Also overseas, countless stakeholders across Brazil, South Korea, France, Qatar, Australia, New Zealand, Switzerland, and beyond made themselves available for interviews. Individuals at the IOC and at FIFA, particularly FIFA's Head of Human Rights and Anti-Discrimination Andreas Graf, over and over proved to me their genuine goodwill, intellectual openness, and a natural receptivity to practical reforms when not presented in a shroud of hyperbolic accusations and bitter cynicism.

And finally, gratitude does not begin to capture my feelings toward my wife, Bethany, who has always seen in me more than I see in myself, and my daughters, Simone, Phoebe, and Bronte, who daily draw it out of me.

The thesis of this book may seem crazy. I would not fault the reader for thinking so. But hear me out. This space is changing.

List of Abbreviations

ACRC	Anti-Corruption and Civil Rights Commission
AFA	Agence Française Anticorruption
APEC	Anti-Corruption Code of Conduct for Business
BMW	Bayerische Motoren Werke
BRIC	Brazil, Russia, India, and China
BWI	Building and Wood Workers International
CAF	Confederation Africaine de Football
CCA	Clean Companies Act
CEO	Chief Executive Officer
COSO	Committee of Sponsoring Organization of the Treadway Commission
CSR	Corporate Social Responsibility
DOJ	Department of Justice
FBPA	The Act on Preventing Bribery of Foreign Public Officials in International Business Transactions
FCPA	Foreign Corrupt Practices Act
FIFA	Fédération Internationale de Football Association
FOI	Freedom of Information
FPRW	International Labour Organization's Declaration on Fundamental Principles and Rights at Work
G8	Group of Eight
G20	Group of Twenty
GDP	Gross Domestic Product
GEMS	Global Education Management Systems
GET	Greco Evaluation Team
GRECO	Europe's Group of States Against Corruption
HRC	Human Rights Council
ICC	International Chamber of Commerce
ICCPR	International Covenant on Civil and Political Rights
ICECSR	International Covenant on Economic, Social and Cultural Rights
ILO	International Labour Organization
IOC	International Olympic Committee
ISO	International Organization for Standardization
ITUC	International Trade Union Confederation
JTBC	Joongang Tongyang Broadcasting Company
KOC	Korean Sport & Olympic Committee
KRW	Korean Won

LG	Lucky GoldStar
LGBT	Lesbian, Gay, Bisexual, and Transgender
LOC	Local Organizing Committee
MNC	Multinational Corporation
MSE	Mega Sporting Event
NATO	North Atlantic Treaty Organization
NCP	National Contact Point
NGO	Nongovernmental Organization
NTR	Non-trial Resolution
O&M	Operations and Maintenance
OCOG	Organizing Committee for the Olympic Games
OECD	Organisation for Economic Co-operation and Development
OSP	Offshore Procurement
PACI	World Economic Forum Partnering Against Corruption Initiative
POCOG	Pyeongchang Organizing Committee
QEC	Qatari Education City
QNV	Qatar National Vision
RDC	Regime Diferenciado de Contratações
ROTC	Republic of Total Corruption
SBM	Sustainable Business Management
SC	Supreme Committee for Delivery and Legacy
SHI	Samsung Heavy Industries
SOE	State-owned Enterprise
SRSG	UN Special Representative of the Secretary-General
TI	Transparency International
UNCAC	United Nations Convention Against Corruption
UNESCO	United Nations, Educational, Scientific and Cultural Organization
UNGPs	United Nations Guiding Principles on Business and Human Rights
USAID	United States Agency for International Development
USWNT	US Women's National Team
WC	World Cup
WTO	World Trade Organization
WWF	Workers' Welfare Forum
WWO	Workers' Welfare Officer
WWS	Workers Welfare Standards

PART I

ORIGINS OF THE NEW LEGACY

1

The Founding through Globalization

Introduction

The Olympic Games and FIFA Men's World Cup are widely regarded as a quagmire of corruption and human rights problems, and for good reason. Corporations and governments defraud taxpayers with inflated construction costs. Top-rank officials peddle their influence in exchange for corporate support of pet projects. The poor are evicted from their homes, without due process, to make way for infrastructure projects of dubious long-term value. Migrant workers labor in conditions that deprive them of their freedom of movement, their safety, and at worst, their lives. And to conceal it all, governments suppress freedom of speech and of the press. The myriad ways that megasports induce corruption and human rights violations are well-documented and undeniable.

For these reasons the International Olympic Committee (IOC) candidly acknowledged that "the perception of the legacy of the Olympic Games remains challenging."[1] Truer words were never spoken. Exhibit A in support of this statement has been the declining number of countries—particularly democratic countries—interested in hosting the Games.

But crisis creates opportunity. Another dynamic is now emerging, an interaction between megasports and their host countries that is as counterintuitive as it is unknown. Mega sporting events (MSEs) are accelerating the adoption of anti-corruption and human rights norms, practices, policies, and even laws in the host countries. These reforms are not limited in scope to the preparations for or the hosting of the event; they extend well beyond the events themselves, embedded in broader public- and private-sector governance in ways that seem likely to remain for years after the games are done.

Modern megasports are presenting a paradox, one that would seem impossible or even ridiculous were it not grounded in fact. The Olympics and the FIFA World Cup, while undeniably fraught with egregious corruption and human rights violations, are at the same time becoming a catalyst to host-country corruption and human rights reforms. The first half of this

A New Megasport Legacy. Andrew Brady Spalding, Oxford University Press. © Oxford University Press 2022.
DOI: 10.1093/oso/9780197503614.003.0001

paradox is widely known; the second is the subject of this book. The Olympic Games and the FIFA World Cup are beginning to generate what this book calls a human rights and anti-corruption legacy: a series of norms, policies, practices, and laws, promoting transparency, accountability, and human rights, that have effect beyond the sporting events themselves, are likely to remain in place after the event is over, and the implementation of which is accelerated by hosting the event.

No nation or person—and certainly not this author—can claim to have invented this new legacy. The concept that megasports can leave a legacy of lasting host-country anti-corruption and human rights reforms is less invented here than it is discovered. This legacy emerges organically and gradually, through a series of historical developments in geopolitics, in international law, and in megasport governance. It arises naturally from the conditions of modern megasports and the historical currents that precede it. This book identifies a pattern and names it; traces its origins and projects its future; and suggests reforms that might expand, support, and direct it.

We should remember that megasport governance problems are not new; they are as old as the Olympics themselves. Reports of Olympic bribery date back to the fourth and fifth centuries BC and continue to this day. What's new is our ability, and resolve, to investigate, prosecute, and deter this behavior. The decades following World War II saw the steady rise in global standards: new human rights and anti-corruption norms, increasingly embraced on a global scale, with application to both the public and private sectors. These new norms were not uncontested, and are not now; neither are they without cultural variants. Nonetheless, core principles emerged that increasingly commanded universal assent to a degree unique in history. On the human rights side, beginning in the 1960s, two foundational covenants would be adopted and then eventually ratified or signed by an overwhelming majority of the world's nations. Then, just two decades later, the 1990s gave rise to the "Corruption Eruption"—a new global consensus that corruption is bad, and even more, that it can and should be changed through legal reform. Academic studies on the causes and forms of corruption proliferated; diplomats negotiated landmark international instruments; policymakers enacted and prosecutors enforced important new laws; and citizens spoke out.

These new norms are manifest in megasports in a way no one expected and few are noticing. For example, ask any anti-corruption expert to list the major economies that, in the last decade or so, have implemented the most meaningful anti-corruption reforms and enforcement initiatives. Four of them would likely be Brazil, South Korea, China, and France. Each has seen a recent groundswell of public discontent with endemic corruption. Each responded with major statutes that give enforcement agencies new tools to curb the problem. Enforcement agencies then used these tools to win high-profile prosecutions of corporate leaders, government officials, and even past or current presidents. To the casual onlooker these events may seem evidence of a state in decline. But whatever temporary political instability they may cause, these enforcement actions are achievements for the long-term rule of law. By this standard, Brazil, South Korea, China, and France are global leaders in adopting effective governance reform. And notice the pattern: Brazil, South Korea, China, and France are also hosts, respectively, of the 2016, 2018, 2022, and 2024 Olympic Games. We appear to be witnessing a historical moment, not yet recognized, in which hosting megasports often coincides with remarkable and momentous host-country governance reform.

An even deeper irony lies in Qatar. As a case study, this country's experience is perhaps the most surprising and certainly the most instructive. Its shocking success in winning the hosting rights to the 2022 FIFA World Cup immediately gave rise to bribery suspicions, but this did not turn out to be Qatar's biggest social problem. Corruption allegations were soon dwarfed by reports of egregious labor abuses. In a country where 95 percent of its workforce are migrants, reports surfaced of recruitment with false promises about levels of pay and the nature of the work. Once in Qatar, employers would confiscate the workers' passports, effectively reducing them to forced labor. Accommodations were filthy and cramped, and workers endured life-threatening heat and humidity without work breaks. These abuses remain salient in the consciousness of sports commentators and casual fans, as well they should.

Though Qatar is for the moment perhaps the most salient example of governance abuses in megasport, it may be for that same reason the most underappreciated legacy. Few realize under criticism from civil society, the global media, and the United Nations, Qatar agreed to cooperate with the International Labour Organization (ILO) to design and institute a number of significant labor reforms. Qatar adopted a minimum wage. It agreed to the monitoring of its labor conditions by independent experts. It agreed to reform the employer sponsorship system, known as the *kafala*, which was the source of many employer abuses. Ironic as it is, Qatar is poised to emerge from the 2022 FIFA World Cup with a vastly improved human rights regime firmly in place. And unlike Brazil or South Korea, where megasports were only one of many causal factors, hosting an MSE may deserve the largest share of credit for catalyzing Qatar's reforms. In Qatar, we see lasting and positive changes to the laws, practices, and cultural norms surrounding labor rights as a direct result of hosting an MSE. Put another way, we see a megasport human rights legacy.

This emergent legacy is driven in large part by a worldwide crescendo of criticism focusing on megasport human rights and anti-corruption abuses. It may at first appear that we do not, and could not, believe megasports can comply with anti-corruption and human rights norms. The opposite may be true. When we express outrage, we tacitly express an underlying ideal: megasports ought not to violate human rights or induce corruption. The outrage is itself evidence that we still believe at least the normative dimension: megasports ought to be better. As advocates and scholars we all wish, and some still hope, that megasports can affirm these deeper values.

This book argues that megasports can and indeed do now go further. MSEs are doing more than merely avoiding violations of modern anti-corruption and human rights norms and laws. They are accelerating the implementation of those norms and laws in the countries where the events take place. This has already begun to happen, and with foresight and thoughtfulness MSEs can do an even better job of catalyzing enduring reform. This book's argument is thus both descriptive and normative. It identifies the dynamic that has occurred and is now occurring in countries as diverse as Brazil, South Korea, Qatar, and France. So too does it offer suggestions on how this dynamic can inure to even greater host-country benefit.

A Founding Idea, Frustrated by History

Though human rights and anti-corruption legacy is new, it has not emerged out of nowhere, suddenly springing from thin air. Quite the contrary: it is the natural outgrowth of a series of ideas and historical forces that have impacted megasports since their revival in the late nineteenth century. The trajectory is of course not without outliers: China's hosting of the 2022 Beijing Winter Olympics is fraught with human rights controversies and as of press time shows little promise of reform. Still, look closely and a rough trajectory appears, originating at least in the late nineteenth century. This section describes the founding ideals of megasports and how global political and economic forces during the world wars and the Cold War largely frustrated their realization. The emerging human rights and anti-corruption legacy may provide a window for redeeming those seemingly distant ideals.

A commitment to promoting broader social goals through sport may be traceable to the ancient origins of megasports. The original Olympic Games began in 708 BC as part of a religious festival for the Greek god, Zeus Olympios. By one account, offered by the Director of the International Olympic Truce Centre at the 2002 IOC Legacy Convention, the Games were conceived expressly as an antidote to the otherwise chronic warring among Greek city-states. One of these state's kings asked the Oracle of Delphi for advice on ending the cycle of violence. The Oracle advised the king to organize an athletic and cultural festival to occur in the summer of every fourth year, during which all participating states should declare a truce. An existing peace treaty was in fact expanded to apply to the three-month period in which the Games were held, at least to allow visitors to travel to and from the event. During this period, no military action was allowed in and around Olympia, and legal disputes and executions were suspended.[2] The Games continued for one thousand years until, in 294 AD, the newly Christianized Roman Empire disbanded the Games as pagan rituals.[3]

After a gap of nearly fifteen hundred years, in the mid-nineteenth century, diverse movements to resurrect the Olympics appeared. In Sweden, the Jeux Olimpiques Scandinaves occurred in 1834 and 1836; in England, multiple minor Olympic Games were staged in the mid-nineteenth century; the "Montreal Olympic Games" took place in 1844; in Germany, in 1852, the call was made to excavate the original site of the ancient Greek games (which the Germans took up in 1875); and the Greeks sought to revive the Games and staged minor events between 1859 and 1889.[4]

The idea of an international sporting event would not gain momentum until seized by the French nobleman Pierre de Fredy, Baron de Coubertin. Biographers trace Courbertin's motivation to revive the Olympic Games to a formative event of his youth. In 1870, as a very young boy, he was traumatized by his country's defeat at the hands of the Prussians and the loss of the Alsace and Lorraine provinces.[5] This event seems to have affected Coubertin in at least two ways. First, he attributed these defeats to the physical inferiority of the French youth, and as an adult went about looking for ways to cultivate physical development in the youth. He first turned to the German educational system, which included a component of strenuous physical exercise unknown in the French system. So too did he study, and admire, the emerging love of sport among the English. And in a visit to the United States, he observed its intercollegiate athletic competitions and the extraordinary degree of institutional support those colleges and universities provided.[6] He would also befriend the not-yet-President Theodore Roosevelt, whose belief in the "strenuous life" impressed him.[7]

However, Coubertin was struck chiefly by the potential of sport to promote strength of both body and character, by its promotion of moral as well as physical development. Sports, he felt, taught youth how to compete, with all that competition entails: discipline and hard work, but also the ability to collectively agree on rules, to gather together to play by those rules, and to compete with collegiality. Athletics were thus a vehicle for promoting the moral attributes of fair play, and of global integration through competition. As one historian noted, Courbertin's motives in organizing international athletic competitions were "at once practical and noble";[8] he sought to strengthen French youth but also educate a new generation of global leaders. In the words of Allen Guttmann, "the political purpose of the games—the reconciliation of warring nations—was more important than the sports. They were merely the competitive means to a cooperative end: a world at peace."[9] Coubertin hoped that the modern Olympics would help to build bonds between ruling elites and contribute to the peaceful resolution of conflict.[10] Similarly, the Olympics would be "making French youth more robust, healthy and physically fit" but also creating "a communion of nations in the name of peace, fraternity and goodwill."[11]

Coubertin thus believed megasports could promote two related principles that are relevant to today's human rights and anti-corruption legacy: fair play, and cooperation through competition. Anti-corruption and human rights norms are in large part (but of course not exclusively) both. The norm that companies ought not to gain competitive advantage by paying bribes, or violating labor rights, is a norm of fair play. We likewise believe judges ought not to violate due process nor ministers award contracts without a transparent bidding process, and for the same reason. So too do these same principles promote international cooperation through competition. As the next chapter will show, anti-bribery laws in international business have been a principal driver of the modern anti-corruption consensus. The UN Guiding Principles on Business and Human Rights (UNGPs) are similarly designed to impose human rights norms on firms engaged in competitive international business. Put another way, the modern governance standards that undergird the human rights and anti-corruption legacy are themselves principles of fair play and of cooperation through competition. Chapters 4–8 will show how megasports are today promoting these principles. In so doing, they give modern credence to Coubertin's original idea.

Animated by these motives, Coubertin organized the first International Olympic Committee, comprised of individuals from Sweden, Russia, Bohemia, Hungary, Britain, France, and the United States. The original modern Games would then occur in 1896, in Athens, Greece. Shortly thereafter, in 1904, the Fédération Internationale de Football Association (FIFA) would form, with its founding nations of France, Belgium, Denmark, Netherlands, Spain, Sweden, and Switzerland. After a couple of minor events, FIFA's first major international competition was connected with the 1908 London Olympics. In the next few years, its originally all-European membership would extend to South Africa, Argentina, Chile, and the United States.[12]

The era of globalized megasports had begun and was infused with an idea that sports can teach nations how they ought to conduct their affairs. How salient this particular element was in the complex array of motives that drove Coubertin and his colleagues is interesting, but may be ultimately irrelevant. Megasport ideals do not depend on the idolization of historical figures or events. It is interesting, but not essential, to recognize that megasports' founder appears to have envisioned that which modern critics of MSE governance tacitly affirm: megasports ought to represent standards of good governance.

The world would prove largely inhospitable to these ideas of integration through competition in accordance with agreed-upon standards. Since the founding era, the social or political history of megasports has fallen into roughly three main eras. The first was the world wars. In megasports, the wars were first about excluding aggressor nations, and then about the struggle to reintegrate those nations into the global order. The second era was the Cold War, in which political ideologies played out on the pitch, nations were again excluded, and tensions were high. The third era would emerge from the demise of the Cold War, as nations became less polarized by political ideology, and uniform standards of fair play and competition came to be expected among citizens, governments, and transnational business enterprises. This is the era of globalization. This third era gave rise first to the idea of a legacy, and now, to the human rights and anti-corruption legacy. So too does it present an opportunity to further realize the founding vision of megasports.

The first of these periods of frustration commenced with the Sixth Olympic Games, of 1916, scheduled to occur in Berlin, Germany. With the outbreak of the First World War, those Games were canceled. So too did World War I nearly destroy FIFA. The FIFA Congress could not convene because certain members could not cross borders, and Britain withdrew partly out of a refusal to compete against wartime enemies.[13] It would turn out that canceling the Berlin Games would be a relatively easy question to answer; the harder question concerned whether and when to invite Germany to rejoin the Olympic movement. After a decade of ostracization, that invitation would come in 1928. And by 1931, the IOC would even decide that Berlin would be a suitable host for the 1936 Games.[14]

In 1931, Germany was ruled by a fragile centrist coalition that would not survive until the 1936 Games. That coalition was of course displaced by the Third Reich, and thus megasports were already pulled into the quagmire of an impending second world war. The Nazis initially resisted hosting the Games and all of modern sports—the Olympic ethic of universalism and equality were antithetical to Nazi Aryan supremacy. Indeed, one Nazi government spokesperson condemned the Olympics and sport generally because they were "infested" with "Frenchmen, Belgians, Pollacks, and Jew-Niggers" who were allowed to "start on the tracks, to play on the soccer fields, and to swim in the pools."[15]

However, Nazis quickly realized the Games' potential to create what we would later call a political legacy: a projection of the Third Reich's supposed strength and organizational skill, not to mention Aryan racial superiority. The IOC was predictably concerned that Nazi Germany would systematically prevent German Jews from competing in these Games. In an effort to allay these concerns, Germany pledged to not discriminate, and twenty-one Jews were invited to try out. None made the team. Regardless, organizationally the Games set an historic precedent, widely perceived as the most magnificent Games of the modern era to date. Among other things, the 1936 Berlin Games were the first to receive large-scale organizational and financial support from a national government.[16]

Hitler's envisioned political legacy was famously defeated by Jesse Owens' winning of a historic four gold medals. Notably, his was not the only non-Aryan achievement; African-Americans won a total of thirteen medals. The Nazi propaganda regime rushed to reframe the success of African-American athletes as a symbol of their own moral inferiority, attributing their success to a "jungle inheritance."[17] Though an obvious repudiation of Aryan supremacy, stories of Hitler's refusal to personally congratulate Owens are exaggerated. In truth, Hitler's practice, irrespective of Owens' racial challenge, was to extend personal congratulations only to the German winners.[18] Although Owens took no offense at Hitler's habits, he publicly spoke of his offense at never receiving congratulations from his own president, Franklin Delano Roosevelt. Said Owens, "Hitler didn't snub me—it was our president who snubbed me. The president didn't even send me a telegram."[19]

The Third Reich's racist ideology would prove to be but one component of this era's threat to the Olympic Movement. Militarism would be the other. Following 1936, the next scheduled Olympic host was Japan, slated for 1940. That country's prior invasion of Manchuria was not thought to be an act of sufficient aggression to disqualify its bid. Indeed, when Japan then invaded China in 1937, the IOC still seemed unfazed. External pressure mounted, first from Australia and then Great Britain, to boycott the 1940 Games if Japan were still at war. The boycott question was avoided when in 1938, Japan decided the Games were a mere distraction and, two years prior to the event, announced that it would not host them. The IOC first moved the Summer Games to Finland and the Winter Games to Germany, but the Games were ultimately canceled in 1940, and then again in 1944.[20] These same political forces would prove equally disruptive on the FIFA side. World War II would lead to the cancellation of both the 1942 and 1946 FIFA World Cups.

Both Germany and Japan would suffer the consequences of their ambitions, in the form of a temporary exclusion from both FIFA and the Olympic Movement. Immediately following World War II, the majority of the international community opposed the inclusion of the Axis Powers countries in the Olympics.[21] This forced the IOC to choose between excluding countries for political reasons or accepting their participation in the face of international political pressure. The IOC decided to respect international opinion. In the first postwar Olympics, the 1948 London Games, neither Germany nor Japan was invited to participate.[22] Further, even though the IOC invited the Soviet Union, it refused to attend.[23] So too was Germany banned from the 1950 FIFA World Cup.

The world war era of megasport history is defined not just by its divisions but also by their eventual healing. Just as with World War I, the IOC would commit to reintegrating both Japan and Germany back into the global Olympic order. Indeed, Tokyo would ultimately host the Summer Games in 1964, and Munich in 1972. The latter, in particular, would have been a success story but for the tragic events that unfolded. Wishing to change the country's image, the Munich organizers elected to reduce the police presence at the Games, attempting to atone for their past and create an atmosphere of openness and trust. This trust would be violated in the most horrific of ways when a Palestinian terrorist group took hostage, and eventually murdered, eleven Israeli Olympic athletes.[24] On the FIFA side, Germany would return from its 1950 ban to win the 1954 FIFA World Cup under the West German flag, and West Germany would win again in its own country when hosting the 1974 FIFA World Cup. Japan would also start competing in FIFA World Cups beginning in 1954.

With the passing of the world wars and the reintegration of Japan and Germany into both IOC and FIFA, a new megasport era commenced. This second major era was the Cold War, characterized by deep politicization, national and ideological rivalries, and the rise of commercialism. In this era, nationalism would become a dominant influence in the Games, and journalists began tallying national medal counts.[25] The Cold War would thus produce a peculiar new theme to megasports: competition among nations that did not promote integration but instead celebrated division.

These new political divisions would pose a host of novel policy questions. The first concerned divided Germany. Initially, the IOC required Germany to field a united team, despite its political division into West and East Germany.[26] The IOC made the decision citing political neutrality and the Olympic ideals of peace and inclusiveness. However, the "united German team" was fielded under the name of West Germany. It was not until 1955 that the IOC accepted the reality of international politics and allowed West and East Germany to field separate teams.[27] However, it would be thirteen more years before West and East Germany would actually field separate teams at the 1968 Mexico City Games.[28] In 1974, separate West and East German national football (or "soccer," as some countries still prefer) teams would play each other in the FIFA World Cup that West Germany hosted. The game, which East Germany won 1–0, was widely regarded as a symbol of the softening relations between the two countries.[29] The Cold War would raise a series of additional questions for the IOC and FIFA. Should they tolerate the Soviet Union's state-sponsored athletes? If Germany would be divided into two teams, what about North and South Korea, or China and Taiwan?

Cold War tensions reached their Olympic apex when, in 1979, the Soviet Union invaded Afghanistan. President Jimmy Carter, unwilling to counter with military action but needing to do something, proposed a boycott of the Soviet Union's 1980 Games. Great Britain and then West Germany aligned with the United States, and eventually 62 of the 143 invited nations joined the boycott. In apparent retaliation (there was no other catalyst or credible proffered justification), the Soviet Union boycotted the 1984 Games hosted by the United States; sixteen of its allies joined. The divisiveness of megasports, and the frustration of Coubertin's vision, was arguably never more pronounced.

Unlike the world wars era, the IOC and FIFA never had to resolve the question of how and when to reintegrate these divided countries. With the collapse of the Soviet Union in 1991, the Cold War divisions would organically subside. The third era of megasport history—globalization—would thus begin. This era gave rise to more globalized standards of governance and, quite relatedly, the megasport legacy movement.

Globalization, Globalized Standards, and Legacy

Beginning with the fall of the Berlin Wall in 1989 and continuing to this day, three closely connected developments are occurring at the same time. Collectively, they are reworking our expectations of megasport governance. First, the world has entered, and remains in, a period now called globalization—the increasing interconnectedness of peoples, businesses, and governments. Second, with globalization comes the rise of common standards of public- and private-sector governance: anti-corruption and human rights conventions and standards that may be poorly implemented but that nearly every country feels obliged to at least appear to accept. Third, in this era of interconnected countries and increasingly agreed-upon governance standards, megasport stakeholders have turned their attention to legacy: the notion that we ought to care about the event's long-term impacts on a host country or city, and that we can use a common metric to measure those impacts. These three coinciding developments created the conditions in which the human rights and anti-corruption legacy has emerged.

As this book goes to press, globalization is rhetorically out of fashion. But despite the present glitches of recent populist movements, globalization is an inexorable feature of modern life. We will never cease to purchase foreign-made goods, and we will never abandon the notion that there are certain things all governments must do and no government may do. We will argue at the margins—Is voting a universal right? Can we distinguish between a bribe and a grease payment?—but nearly every country concedes that corruption should be deterred and human rights, however defined, should be protected. In this era, megasports have become truly global, hosted around the world. Globalization also produced a gradual and of course still-ongoing formation of global governance standards. Those standards—their history, content, and application to both government and business—is the subject of Chapter 2. Globalization has hit megasports in demonstrable ways. For starters, consider host locations. The Olympics have moved way beyond Western Europe and North America, as successive Games are being hosted by Brazil, Russia, South Korea, Japan, and China. So too would the first FIFA World Cup in history be hosted on the African continent, in South Africa, shortly followed by the Middle East's first MSE in Qatar.

Globalization has several components. Economically, it has entailed a move toward market economies and diminished state control. Relatedly, trade barriers have dropped as nations committed to freer international trade and foreign direct investment. Politically, more nations came to be classified as democracies than at any point in history. In international politics, a previously bipolar world has become far more pluralistic and inclusive of developing countries. The once-powerful G8 (France, Germany, Italy, the United Kingdom, Japan, the United States, Canada, and Russia) was largely displaced by the G20 (which adds Argentina, Australia, Brazil, China, India, Indonesia, Italy, South Korea, Mexico, Saudi Arabia, South Africa, and Turkey, as well as the European Union).

Much globalization commentary is written by economists, focusing on the transitions to variants of a free market economy. Joseph Stiglitz, author of the landmark books *Globalization and Its Discontents*[30] and *Making Globalization Work*,[31] is a rigorous critic of globalization's economic damage but believes the problems lie not in globalization per se but in the clumsy management of its early decade or two. By this view, globalization is inevitable, but if well-managed will tend to ultimately deliver on its promises of decreased poverty and greater economic stability. Looking at globalization in a broader historical perspective, Fareed Zakaria chronicles the three great power shifts of the modern era: the rise of the West, beginning in the fifteenth century and accelerating in the eighteenth; in the nineteenth century, the rise of the United States, which he calls the most powerful nation since imperial Rome, and then, with globalization, "the rise of the rest,"[32] in which leadership is more diffuse and standards of governance cease to be associated with a country or region. Here, norms of good governance become more universal.

Surely the most famous of globalization's commentators is Thomas Friedman. His popular book, *The World Is Flat*, describes the components of the globalization process that, working together, "flattened" or integrated the world.[33] He observes that the collapse of the Soviet Union did not merely liberate the Eastern bloc but "tipped the balance of power across the world toward those advocating democratic, consensual, free-market-oriented governance." Not that practices were instantly universal or consistent, or that there were not utterly illiberal belief systems that still held sway in countries or regions, but that "if you continued to hold fast to [nonliberal rule], you were seen as being on the wrong side of history." In this period of history we began to think of the world as "more of a seamless whole . . . a single market, a single ecosystem, and a single community." As the world became integrated, or as he says, flattened, it "paved the way for the adoption of common standards—standards on how economies should be run."[34]

To be sure, dramatic disagreements remain on the proper degree of both economic and political liberalization; major countries or even regions are still characterized by principled disagreement with certain components of the globalization agenda. However, these disagreements are less radical, and less ideological, than at any point in world history, let alone megasport history. Major developing countries practice variants of "state capitalism," in which the state more heavily regulates or even monopolizes major sectors of the economy. As the grammatical structure of the phrase plainly implies, this is but a variation on the fundamental principles of capitalism. East Asian countries may continue to push against the individualism of human rights and democracy, but few would attempt to justify in principle the authoritarianism of North Korea. Similarly, mainstream Islamic cultures may reject the separation of church and state, certain aspects of gender equality, and the modern right to privacy in procreation. But radicalized militant Islam, however violent and destructive, does not pose a threat to global liberalism on the scale of the former Soviet Union. Indeed, the twenty-first century is characterized by remarkable degree of globalized agreement-in-principle. Were that not the case, we could not speak of a prospective human rights and anti-corruption legacy now.

Though globalization is recognized as a distinguishing feature of the context in which modern megasports occur,[35] commentary on globalization and megasports has primarily emphasized the excessive power of corporations, restrictions on civil liberties, and disenfranchisement.[36] But there is more going on here. First, the globalization era has led to the rise of developing nations in hosting the Games. Between 2014 and 2022, for example, the Olympics will be hosted by three of the four BRIC nations—Brazil, Russia, India, and China. In this eight-year period, host countries will include Russia, Brazil, South Korea, and China (twice). The only highly developed country in this span is Japan (2020), which is a country that was once banned from the Olympics for World War II–era military aggression. Similarly, successive FIFA Men's World Cups have been hosted by South Africa, Brazil, Russia, and Qatar. It seems the old order, in which the wealthiest European and North American countries dominated megasports, is far gone.

At least as importantly, globalization has led megasports to embrace political norms that in a prior historical era would have been deemed a compromise of their commitment to political neutrality. That commitment must be honored, as it has deep roots in megasport governance. The IOC Olympic Charter contains multiple references to political neutrality, prohibiting political demonstrations in Olympic sites, and remaining free of political influence.[37] Similarly, the FIFA Statutes provide that "FIFA remains neutral in matters of politics and religion," and that member associations and confederations must do the same.[38] FIFA's Code of Conduct likewise requires political neutrality, but in furtherance of that neutrality, "strictly prohibits discrimination in employment or employment-related decisions based on any concept of race, skin color, gender, age, national or ethnic origin, religion, ideology, disability, sexual orientation, political opinion, social status, marital status, citizenship or any other status protected by law."[39] Notice the shift here: these principles of nondiscrimination are not political; they are apolitical. They are themselves neutral; they are globalized values.

As powerful evidence of this new commitment to globalized values, the IOC and FIFA have increasingly affiliated with the United Nations or other intergovernmental organizations, entering into agreements that may at one time been perceived as politically divisive: gender equality; workers' rights; human rights generally; anti-corruption measures. Human rights and anti-corruption norms are no longer deemed a violation of megasports' historic commitment to political neutrality; to the contrary, these norms are themselves now neutral, and the failure to honor them becomes political. Since as early as 1992, megasports have sought to boost their legitimacy by engaging with governance issues through agreements with UN or other intergovernmental organizations. The timing is telling—this began occurring just after end of the Cold War and the advent of globalization.

Admittedly, certain of these agreements do not raise particularly divisive policy issues. One of the earliest of these agreements with the IOC was established with the Environmental Programme (1994). This agreement was created to promote a more sustainable environment and development for the twenty-first century and beyond. In that vein, careful environmental considerations now serve as a prerequisite to host country candidature.[40] Addressing the somewhat more sensitive topic of political refugees, the IOC and the United Nations signed a memorandum of understanding on the "role of sports in development and peace" in 2014. The purpose of this memorandum was to promote sports in parts of the world that are hosting refugees displaced by political conflict.[41] In the area of public health, FIFA and the World Health Organization signed a memorandum of understanding in 2019 to promote global health and well-being. The organizations plan to work toward this goal through public awareness campaigns and by creating a healthier and safer environment at the physical sporting events.[42]

However, issues that just a few decades ago seemed more politicized likewise became the subject of international agreements. The IOC signed a cooperative agreement with UN Women in 2012 to advance the empowerment of women through sport.[43] FIFA and UN Women signed a similar memorandum of understanding just before the FIFA Women's World Cup began in 2019.[44] Likewise, FIFA and the French Development Agency signed an agreement to focus on gender equality and women empowerment through football.[45]

Similar agreements have extended beyond the specific topic of gender equality to human rights and governance generally. The Council of Europe and FIFA signed a memorandum of understanding focusing on four specific areas: human rights, integrity and good governance, safety and security, and cooperation in operations.[46] The IOC signed a cooperative agreement with the ILO in 1998 to promote social justice and human dignity and to reduce poverty and child labor around the globe.[47] FIFA signed a similar agreement with the European Union that used football to aid the fight against poverty and worked to support the world's poor and struggling countries. This memorandum of understanding specifically focused on eliminating poverty in the poorest countries of Africa, the Caribbean and the Pacific.[48] In 2019, FIFA, the Confederation Africaine de Football (CAF), and the African Union signed a memorandum of understanding focusing on education, governance against corruption, and safety at football games.[49] These various agreements illustrate the increasing tendency of the IOC and FIFA to join intergovernmental organizations in promoting human rights and good governance generally. As globalization produced increasingly global standards, sports organizations felt they could embrace these standards without compromising their commitment to neutrality.

As the standards became more globalized, megasports stakeholders turned their attention to how the events can be governed to produce effects that align with these standards. In this era, notions of legacy would proliferate and diversify. Of course, legacy talk begins with economic legacy: the projected long-term economic benefits weighted against the initial costs. Sadly, most economists, most of the time, find this legacy to be negative. However, legacies are not exclusively economic. A "sporting" legacy refers to athletic facilities, levels of participation and popularity of sports following the games. "Urban" legacies might include beautification, regeneration, and improved infrastructure improvements. "Social" legacies can involve the rediscovery of indigenous culture or global recognition of that culture, integration of minority or marginalized populations, educational programs promoting the virtues of excellence, friendship, respect, and volunteerism; and cooperation among sectors and social groups. The notion of an "environmental" legacy has steadily gained support and reached a zenith in Pyeongchang: the host city produced zero net-carbon emissions in part by building a wind farm and utilizing a 300-vehicle fleet of electric cars. Though less widely appreciated than the high-profile corruption scandals, megasports are starting to build a track record of benefiting, at least in modest part, the host country.

To be clear, the concept of a legacy was not invented during globalization: the term first appeared in an early Cold War–era candidature document for the Melbourne Olympic Games in 1956, and again appeared in Calgary's 1981 candidature file for the 1988 Winter Games. But there is no question that globalization, and the closely related focus on governance, provided a sort of fertilizer in which the legacy concept grew exponentially, as will be explained later. What is the link? As Thomas Friedman explained, globalization is largely about governance. As the world came to focus on governance, the governance of MSEs naturally made its way onto the radar. Legacy is, to a significant degree, about how well the events are governed. Economic legacy most definitely is. Once a global consensus emerges that governments ought to promote sustainable economic development, the role of MSEs in that economic development is inevitably engaged. So too did globalization promote a kind of commercialism that, in the eyes of many commentators, drove MSE's to economic excess, in turn raising questions of economic sustainability. The focus on economic legacy in turn drove commentators to develop additional dimensions of legacy, as this chapter will later explain.

At least in part due to globalization and increasingly accepted standards of governance, during the last thirty years the legacy concept has shot off like a rocket. In 1991, the Organizing Committee for the 1996 Centennial Olympic Games in Atlanta included the goal to "leave a positive physical and spiritual legacy" in its mission statement. In 1997, Athens' candidature file for the 2004 Olympic Games entitled a brochure "A legacy for Olympism." The legacy concept then gained considerable steam in the following decade in the context of heavy critique of "commercialization, 'gigantism,' political vicissitudes and a history of boycotts," not to mention, the endemic corruption that the 1998 Salt Lake City bid scandal (described in detail later) exposed.[50] In this context critics wondered just what the lasting benefits to the host city and country might be. To that end, in 2000 the IOC modified its charter to establish a commitment "to promote a positive legacy from the Olympic Games to the host cities and host countries."[51] This same year, the IOC began requesting a legacy plan from each applicant as part of the bid process.[52]

In 2002, the year of the pivotal Salt Lake City Winter Olympics, the IOC organized an International Symposium to discuss the legacy of the Olympic Games, bringing together 150 experts, representing Olympic bid committees, Olympic Games Organising Committees, International Sports Federations, National Olympic Committees, and researchers from different countries and disciplines. The IOC Olympic Games Study Commission issued a report in July 2003 which referenced the importance of Olympic legacy and recognized the need to ensure that host cities and their residents are left with a significant legacy of venues, infrastructure, expertise, and experience. The report officially recognized the nonphysical and perhaps even noneconomic dimensions of legacy. Finally, the importance of legacy was specifically addressed in Rule 2 of the Olympic Charter, which is the codification of the Fundamental Principles of Olympism, Rules and Bye-laws adopted by the IOC. The legacy concept gained further momentum with the 2012 London Games, sometimes referred to as the "Legacy Games."[53] In 2015, the IOC founded the Sustainability and Legacy Commission to help improve the prospects of positive legacies.

Legacy scholarship followed, initially focusing on the economic dimension of legacy. Infrastructure costs are of course foremost to these analyses and are weighed against the economic benefits of new infrastructure but also tourist revenue and enhanced business relationships.[54] This research has generally yielded significant skepticism concerning the economic benefit of these events, leading many cities—Vienna, Munich, Hamburg, Stockholm, Oslo, Lviv, Krakow, Boston, and others—to recently withdraw their candidacies.[55] The economic dimension of legacy remains, as it should, central to both popular discourse and the academic study of legacy.[56] However, the viability of the concept, if not of megasports themselves, depends on recognizing other forms of legacy. Indeed, as far back as the 2002 conference, policymakers recognized that legacies can take any of a number of forms: social, cultural, educational, and political.

Where globalized standards intersect with a focus on legacy, a new kind of legacy emerges. This is the human rights and anti-corruption legacy: a series of laws, procedures, and cultural norms, promoting transparency, accountability, and human rights, that have application beyond sport and remain after the games are over. It could not occur without the perception that human rights and anti-corruption, as core principles, are essentially universal values, and that these values ought to be integrated into megasports. For specific evidence of the way these norms can transcend countries with vastly different political cultures and histories, one need only compare two countries: France, and Qatar. Despite their differences, talk to officials in either country and you'll find absolute agreement on this point: there is no question that megasports should avoid violating human rights, and there is no doubt these events should minimize corruption. It may be fairly said that the agreement of these two countries on standards of governance is itself a powerful symbol of what globalization has done to megasport governance. These globalized values form the conceptual foundation for the human rights and anti-corruption legacy.

The Crisis of Megasport Governance: Corruption and Human Rights Violations

With the preceding three pieces in place—globalization, increasing acceptance (at least optically) of anti-corruption and human rights principles, and a focus on the legacies of sport—climatic conditions were just right for a megasport governance storm to erupt. The epicenter of that storm would prove to be Salt Lake City, host of the 2002 Winter Olympics. The Salt Lake City bribery scandal released a deluge of crisis-level attention paid to megasport host-country governance that continues to this day. This flood of criticism would steadily rise, and the high-water mark may have been Russia in 2014. Again, this criticism emerged not because anti-corruption and human rights violations suddenly began occurring; these are as old as the Games themselves. What was new, rather, was the notion that megasports ought to be otherwise. The Games may or may not have changed, but the standards by which we judge them surely have.

It would of course be historically incorrect to suggest that megasports were devoid of such scandals prior to Salt Lake City. While the governance critiques gained ascendancy post-globalization, their origins date back at least to the 1960s, the decade in which the two major human rights covenants would be adopted. Perhaps the clearest early statement that megasports would begin to look at human rights came in 1961. FIFA suspended South Africa from global football due to apartheid, a suspension that would last into the 1990s.[57] Similarly, in 1968, police shooting into a crowd of student democracy protestors just ten days before the Mexico City Olympics would similarly give rise to a rights-based critique of host-country governance.[58] In 1978, commentators spoke of Argentina hosting the FIFA World Cup during its so-called "Dirty War" of 1976–1983 in which over thirty thousand political activists disappeared or were imprisoned.[59] Years later, the IOC selected Sydney to host the Summer 2000 Olympics over Beijing in a narrow vote of 45–43.[60] This decision is credited as one of the most contentious bidding processes by the IOC, which took into account China's human rights abuses from the 1989 Tiananmen Square massacre to ultimately determine that China would not be fit to host the Games.[61]

However, the sports governance tipping point occurred in 1998, when host-country corruption galvanized global attention. The historian Richard Espy observed that the modern Olympic Games represent the struggle between our ideals and the reality in which we live.[62] Perhaps nowhere did that prove truer than in Salt Lake City, host of the 2002 Winter Olympics. The Games' official slogan, "Light the Fire Within," was likely meant to have a double meaning: it connotes the passion of athletic competition and also seems a subtle reference to the region's characteristic religious beliefs. But no one could have known that it would take on a third meaning. The decades-old process of awarding Olympic Games to bid cities would turn out to be a bomb waiting to explode. Salt Lake City unwittingly lit the fuse.

The city had been trying to win the Winter Olympics for half a century. Following more distant failures in 1932, 1972, and 1976, the city would lose the 1998 bid to Nagano, Japan, by a mere four votes. This failure particularly hurt, and sentiment arose that Salt Lake City simply wasn't playing the kind of hardball that a successful effort required. A Salt Lake City bid committee member complained, "We were giving out saltwater taffy and cowboy hats, and they were giving out computers. IOC members who came to inspect Nagano were put up in ritzy hot spring resorts, where they washed down expensive sushi with sake poured by kimono-clad geisha. They went home laden with souvenir gifts and expensive paintings."[63] Surrounding these and other bid efforts, rumors had circulated for years that bribery was occurring in relation to the bids. But no evidence had ever been produced, and indeed, corruption in the bidding might not have been thought entirely shocking or scandalous.

Salt Lake City's disappointment would end on June 16, 1995, when the International Olympic Committee announced that the Utah city had won the 2002 Winter Games. This victory made heroes of the two local businessmen who led the effort: Thomas Welch and David Johnson. These two men would continue to serve in leadership roles in the Games' preparation. Word on the street was that they simply did not get along. After four years of rumored tensions between the two men, a curious thing happened. An unidentified source released to Salt Lake City news correspondent Chris Vanocur (son of well-respected Washington, DC, correspondent Sander Vanocur) a draft copy of a 1996 letter. Written on the stationery of the Salt Lake City Organizing Committee, the letter was addressed to Sonia Essomba, a student at American University in Washington, DC, and daughter of an influential member of the IOC. The letter read, "the enclosed check for $10,114.99 will have to be our last payment for tuition." The letter bore the signature of David Johnson.[64]

To this day, the precise reason why the letter was leaked remains unknown. It seems likely that whoever did it could not have anticipated what happened next. On November 24, 1999, Vanocur revealed the letter on the evening news. The *New York Times* and National Public Radio quickly picked up the story. Then the issue exploded. An investigation would eventually reveal that Essomba had received a total of US$108,350 over the course of several years. Swiss IOC member Marc Hodler, head of the committee overseeing the organization of the 2002 games, publicly accused a group of IOC members of having taken bribes for years.[65] The scandal had begun.

The US Attorney's Office eventually indicted both Welch and Johnson for conspiracy, mail fraud, wire fraud, racketeering, and interstate travel in aid of racketeering. It alleged that Welch and Johnson had improperly influenced more than a dozen delegates of the IOC. An independent ethics panel investigating Salt Lake City's bid concluded that officials had lavished more than US$1.2 million in cash, scholarships, jobs, medical treatment, shopping sprees, luxurious travel, and expensive gifts on IOC delegates and their families. But Welch and Johnson were not the only ones indicted. David Simmons, a Salt Lake City businessman, pleaded guilty to tax offenses related to a sham job provided to the son of a South Korean IOC delegate. The son, John Kim, was also indicted but left the country. Similarly, Alfredo La Mont, formerly in charge of international relations for the US Olympic committee, pleaded guilty to tax charges related to payments he received from Salt Lake City bid committee as consultant to help win 2002 bid. Further investigations would reveal allegations related to the 1996 Summer Olympics in Atlanta, the 1998 Nagano Winter Games, and the 2000 Sydney Summer Games. It seemed that bribery in the Olympic bidding process was endemic.[66]

Salt Lake City locals will be quick to point out that Welch and Johnson were acquitted of all criminal charges. In December 2003, federal Judge David Sam granted a rare motion for acquittal without sending the case to the jury, ruling that there was insufficient evidence to sustain a conviction on any of the fifteen counts.[67] The judge sharply criticized the government's case, saying that in forty years of working in the criminal justice system, he had never seen a case so lacking in "criminal intent or evil purpose." According to the *New York Times* reporter, Judge Sam indicated in his oral comments from the bench that his "sense of justice was offended by the bringing of felony charges against Welch and Johnson while the rest of Utah enjoyed the fruits of their Olympic efforts."[68]

Despite the acquittals, the Salt Lake City scandal marked the genesis of the modern megasport corruption narrative. Though Marc Holder, then IOC vice president, admitted in 1998 that "to my knowledge, there has always, always, been a certain part of the vote given to corruption,"[69] not until Salt Lake City did Olympic corruption become the subject of substantial international commentary and aggressive criminal prosecutions. Why was Salt Lake City's corruption any different? It may be tempting to say the United States had a lower level of tolerance for corruption—that cultural norms more strongly frowned upon this conduct. So too might it be said that the US law enforcement agencies took corruption more seriously than other countries at that time. But neither explanation holds up. Nobody seems to suspect that the original incriminating letter was leaked to the press due to moral disapproval of the underlying conduct. Rather, suspicions (admittedly speculative) focus on the power struggle within the Salt Lake City Olympics leadership, as will be explained later. Neither do US government agencies deserve credit for blowing the case open. The story had become a global phenomenon long before the US Attorney's Office got involved, and their prosecution ultimately became something of an embarrassment.

It would seem that uniquely American norms or institutions simply cannot explain why Olympic corruption became a big deal in the late 1990s. Rather, the explanation lies in global legal and cultural changes occurring in this time. Perhaps neither Welch nor Johnson appreciated the worldwide "Corruption Eruption" (discussed in Chapter 2) that had only recently been named and was occurring all around them. They likely appreciate it now.

The Salt Lake City scandal would first produce a shock at the IOC, and then systemic reforms. Ten IOC delegates resigned or were forced out. The IOC then appointed the IOC 2000 Commission (more popularly known as the Reform Commission) to study Olympic governance. It made fifty recommendations, all of which the IOC adopted in 1999. The reforms dramatically changed the appointment and terms of IOC members and the appointment of National Olympic Committee and International Federation presidents, created eight-year terms (renewable) for IOC members, set a mandatory retirement age of seventy, and established new rules for the selection of host cities, including a prohibition on IOC travel to candidate cities.[70]

The era of training the world's eye on host country governance failures had begun. What followed was a series of MSEs eliciting worldwide criticism for human rights and/or corruption violations. The 2008 Beijing Summer Olympic would see the detention and deportation of journalists, a prohibition on coverage of sensitive political issues such as Tibet or Xinjiang. Human rights activists were detained or removed during Games. The government denied protestors promised permits. As many as one million people were forcibly relocated, albeit with assistance, from their homes. Global attention would also be paid to broader human rights issues: lack of elections, free speech and religion, forced abortions for violations of the one-child policy, aggressive use of the death penalty, environmental degradation, support of authoritarian regimes and dictators around world, and the like.[71]

The first megasport on the African continent—South Africa's 2010 FIFA Men's World Cup—would embody globalization in a variety of ways. Not only did it symbolize just how globalized megasports had become, but it marked this specific country's reintegration into the megasport movement after decades of exclusion under apartheid. The awarding of the 2010 World Cup was therefore something of a triumph for globalized standards. But so too did it elicit governance criticism, in ways quite typical of this era. Informal housing, such as shelters and hostels, was destroyed to create a better image and clean up areas near the World Cup stadiums.[72] Individuals were evicted and relocated to what is known as Tin Can Town, or Blikkiesdorp, which the residents compared to a concentration camp. Residents reported that police came each night and beat them, forcibly enforced a curfew, pepper-sprayed them, and abused their authority. Thousands of people were forced into tight living corners where disease was rampant and unsanitary conditions led to foreseeable sickness. With no money, means for food, running water, or employment opportunities, these individuals were hungry, dirty, helpless, and frustrated with the deceitful image the South African World Cup was portraying to the rest of the world.[73]

Russia's 2014 Sochi Winter Olympics and 2018 FIFA Men's World Cup may well have been the low point for host-country governance. The events elicited a dizzying array of corruption and human rights allegations: clampdowns on dissent, discrimination against minorities, and Russian oligarchs embezzling tens of billions of US dollars. Forced evictions occurred with little or sometimes no compensation. Migrant workers were exploited, and speech was suppressed. Perhaps most egregious was the persecution of LGBT individuals, going so far as to include a law, signed by Vladimir Putin in 2013, banning the promotion of "non-traditional" sexuality. In preparations for Olympics, an estimated US$50 billion were allegedly embezzled, and the 2018 World Cup was the most expensive in history. But Russia did not, and has not, responded with meaningful governance reforms. We do not see the enactment and effective enforcement of impactful laws prohibiting these forms of corruption or human rights abuses. From a governance perspective, Russia amounted to a nonresponse. Russia represents, quite conspicuously, the absence of a human rights and anti-corruption legacy.[74]

Though Russia may seem the norm, it would prove to be the exception. Subsequent to the 2014 Olympics, a remarkable pattern emerged. Host countries began adopting major reforms concurrent with their preparation for the megasport events. These reforms were never planned by the host-country organizers, the IOC, or FIFA. But nor were they unrelated to, and merely coincidental with, the mega events. Rather, the reforms occurred in part as a kind of backlash against the abuses the events exposed. Obviously, the sporting events were not the only and certainly not even the primary cause.

However, in each case, they were part of a constellation of events that triggered governance reforms. As Chapter 3 explains, this pattern begins in Brazil, host of the 2014 FIFA World Cup and 2016 Rio de Janeiro Summer Olympics. As if by script, the host of the very next Olympic Games would see an astonishingly similar pattern play out. Chapter 4 describes how South Korea, host of the 2018 Pyeongchang Winter Olympics, would continue the pattern of a megasport host country, producing scandals that accelerated lasting anti-corruption reforms. And then Qatar's controversial winning of the rights to host the 2022 FIFA Men's World Cup, followed by widespread allegations of bribery and then labor abuses, would catalyze systemic labor rights reforms. This astonishing story is told in Chapter 5.

These events create a pattern, within which lurks an opportunity. Given the demonstrated capacity of megasports to expose host-country governance weaknesses, and the host countries' demonstrated willingness to institute reforms, could we transition from the reactive to the proactive? From legacies by accident to legacies by design? Can we build governance legacies in a preventative fashion, avoiding the collateral damage of impeached presidents, criminally convicted business leaders, and the severe tarnishing of the Olympic and FIFA brands? Events in Brazil, South Korea, China, and Qatar intimate a new possibility: that megasports could, with careful design, become a deliberate, intended catalyst for host-country anti-corruption and human rights reform.

Defining the Human Rights and Anti-Corruption Legacy

As mentioned in the preceding section, legacy literature has exploded in the globalization era. Academics, as well as the IOC and FIFA themselves, have produced an abundant and helpful body of commentary on how legacy might be understood.[75] A comprehensive review of the literature would be nearly impossible. But this section pulls out certain of the more relevant ideas from legacy scholarship to then provide a more fulsome description of what the human rights and anti-corruption legacy is and what it might become.

The legacy concept is inherently forward-looking; interestingly, peculiarities of the English language may have helped to make it so. J.J. MacAloon has noted that the equivalent word in French, "heritage," emphasizes "the accumulated capital of the past arriving in the present," while the English term "legacy" generally refers to the "present's contribution to the future."[76]

Though the megasport movement recognizes both official languages, the legacy scholarship tilts heavily toward the English meaning, focusing on the future benefits of the events.

Laurence Chalip wrote that "events should be planned and administered in a manner that will engender positive outcomes which will last beyond the time of the event."[77] Three themes are sounded here. First, Chalip believes that the legacy must be planned, and not an accident. Martin Polley sees it otherwise, coining the term "accidental" or "incidental" legacy,[78] and using London 1908 as a case study to illustrate how physical and sporting legacies may result even where "legacy" was no part of planners' thinking. As subsequent chapters of this book will explain, governance legacies in Brazil and South Korea were similar accidents. But in Qatar and France we are moving toward planned legacies. Chalip further suggests that a legacy should be positive. This is largely a corollary of the planned component, as none would plan a negative legacy; the negative legacies, economic and otherwise, were certainly not planned (though many planners may have suffered from a kind of deliberate ignorance). Finally, the legacy must endure beyond the event; this, of course, is the very meaning of legacy.

Richard Holt and Dina Ruta distinguish between "hard" legacy—the traditional infrastructure focus—and "soft" legacy, which may include the increase of human capital through training in management or security, reputational gains, the promotion of grass-roots participation in sports, or the acceleration of urban planning.[79] The human rights and anti-corruption legacy is, in this framework, a soft legacy. Jean-Loup Chappelet finds three dimensions of legacy: tangible versus intangible (hard versus soft); territorial versus personal (limited to country versus affecting people that will leave the country); and direct and indirect relation to sport (sports buildings, for example, versus transportation infrastructure).[80] Richard Cashman finds six categories of legacy: an economic legacy; a legacy of the built and physical environment; an information and education legacy; a legacy of public life, politics, and culture; a legacy of sport; and a legacy of symbols, memory, and history.[81]

Ultimately, Professor Holger Preuss has built out the legacy concept in ways that best highlight what the human rights and anti-corruption legacy is, and what it can become. Having surveyed the abundant legacy literature, he defines the term to refer to "all changes created for and by a sport event that remain[] longer than the event itself as well as all future impacts created by those changes."[82] As he notes, previous literature had identified a plethora of legacies, with examples ranging from the obvious infrastructure and urban planning to intangible legacies such as urban regeneration, enhanced international reputation, increased tourism, improved public welfare, additional employment, more local business opportunities, better corporate relocation, opportunities for city marketing, renewed community spirit, better interregional cooperation, production of ideas, production of cultural values, popular memory, opportunities for education, emotional experience, and additional know-how.[83]

Preuss effectively organizes this diffusion of practices, ideas, and writings into a framework. Distilling these and other diverse examples, Preuss finds three dimensions of legacy, represented in a "legacy cube": planned versus unplanned, negative versus positive, and tangible versus intangible.[84] He ultimately defines legacy as "all planned and unplanned, positive and negative, tangible and intangible structures created for and by a sport event that remain longer than the event itself."[85] The human rights and anti-corruption legacy, ideally, is a planned, positive, intangible legacy.

If these concepts go to the definitions of legacy, helpful work has also been done on the "facets" of legacy. Scheu, Preuss, and Konecke identify six overlapping facets of legacy: urban development; environmental enhancement; policy and governance; skills, knowledge, and networks; intellectual property; and beliefs and behavior. Human rights and anti-corruption legacy spans three facets: policy and governance; beliefs and behavior; and skills, knowledge, and networks. Reviewing the scholarship on these dimensions provides helpful context for understanding the human rights and anti-corruption legacy.

The second facet—beliefs and behavior—has proven to be the facet of legacy most often studied by researchers. They can focus on changes in the city's self-image (mostly positive), or on the city residents' perception of the Games' legacy (mixed), or on changing attitudes and behaviors toward physical activity (mostly positive).[86] These beliefs can more generally include a "feel-good factor."[87] It might also include states' pursuit of mega events to further what the political scientist Joseph Nye called "soft power" in international relations.[88] This is the older political legacy. Human rights and/or anti-corruption norms do not yet seem to have been the focus of study; they are not yet on our legacy radar. But this commentary illustrates that changing norms are themselves an important and well-established facet of legacy. Changing a country's anti-corruption and human rights norms are a key component of the human rights and anti-corruption legacy.

The skills, knowledge, and networks facet can encompass building partnerships and local or international partnerships, the capacity to host mega events, or language skills.[89] These can encompass: basic manual labor skills; cooking or driving; or sports management, tourism, and hospitality. The human rights and anti-corruption legacy will also include skills in implementing governance best practices, knowledge about those best practices and the laws that underlie them, and in some cases, networks of trained professionals.

Policy and governance—referring to laws, regulations, guidelines, and policies—has been a minor field of research.[90] This dimension seems to have been first added to the legacy scholarship by Leopkey and Parent in 2012.[91] The policy and governance they have in mind is oriented almost entirely toward sports. Examples include policies increasing sport participation in London 2012, and national policies of sport management following Beijing 2008. Non-sport policies have concerned security (Vancouver 2010); the environment (emission standards in Beijing); and food (sustainable food policies following London 2012).[92] So too has a cultural legacy encompassed greater inclusion of marginalized social groups.[93] Other examples are the quality charter for sport events (Vancouver 2010) and sustainable food policies from the London 2012 Games. They can include new anti-doping policies after the Russian doping scandal (Sochi 2014), better governance structures of national/international sport federations, or new police crowd-control regulation (Germany WC 2006).[94]

While these forms of policy and governance are important facets of legacy, they do not approximate the human rights and anti-corruption legacy. They do not concern core governance principles concerning transparency, accountability, and human rights that have application beyond sports in the broader public- and private-sectors. The new human rights and anti-corruption legacy is significantly bigger and, arguably, of greater social significance.

A comparison to a once-recognized legacy with a similar name, but of a very different substance, may prove helpful. Olympic stakeholders once spoke of a "political legacy," though that phrase has more recently fallen away from megasport discourse. While the political legacy may seem closely akin to the human rights and anti-corruption legacy, they are materially different. At its inception, the political legacy was mainly about perception. Surveying some of the academic commentary on "political legacy" helps us to see how the modern human rights and anti-corruption legacy is essentially different. In the words of Graeme Hayes and John Karamichas, the political legacy is about "the generation and projection of symbolic meanings."[95] It is about perception, both domestically and internationally, and often tied to the vanity of the country's leadership. It tends toward megasports that are grandiose and showy, less about what they are than how they look.

By contrast, the new and nascent human rights and anti-corruption legacy is less about image than it is about substance. It concerns how a country is actually governed, not just how it appears to be governed. John Horne has distinguished between selective legacies, which are "particular, individualist, and elitist, and tend to serve the interests of those dominating powerful political and economic positions in society," and universal legacies, which are "communal, collectivist, and inherently democratic, available to all by virtue of being made freely accessible."[96] The political legacy tends to be selective; the human rights and anti-corruption legacy is inherently universal.

Perhaps the first and most oft-cited example of a political legacy is Hitler's extravagant 1936 Berlin Olympics, in which he sought to establish the Third Reich as a leading global power. Decades later, the 1984 Los Angeles Games were, in the words of the vice president of the Salt Lake City 2002 Organizing Committee, "identified with the American political establishment" and were a "strong platform for carrying a political message" which was "tied to patriotism."[97] The 1996 Atlanta Games were similar in the way then-President Bill Clinton, up for re-election just months before the Games, recognized the Games' "political capital"—their potential to project a positive political image for the country and himself. To this end, he became the first US president to visit the athletes on the eve of the Games and explicitly told them that their performance in the Games would impact the country's image.[98] Of course, the bribery scandal that would erupt just a few years later in relation to the Salt Lake City 2002 Games would undermine this effort, ironically proving the president's point. More recently, the 2014 Winter Olympics in Sochi appeared to be part of Vladimir Putin's broader effort to reassert Russia in global politics.[99] Writing about Australia, Kristine Toohey briefly refers to the "political legacy" of the Sydney 2000 Games, referencing the political leaders and parties whose reputations the Games most impacted.[100]

Political legacy thus referred primarily to a country's image: how the world perceives the host country, and how that country perceives itself. It is for this reason inherently distasteful: about optics, not substance; about manipulated images, not enduring, meaningful reform. Perhaps for this reason, the political legacy concept would largely drop out of the IOC's typology. Soon after the 2002 conference, the IOC seemingly sought to steer clear of any references to the political structure of the host country. Scholars would continue to talk about it, but not the IOC or even the bidding countries. Following the conference, the IOC explicitly incorporated the legacy concept into the bidding process, though in depoliticized fashion. The promise of a positive legacy would become a key factor in London winning in 2005 the bid for the 2012 Games, and London viewed the Games not just as an athletic event but as a "catalyst for change." London introduced the term "sustainability" into the megasport lexicon, which meant that the Games "must produce long-lasting social, economic, environmental and sporting benefits."[101] This sustainability concept did not include the original political dimension.

In 2012 the IOC would affirm this newly edited concept of legacy by publishing a document, "Olympic Legacy."[102] Notably, the document contains no mention of the Games' effect on governance. Though it recognized five dimensions of legacy; the political is not among them. Directed to host cities, it read, "a potential host city must have a strong vision and clear objectives of what the Olympic Games, and even bidding, can do for its citizens, city and country."[103] The most obvious dimension, "sporting," refers to athletic facilities, levels of participation and popularity. "Economic" legacies include increased economic activity in the form of job creation, tourism, infrastructure, and foreign investment. "Urban" legacies include beautification, regeneration, and improved infrastructure improvements. "Environmental" includes a heightened environmental awareness and level of protection and sustainability, to include urban revitalization and new energy sources. "Social" legacies include rediscovery of indigenous culture or global recognition of that culture; integration of minority or marginalized populations; educational programs promoting the virtues of excellence, friendship, respect, and volunteerism; and cooperation among sectors and social groups. These five categories both originated in, and are reproduced in, the legacy scholarship.[104] None concerns politics, let alone governance.

The disappearance of political legacy leaves a gaping hole in our legacy framework. That hole keeps us from recognizing the distinctive developments in Brazil, South Korea, Qatar, and France. Recent megasport developments require that we distinguish between the symbolic projections typically implied in the "political legacy," and the systemic governance reforms now occurring. Fashioning a new dimension of legacy is the purpose of this book.

Drawing on this legacy scholarship, the IOC in 2017 produced its landmark legacy document, "Legacy Strategic Approach: Moving Forward." To the IOC's credit, the document acknowledges that "the perception of the legacy of the Olympic Games remains challenging."[105] The Strategic Approach is the IOC's effort to develop and then implement a more effective legacy strategy. The document explains that the IOC developed a series of definitions beginning in 2008.[106] Today, it "proposes" this definition:

> Olympic legacy is the result of a vision. It encompasses all the tangible and intangible long-term benefits initiated or accelerated by the hosting of the Olympic Games/sport events for people, cities/territories and the Olympic Movement.[107]

This definition provides a helpful context for understanding the human rights and anti-corruption legacy. First, the human rights and anti-corruption legacy must be envisioned; put another way, it must be planned. In this sense, Brazil and South Korea are not quite legacies; because they were not planned, their reforms may not quite count in the eyes of the IOC as legacies. They may instead be impacts. But envisioned by whom? The IOC further provides that the legacy must "originate[] in the expectations of local society." Where local society—to include civic society activists, residents, and perhaps even academics—gives rise to an idea that the organizing committee or others eventually embrace, this would count as legacy. The human rights and anti-corruption legacy is plainly a benefit, and of the intangible variety. These benefits will be long-term, barring sudden shifts in the political winds; governance reforms that last only as long as the spotlight shines on the host is no legacy at all.

A key concept to the human rights and anti-corruption legacy is "accelerated." Megasports do not have the capacity to become the original impetus to adopt anti-corruption or human rights reforms. Put another way, nobody proposes bidding for the Olympics or FIFA World Cup in order to spur an anti-corruption and human rights reform movement. The careful reader will notice the absence of the word "causation" in the following pages. Causal claims are difficult methodologically and invariably disputed. Fortunately, the literature on legacy does not require such claims. This book does not attempt to make a hard argument that hosting an MSE "causes" legacies. It instead makes the more modest claim that MSEs have accelerated the adoption of these norms, policies, practices, and laws. Social scientists may yet quibble with that argument. But without purporting to provide scientific proof, this book marshals considerable evidence that hosting these events has already had the effect of accelerating the implementation of anti-corruption and/or human rights reforms. These accelerated benefits come to the city/territory, people directly involved, and the broader Olympic Movement.[108]

The IOC legacy document contemplates various long-term benefits, similar to the above-mentioned facets: economic value and brand recognition for city/territory, environmental enhancement, urban development, culture and creative development; human skills, networks, and innovation; social development through sport. The last two are particularly relevant. Human skills, networks, and innovation can include producing a new generation of talent in a given field, developing soft skills, creating professional networks, and innovating in different fields. Social development presently includes the health benefits of sport, education in Olympic values, peace-building and international cooperation, and gender and inclusiveness.[109] There is room to add anti-corruption and human rights values, practices, and laws to both these categories.

The legacy concept figures perhaps somewhat less prominently in the FIFA space—FIFA publications and academic commentary on FIFA legacy are far more scarce than for the Olympics. FIFA does not appear to publish a single publication comparable to the IOC's "Legacy Strategic Approach." Rather, it has published legacy policy in connection with specific FIFA events. The 2014 Brazil Sustainability Strategy, for example, provides, "The sustainability efforts of the FIFA World Cup are guided by the principles of accountability, transparency, ethical behavior and respect for stakeholder interests, the rule of law, international norms of behavior and human rights. Furthermore, FIFA and the LOC aim to leave a positive legacy in the host country."[110] Whether the positive legacy is one of anti-corruption and human rights norms, practices, and laws is unclear. Still, this document provides a conceptual foundation for the modern human rights and anti-corruption legacy. Fittingly, that foundation comes out of Brazil, the first of the four case studies in this book of an MSE producing (albeit unwittingly) lasting reforms.

In the subsequent FIFA Men's World Cup—2018, in Russia—the "Sustainability Strategy" mentions issues of nondiscrimination, human rights, and anti-corruption. But more importantly, FIFA formulates in this document a definition of legacy (though somewhat buried in the glossary):

> The legacy of the FIFA World Cup is about leaving a lasting and positive impact with a focus on the host country which is achieved through the sustainable organisation of the event. It requires the contribution of all actors involved in organising the event, including FIFA, the LOC, government

> authorities, host cities and commercial affiliates. The impact can include material (e.g. sports facilities, airports, public transport, IT equipment, etc.) and non-material (capacity building, best practices, environmental regulations, processes, innovations, etc.) elements.[111]

Though not adding much to the legacy literature, this definition signals FIFA's commitment, at least in principle, to a multifaceted definition of legacy, and its openness to the concept of a human rights and anti-corruption legacy. Indeed, the human rights and anti-corruption legacy has found its fullest expression in a FIFA event, Qatar 2022.

FIFA would then make history with its hugely successful 2019 Women's World Cup. Hosted in France, the event brought unprecedented attention to women's soccer/football and was utterly devoid of the scandals that plague men's megasports. FIFA's Sustainability Strategy[112] for the event, while less developed than those of Brazil or Qatar, would nonetheless sound themes of governance broadly and human rights specifically, fitting to this powerful symbol of women's equality. Future Women's World Cups will hopefully bear the influence of France's example.

Appropriately, FIFA intimations of a nascent human rights and anti-corruption legacy are clearest in its Qatar literature. FIFA states the World Cup will "build a sustainable and lasting legacy that contributes both to FIFA's vision and Qatar's national development goals." It will create a Qatar that is "more equitable" and "free from discrimination." The Sustainability Strategy has five pillars: Social (providing an inclusive tournament experience); Environmental (delivering innovative environmental solutions); Economic (focusing on economic development); Governance (setting an example of good governance and ethical business practices); Human (develop human capital and safeguard workers' rights). These last two, of course, are all about anti-corruption and human rights norms, policies, and practices, if not laws. The document details various ways the event would promote norms and practices in ways that would likely endure after the event.[113] Of course, Qatar's accomplishment lies not in its brochures but in the reforms actually adopted. The details of Qatar's successes are discussed in Chapter 4.

Collectively, this literature provides a number of useful concepts and terms for fleshing out what the human rights and anti-corruption legacy is, and what it can become. Again, we are defining it as a series of norms, standards, policies, practices, or laws, promoting transparency, accountability, and human rights, that have application both in and beyond sports, in the host city or country, and remain in effect after the event is over. In the context of this literature, the human rights and anti-corruption legacy can be said to have the following elements.

It is planned. Members of the host community must undertake to build this legacy. The legacy visionaries need not be the IOC, FIFA, or the organizing committee, though ideally they would be. They may also include businesspersons, municipal government officials and/or employees, national government officials and/or employees, civil society advocates, and academics who envisioned this legacy and pushed for reforms that eventually became a legacy. A planned human rights and anti-corruption legacy occurs when megasport organizers and/or national lawmakers formulate an intention to build a legacy of improved human rights and/or anti-corruption norms, practices, policies, or laws. We might call the legacy accidental when the event leave long-term anti-corruption and/or human rights impacts that no one intended the event to produce. Brazil and South Korea accidental legacies, while Qatar's is planned.

It is positive. The laws, policies, practices, and norms promote the anti-corruption and human rights agendas. They encourage people that governments, businesses, and other organizations are in fact capable of adopting practices that will tend to protect these values. The sports become a symbol of our capacity for reform. They become an antidote to the view, now widely held in parts of the world, that endemic corruption and human rights violations are simply inherent in human society, that where power is wedded to profit or prestige, systemic violations are inevitable. Megasports, to date, have been a symbol of this very thing, a source of widespread cynicism and despondency. The human rights and anti-corruption legacy holds that this need not be. These events have the potential to have the opposite effect, to catalyze meaningful reforms and to symbolize to the host and the world the capacity of organizations to do so.

It is intangible. A human rights and anti-corruption legacy need not produce observable physical differences in infrastructure. It lies in the norms, skills, practices, policies, and laws, both in the public and private sectors.

It will typically accelerate, rather than independently cause, change. No one will pursue the rights to host an MSE as a means to instigating national human rights or anti-corruption reforms. The notion is absurd. But where a bid committee is putting together a bid, it will eventually realize that anti-corruption and human rights risks are significant, that preventative measures must be put in place, and that these measures can leave lasting reforms. This is the point at which the human rights and anti-corruption legacy arises: organizers realize the games can be used to improve national standards. This is precisely what happened in Qatar; it could yet happen in France. For this reason it is what I will call a secondary legacy, rather than what we might call a primary legacy. The potential for a human rights and anti-corruption legacy is not, itself, a reason to pursue a bid, as economic growth, urban renewal, or infrastructure often are. Rather, it arises in the course of preparing the bid.

Which "facets" of legacy does the human rights and anti-corruption legacy encompass? First and most obviously is policy and governance. It can produce written policies and laws, but not just in sports organizations. These can, and have, emerged in both the public and private sectors. Second is beliefs and behavior, or what the IOC calls "social development." Global norms of good governance will be internalized among volunteers, business persons, government officials, and spectators. Third is skills and knowledge, or what the IOC calls "network and innovation." Persons working with the event will learn what the laws are and how to comply with them. Best practices will disseminate.

Beyond these above-mentioned legacy distinctions widely recognized in the literature, tracing the evolution of the human rights and anti-corruption legacy requires two additional binary distinctions: reactive versus proactive; and one-dimensional versus two-dimensional. A reactive human rights and anti-corruption legacy occurs in reaction to scandals: only after an incident occurs, a protest is waged, a report is published, or a complaint is filed, does the organizing committee begin to adopt the reforms that can leave legacies. By contrast, we might use the term "proactive" to describe a legacy that arises in an anticipatory and preventative way; policies and plans form without the catalyst of scandal. Additionally, these legacies may have only a human rights or an anti-corruption legacy, in which we might call them one-dimensional, or they include both.

What then does the optimal human rights and anti-corruption legacy look like? It is of course intangible and positive. It is planned rather than accidental, and proactive rather than reactive. It includes both an anti-corruption and a human rights dimension. It touches on several recognized facets of legacy: policy and governance; norms, beliefs, and behavior (sometimes called social development); and skills and knowledge. The MSE would have accelerated, and likely not caused, these impacts.

Subsequent chapters will show a pattern of impacts that satisfy many or most of these criteria, and future aspirations to satisfy all. All are intangible and positive. Brazil and South Korea left one-dimensional anti-corruption legacies that were both reactive and accidental. Qatar's human rights legacy is intentional and proactive, but still one-dimensional. France, Australia and New Zealand, and Italy still have opportunities to leave more fulsome legacies than their predecessors. And in the United Bid, we see aspirations to the first intentional, proactive, and two-dimensional human rights and anti-corruption legacy. If megasport stakeholders—to include the IOC and FIFA, NGOs, academics, national and city government officials, and national sports organizations—were to recognize not just the appeal, but the practical viability, of a human rights and anti-corruption legacy, these aspirations may yet be fulfilled.

Brief Outline of This Book

This book is organized into four parts. Part I, entitled "Origins of a Human Rights and Anti-Corruption Legacy," maps out the historical, legal, and conceptual context that enables the human rights and anti-corruption legacy. Part II, "Early Intimations of a New Legacy," describes the reactive, accidental, and one-dimensional legacies that arose in Brazil in connection with the 2014 FIFA Men's World Cup and 2016 Rio de Janeiro Summer Olympics, and in South Korea in connection with the 2018 Pyeongchang Winter Olympics. Part III, "Progressing Toward a Proactive, Intentional, and Two-Dimensional Legacy," begins with the astonishing story of Qatar's proactive and intentional, but still one-dimensional, labor rights legacy. It then shows the still unrecognized opportunity in France, as it prepares to host the 2024 Paris Summer Olympics, to build a proactive, intentional, and two-dimensional legacy. After briefly exploring legacy opportunities in Australia and New Zealand (co-hosts of the 2023 FIFA Women's World Cup) and Italy (2026 Milan Cortina Winter Olympics), it concludes by identifying the first promised proactive, intentional, and two-dimensional legacy in the aspirations of the United Bid of Canada, the United States, and Mexico, co-hosts of the 2026 FIFA Men's World Cup. Part IV, "Building a Framework," concludes with a detailed analysis of existing megasport human rights and anti-corruption policies and practices, then suggests reforms to acknowledge, support, and expand these new legacies.

Notes

1. Int'l Olympic Comm., Legacy Strategic Approach: Moving Forward 2 (2017), https://www.olympic.org/-/media/Document%20Library/OlympicOrg/Documents/Olympic-Legacy/IOC_Legacy_Strategy_Full_version.pdf?la=en&hash=0BCD9D4723539CDC8495FE1AE6AC562BCBDAF316.
2. Christopher A. Shaw, Five Ring Circus: Myths and Realities of the Olympic Games 59 (2008).
3. Richard Espy, The Politics of the Olympic Games vii (1979).
4. Allen Guttmann, The Olympics: A History of the Modern Games 11 (1992).
5. *Id.* at 8.
6. *Id.*
7. *Id.* at 10.
8. Espy, *supra* note 3, at vii.
9. Guttmann, *supra* note 4, at 1.
10. Mark Golden, *The Ancient Olympics and the Modern: Mirror and Mirage*, *in* The Palgrave Handbook of Olympic Studies 20 (Stephen Wagg & Helen Lenskyj eds., 2012).
11. Dikaia Chatziefstathiou, *Pierre de Coubertin: Man and Myth*, *in* The Palgrave Handbook of Olympic Studies 26 (Stephen Wagg & Helen Lenskyj eds., 2012).
12. *History of FIFA—The First FIFA World Cup*, FIFA, https://www.fifa.com/news/history-fifa-the-first-fifa-world-cuptm-451.
13. *Id.*
14. Guttmann, *supra* note 4, at 37.
15. *Id.* at 54.
16. David C. Large, *The Nazi Olympics: Berlin 1936*, *in* The Palgrave Handbook of Olympic Studies 60 (Stephen Wagg & Helen Lenskyj eds., 2012).
17. *Id.* at 65.
18. Guttmann, *supra* note 4, at 68.
19. David C. Large, Nazi Games: The Olympics of 1936, 65 (2007).
20. Espy, *supra* note 3, at 21.
21. *Id.*
22. *Politics and the Olympics*, The Guardian (2011), https://www.theguardian.com/politics/politicspast/page/0,9067,892902,00.html.
23. *Id.*
24. *Id.*
25. *See id.*
26. *Id.*
27. Kenneth Garrett, The International Olympic Committee and the German Question: A Case Study of the Role of Transnational Organizations in International Relations (Honors Thesis, Stanford University, June 2002), at 12–19 (available at https://web.stanford.edu/class/ips198/docs/olympic.pdf).
28. *Id.*

29. The FIFA World Cup, 1930–2010: Politics, Commerce, Spectacle, and Identities 231 (Stefan H. Rinke & Kay Schiller eds., 2014).
30. Joseph Stiglitz, Globalization and Its Discontents (2002).
31. *Id.*
32. Fareed Zakaria, The Post-American World 1–5 (2008).
33. Thomas Friedman, The World Is Flat (2005).
34. *Id.* at 49–52.
35. *See, e.g.*, Olympic Games, Mega-Events, and Civil Societies: Globalization, Environment, and Resistance (Graeme Hayes & John Karamichas eds., 2012).
36. *Id.*
37. *See Olympic Charter*, Int'l Olympic Comm. 12, 33, 91 (2017), https://stillmed.olympic.org/media/Document%20Library/OlympicOrg/Olympic-Studies-Centre/List-of-Resources/Official-Publications/Olympic-Charters/EN-2017-Olympic-Charter.pdf#_ga=2.130046479.1093471631.1593452329-1984804538.1593452329.
38. *FIFA Statutes*, FIFA 11 (2019), https://resources.fifa.com/image/upload/fifa-statutes-5-august-2019-en.pdf?cloudid=ggyamhxxv8jrdfbekrrm.
39. Code of Conduct: Playing by the Rules, FIFA 11 (2017), https://resources.fifa.com/image/upload/fifa-code-of-conduct-2929214.pdf?cloudid=wfomatimtwtql2kogyxr.
40. *See generally* Int'l Olympic Comm., Manual on Sport and the Environment (2005), https://stillmed.olympic.org/media/Document%20Library/OlympicOrg/Documents/Olympism-in-Action/Environment/Manual-on-Sport-and-the-Environment.pdf.
41. Constance Johnson, *United Nations: Agreement Signed with Olympic Committee*, Libr. of Cong. (Apr. 30, 2014), http://www.loc.gov/law/foreign-news/article/united-nations-agreement-signed-with-olympic-committee/.
42. Memorandum from the World Health Org. & Fed'n Internationale de Football Ass'n (Oct. 4, 2019) (on file with author).
43. *UN Women Signs Partnership Agreement with the International Olympic Committee to Advance Gender Equality*, UN Women (Aug. 23, 2012), https://www.unwomen.org/en/news/stories/2012/8/un-women-signs-partnership-agreement-with-the-international-olympic-committee-to-advance-gender-equa.
44. Press Release, UN Women, FIFA and UN Women Sign First-Ever Memorandum of Understanding (June 7, 2019) (on file with author).
45. Anthony Kohoi, *Raji Attends FIFA, French Development Agency's Landmark Agreement*, Daily Observer (June 6, 2019), https://www.liberianobserver.com/news/raji-attends-fifa-french-development-agencys-landmark-agreement/.
46. Press Release, Council of Europe, Council of Europe and FIFA Sign Memorandum of Understanding (Oct. 5, 2018) (on file with author).
47. Press Release, Int'l Labour Org., Cooperation Agreement Between the IOC and the ILO (Jan. 19, 1998) (on file with author).
48. *FIFA to Assist Poor Countries*, The World Game (Apr. 23, 2014), https://theworldgame.sbs.com.au/fifa-to-assist-poor-countries.
49. Media Release, FIFA, FIFA, CAF, and African Union Sign Historic Memorandum of Understanding on Anti-Corruption and Safety (Feb. 11, 2019) (on file with author).

50. Valeria Viehoff & Gavin Poynter, Mega-Event Cities: Urban Legacies of Global Sports Events 24 (2015).
51. Anja Scheu et al., *The Legacy of the Olympic Games: A Review*, J. Global Sport Mgmt. 6: 212, 213 (2019).
52. *See generally* Holger Preuss, *Event Legacy Framework and Measurement*, 11 Int'l J. Sport Pol'y & Politics 103 (2019).
53. Scheu et al., *supra* note 51, at 1, 2.
54. *See, e.g.*, Wolfgang Maennig & Andrew Zimbalist, International Handbook on the Economics of Mega Sporting Events (2012).
55. *See* Leveraging Legacies from Sports Mega-Events: Concepts and Cases 2–12 (Jonathan Grix ed., 2014).
56. *See, e.g.*, Maennig & Zimbalist, *supra* note 54.
57. *Defining Moment: South Africa Is Suspended From World Football. September 1961*, Fin. Times (Aug. 21, 2009), https://www.ft.com/content/bfdc8150-8c57-11de-b14f-00144feabdc0.
58. *Mexican Police Exposed as Killers*, The Guardian (Dec. 10, 2001), https://www.theguardian.com/world/2001/dec/11/mexico.
59. Jonathan Stevenson, *The Story of the 1978 World Cup*, BBC (May 18, 2010), https://www.bbc.co.uk/blogs/jonathanstevenson/2010/05/the_story_of_the_1978_world_cu.html.
60. Paul Mastrocola, *The Lord of The Rings: The Role of Olympic Site Selection as a Weapon Against Human Rights Abuses: China's Bid for the 2000 Olympics*, 15 B.C. Third World L.J. 141, 141 (1995).
61. *Id.* at 142.
62. Espy, *supra* note 3, at vii ("The modern Olympic Games symbolize the struggle between man's ideals and the reality within which he must live.").
63. Donald Macintyre, *Japan's Sullied Bid*, Time (Feb. 1, 1999), http://content.time.com/time/world/article/0,8599,2053970,00.html.
64. *Id.*
65. *Id.*
66. Lex Hemphill, *OLYMPICS; Acquittals End Bid Scandal that Dogged Winter Games*, N.Y. Times (Dec. 6, 2003), https://www.nytimes.com/2003/12/06/sports/olympics-acquittals-end-bid-scandal-that-dogged-winter-games.html.
67. *Id.*
68. *Id.*
69. Olympic Reform Ten Years Later (Heather Dichter & Bruce Kidd eds., 2012).
70. *Id.*
71. *See, e.g.*, Allison Welch, *Human Rights in China: 2008 Beijing Summer Olympics*, *in* Topical Research Digest: Human Rights in China 211–13 (2009), https://www.du.edu/korbel/hrhw/researchdigest/china/OlympicsChina.pdf.
72. Press Release, *Human Rights Concerns in South Africa During the World Cup*, Amnesty Int'l (June 4, 2010)(on file with author).
73. David Smith, *Life in "Tin Can Town" for the South Africans Evicted Ahead of World Cup*, The Guardian (Apr. 1, 2010), https://www.theguardian.com/world/2010/apr/01/south-africa-world-cup-blikkiesdorp.

74. *See, e.g.*, *Russia: IOC Acts on Sochi Abuses*, HUM. RTS. WATCH (Feb. 11, 2014), https://www.hrw.org/news/2014/02/11/russia-ioc-acts-sochi-abuses.
75. Scheu et al., *supra* note 51, at 4.
76. OLYMPIC LEGACIES: INTENDED AND UNINTENDED: POLITICAL, CULTURAL, ECONOMIC, AND EDUCATIONAL 184 (J.A. Mangan & Mark Dyerson eds., 2013) (citing John J. MacAloon, *"Legacy" as Managerial/Magical Discourse in Contemporary Olympic Affairs*, 25 INT'L J. HIST. SPORT 2060 (2008)).
77. Laurence Chalip, *From Legacy to Leverage*, *in* LEVERAGING LEGACIES, *supra* note 55, at 6.
78. Martin Polley, *The 1908 Olympic Games: A Case Study in Accidental and Incidental Legacies*, *in* ROUTLEDGE HANDBOOK OF SPORT AND LEGACY 59 (Richard Holt et al. eds., 2015).
79. *See* Richard Holt & Dino Ruta, *Introduction: Sport, Legacy and Leadership*, *in* ROUTLEDGE HANDBOOK OF SPORT AND LEGACY 1–16 (Richard Holt et al. eds., 2015).
80. Jean-Loup Chappelet, *Mega Sporting Event Legacies: A Multifaceted Concept*, 25 PAPELES DE EUROPA 76, 77–80 (2012).
81. Richard Cashman, *What Is "Olympic Legacy"?*, *in* THE LEGACY OF THE OLYMPIC GAMES 1894–2000 (2003).
82. Holger Preuss, *"Legacy" Revisited*, *in* LEVERAGING LEGACIES, *supra* note 55, at 25.
83. Holger Preuss, *The Conceptualization of Measurement of Mega Sport Event Legacies*, 12 J. SPORT TOURISM 207, 209–10 (2007).
84. OLYMPIC LEGACIES, *supra* note 76, at 41 (citing Chris Gratton & Holger Preuss, *Maximizing Olympic Impacts by Building Up Legacies*, 25 INT'L J. HISTORY SPORT 1922 (2008)).
85. Preuss, *supra* note 83, at 207, 211.
86. Scheu et al., *supra* note 51, at 1, 10.
87. Wolfgang Maennig & Marcel Porsche, *The Feel-Good Effect at Mega Sports Events—Recommendations for Public and Private Administration Informed by the Experience of the FIFA World Cup 2006*, at 1 (INT'L ASS'N OF SPORTS ECONOMISTS, WORKING PAPER NO. 08-17, 2008).
88. *See generally* Jonathan Grix & Paul Michael Brannagan, *Of Mechanisms and Myths: Conceptualizing States' "Soft Power" Strategies through Sports Mega-Events*, 27 DIPL. & STATECRAFT 251 (2016).
89. Scheu et al., *supra* note 51, at 1, 12.
90. *See generally* Becca Leopkey & Milena M. Parent, *Olympic Games Legacy: From General Benefits to Sustainable Long-Term Legacy*, 29 INT'L J. HIST. SPORT 924 (2012).
91. *Id.*
92. Scheu et al., *supra* note 51, at 1, 12.
93. *See generally* Lynn Minnaert, *An Olympic Legacy for All? The Non-infrastructural Outcomes of the Olympic Games for Socially Excluded Groups (Atlanta 1996–Beijing 2008)*, 33 TOURISM MGMT. 361 (2012).
94. *See generally* Preuss, *supra* note 52, at 103.
95. OLYMPIC GAMES, MEGA-EVENTS, AND CIVIL SOCIETIES, *supra* note 35, at 2.
96. ROUTLEDGE HANDBOOK OF SPORT AND POLITICS (Alan Bairner et al. eds., 1st ed. 2016).

97. Philip K. Porter & Daniel M. Chin, *Economic Impact of Sports Events*, *in* MAENNIG & ZIMBALIST, *supra* note 54.
98. *Id.* at 260.
99. *Id.*
100. OLYMPIC LEGACIES, *supra* note 76, at 82.
101. Preuss, *supra* note 83, at 207, 210 (citing J.L. Chappelet, *The Tale of Three Olympic Cities—forecast for Torino on Basis of Grenoble and Innsbruck*, TORINO 2006—XX WINTER OLYMPIC GAMES SYMPOSIUM, Feb. 2006); Holt & Ruta, *supra* note 79, at 12.
102. *Olympic Legacy*, INT'L OLYMPIC COMM. (2012), https://stillmed.olympic.org/Documents/Olympism_in_action/Legacy/Olympic_Legacy.pdf.pdf.
103. *Id.* at 6.
104. *See* Holt & Ruta, *supra* note 79, at 2.
105. INT'L OLYMPIC COMM., *supra* note 1, at 2.
106. *Id.* at 12.
107. *Id.* at 3.
108. *See id.* at 16.
109. *Id.* at 17–18.
110. 2014 FIFA World Cup: Sustainability Strategy—Concept, FIFA 10 (2012), https://resources.fifa.com/image/upload/sustainability-strategy-brazil-2014-1651925.pdf?cloudid=pttys42mvib8pdwfmmf0.
111. Sustainability Strategy: 2018 FIFA World Cup, FIFA 25 (2015), https://resources.fifa.com/image/upload/sustainability-strategy-for-the-2018-fifa-world-cup-2666950.pdf?cloudid=h0ysulsujvogspqmnbhl.
112. Sustainability Strategy: FIFA Women's World Cup France 2019, FIFA (2018), https://resources.fifa.com/image/upload/nachhaltigkeitsstrategie-fur-die-fifa-frauen-wm-frankreich-2019.pdf?cloudid=r2sks010xbbqhhobnkq1.
113. *See* FIFA World Cup Qatar 2022 Executive Summary, FIFA 10–11 (2019), https://resources.fifa.com/image/upload/fifa-world-cup-qatar-2022tm-sustainability-strategy-executive-summary.pdf?cloudid=bl0bgeroqdmxjme4sy7h.

2

Globalized Standards

Introduction

As Chapter 1 described, the human rights and anti-corruption legacy could not now emerge without certain preconditions in place. One of those preconditions is widespread agreement, at least in principle, on human rights and anti-corruption standards. We had to arrive at the point that the IOC and FIFA could require host countries to comply with these standards without compromising a commitment to political neutrality.

Arriving at this point in history occurred in three distinct steps. First, anti-corruption and human rights norms had to achieve a measure of global assent. By assent, this book does not and could not mean absolute unanimity and the utter absence of resistance and dispute. Rather, it means a state of affairs in which very nearly every country in the world has joined key anti-corruption and human rights instruments; an agreement in principle that these norms matter.

Second, we had to achieve at least a loose agreement that those norms applied not just to government but to business. This entails an understanding that governments are not the only institutions posing human rights and corruption risks. Businesses have achieved a similar degree of power and salience in society, and citizens are not protected from corruption and human rights abuses unless businesses have legally binding compliance obligations. Third, the norms we applied to business had to then apply to megasports.

This chapter describes these first two steps; the remainder of the book describes the third. These two areas of governance are here discussed in the order in which they emerged historically: first human rights, then anti-corruption. Ultimately, it aims to provide a grounding in the anti-corruption and human rights concepts and instruments that constitute the foundation of the human rights and anti-corruption legacy. It briefly describes the historical origins of human rights and anti-corruption norms and how they became cemented as global political values in the late twentieth century. It then shows how these values came to be extended beyond the operations

A New Megasport Legacy. Andrew Brady Spalding, Oxford University Press. © Oxford University Press 2022.
DOI: 10.1093/oso/9780197503614.003.0002

of government, to business, in the form of anti-corruption compliance and human rights due diligence.

The Post–World War II Global Human Rights Movement

As mentioned in Chapter 1, the worldwide critique that megasports suffer from human rights problems, and require human rights reforms, presumes both that human rights are real and that the institutions involved in producing mega sporting events (MSEs) should protect them. This section explains how something of a loose consensus on key human rights norms came to exist internationally in the late twentieth century. Some may writhe at the notion. Those dedicated to fighting for the progressive realization of these rights may take issue with the suggestion that any kind of consensus now exists, to any meaningful degree. They may look to the abysmal human rights records of the world's largest and most visible countries—such as China, Russia, Saudi Arabia, or the United States—as definitive proof that any such consensus is yet decades away.

To understand what this chapter claims, and what it does not, we might look at rights in three dimensions: as norms, as laws, and as practices. By the last of these three measures, the global record may well be bleak; this book's thesis in no way aims to diminish this fact. However, at the level of laws and of norms the present moment looks different. Consider again the juxtaposition of two consecutive megasport hosts: France, and Qatar. In many respects, these two countries seem about as dissimilar in relation to the global human rights movement as could be. France, since its French Revolution of 1789, has been widely regarded as a pioneer in defining and implementing human rights. Even today, as this chapter discusses, France occupies the very cutting edge of the effort to impose binding legal human rights obligations on companies. In seemingly sharp contrast stands Qatar, a tiny country that did not even exist until fifty years ago, and which sits in a region and a belief system that has historically resisted the global human rights movement. That this country would now be setting the standard for human rights reforms in MSEs is itself powerful evidence of the globalization of human rights norms.

This book thus looks at human rights as norms and as laws. A right can exist, and be said to be "real," in either form.[1] Norms might be understood as the philosophical precursors to laws. Norms about the fundamental purposes of government—to include both the limits on power, and obligations of the state to use its power—are frequently expressed in terms of rights.[2] They may not yet be formalized in law, but that doesn't mean they're not rights. People had rights before governments recognized them; citizens today have rights regardless of whether their government recognizes them. In this regard, a right begins as a norm.

Norms may then become laws. A human rights law can then exist at either the national level or the international level. Lawyers are often cautious to recognize a right before it is formalized in positive law, fearful the right will be dismissed as "soft law," lacking enforcement. But this way of thinking—of validating rights only once formalized into positive law—carries risks of its own. Rights recognized in law, whether national or international, are dependent upon the contingencies of political negotiations. We wouldn't want to delegate the task of defining human rights to politicians and ambassadors. There is a risk of making too little of positive law, but also of making too much.[3]

Whether yet recognized in law or not, a human right is, by definition, universal. All living humans—and in some cases, persons who are not humans, particularly legal persons such as corporations—have rights. These rights are said to exist independently of whether they are recognized in a nation's law, culture, or intellectual traditions. Rights are inherent in being a human being.[4] However, not every right is a human right. Human rights are "intimately connected to human existence in dignity and freedom."[5] They are "of paramount importance" and their violation is a "grave affront to justice."[6] Even so, human rights may not be absolute. They should be "resistant to trade-offs, but not too resistant."[7] In this sense, rights are prioritized and weighed against other governance priorities (like national security or fiscal concerns). Most would agree that some rights can be suspended in times of emergency. For example, though Thomas Jefferson famously declared rights "inalienable,"[8] one who endorses both human rights and the legitimacy of imprisoning criminals "must hold that people's rights to freedom of movement can be forfeited temporarily or permanently by just convictions of serious crimes."[9] Rights are of utmost importance, but practically speaking must still be weighed on the scale of governance.

Though rights are often criticized as ethnocentric or a form of cultural imperialism, many of the world's religious and philosophical traditions incorporate some precursor to modern rights talk.[10] Today, three-quarters of the world's countries have ratified the major human rights treaties. Polling shows widespread support across national and cultural boundaries for a variety of human rights, such as freedom of religion, freedom of speech, and racial and gender equality This support has been proven to exist even in countries that have historically resisted rights, such as China and Iran. The resistance to rights may come principally from those in power, not those whom the governments ostensibly serve.

It may be fitting, or at least worth noting, that modern human rights thinking originated in the same two countries that today provide the official languages of megasports: England and France. Still, its origins are ancient. The oldest known document alluding to rights may be the Cyrus Cylinder of 539 BCE, which provides an account of the conquest of Babylon by Cyrus the Great and has been described as the "First Charter of Human Rights."[11] A more familiar dating is the Magna Carta of 1215, which limited the power of the king of England, promising to protect church rights, ban illegal imprisonment—an early precursor to modern due process—and outlaw excessive taxation. From ancient origins, the idea gained momentum in modern world with English philosopher John Locke and his 1690 *Two Treatises of Civil Government*. Locke argues that we can understand the purpose of government by first reflecting on what the human condition is or would be in its absence, a condition he called the state of nature. In the state of nature, we are all free and equal, enjoying our natural right to liberty. However, owing to this absolute freedom and equality, we lack a neutral third party with the authority to resolve disputes. We are therefore each left to enforce the "law of nature" in our own cases. Predictably, this system breaks down, as "self-love will make men partial to themselves and their friends."[12] Humankind thus needs a government, a "common measure to decide all controversies"[13] that will remedy "those evils which necessarily follow from men being judges in their own cases."[14] The French philosopher Baron de Montesquieu, in *The Spirit of the Laws*, approached rights a different way. Eschewing the Anglo, philosophical abstractions of the state of nature and the social contract, he defined liberty as "a tranquility of mind arising from the opinion each person has of his safety."[15] Liberty, for Montesquieu, is the aim of government. For both thinkers, the administration of justice is easily tainted or, if you will, corrupted, by self-interest. Persons in power are prone to abuse it. This theme should resonate strongly to fans of megasports.

The eighteenth century produced two human rights documents, justifying revolutions in the British Empire and in France. The US Declaration of Independence, written in 1776 and squarely in the Lockean tradition, famously proclaimed the "self-evident truth" that all persons had rights.[16] The US Constitution would be written in 1787, and two years later, in 1789, its Bill of Rights. That same year, France's National Assembly would adopt the Declaration of the Rights of Man as a core statement of the ideals justifying its own revolution. This latter justification may have commanded more credibility, then and well into the future, untainted as it was by slavery. The Declaration proclaimed the "natural, unalienable, and sacred rights of man," arguing that all humans are free by birth and endowed with equal rights, including freedom of political association and participation in government, unjust detention, excessive punishment, due process, freedom of belief and expression, equitable taxation, property, and interestingly, a right to "require of every public agent an account of his administration," that is, a right to be free from endemic official corruption.[17] The enumeration of universal human rights had begun.

Though French and Anglo-American traditions had begun to embrace at least the principle of human rights, this ethic of universalism would not itself become universal until much later. The movement would again be infused with momentum following World War II and the Holocaust. Professor Louis Henkin said that human rights were "born in, and out of, World War II."[18] Previously, throughout the nineteenth century, states were widely viewed as sovereign and the treatment of their citizenry a domestic matter. In the wake of World War II, states would lose their status as the embodiment of the highest social values. At least one historian, Daniel Cohen, has challenged this narrative. Though questioning how explicitly the Holocaust was invoked in UN promotional materials, he does not doubt that the event was the principal psychological impetus. Still, World War II "paved the way for a new understanding of the relationships between the individual, the state, and the international community."[19] Experience showed, through the tragedies of two world wars, that governments alone were seemingly incapable of protecting—or even properly interpreting—the human rights that all human beings possess.

The postwar era would thus give rise to instruments that are now integrated into Olympic host-city contracts and that form the basis for the human rights obligations of sport organizers. As megasports exploded in popularity and magnitude following World War II, so too did the governance standards that would ultimately apply to megasports. In the years after World War II, support rose for an intergovernmental organization that would put human rights at the fore of its focus. A number of NGOs and interested parties successfully lobbied for a rights-based amendment of the UN Charter. Like the US Constitution, the original UN Charter did not include a Bill of Rights.

The Human Rights Commission, headed by Eleanor Roosevelt, had the difficult task of articulating to a battered and skeptical world just what values the newly constituted United Nations would espouse—which natural rights it would endeavor to protect. On December 10, 1948, the Universal Declaration of Human Rights[20] was adopted. Eleanor Roosevelt expressed hope that it would become "the international Magna Carta for all [persons] everywhere." The Commission included members from eighteen countries, and incorporated many rights traditions.[21] Membership in United Nations at the time was only fifty-six states, representing a very different world order from the one in which we now live. Forty-eight states voted in favor and eight abstained, including the Soviet Union, Saudi Arabia, and South Africa.

As a General Assembly Declaration, the document lacks the force of an international treaty, but it provides a conceptual and political foundation for subsequent covenants. It covers civil and political rights such as the rights to life, anti-discrimination, protection against cruel or unusual punishment, equality before the law, due process, freedom of movement, freedom of thought, expression, and worship, and participation in government. So too does it cover economic, social, and cultural rights, such as the right to work by choice and in safe conditions with limited hours and paid vacation; the right to a standard of living including food, clothing, housing, and medicine; the right to education and enjoyment of arts and sciences; the right to intellectual property; and beyond.[22]

The General Assembly Declaration was meant to be immediately followed by a more detailed human rights instrument. But as the Cold War intensified, both the Soviet Union and the United States became, in their own ways, sources of resistance. The world would have to wait eighteen years. Rather than a single, unified covenant, the United Nations produced two: the International Covenant on Civil and Political Rights, and the International Covenant on Economic, Social, and Cultural Rights. Both were opened for ratification in 1966 and entered into force in 1976.

The International Covenant on Civil and Political Rights recognizes five groups of rights:

> the individual's physical integrity, including torture, arbitrary arrest, and deprivation of life; procedural fairness in arrest, trial, and imprisonment; equal protection without regard to race, religion, gender, and other categories; freedom of belief, speech, and association; and the right to political participation.[23]

Today, 173 states are full parties, while 6 are mere signatories, and 18 have taken no action. The conspicuous outlier is China, which is a signatory but not yet a state party.

Complementing this instrument is the International Covenant on Economic, Social, and Cultural Rights. These rights tend to impose obligations on states not merely to refrain from interfering in a sphere of liberty but to affirmatively create conditions for its preservation. The covenant includes the rights to: work freely; education and training; fair wages and safe conditions; limited hours and paid vacations; enter trade unions and right to strike; social security, including insurance; have a family, with paid maternity leave; protections against child labor; adequate food, clothing, and housing, and the continuous improvement of living conditions; physical and mental health; and cultural and scientific participation and protection of intellectual property rights. This covenant would eventually command the assent of 170 state parties, with 4 signatories, and 23 that have taken no action. Here the conspicuous outliers are the United States, which is a signatory but not a state party, and Saudi Arabia, which has taken no action.

The difference between these two categories of rights is sometimes styled as "negative" versus "positive" rights: the civil and political are characterized as rights against the state, that limit or negate state power, while positive rights place affirmative duties on the state. Others might describe it as the difference between "freedom from" and "freedom to." However, a more careful consideration shows that these distinctions ultimately break down. The right to a fair trial, quintessentially a civil and political right, obviously imposes an obligation on the state to act, rather than to not act. Still, both kinds of rights have worked their way into our collective consciousness, and both are included among the rights that megasports must now address.

Following these covenants were a series of more specialized international human rights instruments. While these instruments are, for a variety of reasons, less explicitly integrated into megasports governance standards, they nonetheless illustrate the emerging global human rights norms. The Convention on the Prevention and Punishment of the Crime of Genocide was enacted by the United Nations in 1948. This was the first human rights treaty to be adopted by the UN General Assembly, which codified genocide as a crime during times of war and peace. Its adoption solidified the United Nations' commitment to make genocide a crime in hopes to "never again" the atrocities of World War II. To date, the only state that has not ratified this treaty is the Dominican Republic.[24] The International Convention on the

Elimination of All Forms of Racial Discrimination, which certainly wields an influence in megasports, was enacted by the United Nations in 1965. This treaty was formed to prohibit states from engaging in racial discrimination to secure equal rights, freedoms, and protections for all. These protections also prohibit discrimination based on sex, language, color, religion, and national origin. Currently only Bhutan, Nauru, and Palau have signed but not yet ratified the treaty.[25]

Similarly, the Convention on the Elimination of All Forms of Discrimination Against Women ("the Convention") was enacted by the United Nations in 1979. Its passage aims to ensure equality between men and women in an effort to eliminate discrimination on the basis of sex. The Convention devotes major attention to discrimination against women in areas such as their reproductive rights, cultural relations, and political participation. The United States has signed but not yet ratified the treaty; this could prove a source of major embarrassment to the host of the 2026 FIFA Men's World Cup and the 2028 Summer Olympics.[26] The Convention Against Torture and other Cruel, Inhuman, or Degrading Treatment or Punishment was enacted by the United Nations in 1984. This treaty prohibits state parties from engaging in intentional torture tactics to induce a confession, punishment for an act by a third party, or intimidating acts by an actor or third party to achieve such a result. Consequently, its adoption aims to promote universal respect across state lines to protect the dignity of all humans. Brunei Darussalam, Haiti, India, Palau, and Sudan have signed but not yet ratified the treaty.[27] The Convention on the Rights of the Child was enacted by the United Nations in 1989. Its adoption emphasizes the importance of the growth of children to flourish in society, in hopes for children to grow up in an environment centered around love, peace, and equality. This treaty strives to improve the livelihood of children around the globe, in particular the lives of those living in developing countries, who arguably face disparate conditions incomparable to the developed world. Again, the United States has signed but not yet ratified the treaty. One might hope that hosting upcoming MSEs will produce international pressure on the United States to join the rest of the world and ratify these treaties.[28]

Following these came an instrument that is now central to the megasports human rights framework. The International Labour Organization's Declaration on Fundamental Principles and Rights at Work (FPRW) was passed by the ILO in 1998. Global gaps in working conditions became the topic of conversation at the World Summit in Copenhagen in 1995. These conversations paved the way for the Declaration's adoption in 1998, which defined a standard of rights to be respected by all ILO members, regardless if they have not ratified its fundamental conventions.[29] Its adoption signifies each member state's commitment to endorsing four core principles: freedom of association and the effective recognition of the right to collective bargaining; the elimination of all forms of forced or compulsory labor; the effective abolition of child labor; and the elimination of discrimination with respect to employment and occupation.[30]

Critics note that the passage of the FPRW has shown the ILO's significant shortcomings in enforcing the four principles. Despite satisfactory ratification rates, half of the world's workers are not protected by two of the ILO's fundamental conventions; namely, the freedom of association and the freedom of collective bargaining. If the ILO's fundamental conventions truly aim to enforce the four principles, critics argue that universal ratification is necessary to achieve this result. Moreover, bilateral and multilateral trade agreements are seeming to take the place of the four principles and the ILO's fundamental conventions. And until the FPRW becomes enforceable treaty law, provided with sanctions for noncompliance, members seldom have incentive to ensure the same compliance that the ILO seeks.[31] To the surprise of many, megasports are helping this process.

The ILO Declaration, combined with the International Covenant on Civil and Political Rights and the International Covenant on Economic, Social, and Cultural Rights, form the foundation of human rights standards now applied to megasports. But all these developments, standing alone, would not have gotten us there. If megasports are to make any progress in preventing systemic human rights abuses, their standards must apply not just to governments but to businesses. The next section describes how this occurred.

Where Human Rights Meet Business: The UN Guiding Principles

Historically, human rights claims were made only against states. States have the power to significantly encroach upon our freedom, and rights are the way we define the limits on legitimate state authority. However, many of the key actors in the MSE space—especially organizing committees and the companies doing business with them—are not state actors. If we still believed that rights claims make sense only vis-à-vis governments, there would be little to say here about how the MSEs can embody, let alone promote, our human rights standards and practices. An essential conceptual precondition for the human rights and anti-corruption legacy is the notion that businesses also have the power to violate rights, and that we can legitimately impose responsibilities upon businesses to protect those rights. Enter the UN Guiding Principles on Business and Human Rights (UNGPs).

Just as the crisis of World War II would produce the international human rights instruments relating to governments, a series of corporate scandals would catalyze the extension of these norms to the conduct of business. At the end of the twentieth century, the role of multinational corporate operations in the everyday lives of global citizens expanded in ways that existing human rights norms and instruments could not address. Emblematic scandals such as Nike's debacle with low wages and abusive working conditions, the Union Carbide chemical leak in Bhopal, and Yahoo! sharing sensitive customer information with the Chinese government demonstrated that the interplay of corporate entities across borders and jurisdictions had outpaced the development of institutions to deal with human rights transgressions.[32] Companies attempted to exculpate themselves on legalistic and jurisdictional grounds, blaming their supply-chain partners or other third parties or hiding behind contracts and investment agreements with host countries. A unified vision for corporate human rights governance was lacking.[33]

To address this gap, the UN Commission on Human Rights (later the Human Rights Council, or HRC) created in 2005 a mandate tasked with identifying and clarifying the major issues facing corporations and their responsibilities to the global human rights regime. Professor John Ruggie, as Special Representative, conducted dozens of consultations all over the world with government officials, NGOs, corporations, and lawyers. His research identified the extent of the problem: confusion over which rights were implicated and where.[34] The mandate was then extended, allowing Ruggie to draft the Protect, Respect, and Remedy Framework, which identifies the legal obligations of states with respect to business and human rights, the corporate responsibility to respect human rights, and the vehicles for remedy that apply to both.[35] Finally, the mandate was extended once more to allow for the development and ultimately unanimous endorsement of the UNGPs, which operationalized the Framework. In Ruggie's own words, this was "the end of the beginning."[36]

In the initial phase of the mandate, Ruggie and his team found that corporations affect the entire range of recognized human rights. Their research indicated that companies negatively impacted rights related to health, housing and safe drinking water, security of the person, indigenous peoples, free speech, assembly, and fair trials. This contravened the general operating assumption that companies' adverse effects on human rights were limited to workplace rights and those related to labor and employment. Another important finding revealed that incidents of reported abuses increased significantly in host countries with inadequate governance and sporadic rule of law. Because of this, it became a priority to formulate a basis for corporate responsibility that did not depend on the host country fulfilling its own obligations. Differentials between international and local standards required a nuanced approach. Finally, the mandate's initial research found that the worst incidents of corporate abuse of human rights occurred in conflict zones. Partially, this could be attributed to armed conflict attracting illicit actors, but even global brands were not immune to this propensity. Because countries involved in armed conflict are often not in a position to fulfill their obligations, it became obvious to Ruggie and his team that these scenarios were instances in which the home state of incorporation could and should assume a more primary regulatory role.[37]

The HRC extended Ruggie's mandate in 2007 and tasked him with taking his findings and prescribing a path forward. Historically, advocacy groups had supported mandatory measures, believing them to be the only option with enough teeth to break the inertia exhibited by governments and corporations. By contrast—and not surprisingly—governments and corporations traditionally supported voluntary measures, arguing that the situation was too complex for one-size-fits-all, mandatory measures to tackle. A mandatory framework would take the form of a negotiated treaty agreement between state parties, while a voluntary one would necessitate a substantive beefing-up of the corporate social responsibility (CSR) programs already gaining in popularity. Ultimately, Ruggie concluded that a polycentric governance model was most suited to the task, neither wholly mandatory nor simply voluntary, and comprising aspects of both corporate and civil governance.[38] In 2011, six years after the initial mandate had been granted, the HRC unanimously "endorsed" the UNGPs.[39] The UNGPs were never codified and did not quite become "hard law" at the international level. Still, they became a standard that has been integrated into other negotiated agreements. The IOC Host City Contract is a powerful example of precisely this process—the UNGPs becoming enforceable law through their incorporation into a legally binding contract.

The UNGPs draw on the terminology of the two international human rights covenants to create a three-part framework: "protect" human rights, "respect" human rights, and "remedy" violations. Chapter 8 further explains these principles; this chapter simply introduces them.

The duty to protect requires states to take measures to protect the human rights of individuals from the conduct of third parties, such as other individuals and corporations. States must do more than simply refrain from engaging in human rights abuses; they must take affirmative measures to prevent, investigate, punish, and provide remedy for third-party abuses within their jurisdiction. To protect means to prevent, investigate, punish, and redress through policies, laws, adjudication, and enforcement. The UNGPs elaborate on what each of these mean.

States "should set out clearly the expectation" that businesses "respect" (defined later) human rights in their operation.[40] Applied to the megasport context, this means that the host country or city should establish and enforce this expectation vis-à-vis organizing committees as well as third parties. Businesses (and other non-state actors) have the responsibility to "respect" human rights, with this duty being most fully articulated under the UNGPs. The responsibility to respect requires parties to refrain from acts or omissions that harm the human rights of a person or people. To respect is to prevent, to mitigate, and to remedy abuses that the company is "involved in," either through its own activities or those "directly linked" to is operations. This linkage is key to understanding the difference between the state's duty to protect and the corporation's responsibility to respect. While the scope of a state's duty is defined by its jurisdiction, the scope of the business' responsibility is defined by linkage to its operations. The "directly linked" provision, in effect, becomes a kind of jurisdictional provision for these non-state entities. The core components of the responsibility to respect are essentially three: a company-wide policy commitment to preventing human rights abuses; conducting meaningful due diligence to identify, prevent, and mitigate abuses within activities directly linked to its operations; and a process of remediation. The UNGPs provide further descriptions of each. This responsibility applies to all businesses regardless of size, sector, or context, but the extent of measures required will vary with the company's size and riskiness of operations. While the UNGPs do not provide a comprehensive list of the rights businesses must respect, the document does suggest that, at a minimum, it include the International Bill of Human Rights as well as the International Labour Organization's Declaration on Fundamental Principles and Rights at Work.[41] In summary, the corporate responsibility to respect human rights exists independently of, and complements, the state's duty to protect, includes the whole array of internationally recognized human rights, and includes in scope any potential impact deriving from the company's activities or impacts that flow from its business relationships.[42]

Finally, both states and businesses must "remedy" human rights violations. Effective remedies must be provided to victims of business-related human rights abuses. Appropriate grievance mechanisms must therefore be established. The character of the grievance mechanism, and the remedy, can vary according to the authority and capacity of the organization, as well as the nature of the harm. Grievance mechanisms may be judicial or nonjudicial. They can include civil and/or criminal courts, arbitration or other alternative dispute resolution methods, labor tribunals, national human rights institutions, Organisation for Economic Co-operation and Development (OECD) National Contact Points, and various government-sponsored mechanisms like ombudsperson offices and government-run complaint offices. Remedies can include apologies, restitution, rehabilitation, financial or nonfinancial compensation, and punitive sanctions.

The UNGPs have not proven entirely satisfactory to human rights advocates and scholars, nor will they to the MSE community. The document is variously criticized in regards to process, substance, and enforcement.[43] Some argue that Ruggie's process and methodology valued consensus over substance. They contend that the UN Special Representative of the Secretary-General (SRSG) ensured the support of the business community by employing language that would appeal to them. In particular, by connecting the corporate responsibility to respect with "social expectations" and the "court of public opinion," the SRSG emphasized economic incentives to respect human rights. The due diligence framework also spoke to business, as it suggested that familiar methods could be brought to bear in fulfillment of these responsibilities.[44] Others posit that the UNGP's consensus-driven methodology forced a shift toward CSR and a voluntary framework. The debate that surrounded the UNGPs avoided the implementation of any legally binding framework, opting instead to ground the responsibility to respect as a "social norm." This line of criticism also wonders if we are any closer to answering the question of whether businesses are bound by international human rights law than we were when the process began.[45]

Some critics believe that corporations should, and might now, have stronger responsibilities than the UNGPs acknowledge. David Bilchitz disagrees with the SRSG's rejection of international law as a source of binding authority for the corporate responsibility to respect and believes that corporate responsibilities in the realm of human rights actually go beyond the responsibility to respect.[46] Similarly, Justine Nolan acknowledges that "soft law" can at times be more than voluntary, especially if it is "consistent, comprehensive, and implemented." However, she criticizes the UNGPs as too soft; the source of their authority is ill-formed, the language too lenient and suggestive.[47] Still others take issue with the SRSG's decision to move away from the legally binding, international treaty route. Anita Ramasastry discusses other spheres of practice, such as logging and conflict minerals, where binding international agreements have become the norm. This suggests that the same path might have been pursued in the area of human rights, and that the foreclosure assumed by the SRSG in that regard may have been an illusion.[48] Scholars have also asked whether human rights due diligence—the major practical implication of the responsibility to respect—can adequately prevent a corporation from being complicit in human rights violations. Moreover, the UNGPs fall short of making adequate due diligence a defense to corporate liability, and this oversight might have the unintended effect of discouraging robust due diligence systems.[49] Finally, some believe more guidance is needed on how to enhance access to, and the efficacy of, nonjudicial grievance mechanisms. Empirical analysis has found them wanting.[50]

As a general rule, negotiated international agreements fail to satisfy all stakeholders. The UNGPs are no exception. As the UNGPs are increasingly integrated into MSE governance, human rights critics will point out, perhaps rightly, their various shortcomings. Still, invoking the UNGPs in MSE contracts represents a substantial step forward for MSE governance specifically and for the human rights movement generally. That step has of course occurred side by side with another—the incorporation of anti-corruption standards—as the next section explains.

The 1990s Corruption Eruption

Corruption in government, and in commerce, is as old as government itself. But binding international anti-corruption instruments, and widely recognized standards of corporate anti-corruption governance, are relatively new.

While the human rights instruments were born between World War II and the 1960s, international anti-corruption law and best practices emerged in the 1990s and 2000s. The economist Moises Naim coined the term "corruption eruption" in 1995 to describe that decade's extraordinary surge in attention among lawmakers, commentators, and citizens to the problem of public corruption.[51] This so-called eruption occurred along several dimensions and was due to a variety of cultural, legal, and economic changes that, as this section explains, largely sprang from the end of the Cold War. Like human rights before them, international instruments first codified binding obligations on governments. Then, less formal (but nonetheless impactful) "soft law" created a regime of best practices for businesses.

The term "corruption" is thrown around quite loosely; indeed, it is too easy to deem every abuse of power as corrupt. This tendency was on display in commentary surrounding the Rio 2016 Summer Olympics, in which every governance problem—from the Zika virus to water pollution—was seemingly taken as evidence of corruption. If the word is to mean anything, we must distinguish it from simple bad government. In fairness, no single, universally accepted definition of corruption exists. The term "corrupt" derives from a Latin word that means to decay or to rot. Interestingly, at a recent conference in Russia, a local scholar suggested that the term "corruption" does not apply to the Russian government because a rotting or decaying process presumes the existence of something originally healthy, which the Russian government never was. Historically, the term referred to both political and sexual behavior; this study will obviously avoid the latter. A broader, more contemporary analogue would be the distinction between institutional and moral corruption. This study obviously focuses on the former.

Notably, the world's most prominent anti-corruption document, the UN Convention Against Corruption (UNCAC), makes no effort to define the term.[52] Rather, it seemingly takes the same approach that US Supreme Court Justice Potter Stewart took in relation to obscenity. Admitting his inability to render a definition, he famously wrote, "I know it when I see it."[53] Still, a definition is in order.

Probably the most widely cited definition is "the abuse of public office for private gain." This formulation was first developed by the legendary Harvard political scientist Joseph Nye in the 1960s.[54] The World Bank, whose anti-corruption effort is perhaps second in the world only to US enforcement of the Foreign Corrupt Practices Act (FCPA), has adopted this definition; or rather, in their words, they have "settled" on it.[55] Transparency International, the world's leading anti-corruption NGO, uses a variation thereof: "the abuse of entrusted power for private gain."[56] Similarly, the US Agency for International Development uses "the abuse of entrusted authority for private gain."[57] Note the subtle but important differences in these definitions, particularly the usage of "public office" versus "entrusted power" versus "entrusted authority."

These definitions have three essential elements. The first is "abuse." This term is potentially very broad. Indeed, when scholars were wrestling with how to define this term back in the 1960s and 70s, the question of whether anti-corruption efforts were better served by a wider or more narrow definition of abuse was widely debated, without resolution.

The second is "public office," "entrusted authority," or "entrusted power." Here lies a crucial difference among the variants on the definition. Note that the first term contemplates abuse only by public officials—that is, government officials. It does not try to encompass private conduct. This has the benefit of confining the inquiry to a more discrete field, but has two limitations. First, where a private party has participated in the corruption say, by bribing a government official, the private party's offer or payment of the bribe is not itself corrupt. At most, it is the inducement or aiding and abetting of corruption. Second, some conduct associated with the Olympics that we might call corrupt does not involve public officials at all; match fixing, for example. Appropriate to our purposes, "entrusted authority" is broader. Any actor with authority, including a company employee tasked with negotiating contracts, or an Olympic games referee, has "authority." Finally, "power" is broader yet, as it does not refer exclusively to a kind of formal relationship with delegated authority. Any person with the ability to coerce may be said to possess power.

The third element is "private gain." The original meaning of this phrase has become somewhat obscured in contemporary anti-corruption discourse. Today, most equate "gain" with financial profit. However, earlier definitions, particularly Professor Nye's, contemplated status, prestige, or power in addition to money.[58] Indeed, the Olympic Games provide opportunities for all these forms of private gain: substantial sums of money pass hands, and much prestige is at stake.

Other definitions have gained less traction, but may prove nonetheless illuminating. These include "behavior which deviates from the formal duties of a public role because of private-regarding (personal, close family, private clique) pecuniary or status gains; or violates rules against the exercise of certain types of private-regarding behavior."[59] Another is "a public official, acting for personal gain, violates the norms of public office and harms the interests of the public to benefit a third party who, having received access to goods or services she would not otherwise obtain, rewards the public official."[60] Yet a third is "conduct by a public or private actor that is intended to procure some benefit, either personally or for someone else, the granting of which would contravene official or fiduciary duty and the rights of others."[61]

This book is framed by all these definitions. It will focus on corruption among government officials as well as the private (or semi-private) individuals and organizations that are complicit in megasport corruption. As is appropriate to megasports, we should acknowledge the opportunities for both pecuniary and nonpecuniary gain; these events involve enormous amounts of both money and prestige. We should consider any conduct that violates positive law or widely established norms of official conduct as abuse.

Corruption thus defined can take on a number of forms, all of which may arise in megasports. Perhaps most salient in the international legal landscape today is bribery, which has been defined as an illegal payment made to a government official in return for official, state-sanctioned, authoritative act that produces a selective and tangible impact and that in the absence of the secret payment would not otherwise have been made.[62] A kickback, by contrast, is a payment that is made after, rather than prior to, conferring the benefit, and usually as a portion of the payment from the government to the individual (for example, as the percentage of a contract award). Extortion involves a public official threatening the abuse of power to induce a payment, while embezzlement involves officials, acting alone, to misappropriate public funds. Nepotism consists of decisions illegally benefiting family or friends. Illicit enrichment, an increasingly popular tool for prosecuting public officials, is the significant increase in assets that cannot be reasonably explained by lawful income. Abuse of functions is a generic term for the improper use of office for personal gain. Note that most commentators would consider this a definition of corruption, while UNCAC lists it as a distinct form of corruption.[63]

The abundant academic literature on corruption contains a number of concepts, or distinctions, which will help us think about megasport corruption. Professor Sayed Alatas[64] has developed a typology of corruption that proves helpful in thinking about corruption's various manifestations. He distinguishes between transactive corruption (done by the mutual agreement of two or more parties); extortive corruption (when one party, usually a government official, uses her power to compel conduct that the private party would not otherwise participate in); defensive corruption (where the victim must engage in the corrupt act for self- protection); and investive corruption (where there is no immediate reward to the payor, but a promise of future gains).

Similarly, Professor Mark Robinson draws a useful distinction between three forms of corruption: incidental, which is confined to individuals and rare; institutional corruption, which pervades institutions, but is not necessarily accepted or practiced in the wider society; and systemic corruption, which pervades nearly every aspect of society.[65] In a similar vein, Professor Alvaro Cuervo-Cazurra developed a distinction between pervasive corruption, which is predictable and known, and arbitrary corruption, which is uncertain and unreliable.[66] Legendary corruption scholar Susan Rose-Ackerman, of Yale Law School, drew a distinction between bribery intended to obtain a deviation from the application of existing rules or laws versus bribery that aims to change the existing rules or create new rules or laws.[67] Similarly, the World Bank has developed the notion of "state capture": corruption that is aimed at changing the rules and regulations to favor the interests of the corruptor.[68] While this book may not use these terms explicitly, they are useful in sharpening our understanding of what megasport corruption is and the many forms it takes.

The anti-corruption reform movement, at both the academic and practical levels, lends itself to a unique species of zeal which a careful study of the phenomenon must be careful to avoid. It may be tempting to believe, as many an advocate has claimed, that the law's goal is to rid of the world of these various forms of corruption—to create a world "free from corruption." Cynics will respond that such goals are impossible, as corruption is as old as human society and simply cannot be eliminated. The realistic aim of anti-corruption law is no more to rid the world of corruption than is the aim of laws prohibiting murder or assault to completely eliminate those harms. Indeed, many economists have argued that the optimal of level of corruption in society is actually not zero because the enforcement costs would greatly exceed the social benefit.[69] Accordingly, the aim is to find that equilibrium in which the corruption prevention measures justify the public expense. The goal of the anti-corruption movement, then, is to meaningfully deter corruption.

The world's focus was trained on corruption starting in the 1990s and the "corruption eruption" that continues to this day. Societies that to varying degrees had historically tolerated corruption were suddenly protesting, forcing high-profile resignations and impeachments around the world. These occurred both in countries with relatively strong rule-of-law traditions, such as Great Britain, France, and the United States, as well as in countries still seeking to build such traditions, like Venezuela. The eruption even spilled over into Brazil, with the impeachment of President Fernando Collor de Mello, who claimed to be a "cacador de marajas" (hunter of overpaid bureaucrats). So too did anti-corruption scholarship explode during this time. After the foundational work of political scientists Joseph Nye and Samuel Huntington in the 1960s, economist Susan Rose-Ackerman in the 1970s, Robert Klitgaard in the 1980s, the interdisciplinary study of corruption began to produce innumerable articles in the 1990s.[70]

If scholars had been talking about corruption as far back as the 1960s, why did the full "eruption" occur in the 1990s? The first and most obvious reason was the collapse of the Soviet Union and the rapid transition to free markets and elected government. With the end of communism as a formidable global force (Chinese communism, of course, is not communism by any meaningful definition of the word) came a diminished sense of our resignation to the inevitability of corruption. This occurred both among citizens, whose expectations changed, and among states and international organizations that no longer needed to tolerate corrupt dictators to further Cold War goals. As Naim explained, "secrecy and Orwellian manipulation of the truth—those cornerstones of authoritarian and totalitarian rule—have become increasingly difficult to maintain"[71] in the face of ever-expanding liberalization. This connection between centralized authority and corruption has long been recognized and most famously articulated by the Harvard professor Robert Klitgaard. He wrote that corruption depends on three variables: the monopoly (M) on the supply of a good or service; the government's discretion (D) in allocating that good or service; but which can be checked by the officials' accountability (A) for such allocations, creating a memorable equation: $C = M + D - A$.[72] Where the government monopoly is weakened, corruption is expected to decrease.

So too did liberalization bring an increase in international trade, and with it, increased expectations concerning the business environments of other countries. As major companies increasingly invested overseas, the degree of corruption became of paramount concern. The governments of developed countries become interested in how their companies were behaving overseas and began enforcing prohibitions on foreign bribery. With global interdependence came an expectation of sameness, and of fairness, as described in more detail in Chapter 1.

Finally, liberalization brought much higher scrutiny of government and business conduct from the mass media. This occurred both because countries became more open and the press had greater freedom, but also because technological developments made possible the rapid spread of information. Media conglomerates emerged, satellite broadcasts became commonplace, and the internet continued the trend of drawing people into more regular interaction.[73] So too have some observed that the culture of journalism changed in this era, becoming increasingly aggressive and doing more probing, investigative reporting.[74]

Among the most impactful features of this eruption was a series of international anti-corruption conventions that provide the foundation for anti-corruption initiatives today. That story starts with the OECD, which was established after World War II to encourage cooperation and postwar reconstruction among its members.[75] The OECD promotes policies that spur economic growth and financial stability by creating a forum for its thirty-six members' governments to converse about common problems.[76] The group also publishes statistics and overviews of countries discussing their economic development[77] and conducts peer reviews of member states.[78]

In 1997, the OECD produced its watershed Convention on Combating Bribery of Foreign Officials in International Business Transactions.[79] The convention's breakthrough was its focus on foreign, rather than domestic, corruption and the new obligation that signatories prohibit the bribery of foreign officials. Each signatory is required to create an offense for bribery of a foreign public official; the article provides a meaning for bribery and a definition of foreign public official.[80] Bribery, as defined by the convention, means offering, directly or indirectly, an official pecuniary or other advantages to either act or refrain from acting in a way that would advantage the briber.[81] A foreign public official is defined as a person who holds a "legislative, administrative or judicial office, whether appointed or elected[,]" and exercises a public function.[82] Though this convention has a more limited connection to megasports, anti-bribery enforcement became a principal catalyst to the growth of the global compliance movement, and more generally to global sea change about the importance and feasibility of reducing corruption that occurs between corporations and governments.

The next major international instrument was UNCAC.[83] Substantially broader than the OECD Convention in both its prohibitions and its signatories, UNCAC covers both the public and private sectors and addresses international cooperation and recovery of stolen assets. UNCAC addresses five main areas: preventive measures, criminalization and law enforcement, international cooperation, asset recovery, and technical assistance and information exchange.[84] UNCAC encourages members to implement anti-corruption policies and bodies to govern these policies and disseminate information.[85] The terms are loose and include "non-mandatory language," which may undermine the convention's effectiveness.[86]

As is always the case with negotiated international instruments, commentators have noted the document's shortcomings. Some have argued that the UNCAC convention does not do enough to advance international anti-corruption because of its imprecise and qualified language.[87] Some find UNCAC's language to range from "mandatory to non-mandatory, precise to vague, and absolute to qualified." Cecily Rose argues that these provisions dilute the UNCAC's legitimacy, which leaves state parties little guidance regarding compliance requirements, and furthermore, causes conflicting interpretations between them. These provisions thus "lack firm content," and "look more like sketches than complete pictures of anti-corruption norms." She notes that the drafters intentionally left certain provisions vague to "allow[] State Parties an appropriate degree of freedom to make their own choices," but these indefinite provisions "do little to constrain or guide interpretations by State Parties." As a result, "[t]he prevalence of non-mandatory, qualified, and vague provisions impedes the implementation and enforcement of the norms set forth in the Convention."[88]

In addition to UNCAC and the OECD Convention, several regional agreements were adopted around this time. These include the Inter-American Convention Against Corruption (1996); the African Union Convention on Preventing and Combating Corruption (2003); and the Asia Pacific Economic Cooperation Course of Action on Fighting Corruption and Ensuring Transparency (2004).[89] Principal among these is Europe's Group of States Against Corruption (GRECO), with its Criminal Law Convention (2002) and Civil Law Convention (2003).[90] GRECO was created by, and falls under, the Council of Europe, a human rights group.[91] The conventions were established in 1999 to help fight corruption of its signatory members. The Civil Law Convention focuses on providing compensation to victims of corruption, which is defined in terms of bribery. The Civil Convention encourages legislation that makes contracts based on corruption void, provides protection for whistleblowers, and encourages annual accounts by corporations. The Criminal Convention is much more expansive in its definition of corruption and requires implementing legislation that prohibits active and passive bribery of both domestic and foreign public officials, as well as in the private sector. The Criminal Convention also mandates that trading in influence and money laundering be disallowed. Moreover, the Criminal Convention requires that corporations be held liable for the listed offenses.[92] Similar to the OECD Convention, member countries are monitored and evaluated on a peer review basis by the GRECO Evaluation Team. This team, unless decided otherwise, is made up experts chosen by GRECO.[93]

With the adoption of these instruments, anti-corruption law achieved a status comparable to human rights law. Indeed, the two movements have proceeded side by side into the megasports space, becoming two facets of the governance reform movement as the balance of this book explains. How have these two concepts become, in effect, kindred movements? What is the connection between them? That connection does not lie in the international instruments. The anti-corruption conventions do not frame corruption as a rights violation, and the human rights instruments do not even mention corruption. The principal international anti-corruption instrument, UNCAC, enumerates diverse forms of corruption such as bribery, embezzlement, trading in influence, and others. However, the document only makes passing references to various discrete human rights, and they are generally in reference to the collateral impact of anti-corruption enforcement measures on other rights. This pattern is likewise observed in the OECD Convention. So too do the human rights instruments fail to mention corruption. In the Universal Declaration of Human Rights, the International Covenant on Civil and Political Rights, and the International Covenant on Economic, Social, and Cultural Rights, the word "corruption" does not even appear, nor does freedom from corruption by any other name. This is likewise true of the European Convention for the Protection of Human Rights, the American Declaration of the Rights and Duties of Man, the American Convention on Human Rights, and the African Charter of Human and Peoples' Rights.

The same philosophers who provided the conceptual foundations of the human rights movement likewise laid the foundation for the modern anti-corruption movement. First, consider again John Locke. Though Locke did not use the term "corruption," the concern with protecting citizens from the abuse of public office pervaded his rights theory. Indeed, a close reading reveals that the well-known Lockean right to liberty is actually but another name for the right to be free of corruption. Locke argues that we can understand the purpose of government by first reflecting on what the human condition is or would be in its absence, a condition he called the state of nature. In the state of nature, we are all free and equal, enjoying our natural right to liberty. However, owing to this absolute freedom and equality, we lack a neutral third party with the authority to resolve disputes. We are therefore each left to enforce the "law of nature" in our own cases. Predictably, this system breaks down, as "self-love will make men partial to themselves and their friends."[94] Humankind thus needs a government, a "common measure to decide all controversies"[95] that will remedy "those evils which necessarily follow from men being judges in their own cases."[96] The administration of justice is tainted or, if you will, corrupted, by self-interest.

What Locke calls "civil society" is thus formed by creating a government that is "bound to govern by established standing laws, promulgated and known by the people." Such a government does not compromise our natural liberty; to the contrary, it guarantees it: "For in all the states of created beings, capable of laws, where there is no law there is no freedom. For liberty is to be free from restraint and violence from others, which cannot be where there is no law." Liberty, by definition, is "to have a standing rule to live by, common to every one of that society, and made by the legislative power . . . not to be subject to the inconstant, uncertain, unknown, arbitrary will of another man."[97]

In more contemporary terms, our right to liberty only exists where government officials do not abuse their public office for private gain; that is, where they do not act corruptly. Where officers do so act, citizens "have no such decisive power to appeal to, [and] they are still in the state of Nature."[98] Corruption thus voids the social contract, destroys civil society, violates our right to liberty, and returns society to a state of nature. Indeed, when Locke defines tyranny as "making use of the power any one has in his hands not for the good of those who are under it, but for his own private, separate advantage,"[99] he is describing what we today call corruption.

The conviction that our natural right to liberty can only exist in the absence of corruption was a dominant intellectual influence at the American founding. The Declaration of Independence's promise of "life, liberty, and the pursuit of happiness" is derived directly from Locke's writings. Indeed, corruption was discussed at the Constitutional Convention more often than factions, violence, or instability; James Madison recorded the term fifty-four times.[100] Historian Bernard Bailyn observed that the very "heart of the revolutionary movement" was the "fear of a comprehensive conspiracy against liberty . . . nourished in corruption."[101] Legal scholar Zephyr Teachout thus finds that the US Constitution "carries within it an anti-corruption principle, much like the separation-of-powers principle, or federalism."[102]

A reliance on Anglo-American thought alone would make the anti-corruption movement seem yet another form of cultural imperialism. However, the notion that entrusted authority ought not to be abused for private gain commands a far broader and deeper support. There may be no better place to start than that eminently non-Western political philosopher most closely associated with Asian values: Confucius. Though an ancient philosophy, modern China is seeing a revival of Confucianism, as the Chinese state gradually distances itself from Marxism. China's proudly ancient, intellectual traditions (and more modern Marxist legacy) would both seem to situate the country well outside the Western liberal paradigm. However, there is no value more fundamental to Confucian ideals of good government than the absence of corruption.

The pervasiveness of corruption in sixth century BC China was among the chief sources of Confucius' political thought.[103] This state of affairs found some support in a political philosophy which taught that "virtue as a basis for the State was not practicable," that the "State was not bound by ordinary moral rules," and a state that attempted to achieve ethical ideals "would thereby only commit suicide."[104] Writing to counter this pernicious view, Confucius taught that the first requirement of good government is "the rule of virtue." The government is thus subject to the same ethical rules that apply to individuals. The legitimate ruler does not separate ethics from politics, and the ends do not justify the means.[105] Indeed, the government's example should be the starting point for the establishment of a harmonious and prosperous society; the ruler's virtue was to "sweep over the people and transform them just as the wind blowing over longs stalks of grass bends them as it passes."[106] Only a person of great virtue, then, could be qualified to become the ruler, the "Son of Heaven"; without virtue, he loses his legitimacy.[107] Corruption was thus a fundamental, if not the most fundamental, principle of good government. To Confucius, there could be no legitimate government without the absence of corruption. In contemporary Western parlance, the absence of corruption was a public policy trump, its presence a grave affront to justice.

Another region of the world that possesses a proud, ancient, and eminently non-Western intellectual tradition, and that has resisted the embrace of Western political values, is the Islamic Middle East.[108] Islamic law is widely incorporated into civil law systems across the Middle East (and

South Asia as well) and significantly frames public policy discussions.[109] Like Confucianism, traditional Islamic law holds that among the most fundamental principles of governance, and the important functions of government, is to secure the freedom from corruption.

The term "Islamic law" refers to the cumulative body of thought of numerous communities and schools, and its core is the concept of sharia.[110] "Sharia" means the "path to the watering place," referring to the divine will and connoting a path of discipline and virtue.[111] Based on the Qur'an as well as the traditions and teachings of Muhammad (*sunnah*), sharia teaches that humankind is "entrusted with the responsibility to establish justice and good governance."[112] Islamic doctrine thus in the first instance seeks to cultivate self-discipline and morality, through such virtues as honesty (*sidq*) and the fulfillment of promises (*wafa bi'l-'ahd*), as well as the avoidance of lying (*khidhb*) and perfidy (*radha'il*).[113] Islamic jurists have further taught that internal accountability must be supplanted by external checks and balances. Accordingly, Muslim jurists have historically taught that law must prohibit various forms of corruption, including the acceptance of gifts, embezzlement, compromising official duties in exchange for bribes, or basing official decisions on family or tribal considerations.[114]

As one Muslim legal scholar laments, "unfortunately, Islamic standards and norms are not often appreciated by states in the Muslim world."[115] These states' failures, however, have no bearing on whether corruption is rightly understood as a rights violation or its structural equivalent. Traditional Islamic thought, much like Confucian thought, recognizes corruption as a violation of the most fundamental principles of good governance. Indeed, the disconnect between traditional jurisprudence and contemporary practice itself underscores the need to recognize that freedom from corruption is held by all persons irrespective of what their governments may now do or say.

While many asserted rights tend to accentuate differences in worldviews, the right to be free from corruption does not. In such diverse traditions as Anglo-American liberalism, East Asian Confucianism, and Middle Eastern Islamic law, freedom from corruption is deemed among the first principles of government. Indeed, of the various candidates for a universal moral principle, one that all persons have by virtue of being human, the freedom from corruption may well be the strongest and most fundamental. It is hardly surprising, then, that the anti-corruption conventions have commanded universal assent, again a kind of agreement in principle.

These instruments, and the national laws that result, generally recognize the contributions of both public and private sector actors to corrupt transactions. They call on states to prohibit both actors' contributions. However, these prohibitions, standing alone, will not curb corporate corruption. Rather, the catalyst to the meaningful reduction in corporate corruption has been the phenomenon of compliance, as the next section shows.

Where Anti-Corruption Meets Business: Compliance

Compliance is a buzzword to many, but empty verbiage to others. Recently, a colleague in the compliance field was contacted by an Organizing Committee for the Olympic Games (OCOG) general counsel and asked, "So what is compliance?" But the tide of compliance is inexorably moving around the globe. Part of building the human rights and anti-corruption legacy is making compliance clear, familiar, and, above all else, practical to persons and jurisdictions whose compliance industries are still fledgling. To the extent the Olympic Movement can effectuate this change, it will make a substantial contribution to governance.

Anti-corruption compliance differs from human rights compliance (also known as human rights due diligence) in at least one key respect. As this chapter has explained, there exists in the human rights space a single, internationally recognized, authoritative standard: the UNPGs. The document has been approved by an international body (the UN Human Rights Council) and is now specifically and explicitly incorporated into the IOC's host-city contract. Anti-corruption compliance is much more pluralistic. Its standards are diverse, emanating from a variety of sources. Those sources may fall into three categories. The first, and probably most authoritative, compliance standards tend to be those issued by national enforcement agencies. These would include the US Department of Justice's "Evaluation of Corporate Compliance Programs,"[116] the UK Ministry of Justice's "Bribery Act 2010 Guidance,"[117] and, more recently, the Agence Française Anticorruption's "Guidance."[118] The second is the guidance developed by nongovernmental associations such as the International Organization for Standardization or the Committee of Sponsoring Organizations of the Treadway Commission. The third may be the nonbinding guidance provided by an almost-dizzying variety of intergovernmental organizations. The UN Office of Drugs and Crime's "Anti-Corruption Ethics and Compliance

Programme for Business"[119] may be the most visible of these globally. It, in turn, incorporates standards from a variety of sources, including the Asia-Pacific Economic Cooperation Anti-Corruption Code of Conduct for Business; the International Chamber of Commerce Rules on Combating Corruption; the OECD Good Practice Guidance on Internal Controls, Ethics, and Compliance; the World Economic Forum Partnering Against Corruption Initiative Principles for Countering Bribery; Transparency International's Business Principles for Countering Bribery; and the World Bank Group Integrity Compliance Guidelines.[120] Ironically, in marked distinction to the human rights space, the intergovernmental organization publications may actually command substantially less attention among compliance professionals than the national guidelines and private organization publications. Pluralism can be good for innovation, but can complicate the effort to incorporate a single standard into MSEs.

Though no single definition exists, corporate compliance generally refers to the systems of self-governance a company puts in place to prevent, detect, and respond to violations of law or of self-defined standards of conduct. Sometimes these systems are required by law, as France has done with its 2016 law Sapin II (see Chapter 6). In other jurisdictions, they are not quite required, but are highly encouraged and rewarded, as is the case in both the United States and the United Kingdom. This means that some host cities/countries will already have laws in place requiring the adoption of compliance, while others may not. Indeed, it may be a surprise to many to know that the United States, which has long been a leader in the compliance industry, has not adopted a general requirement that companies adopt compliance programs. Corporations participating in the preparation and hosting of the Los Angeles 2028 Summer Olympics will not already be subject to mandatory compliance. It will fall to the OCOG to ensure that its companies have strong anti-corruption and human rights programs in place.

Defining compliance this way, compliance has several components. First, it is a system of self-governance. It is not merely an admonition that employees ought not to break the law. Nor is it a simple declaration of values. Rather, it is a system, with multiple working parts and an abundant literature on how to design, operate, and monitor those parts. For this reason, compliance is an investment of resources, one that requires a long-term view of the company's operations, goals, and return on investment. In megasports, the harms of scandal are all too well known; the value of compliance should be a relatively easy sell.

It may be said that compliance's three principal goals are prevention, detection, and response. Prevention is obvious and best—we should endeavor to keep our operations from running afoul of the law. However, no compliance system is perfect. A 100 percent effective program would be prohibitively expensive; it would put companies out of business. Even the most demanding enforcement agencies will readily concede that with a compliance program in place, violations can still occur. So all of us, even corporations, live with risk. This leads us to the next goal of compliance.

A compliance system must detect violations, or potential violations, when they occur. The potentially "noncompliant event" should be flagged and brought to the attention of the appropriate people within the entity. Whether the misconduct occurred intentionally or not, the employees, managers, or even executives implicated in the misconduct should not be able to hide it from the rest of the company. Someone who is equipped to handle the allegation appropriately needs to know.

Accordingly, the third goal of any compliance program is response. The program must respond to the detected violation in a principled, organized, and constructive manner. This response might take several forms and should occur in several steps. The first step is an investigation. The company must investigate all credible allegations of internal misconduct. The scope and structure of the investigation will vary with the nature of the allegation and the company's resources. A minor allegation might be investigated through an informal investigation led by the company's general counsel or chief compliance officer. More substantial allegations might require a more formal and extensive investigation. The investigation might even require the assistance of outside counsel and, in cases of more elaborate and high-stakes financial crime, outside forensic accountants. Where executives or upper management is involved, the investigation might require establishing a special committee of independent board members who will retain outside counsel and oversee the investigation.

Whatever the scope and structure of the investigation, the company must then determine what to do, internally, with the investigation's findings. The violation might have resulted from the innocent misstep of a well-meaning employee. Or it might have been the premeditated crime of a bad actor. Employees may need to be trained, or even disciplined. Some may need to be terminated. Operations might need restructuring to create internal checks that will make future violations less likely. These steps, generally referred to as "remediation," are essential not only to the company's future operations but to its potential legal liability; enforcement agencies are generally far more lenient with a company that takes remediation seriously than with one that doesn't. Finally, the company will have to decide whether to voluntarily report its findings to the enforcement agencies. Self-reporting, also known as voluntary disclosure, is increasingly the favored practice of enforcement agencies. Those agencies will offer benefits to the defendant, including penalty reductions or even a declination (letting the company off without penalty). Companies have to weigh the benefits of disclosure against the risks. Good compliance programs will be equipped to participate in all of these assessments.

The "violations" that a compliance program should prevent, detect, and respond to may be violations of law, but not necessarily. Companies might also define certain best practices, or particular values, that they intend to uphold in their operations regardless of whether strictly required by law. Companies will define these standards with various concerns in mind. Beyond legal liability, they may risk financial liability if operations are inefficient. So too do companies face reputational risk, as misconduct can cause substantial public embarrassment. Finally, companies might have ethical values that they simply value for their own sake. The violations that compliance should prevent are thus a combination of laws and norms.

Corporate compliance may be new, but its conceptual and historical roots run deep. The notion that business misconduct threatens social well-being and must be deterred through law has existed since the earliest civilizations.[121] The Code of Hammurabi was written by King Hammurabi of the Babylonian dynasty, who ruled over central Mesopotamia (present-day Iraq) from 1792 to 1750 BC.[122] The Code was one of the world's first known and complete written legal codes to be established in a civilization. A substantial portion of the Code is focused in the area of regulating business activities, such as construction, medical malpractice, minimum wage requirements, and establishing gross negligence for business operations that led to the injury of another party.[123] Self-regulation of business, the precursor to compliance, began with the Middle Age merchants and craft guilds, who set business standards for themselves.[124] During the Enlightenment, large businesses became symbols of hierarchical privilege on both sides of the Atlantic. James Madison, in defending the need for a constitution in the United States, wrote of the need for strong limitations on corporations.[125] With industrialization, the rising power of large corporations created a more pressing need to align corporate behavior with social values. The post–World

War II economic boom and the state-sponsored investment in Europe would bring about another surge in corporate activity. As Chapter 1 of this book explains, the collapse of the Soviet Union and the advent of globalization brought about a heightened sense that values were more common, that international business can help to build a more stable and prosperous global order, and that the rules of competition should be consistent.

Around the turn of the millennium—the year 2000—three major events occurred that would prove powerful catalysts to the global compliance industry. For better or for worse, the United States was central to each. The first was a series of US fraud scandals involving now-familiar corporate names such as Enron, World Com, and others. This wave of corporate scandals precipitated a crisis of faith in corporate conduct which demanded a response. That response came in 2002 in the form of the Sarbanes-Oxley Act, a federal law including a variety of provisions that would force publicly traded companies to take compliance more seriously.[126]

The second event was the horrific attack on the World Trade Center in New York City on September 11, 2001. This event would heighten concern about the threat of terrorism to the United States and the rest of the world. Terrorism, of course, is funded in part through corruption, especially money laundering. Financial institutions and other corporations often enable, knowingly or not, these illicit transfers of money. The need to prevent terrorism became a need to deter corporate corruption. The third, which flowed from the first two, was the onset of the enforcement of laws prohibiting foreign bribery. As far back as the 1970s, the United States had enacted a law prohibiting its companies from bribing foreign officials, called the US Foreign Corrupt Practices Act.[127] The law would lie dormant for a quarter century, in part because countries that competed commercially with the United States had not passed similar laws, and the United States feared a competitive disadvantage. Then, in the late 1990s, the OECD passed the Anti-Bribery Convention previously discussed. The playing field in international business was thus becoming more level.

Anti-bribery enforcement, motivated as it was by these two prior events, would prove a catalyst to the global adoption of compliance programs. Two features of US enforcement particularly had this effect. One was the incentivization of compliance. The US Department of Justice (DOJ) would make liberal use of provisions in the US Sentencing Guidelines authorizing penalty reductions for compliance.[128] Given the obvious bribery risks for

Western companies doing business in countries lacking the strong rule of law, combined with aggressive enforcement of the criminal prohibition on bribery and liberal penalty reductions for compliance, compliance started to become a good investment. However, this alone could not have catalyzed a global compliance movement without a second feature of FCPA enforcement, which is the aggressive prosecution of non-US companies. Flagship corporations such as Germany's Siemens, Brazil's Petrobras, South Korea's Samsung, and France's Airbus have found themselves subject to FCPA enforcement. While the statute was drafted to focus on US companies, a jurisdictional provision allowing enforcement against any company with shares traded on a US exchange would prove to cast a very wide net.[129] Corporations around the world were put on notice that US enforcement of its anti-bribery law was not limited to US companies.

The DOJ's efforts to incentivize compliance thus had global effect. Not only did companies get on board with compliance but other jurisdictions began enforcing anti-bribery laws with their own approaches toward incentivizing compliance. The United Kingdom would soon follow with its 2010 Bribery Act.[130] Rather than the penalty reductions of the US Sentencing Guidelines, the UK Act provided a statutory defense for "adequate procedures," that is, reasonable compliance programs in place at the time of the violation.[131] That is, proving to the prosecution that the defendant company had an adequate compliance program in place at the time of the violation would provide a complete defense to corporate liability, even if individuals in the company may be guilty. France would then develop yet a third approach with its revolutionary Sapin II: creating a freestanding requirement that companies over a certain size adopt compliance programs (see Chapter 6 for further description of this innovative statute). France would also create an enforcement agency, the Agence Française Anticorruption to investigate companies for the adequacy of their compliance programs and administer modest fines. Brazil would become a major regional leader in South America in anti-corruption enforcement and compliance with its Clean Companies Act (see Chapter 3), as would South Korea in East Asia (see Chapter 4) with its Kim Young Ran Act.

Although there exists no single authoritative account of what constitutes good compliance, any set of standards would include at least five elements. The first element is leadership. This is sometimes described as "tone at the top," referring to the example set by senior leadership. Other expressions circulating in the compliance space are "tone at the local top" (referring to leadership in more localized departments or operations), "tone in the middle" (referring to the leadership of middle management), or "conduct at the top" (referring not merely to words but to behavior). Regardless of these formulations, the concept is the same: compliance begins with leadership creating a culture of good-faith compliance, providing the resources necessary to implement compliance, and rewarding individuals for participating in compliant behavior.

The second element is a risk assessment. A company will go through a risk assessment to identify how its operations intersect with laws and cultural norms to create legal, operational, or reputational risk. Once the company is in a position to survey all potential risk, it must then prioritize those risks to effectively allocate compliance resources that are inherently scarce. No company can implement perfect compliance in relation to all risks in all partnerships, transactions, and operations. It would be too costly; it would drive most any company out of business. Rather, the risk map enables the company to identify those risks most deserving of compliance resources. Risk maps should be periodically updated as operations and legal enforcement trends, if not the laws themselves, evolve.

The third element might be generally described as standards and controls. These include a code of conduct, as well as company policies and procedures. A code of conduct is something like the preamble to a constitution, while the policies and procedures are the constitution itself. The code declares the laws and norms which the organization is committed to following. It should be impactful and memorable but clear and accessible, tailored to the company's unique operations and culture. It should leave a lasting impression. That code of conduct must then be rolled out and continually referenced and followed in a way that cements its values in the company's culture and operations. Policies and procedures might be the "how" to the code of conduct's "what"—the more specific rules and processes for keeping the company's employees within the code's boundaries.

The fourth essential element of compliance is training. Once leadership has composed the code and policies and identified its risks, employees must be taught how to implement the company's policies. The training should cover the company's core beliefs, how those beliefs inform its operations, the risks that inherently arise, and what each employee must do to manage those risks. Ideally, training is in-person rather than remote, with opportunities for employees to engage and ask questions. It should provide practical scenarios that employees must learn to handle. It should be periodic, so the lessons remain current, and it should be mandatory. Without effective training, compliance is a mere "check the box" exercise. It is form without substance.

Finally, the fifth essential element is oversight. Once procedures are designed and employees are trained in how to implement them, that implementation must be regularly watched and periodically evaluated. Words used in this space include "monitoring," "auditing," and "reporting." Monitoring is an ongoing process of identifying gaps in compliance procedures with the aim of immediate remediation. While monitoring is focused on the present, auditing is a backward-looking process, evaluating past performance. Auditing might be performed internally or by an external firm, weighing cost, control, and the learning opportunities for staff against the credibility, expertise, and objectivity of external auditors. Finally, reporting refers to the mechanisms for employees to anonymously, safely, and effectively report potential misconduct. Such reporting hotlines can exist within the entity or can be hosted by an outside firm. Either way, the credibility of reported allegations must be assessed by competent and high-ranking people in the organization. Retaliation against the reporting employee must be strictly prohibited and strongly punished. A company should build a culture around reporting, in which employees reporting potential misconduct are perceived as advocates or guardians rather than as snitches or traitors. Finally, where allegations seem credible, the entity must mount a swift and effective response, including an appropriate investigation and remediation. Responses should be visible within the organization, helping to establish the compliance program's credibility.

As mentioned, these five essential elements can be found in any of a number of the myriad guidance documents previously discussed. The variety of national and international standards and laws has produced a global web of anti-corruption compliance.

Alongside human rights due diligence, we now have a paradigm that applies to both public and private sector governance. To varying degrees, and in various ways, countries around the globe are buying into this paradigm. That much is widely known. What may not be known, and what the rest of this book endeavors to show, is the role of megasports—both their actual role now, and their potential role moving forward—in accelerating this global reform movement.

Notes

1. James Nickel, *Human Rights*, *in* The Stanford Encyclopedia of Philosophy (Edward N. Zalta, rev. ed. 2019), https://plato.stanford.edu/archives/sum2019/entries/rights-human/.
2. Steven Wheatley, The Idea of International Human Rights Law 17 (2019).
3. Irwin P. Stotzky, *The Rights of Man Today. By Louis Henkin*, 11 U. Miami Inter-Am. L. Rev. 229, 235 (1979).
4. Johannes Morsink, Inherent Human Rights: Philosophical Roots of the Universal Declaration 1, 14 (2009).
5. Christian Tomuschat, Human Rights Between Idealism and Realism 4 (3d ed. 2014).
6. David Daiches Raphael, Political Theory and the Rights of Man 1, 52 (1967).
7. James Griffen, On Human Rights, at § 2.4 (2008).
8. The Declaration of Independence, para. 2 (U.S. 1776).
9. Nickel, *supra* note 1, at § 1.
10. Micheline R. Ishay, The History of Human Rights: From Ancient Times to the Globalization Era 16–22 (2008).
11. Wheatley, *supra* note 2, at 19 n.11.
12. John Locke, The Second Treatise on Civil Government 1, 13 (1986).
13. *Id.* at 70.
14. *Id.* at 13.
15. Stan. Enc. Montesquieu 4.2, https://plato.stanford.edu/entries/montesquieu/.
16. The Declaration of Independence, para. 1.
17. Declaration of the Rights of Man—1789, https://avalon.law.yale.edu/18th_century/rightsof.asp.
18. Louis Henkin, The Rights of Man Today 1, 92 (1978).
19. Tomuschat, *supra* note 5, at 27.
20. G.A. Res. 217 (III) A, Universal Declaration of Human Rights (Dec. 10, 1948), https://undocs.org/A/RES/217(III) [hereinafter UDHC].
21. Ishay, *supra* note 10, at 218–19.
22. UDHC, *supra* note 20.
23. Phillip Alston & Ryan Goodman, International Human Rights 1, 160 (2012).
24. *The Genocide Convention*, United Nations (Dec. 9, 1948), https://www.un.org/en/genocideprevention/genocide-convention.shtml. *See Treaty Collection*, United Nations, https://treaties.un.org/Pages/ViewDetails.aspx?src=TREATY&mtdsg_no=IV-1&chapter=4.
25. *International Convention on the Elimination of All Forms of Racial Discrimination*, United Nations Hum. Rts. Off. High Commissioner (Dec. 21, 1965), https://www.ohchr.org/en/professionalinterest/pages/cerd.aspx. *See* United Nations, *Treaty Collection*, https://treaties.un.org/Pages/ViewDetails.aspx?src=TREATY&mtdsg_no=IV-2&chapter=4.

26. *Convention on the Elimination of All Forms of Discrimination against Women New York*, United Nations Hum. Rts. Off. High Commissioner (Dec. 18, 1979), https://www.ohchr.org/en/professionalinterest/pages/cedaw.aspx. *See* United Nations, *Treaty Collection*, https://treaties.un.org/Pages/ViewDetails.aspx?src=TREATY&mtdsg_no=IV-8&chapter=4.
27. *Convention against Torture and Other Cruel, Inhuman, or Degrading Treatment or Punishment*, United Nations Hum. Rts. Off. High Commissioner (Dec. 10, 1984), https://www.ohchr.org/en/professionalinterest/pages/cat.aspx. *See* United Nations, *Treaty Collection*, https://treaties.un.org/Pages/ViewDetails.aspx?src=TREATY&mtdsg_no=IV-9&chapter=4&clang=_en.
28. *Convention on the Rights of the Child*, United Nations Hum. Rts. Off. High Commissioner (Nov. 20, 1989), https://www.ohchr.org/en/professionalinterest/pages/crc.aspx. *See* United Nations, *Treaty Collection*, https://treaties.un.org/Pages/ViewDetails.aspx?src=IND&mtdsg_no=IV-11&chapter=4.
29. *Id. See* International Labor Conference, *Fundamental Principles and Rights at Work: From Commitment to Action* (2012), https://www.ilo.org/wcmsp5/groups/public/---ed_norm/---relconf/documents/meetingdocument/wcms_176149.pdf. *See also* ILO, *Conventions and Recommendations*, https://www.ilo.org/global/standards/introduction-to-international-labour-standards/conventions-and-recommendations/lang--en/index.htm (listing the eight fundamental Conventions of the ILO).
30. *The ILO Declaration on Fundamental Principles and Rights at Work*, International Labour Organization (June 18, 1998), https://www.ilo.org/declaration/thedeclaration/textdeclaration/lang--en/index.htm.
31. *See generally* Philip Alston, *Core Labour Standards and the Transformation of the International Labour Rights Regime*, 15 Eur. J. Int'l Law 457, 515–26 (2004).
32. John Gerrard Ruggie, Just Business: Multinational Corporations and Human Rights 3–18 (2013).
33. *Id.* at intro.
34. *Id.* at ch. 1.
35. *Id.* at 83.
36. *Id.* at 126.
37. *Id.* at ch. 1.
38. *Id.* at ch. 2.
39. *Id.* at 125–27.
40. *Implementing the United Nations "Protect, Respect and Remedy" Framework*, United Nations Hum. Rts. Off. High Commissioner (2011), https://www.ohchr.org/documents/publications/guidingprinciplesbusinesshr_en.pdf.
41. *Id.* at § 2.
42. Ruggie, *supra* note 32, at 100.
43. David Bilchitz & Surya Deva, Human Rights Obligations of Business: Beyond the Corporate Responsibility to Respect? 1–4 (David Bilchitz & Surya Deva eds., 2013).
44. *Id.* at 18.
45. Bilchitz & Deva, *supra* note 43, at 18–19.

46. David Bilchitz, *A Chasm between "Is" and "Ought"? A Critique of the Normative Foundations of the SRSG's Framework and the Guiding Principles*, *in* HUMAN RIGHTS OBLIGATIONS OF BUSINESS: BEYOND THE CORPORATE RESPONSIBILITY TO RESPECT? 114–24 (David Bilchitz & Surya Deva eds., 2013).
47. Justine Nolan, "*The Corporate Responsibility to Respect Human Rights: Soft Law Or Not Law?*," *in* HUMAN RIGHTS OBLIGATIONS OF BUSINESS: BEYOND THE CORPORATE RESPONSIBILITY TO RESPECT? 160–61 (David Bilchitz & Surya Deva eds., 2013).
48. Anita Ramasastry, "*Closing the Governance Gap in the Business and Human Rights Arena: Lessons from the Anti-corruption Movement*," in HUMAN RIGHTS OBLIGATIONS OF BUSINESS: BEYOND THE CORPORATE RESPONSIBILITY TO RESPECT? 184–89 (David Bilchitz & Surya Deva eds., 2013).
49. *Id.* at 21–22.
50. *Id.* at 24.
51. Moises Naim, *Corruption Eruption*, BROWN J. WORLD AFF. (1995), http://carnegieendowment.org/1995/06/01/corruption-eruption/.
52. United Nations Convention Against Corruption, G.A. Res. 58/4, U.N. Doc. A/58/4 (Oct. 31, 2003), *reprinted in* 43 I.L.M. 37 (2004).
53. *Jacobellis v. State of Ohio*, 378 U.S. 184, 197 (1964) (J. Stewart, concurring).
54. Joseph Nye, *Corruption and Political Development: A Cost-Benefit Analysis*, AM. POL. SCI. REV. 61(2), 417–27 (1967).
55. *Helping Countries Combat Corruption: The Role of the World Bank*, THE WORLD BANK GROUP, 8–22 (1997), http://www1.worldbank.org/publicsector/anticorrupt/corruptn/corrptn.pdf.
56. *Corruption and Human Rights: Making the Connection*, INTERNATIONAL COUNCIL ON HUMAN RIGHTS POLICY AND TRANSPARENCY INTERNATIONAL, 16 (2009), http://www.ichrp.org/files/reports/40/131_web.pdf.
57. *An Anticorruption Reader*, UNITED STATES AGENCY FOR INTERNATIONAL DEVELOPMENT, (2005), http://pdf.usaid.gov/pdf_docs/PNADF530.pdf.
58. Nye, *supra* note 54.
59. ROBERT E. KLITGAARD, CONTROLLING CORRUPTION 23 (1988).
60. Mark Philip, *Corruption Definition and Measurement*, *in* MEASURING CORRUPTION 45 (Charles Sampford et al. eds., 2006).
61. Andrew Brady Spalding, *Corruption, Corporations, and the New Human Right*, 89 WASH. L. REV. 1365 (2014).
62. MICHAEL JOHNSTON, SYNDROMES OF CORRUPTION: WEALTH, POWER AND DEMOCRACY (2005).
63. Stephen D. Morris, *Forms of Corruption*, *in* CESIFO DICE REPORT (2011), https://www.econstor.eu/bitstream/10419/167031/1/ifo-dice-report-v09-y2011-i2-p10-14.pdf.
64. HUSSEIN ALATAS, CORRUPTION: ITS NATURE, CAUSES AND FUNCTION (1990).
65. Mark Robinson, *Corruption and Development: An Introduction*, *in* CORRUPTION AND DEVELOPMENT 1–14 (Mark Robinson ed., 2006).
66. Alvaro Cuervo-Cazurra, *Better the Devil You Don't Know: Types of Corruption and FDI in Transition Economies*, 14 J. INT'L MGMT. 12–27 (2008).
67. SUSAN ROSE-ACKERMAN, CORRUPTION: A STUDY IN POLITICAL ECONOMY (1978).

68. *See* Boris Begovic, Corruption: Concepts, Types, Causes, and Consequences, *in* Center for International Private Enterprise Economic Reform 4 (2005).
69. Klitgaard, *supra* note 59, at 25.
70. For a modern bibliography of anti-corruption scholarship, *see* the *Global Anti-Corruption Blog*.
71. Patrick Glynn et al., The Globalization of Corruption, Inst. for Int'l Econ., https://www.piie.com/publications/chapters_preview/12/1iie2334.pdf.
72. Klitgaard, *supra* note 59.
73. Naim, *supra* note 51.
74. *Id.*
75. *About the OECD: OECD 60th Anniversary*, OECD, https://www.oecd.org/60-years/.
76. *Id.*; *About the OECD: How We Work*, OECD, https://www.oecd.org/about/how-we-work/.
77. *Id.*
78. *Id.*; *Bribery and Corruption: OECD Convention on Combating Bribery of Foreign Public Officials in International Business Transactions*, OECD, http://www.oecd.org/corruption/oecdantibriberyconvention.htm.
79. *Id.* at 78.
80. *Id.* at 7.
81. *Id.*
82. *Id.*
83. *Corruption and Economic Crime Branch*, United Nations Office on Drugs and Crime, https://www.unodc.org/unodc/en/corruption/about.html.
84. United Nations Convention Against Corruption, United Nations Office on Drugs and Crime 9 (2004).
85. *Id.*
86. Cecily Rose, International Anti-Corruption Norms (2015), http://www.oxfordscholarship.com/view/10.1093/acprof:oso/9780198737216.001.0001/acprof-9780198737216-chapter-4.
87. *Id.*
88. Cecily Rose, The Limitations of the United Nations Convention against Corruption 97 (2015).
89. Glynn et al., *supra* note 71.
90. *The Fight Against Corruption: A Priority for the Council of Europe*, Council of Europe, https://www.coe.int/en/web/greco/about-greco/priority-for-the-coe.
91. *Id.*
92. *Details of Treaty No. 174*, Council of Europe, https://www.coe.int/en/web/conventions/full-list/-/conventions/treaty/174?_coeconventions_WAR_coeconventionsportlet_languageId=en_GB.
93. *How Does GRECO Work?*, Council of Europe, https://www.coe.int/en/web/greco/about-greco/how-does-greco-work.
94. Locke, *supra* note 12, at 13.
95. *Id.* at 70.
96. *Id.* at 13.

97. *Id.* at 72.
98. *Id.* at 50.
99. *Id.* at 108. *See also id.* at 109 ("Wherever law ends, tyranny begins, if the law be transgressed to another's harm.").
100. James Savage, *Corruption and Virtue at the Constitutional Convention*, 56 J. Pol. 174, 177 (1994).
101. Bernard Baiyln, The Ideological Origins of the American Revolution xiii (1992). Similarly, George Mason said at the Convention, "If we do not provide against corruption, our government will soon be at an end." Notes of Robert Yates, *in* 1 The Records of the Fed. convention of 1787, 392 (Max Farrand ed., rev. ed. 1996) (1937).
102. Zephyr Teachout, *The Anti-Corruption Principle*, 94 Cornell L. Rev. 341, 342 (2009).
103. Leonard Shihlien Hsu, The Political Philosophy of Confucianism 24–25 (1975).
104. *Id.* at 9–10.
105. *Id.* at 111.
106. Randall Pereenboom, China's Long March Toward Rule of Law 32 (2002).
107. Hsu, *supra* note 103, at 79.
108. Though Association of Southeast Asian Nations created a subregional agreement, the Intergovernmental Commission on Human Rights, China is not a member. In the Middle East, the Arab League created the Arab Charter of Human Rights, it has very few ratifications and no international court or active enforcement mechanism.
109. Mohamed A. Arafa, *Corruption and Bribery in Islamic Law: Are Islamic Ideals Being Met in Practice?*, 18 Ann. Surv. Int'l & Comp. L. 183 (2012).
110. *Id.* at 185.
111. Mohammad Hashim Kamali, Shari'ah Law: an Introduction 14 (2008).
112. *Id.*
113. *Id.* at 29.
114. Arafa, *supra* note 109, at 106.
115. *Id.* at 127.
116. Evaluation of Corporate Compliance Programs, U.S. Dep't of Justice, Criminal Division (June 2020), https://www.justice.gov/criminal-fraud/page/file/937501/download.
117. The Bribery Act 2010 Guidance about procedures which relevant organisations can put into place to prevent persons associated with them from bribing (Section 9 of the Bribery Act 2010), Ministry of Justice (Mar. 2011), http://www.justice.gov.uk/downloads/legislation/bribery-act-2010-guidance.pdf.
118. Guidance to help private and public sector entities prevent and detect corruption, influence peddling, extortion by public officials, unlawful taking of interest, misappropriation of public funds, and favouritism, Agence Française Anticorruption (Dec. 2017), https://www.agence-francaise-anticorruption.gouv.fr/files/2018-10/French_Anticorruption_Agency_Guidelines.pdf.

119. An Anti-Corruption and Compliance Programme for Business: A Practical Guide, UNITED NATIONS OFFICE ON DRUGS AND CRIME (Sept. 2013), https://www.unodc.org/documents/corruption/Publications/2013/13-84498_Ebook.pdf.
120. *Id.* at v.
121. Hammurabi, a king who reigned in Babylonia from 1792 to 1750 BC, wrote a collection of rules to govern all of southern Mesopotamia. *See generally Code of Hammurabi*, HISTORY.COM (Nov. 9, 2009), https://www.history.com/topics/ancient-history/hammurabi.
122. *Id.*; *see also* The Code of Hammurabi (L.W. King trans.), THE AVALON PROJECT (2008), https://avalon.law.yale.edu/ancient/hamframe.asp.
123. Karatholuvu Nagarajan, *The Code of Hammurabi: An Economic Interpretation*, 2 INT'L J. BUS. SOCIAL SCI. 108 (2011).
124. Charles J. Walsh & Alissa Pyrich, *Corporate Compliance Programs as a Defense to Criminal Liability: Can a Corporation Save Its Soul?*, RUTGERS L. R. 649 (1995).
125. *Id.*
126. Sarbanes-Oxley Act of 2002, Pub. L. No. 107-204, 116 Stat. 745.
127. Foreign Corrupt Practices Act of 1977, Pub. L. No. 95-213, 91 Stat. 1494 (codified as amended in scattered sections of 15 U.S.C.).
128. Dep't of Justice, Criminal Division, *supra* note 116.
129. 15 U.S.C. § 78m(a).
130. Bribery Act 2010, c. 23 (UK).
131. Bribery Act 2010, c. 23, § 7(2) (UK).

PART II
EARLY INTIMATIONS

3

An Awakening: Brazil

Introduction

There may be no better symbol of globalization's impact on megasports than Brazil. The first South American country to host the Olympics was also only the second country to consecutively host that event and the FIFA Men's World Cup. So too would the forces described in Chapters 1 and 2 come crashing down on Brazil in most dramatic and impactful fashion. Brazil may be understood as an awakening to a historic moment in which hosting megasports coincides with systemic anti-corruption reforms, raising the possibility of a new kind of megasport legacy.

This chapter explores the extraordinary series of events, lying in a line that is straight but certainly not obvious, that connect Brazil's hosting of mega sporting events (MSEs) with enduring and far-reaching anti-corruption reforms. The roots of Brazil's systemic corruption—and the culturally iconic "jeitinho Brasileiro"—run deep in a history of colonization and military dictatorships. After a 1988 constitutional revolution and an era of soaring economic optimism, Brazil would pursue and then win the rights to host the 2014 FIFA World Cup and the 2016 Summer Olympics. Immediately thereafter, an unforeseen series of political and economic developments—including the Mensalao corruption scandal, a sharp downturn in Brazil's economic prospects brought on partly by the 2008 financial crisis, and then the government's increase in public transportation fares—sparked public outrage with bad governance generally, and corruption specifically. The ultra-expensive MSEs became a popular symbol of Brazil's governance failures.

Brazil's public institutions responded in two dramatic ways. First, its Congress adopted a series of four important laws that created a new anti-corruption legal regime. Second, federal prosecutors launched an investigation, utilizing the new legal tools anti-corruption laws created. The investigation would eventually ensnare multiple current or former presidents and a majority of its national legislature, becoming perhaps the most

A New Megasport Legacy. Andrew Brady Spalding, Oxford University Press. © Oxford University Press 2022.
DOI: 10.1093/oso/9780197503614.003.0003

impactful national anti-corruption enforcement effort in any country at any time in history.[1]

When the dust settled, megasports had become a critical part of a constellation of forces that accelerated the implementation of new anti-corruption norms, practices, policies, and laws. These anti-corruption reforms are both culturally and legally radical, and have endured years after the MSEs. Though megasports clearly were not the original or sole cause of these changes, Chapter 1 showed that they need not be the cause; the megasport need only accelerate the changes. Admittedly, neither megasport organizers nor national lawmakers set out to intentionally create a megasport legacy, as Qatar would later do. Brazil's legacy should therefore be understood as accidental rather than intentional. So too were the reforms passed only after scandal erupted; for this reason the legacy is reactive rather than proactive. Finally, Brazil's reforms were essentially one-dimensional, focusing almost exclusively on anti-corruption without comparable human rights reforms. As such, Brazil presents a legacy this book calls reactive, accidental, and one-dimensional. Still, the Brazilian experience is the first in a series of megasport events that collectively suggest the possibility of a new human rights and anti-corruption legacy.

The Context: Colonization, Dictatorship, and the Jeitinho Brasiliero

It is sometimes said there are places in the world where corruption is "cultural." This statement may be true in one sense but false, and dangerously so, in another. No culture teaches that a suitcase full of cash, exchanged under the table for illegal benefits, is a good and proper way to run a country. There is no well-developed and long-standing intellectual or cultural tradition which teaches that corruption is good and that we should not try to reduce it even if we could. However, there are certainly many parts of the world where corruption is pervasive, and where people seemingly perceive it to be a necessary way of surviving in a corrupt world. Not very long ago, Brazil was just such a country, and the cultural manifestation of this social fact was the (in) famous "Brazilian jeitinho."

"Jeitinho" is variously translated as the "little way out," "adroitness," a "knack," or even a "clever dodge" way of accomplishing tasks. It can include "talking yourself out of a fine when paying a bill late, jumping the queue if you see some acquaintance ahead in the queue, or asking for a receipt with a higher amount (than what you actually paid for) so that you can claim more money back for expenses." The Brazilian jeitinho is described as a uniquely "Brazilian way" of doing such things and is seen as integral to the national identity of Brazil, "o pais do jeitinho" or "the land of jeitinho." One group of Brazilian scholars notes a general belief that the Brazilian jeitinho "identifies Brazil as a nation" and is "central to the collective psyche of a whole nation."[2]

Jeitinho's roots can be traced to Portuguese colonization, which created a contrast between the highly hierarchical forms of social control imported from Europe with a more native preference for informal and affectionate social relationships.[3] With the end of colonization in 1822, the country would enter a century and a half of often violent oscillations between highly decentralized and ostensibly democratic but highly ineffective representative governments and highly centralized military dictatorships, neither of which tended to elicit trust in government. This pendulum swung with particular force in the late twentieth century when, after a series of mid-century ineffective governments, the military seized control in 1964. The military created a strong centralized government that was able to stimulate economic growth, but was widely perceived as oppressive and corrupt. The seeds of Brazil's recent push for accountability and transparency were sown in 1988 with the founding of the modern Republic of Brazil, a constitutional government founded on checks and balances, separation of power, federalism, and the protection of individual rights.[4] But the many years of colonization, dictatorship, and highly ineffective government would help precipitate the rise of the Brazilian way.

Brazilians thus learned how to beat the system, even at its own game. This "Brazilian dilemma" between the cultural preference for informal, affective relationships and the impersonal, hierarchical, and ineffective government helped to create the jeitinho, in which interpersonal strategies are used to navigate through hierarchical governmental structures. Jeitinho becomes "a typically Brazilian way to overcome bureaucracy" and to "break laws and norms to attain a certain objective."[5]

Scholars, and particularly Brazilian scholars, have disagreed on the extent to which jeitinho is synonymous with corruption. Brazilian anthropologist Roberto DaMatta distinguishes between "positive jeitinho," which does not cause damage to others, and "negative jeitinho," which knowingly breaks the law and more closely approximates corruption.[6] Professor Lívia Barbosa sees a distinction between "dar um jeitinho" (to have a way out) and "jeitinho

Brasileiro" (the Brazilian way out), where the former refers to corruption while the latter refers to a creativity and pragmatism that do not threaten social order. In particular, Professor Barbosa found that in the abstract, Brazilians tend to clearly distinguish between three categories: jeitinho, favor, and corruption.[7] Favor implies reciprocity and is based on trust and does not involve a violation of established laws or norms; jeitinho may be engaged in with strangers, and involves only a minor infraction; while corruption involves substantial material gain. Some scholars have found that a spectrum exists within the minds of Brazilians, with favor at the positive end, corruption at the negative end, and jeitinho somewhere in the middle.[8] However, those scholars have found through interviews that Brazilians had trouble distinguishing between the three in practical scenarios.

Despite this history of colonization, dictatorships, and corruption, Brazilians hoped that winning and then hosting the Olympic Games would announce a new era in Brazilian history. Against this backdrop, the 2007 and 2009 announcements that Brazil had won the rights to host the world's two premier MSEs were met with large public celebrations.[9] In what was then an era of great optimism, these events were expected to announce to the world Brazil's arrival as a modern, developed, and capable country and to stimulate Brazil's economic development. Carlos Roberto Osorio, Secretary General of the Brazilian Olympic Committee, gave the following interview, showing the depth of Brazil's optimism and the symbolic value of these events:

> Our motivation to participate in this process is to take advantage of an event like the Olympic Games to make a real difference in the city and in the country, in various ways. First, in terms of the city of Rio itself, [it is] the amount of investment in infrastructure that the Games will bring to the city. Actually, Rio didn't ask Brazil for money to do many new things; we are accelerating existing processes. Because of the time frame of the Games, things that would be done in [twenty] years will be done in seven years. We are talking about metro expansion, roads, airport renovation. So, the infrastructure of the city will be transformed—and with that, the quality of life. Also, the ability to attract additional investment. But, these are the tangible [outcomes] of the story—and in our view, the smallest part of the story. We are not shy to say that Brazil is a country that has social problems. One of the biggest problems that we have is the inequalities within our society. We view sports, and the Olympics Games in particular, as an excellent tool to foster social integration, to foster and to motivate young people to join

> sports, and [to make] Olympic values [part] of their future lives. So the social legacy of the Games will be a very, very important part of our project. Everything that is going to be done in Rio [relates to] a vision of physical legacy—that's very important. But more important is this big opportunity to leverage [social] programs that already exist, to foster integration within the society, and to raise a younger generation to a better standard of living. And sports is an excellent tool to foster education and to deliver this legacy. So, we are very thrilled by the legacy potential. And I think that's one of the reasons that Rio was chosen.[10]

Promoters thus touted these events as a way of stimulating economic and cultural development. Indeed, winning the FIFA World Cup and the Summer Olympics would set a kind of high-water mark for Brazil's confidence in its ability to govern. Unfortunately, the next several years brought about something of a confidence drought. MSEs are routinely awarded approximately seven years in advance, giving the host country sufficient time to prepare.[11] In Brazil, this period of preparation would do much more than simply buy time for infrastructure development. It would instead stimulate a historic pivot in approaches and attitudes toward corruption.

When the 2014 FIFA Men's World Cup hosting rights were announced, Brazil's first effort toward mounting an effective legal response to corruption had begun. Mensalão, Portuguese for "big monthly stipend," was a bribery scheme in which President Luiz Inacio Lula da Silva's Workers' Party made secret payments to members of Congress in return for supporting the party's legislative agenda.[12] The scandal erupted in 2005 when an opposing party member claimed the Workers' Party was paying members of congress 30,000 reais a month (around US$12,000 in 2005), and the money had come from the public treasury by way of fake advertising contracts entered into by state-owned companies.[13] From that accusation, the scandal spread to include bribery allegations against the state-run postal system and that the Workers Party was extorting money from illegal betting rings in Rio. The scandal eventually implicated numerous congressmen and Jose Dirceu, then-chief of staff to President Luiz Inacio Lula da Silva. The Supreme Federal Tribunal of Brazil convicted twenty-five people including top legislators, senior Working Party officials, businessmen, and former president da Silva's Chief of Staff; sentencing them to prison for funneling party funds in order to buy votes from legislators.[14] In a country where the legal code offers extraordinary protections to the political and financial elite, the case was a social and legal turning point for Brazil. It was a landmark case, being the first-time high-ranking politicians were found guilty of corruption in a criminal trial and served prison terms.[15]

The convictions gave the Brazilian people and international observers hope that the courts may finally be assuming the role as a legitimate check on government officials' power. This new optimism was joined with an economic optimism. As the lead-off letter in the famous BRIC (Brazil, Russia, India, China) acronym, optimism swirled around Brazil in the first decade of the twenty-first century.[16] The FIFA World Cup and Olympic Games thus found Brazil at a moment when its self-confidence historically high.

The Catalyst and the Reforms: Anti-Corruption Protests and Four New Statutes

Several factors then coalesced in the 2010s to dramatically worsen economic conditions, not to mention the public mood. These factors including a global decline in commodity prices and, in the minds of some, the political strategy of President Dilma Rousseff and the Workers Party of incurring large government deficits to spend heavily on social programs and tax breaks to expand its political support. The economy began to shrink, and credit-rating agencies downgraded the country's debt to junk status. The public's optimism about its economic future, as well as the government's ability to navigate the country through challenging economic times, worsened significantly.[17] At about this time, the populace came to recognize that a cash-strapped government, now proven to be corrupt, would be one of only three countries to host back to back the two most expensive sporting events in the world: the FIFA World Cup and the Olympic Games.[18] The Mensalão scandal injected the issue of public corruption into the public's consciousness and discourse in dramatic ways.

Finally, in June 2013, public discontent would surge when the government announced rate hikes for public transportation.[19] The rate hikes incited protests and even riots across Brazil in more than eighty cities, including Rio, São Paulo, and Brasília, as well as Manaus, Recife, Belo Horizonte, Curitiba, Porto Alegre, and others.[20] Outraged, the public took to the streets in large-scale demonstrations over corruption specifically and government mismanagement generally.[21] Numbering in the hundreds of thousands, protestors voiced their concerns over not just the public transportation rate hikes but poor government and the cost overruns of hosting the upcoming sporting events. As one commentator put it, the protestors spoke out against "poor quality of public services, lavish investment on international sporting events, low standards of healthcare and wider unease about inequality and corruption."[22] Protests continued into 2014, as so many of the infrastructure projects promised for the dual mega-events of the World Cup and Olympics were scaled down, delayed, or canceled.

As public discontent mounted, Brazil's Congress responded by enacting four distinct statutes, two of which were enacted in 2011 just prior to the 2013 protests, and two in 2013, just after. These laws were, to varying degrees, enacted in response to both public concerns about governance generally, and the corruption which grew around the eve of hosting the World Cup and Olympic Games. These "Four Pillars," consist of the following: (1) the 2011 procurement reforms, called the Regime Diferenciado de Contratações and known as the RDC;[23] (2) the 2011 Information Access Law, which functions as a freedom of information law and which addressed the government's role in corruption by obligating agencies to make information available to the public;[24] (3) the 2013 Clean Companies Act, which addressed the corporate sector's role in public corruption by creating corporate liability for bribery, incentivized cooperation with government investigations, and incentivized corporate compliance programs;[25] and (4) an untitled 2013 organized crime bill which authorized the enforcement tools that allowed federal prosecutors to blow open the Petrobras scandal and many other corruption schemes.[26] This combination of laws—enacted in such a short span and to such dramatic effect—is beyond rare; it may well be historically unprecedented. In these reforms, Brazil is consciously addressing a culture that once tolerated corruption and glorified jeitinho, seeking to move beyond a history of official corruption bred under colonization and military dictatorships.

This section will discuss each of the four pillars individually, in order of their enactment: first, the procurement reforms; then the freedom of information law; followed by the Clean Companies Act; and finally, the organized crime law. Where necessary, it provides detailed background on these areas of law, to illustrate just how profoundly these reforms transformed anti-corruption governance in both public and private sectors.

The first pillar was procurement reform. The harms of corruption in the specific realm of government procurement are obvious to all. Government officials may be bribed to accept bloated contracts, or inferior products, or both, all at the public's expense. But in trying to prevent corruption, procurement presents a series of counterintuitive, and underappreciated, policy trade-offs. The first trade-off is between transparency and cost. Transparency is generally thought to be an antidote to corruption: where processes are open to the public, and readily reviewable, the risk of cost inflation would seem to go down.[27] Controlling corruption is generally among the ways to control costs. However, as the Brazilian experience has shown, sometimes transparency can actually exacerbate cost inflation.[28] In this regard, transparency can cause the precise harm that anti-corruption measures are designed, at least in part, to prevent. In fact, a 2011 study by a professor from the Fundação Getúlio Vargas found corruption had cost Brazil approximately US$18 billion in just the six-year window from 2002 to 2008.[29] The relationship between transparency and cost is thus not as simple as may first appear.

So too, in procurement as in government generally, do we suspect that the concentration of power can give rise to corruption. We might assume multiple companies working on a project would be better than a single company with monopolistic control over the project; the various companies might tend to keep each other in check, increasing accountability and decreasing graft. Again however, in the case of Brazil, experience has shown that multiple companies sharing responsibility in procurement projects actually creates inefficiencies and tends to result in increased costs and delays. Such was the case in a number of urban drainage and metro expansion projects.[30] This shows yet another paradoxical example where an effort to reduce corruption actually increases costs to the Brazilian public.

Brazil was keenly aware of these trade-offs and of the challenges inherent in its procurement regime, before the World Cup and Olympics, but the MSEs became an impetus to experiment with a new procurement regime.[31] This new regime was at least designed to make public procurement more streamlined and efficient, however it turned out that the new procurement regime for World Cup and Olympic infrastructure projects was only optional. Indeed, an Organisation for Economic Co-operation and Development's (OECD's) report ultimately found the new procurement regime was not chosen by any of the implementation or oversight authorities for any of the public tenders for the Olympics.[32] The extent to which these efficiency-minded reforms will create corruption risks remains to be seen.

Some draw a distinction between public and private procurement, and others define the term to include only acquisition by a government entity.[33] For the purposes of this chapter, procurement refers to any acquisition by official Olympic organizing entities whether public, private, or a combination of the two.[34] For large-scale events or government projects, such as the Olympic Games, procurement is typically accomplished through a regulated process that requires potential suppliers of goods and services to bid against each other with the goal of maximizing the quality of the good or service offered while minimizing its cost.[35]

It is no secret that procurement is highly vulnerable to corrupt practices, with a lack of transparency and lack of accountability as two of the major threats to corruption in procurement. At all stages, issues like bribery or kickback arrangements could present themselves, with each stage of the procurement process presenting its own unique risks.[36] While some of these issues are specifically addressed in the Clean Companies Act and other various procurement laws, true progress in anti-corruption measures all comes down to oversight and enforcement.[37]

Procurement generally consists of three distinct stages: (1) pre-bidding, (2) bidding, and (3) post-bidding.[38] While the nature and type of corruption differs at each of the various stages of the procurement process, each stage is imbued with the potential for exploitation without proper oversight and management. The pre-bidding stage consists of an initial assessment, general planning and budgeting, and development of specifications/requirements for the various projects (both individually and in toto). Each element is potentially subject to corrupting influence, including: lack of adequate assessment or undue influence in assessment needs, lack of coordination of procurement with larger event organization, publication of design criteria not distributed evenly, or design specifications tailored to fit one particular company, and so forth.[39] The bidding stage consists of the specific procurement procedures, perhaps including specific requests for proposals/bids, the bid submission format and process, the bid evaluation process, and ultimately the awards of the various contracts. This is often seen as the stage with the greatest potential for corruption. Each element can be tailored to favor or discriminate against bidding companies, and various sources of influence can play a strong role for both the bidding companies and the selection committees.[40] Additionally, collusion among bidders to decrease competitiveness and increase bid prices is always a possibility. Lastly, the post-bidding stage, consisting of contract management and performance as well as payment format, is risky in that the accuracy of the quality and amount of labor and materials used in project construction, requests for contract adjustments, delays in construction timeline, and the potential for fraudulent billing practices are all susceptible to corruption.[41] Corruption at any or all of these stages can cause the contracting party, in many cases, the Brazilian people by way of their government in the cases of the 2014 World Cup and 2016 Olympic Games, to pay more than it otherwise would.

Brazil's traditional procurement regime has two features that, at first glance, may appear to promote efficiency and accountability but which have created new and serious problems. The first concerned the pre-bidding and bidding stages. Under the Procurement Law, the technical and procurement phase bids are solicited separately and can therefore be awarded to separate companies.[42] The company helping the government to design the project can thus be different from the company that ultimately builds the project. While this in theory helps ensure against institutional oversights which a single company might miss, the difficulty arises when the construction phase encounters a problem. If the project, as designed and thus far built, proves inadequate or encounters unexpected issues and requires additional time and money to complete, neither the firm that won the bid for the technical project nor the firm that won the construction project will want to accept the blame.[43] Instead, there is a high likelihood each will point the finger at the other: the construction firm might claim that the problem lies with the design or initial planning, while the design firm would attribute the problem to poor execution of a blameless plan. Such a scenario would doubtlessly prompt litigation, which would cause further delays and cost increases. Ultimately, the problem lies in the fact the interests of the design firm and the interests of the construction firm are not aligned. Therefore, if trouble arises, attributing fault will be slow, costly, and imprecise.

The second problem concerned the ironic tension between transparency and inflation. The traditional Procurement Law followed the practice of "open bidding," in which the government publicly announced the project's budget before issuing its request for proposal.[44] Open bidding reflected the default assumption that transparency tends to limit corruption and costs. However, the Brazilian experience proved the opposite to be sometimes true. A bidder that is capable of bidding substantially under the government's budget might inflate the bid to more closely approximate the available government funding.[45] In this way, open bidding can have the effect of driving up costs.

The Regime Diferenciado de Contratações, Law No. 12462/11 and locally known as the RDC, is Brazil's experiment with addressing the inefficiencies with traditional procurement.[46] The law was also aimed to specifically address the procurement needs of the 2014 World Cup and 2016 Olympic Games and was designed to expedite the public procurement process in response to the slow pace of other of massive infrastructure projects previously undertaken, and some which are still underway in Brazil.[47] In many respects, Brazil's hosting of the World Cup and Olympics provided a catalyst to experiment with an alternative procurement regime, which the Brazilian government hoped would prove more efficient.

The RDC modifies the usual procurement process under the Procurement Law in two important ways. First, it allows the government to conduct a single, integrated bidding process for both the design and construction, combining the pre-bidding and bidding phases.[48] The construction bidding no longer depends on the existence of an elaborate design already prepared by a separate design company (who had won the bid in a prior bidding process). Instead, the government provides a general description of what it needs from the project, and companies will simultaneously bid for the design and construction of the project.

Second, the RDC eliminates the requirement for open bidding by no longer requiring the government to make its budget publicly available before issuing the request for proposal.[49] The government has the option of conducting closed bidding and not disclosing the budget, although the government has to justify doing so.[50] Many believed that this process would produce better financial results for the government because the lowest bidder will not be able to allow its bid to creep up to be as close to the budget as possible.

However, skeptics of the RDC were quick to point out that this financial benefit came at the apparent cost of transparency.[51] The instinct that transparency limits corruption, and secrecy exacerbates it, was immediately triggered. Moreover, some critics believed, rightly, that the most powerful companies would use inappropriate influence to find out the budget amount or otherwise affect bid selection, and thus the secrecy would only compound the corruption. While research suggested that companies can no longer expect to obtain that nonpublic information in closed-door private meetings, and perhaps indicating a dramatic change in the mores of Brazilian government, the reality proved otherwise. Following revelations and disclosures as a result of Operation Car Wash, there have been investigations of corruption in all infrastructure constructed for the Rio Olympics and the five top-tier companies involved in the procurement process.[52]

The RDC was originally designed to be used for a limited subset of projects, including the World Cup and Olympic Games, with the mega events being regarded as a kind of experiment in this new procurement regime. Though most Olympic projects did not use the RDC, the Olympics nonetheless served as a catalyst for adopting this new regime. Indeed, initial optimism led to the passage of Law No. 12688/12, which expanded the RDC to contracts which fell under Brazil's federal growth acceleration program.[53] Despite the expansion there has been ongoing debate over whether the RDC did in fact constitute an improvement over the traditional procurement system, and whether further reforms should be adopted. Under current consideration is a bill which would substantially change public procurement laws, including the RDC, not only for the bidding process but also for the insurance industry. While the bill was adopted by the Brazilian Senate in 2016, the Brazilian House of Representatives is still debating it, and it is currently unknown when or if it will come into law.[54]

The second pillar of Brazil's governance reforms is its Freedom of Information Law. Law No. 12.527/2011, widely known as the Information Access Law in Brazil (international audiences might understand it as a freedom of information (FOI) law), was perhaps the first major signal of the government's intention to enact meaningful anti-corruption legislation.[55] While perhaps the least prominent of the four pillars, it would prove a precursor to the extraordinarily impactful statutes of 2013.

Based on the principle, "publicity as the general precept, and secrecy as the exception," the FOI law moves to an era of active transparency, in which the government is obligated to publish certain forms of information without a request.[56] It brings an end to what Brazilians called the "eternal secrecy," in which public documents had an indefinite period of confidentiality because highly classified documents could see their classification renewed ad infinitum. Indeed, when the FOI law was under consideration in Congress, some lawmakers had pushed for keeping the "eternal" classification for certain categories of documents—there were national security concerns about documents and information covering nuclear and aerospace technology, national defense, and diplomatic relations—but the provision was ultimately defeated.[57] So too did the bill create controversy about the potential disclosure of military intelligence concerning human rights violations during the military dictatorship.

The FOI law has three core components. First, it obligates the federal, state, and municipal governments, and all branches thereof, as well as state-owned companies and even non-profits receiving government funds, to publish various kinds of information, including documents on government spending, without a request.[58] These so-called "active transparency" obligations extend to the official contact details of all employees, financial operations, spending, procurement contracts, and answers to frequently asked questions. Second, the law empowers any citizen to request information from the government and obliges the government to provide any such documents that are not classified.[59] Third, it reduces the terms of confidentiality of documents designated as top secret, secret, and undisclosed for twenty-five, fifteen, and five years, respectively, and ends the possibility of renewal of these periods.[60] In what could be construed as a recent step backward from this progressive trend, soon after taking office in 2019, President Jair Bolsonaro signed a decree which expanded the number and scope of public officials who could classify documents at each of the classification levels.[61] Some critics see this as undermining the efficacy of the push for transparency, though it does not alter the sunset periods of the classifications.

Preliminary data suggest that the Brazilian government is starting to comply with the law, although patterns and attitudes will take time to reform. According to one study, of all valid requests for information under the new law, 40 percent were unanswered, 18 percent were partially answered, and 31 percent received full responses.[62] Of the partial or full responses, 51 percent were deemed of good quality. In 2017, two reports were released which analyzed and evaluated compliance with the FOI law after five years of implementation. Those reports revealed that the compliance at the federal level was extremely high (response rates were at 90 percent) due to effective oversight.[63] However compliance and implementation of the law was found to be very weak at the state and municipal levels.

The third, and perhaps biggest, pillar is the so-called Clean Companies Act. While the FOI law targets the public sector, this act focuses on the private sector. Passed in 2013, Brazil's Anti-Corruption Law, also referred to as the Clean Companies Act (CCA), adopts a number of measures to increase corporate liability and accountability, and to incentivize the growth of a compliance industry and culture.[64]

Brazil had a law on the books before the World Cup and Olympic Games that prohibited official corruption; all governments do. However, it failed to create the corporate compliance culture that has proven in other countries to be so critical to anti-corruption enforcement. Accordingly, in response to the Mensalão scandal and public protests, Brazil adopted the CCA. Indeed, the law marks an important milestone in Brazil's fight against corruption and was intended by President Rousseff's administration to send a strong message that the corruption tides have turned in Brazil.

The CCA's essential prohibition is the promising, offering, or giving of an "undue advantage" to a public official or third person related to the public official.[65] This provision mirrors the bribery prohibition in the OECD Anti-Bribery Convention, to which Brazil is a party.[66] The statute also prohibits a number of other forms of corporate corruption concerning public tenders, shell companies, and obstructing public investigations of companies suspected of corporate wrongdoing.

The statute's reforms are both substantive and procedural. First, it prohibits not just the bribing but the solicitation or offer of a bribe.[67] This brings the act into conformity with the OECD Anti-Bribery Convention and obviously serves to prohibit a much broader swath of conduct. Second, the act imposes strict liability on corporations for the acts of employees. That is, when an employee commits a violation, the company automatically becomes liable; the prosecutor need not prove that the company intended, authorized, or even had knowledge of the bribe independently of the employee.[68] This is similar to the US model, but different from the United Kingdom. In the United States, owing to a long-established principle of *respondeat superior*, the company is liable for the acts of its employee as long as the employee was acting in the course of employment (defined very broadly) and intended at least in part to benefit the company.[69] The US statute, like Brazil's CCA, does not require proof that the company was also liable, independently of whatever the employee did; if the employee did it while acting as an employee, the company is also liable. Similarly, under the CCA a company will be liable "for the wrongful acts . . . performed in their interest or for their benefit."[70] The United Kingdom, by contrast, has recently provided companies a defense to liability for the acts of its employees. If the company can prove that it had a good faith compliance program in place—that is, that it took appropriate measures to prevent the violation—but the violation occurred nonetheless, the company will not be liable.[71] Brazil's CCA eschews the British approach, containing an explicit provision holding companies strictly liable.[72] Though time will tell, this will likely mean that a company is liable no matter what the company did or did not do, apart from the employee.

Third, the statute makes clear that companies owned by the government—typically called state-owned enterprises (SOEs)—are deemed an extension of the government, such that these companies' employees are public officials.[73]

In the US context, for example, whether employees of SOEs are foreign officials was a matter of much dispute, as the statute did not explicitly address the question. Only in 2011 did the US courts resolve the question, holding just as the CCA now does that SOE employees are to be treated as officials.[74]

Finally, and perhaps most importantly, the statute imposes two forms of liability on companies: (1) civil, and (2) administrative. Notably, the statute does not impose criminal liability on companies, but this is not inappropriately lenient, much less scandalous. Though the United States, the United Kingdom, and many other jurisdictions around the world hold companies criminally liable, many (such as Germany) do not.[75] And indeed, corporate criminal liability is a relatively new phenomenon in the history of law. International conventions such as the OECD Anti-Bribery Convention require signatory states to hold companies liable in accordance with their underlying principles of law, recognizing that some jurisdictions simply do not recognize the criminal liability of corporations.[76] The CCA should not be thought as somehow less effective in this regard.

The CCA's penalty provisions are especially strong; companies may even say severe. The penalty is to be calculated as a percentage, up to 20 percent, of the gross earnings in the company's most recent fiscal year preceding the onset of enforcement proceedings.[77] Note what the statutory penalty is not. First, it is not calculated based on the amount of the bribe, as some might assume, meaning even a bribe of relatively modest proportions could give rise to a substantial penalty. Second, it is not a function of the earnings which result from the bribe. In the United States, for example, under the Foreign Corrupt Practices Act (FCPA), a company's financial penalty for foreign bribery is calculated based on the profits made possible by the bribe.[78] The CCA, by contrast, disregards both the size of the bribe and the size of the profits made possible by the bribe. Finally, note that this statute does not calculate profits based on annual profits but rather annual gross earnings. Accordingly, a company that is losing money—it is not uncommon for corporations to have years, sometimes consecutively, where they post no profits—can still be fined. Where the bribes proved to be bad business and became a losing proposition, the company may nonetheless be fined. So too may the company be debarred or prohibited from conducting further business with the government, and in some circumstances may even be dissolved.[79]

Just as important as the preceding substantive reforms are the changes the CCA creates for white-collar enforcement. To appreciate the depth of those changes, some background on white-collar anti-corruption enforcement is helpful. Enforcement agencies in even the richest countries have limited budgets. The principal aim of public anti-corruption enforcement is to maximize general deterrence, thereby preventing persons within their jurisdiction from committing similar acts. While specific deterrence refers to preventing recidivism (the defendant's repeated violation), general deterrence refers to preventing persons other than the defendant from committing similar violations. Accordingly, the US enforcement agencies seek to maximize general deterrence while operating on a fixed budget. It might be said that they are looking for the maximum general deterrence return on the dollar.

A traditional way to achieve both specific and general deterrence is to bring wrongdoers to trial. If convicted, the defendant company would face a stiff penalty and considerable reputational damage through the negative press. However, trials present two challenges for the enforcement agencies. First, they are extremely resource-intensive, as the gathering of evidence (discovery) and resulting trials are notoriously drawn out and expensive, consuming vast amounts of the enforcement agencies' time, money, and personnel. Second, because they are so resource intensive, the agency can only practically try a relatively small number of companies. Finally, a trial is unpredictable, and the government can rarely be sure all the money and time spent on trying a case will actually result in a conviction.

Meanwhile, criminal trials are obviously unattractive for the defendant company. The company feels the drain on resources, as key personnel are distracted from their regular duties and high-priced corporate litigators rack up billable hours. The unpredictability of trials is a major down side to the defendant company, as they too cannot be certain of an acquittal, or a conviction with an unexpectedly severe penalty. Finally, trials will generally produce negative press for a company (which can sometimes be worse for a company than the dollar value of an adverse judgment), harming their reputation and, for public companies, their stock value. Even if ultimately acquitted, the reputational damage can be very hard to overcome.

Enforcement authorities are increasingly offering, and companies are generally accepting, an alternative form of investigation and settlement. This alternative route has four core components. The first is the investigation stage. When an allegation of wrongdoing arises, either within a company or publicly, the company will not wait for the government to catch wind of the suspicions and begin to investigate the company. Rather, the company conducts its own investigation into its own potential wrongdoing. With an "internal" investigation, typically for lesser alleged offenses, the company will conduct the investigation in-house. When the misconduct is larger scale, more systemic, or where the in-house lawyers are potentially implicated, the company may conduct an "independent" investigation. Here, the board of directors will retain an outside law firm, one that has not previously represented or been affiliated with the company, to conduct a factual investigation into the wrongdoing and formulate conclusions concerning what wrongdoing may have occurred, the liability the company may face, and which steps the company should take in terms of internal governance and the retaining or firing of implicated personnel. Either way, when the investigation is complete, a substantial factual record, and a report summarizing the factual and legal conclusions, will be compiled. That report is left in the company's possession.

The second core feature of modern anti-bribery enforcement concerns what happens after the final report is delivered to the company. The company has now spent millions, or tens of millions, on an investigation into its own wrongdoing, and possesses a comprehensive report with supporting documentation. The enforcement agency, seeking access to the report, offers the company "cooperation credit."[80] By the terms of this deal, if the company hands over the investigation's findings and makes its employees available to further interviewing, and otherwise cooperates with the government, the government will offer a penalty that, it claims, is substantially less than what the defendant would likely get if convicted at trial. The company must then make a decision. It can risk the unpredictability of a trial, with its exorbitant costs, substantial drain on company resources, and undoubtedly negative press, or, it can accept the government's offer of cooperation credit and turn over to the government the results of its investigation, buying itself a reduced penalty, predictability of outcome, reduced lawyer's fees, and reduced negative press.

Invariably, companies select the latter route, opting to cooperate with the government.[81] The turning over of its investigation conclusions is widely referred to as "voluntary disclosure," meaning the company voluntarily discloses the results of its findings. The return for voluntary disclosure is the cooperation credit. Notably, the government cannot force companies to accept this deal, and yet the companies invariably do. It is perceived to be in the interests of both parties.

This deal culminates in the third core feature of the US anti-corruption settlement process: non-trial resolutions (NTRs). These are forms of settlement, in which the government agrees to either defer prosecution or to forgo prosecution altogether in exchange for the company accepting certain terms of settlement. The terms will include a penalty and might also include disgorged profits, the termination of various personnel, the withdrawal of business from the problematic markets, or acceptance of a government-imposed monitor.[82] Under an NTR, the government in effect gives the company a trial period in which to demonstrate its compliance with the law and the settlement terms.

The fourth unique component of this enforcement procedure concerns the role of compliance programs. Compliance programs are designed to prevent violations of given laws through training, monitoring, and the maintenance of an appropriate company culture.[83] With respect to a given area of federal law (be it environmental, health care, or, in our case, anti-corruption), a company that knows itself to be at risk may invest in compliance to varying degrees. Of course, it may not invest at all, liking its chances that it will not violate the law or, at least, will not get caught. It may create a mediocre compliance program, and may or may not work to support that program by creating a culture within the company that values compliance. Alternatively, the company may take compliance seriously, investing in a first-rate program and taking substantial effort to back up those programs with company culture.

Enforcement agencies generally wish to incentivize the growth of compliance programs and will therefore reward companies for quality programs in several different stages of enforcement. First, the government may decide not to investigate a company at all.[84] Second, the agency may investigate a company but then decide not to penalize it. This formal decision not to penalize a company is often called a declination. Finally, where there is sufficient evidence of culpability to enter into an NTR with the company, a quality compliance program can lead to a penalty reduction.

Brazil's CCA introduces this type of enforcement regime into Brazilian anti-corruption enforcement. Though necessarily announcing that it is eschewing or even discouraging traditional trials, multiple provisions of the CCA are designed to foster the growth of an enforcement regime based on self-investigation, voluntary disclosure, and cooperation credit through settlements.

First, the CCA contains a list of enumerated factors that the government will consider when determining appropriate sanctions.[85] The first six provisions of Chapter III, Article 7 are predictable and rather unremarkable: (1) the seriousness of the offense, (2) the advantage gained by the illicit conduct, (3) whether the illicit act was completed, (4) the degree or risk of damage, (5) the adverse effect of the conduct, and (6) the offending company's economic circumstances.[86] However, the next two provisions are harbingers of a new enforcement era. Article 7.VII provides that penalties will be determined in part based on the "cooperation of the legal entity in the investigation" of the wrongdoing. This is cooperation credit. The next provision, Article 7.VIII, provides that penalties will also be based on the existence of internal procedures designed to promote integrity, including but not limited to auditing, whistleblowing, and self-enforcement of the codes of ethics and conduct. These are all features of what the West (or North, as it were) calls a compliance program.

Additionally, the CCA authorizes the relevant enforcement agency to enter into what the statute calls "leniency agreements."[87] The term "leniency agreement" makes its purpose more explicit: to be lenient on the defendant in exchange for the defendant's cooperation. The CCA establishes several requirements that a defendant company must meet if it is to be entitled to a leniency agreement; these requirements are much more specific, and perhaps more exacting, than anything seen in the US system.[88] Requirements companies must meet include: (1) collaboration must result in identification of the guilty individuals; (2) the rapid exchange of information; (3) the legal entity must have initiated the cooperation; (4) the entity must completely discontinue its involvement in the investigated wrongdoing; (5) the entity must fully admit its participation in the wrongdoing; and (6) fully and completely cooperate with the investigation until its conclusion.[89]

The CCA is thus a bold effort to stimulate the growth of a new corporate enforcement climate—where companies invest in compliance programs, where they investigate their own potential misdeeds, and where they will cooperate with the enforcement agencies to efficiently negotiate settlements.

The final pillar of Brazil's reforms is the Organized Crime Law. Passed in August 2013, this statute is remarkable both for its impact and for the circumstances that led to its enactment. The statute provides a definition of organized crime and authorizes a number of law enforcement methods to investigate and prosecute organized crime. The federal prosecutors' use of these tools led to the Petrobras scandal, discussed in this section.

The bill was supposedly proposed to go after organized crime (e.g., drug trafficking) generally and specifically to target a group of violent protestors known as the Black Bloc.[90] During the early stages of congressional consideration of the bill, there was no mention that these enforcement tools could, or would, be used to go after high-level officials and businesspersons engaged in graft. However conventional understandings indicate that advocates pushing for adoption of the bill may well have understood its potential to convict the very politicians who would vote to support the bill.[91]

Of the organized crime laws various enforcement tools, two have proven of particular significance to anti-corruption enforcement. First, the law provides an obstruction of justice charge; specifically, a person who obstructs investigations is subject to the same punishment range as one who promotes, constitutes, or finances a criminal organization.[92]

Second is the expanded plea bargain. Though plea bargaining previously existed under Brazilian law, it was much more restricted and thus a much less effective tool in the prosecutor's arsenal. Under the previous regime, judges could only reduce the penalty by one to two-thirds, or grant a pardon post-conviction if the judge determined that the defendant's cooperation was useful to the conviction.[93] A defendant could thus not be sure, at the time of confession, of the plea bargain's effects on his or her conviction and sentence. The 2013 organized crime law goes significantly further. It does not merely provide for a sentence reduction or eventual pardon but rather, it allows the prosecutor to not bring charges at all under certain circumstances.[94] Specifically, a prosecutor or judge may grant complete impunity, or reduce a penalty by up to two-thirds, for a defendant who has effectively and voluntarily cooperated with the investigation, provided that the cooperation produces one of five results: (1) the identification of other participants in the crime; (2) information on the structure and control of the criminal organization; (3) the prevention of additional criminal activity by the organization; (4) the complete or partial recovery of the criminal proceeds; or (5) the location of the victim.[95] So too may the prosecutor dismiss the complaint against the defendant if he or she is not the leader of the criminal organization and is the first member of that organization to enter into a plea agreement with the enforcement authorities.

The obstruction of justice charge and the enhanced plea bargain under Brazil's new organized crime law made possible what may be the largest anti-corruption prosecution in history: Petrobras.[96] Former Petrobras executive Paulo Roberto Costa, who was arrested in March 2014 for involvement in a separate money-laundering probe, accused more than forty politicians of participating in a vast kickback scheme designed to benefit the Brazilian oil giant between 2004 and 2012.[97] He alleged that the participants received as much as 3 percent of the value of contracts signed between Petrobras and the Brazilian government in exchange for favorable votes in the legislature.

Prosecutors would eventually uncover a scheme of money laundering, drug trafficking, tax evasion, foreign exchange evasion, and smuggling valued at over US$3 billion.

This author's interviews with Brazilian prosecutors disclosed that the organized crime law of 2013 made this prosecution possible.[98] Costa was at first questioned about a minor violation and was reportedly revealing little of what he seemed to know. Prosecutors then used their new tool, an obstruction of justice charge, which they threatened against both Costa and his family if he did not disclose further information. The threatened obstruction charge flipped Costa and broke open "Operation Car Wash."[99] Prosecutors have also made liberal use of their new plea bargaining authority, again authorized by the organized crime bill. As of March 2017, sixty-five plea deals had been signed; by July 2019, the number of plea deals had reached 184.[100]

Most significant for the Olympics is the central role of Brazil's major construction companies, which obviously figured prominently in preparations for the World Cup and Olympics. These construction companies were funding the political parties' campaigns in exchange for illicit benefits in the bidding of construction projects, including but not limited to World Cup and Olympic venues.[101] As of 2017, 109 persons were already convicted in first instance and sixty signed plea deals with the Ministério da Justiça. Alberto Youseff, former black-market money dealer and suspected to be one of the leaders of the scheme, said in his deposition that he collected close to US$60 million in bribery.[102]

Most of the people who signed the plea deals are executives or former executives and former directors of big construction companies. For example, Clóvis Peixoto Primo, former president of the construction company Andrade Gutierrez, said in his deposition that he paid bribes to the former Rio de Janeiro governor, Sergio Cabral, and the owner of the Delta construction company, relating to the Maracanã Stadium renovation. Augusto Mendonça, Toyo Setal executive, said in his deposition that between 2008 and 2011, he paid around US$15 million to the former Services Director of Petrobras. Claudio Melo Filho, former director of institutional relations of Odebrecht, showed in his depositions the values that were given to fifty-one politicians of eleven political parties for the purpose of getting illicit benefits to the construction company. These politicians included the former president of the Senate, Renan Calheiros, Worker's Party leading Senator Delcídio do Amral, and former Brazilian President, Michel Temer. Other executives or former executives and former directors of large construction companies that signed plea deals, include Eduardo Hermelino Leite, former vice president of Camargo Correia; Hamylton Pinheiro Padilha Junior, former representative of Vantage Drilling Corp; and João Carlos de Medeiros Ferraz, former president director of Sete Brasil.[103] As an example of how impactful these plea deals were, Odebrecht would eventually enter into a US$3.5 billion settlement with authorities in Brazil, the United States, and Switzerland for paying bribes around the world.[104]

Operation Car Wash would eventually bring the Olympic Games themselves within its snare. The most expensive construction project undertaken for the Games was the US$2.5 billion revitalization of the port region of Rio de Janeiro, known as "Port Maravilha." The Car Wash investigation has uncovered a suspicious payment of US$300,000 to a code name "Turquesa 2."[105] The Engenharia and OAS construction firms are also implicated and under investigation for participation in the project. This particular scheme allegedly involved then-president of the Brazilian House of Representatives, Eduardo Cunha, who received around US$700,000 to provide the construction companies special tax breaks in relation to the Olympic construction.

Not surprisingly, on the eve of the Games, 63 percent of Brazilians surveyed thought hosting the Olympics would hurt the country.[106] There is overwhelming evidence to suggest they were right. Six months later, the *New York Times* would run a jarring article entitled "Legacy of Rio Olympics So Far Is Series of Unkept Promises," detailing the economic waste and incomplete projects left in the Olympics' wake, and the eventual tally would show that hosting the Games cost Brazil over US$20 billion, with at least US$13 billion falling on Rio de Janeiro.[107] Additionally, while Operation Car Wash revealed a history of corruption which existed well before Rio won either the World Cup or Olympic Games, the infrastructure projects which those two mega events necessitated proved to be fertile fodder for even greater corruption, among both corporations and politicians.

The fallout from Operation Car Wash has spread far beyond the already vast scope from just a few years ago. Not only was the stain of alleged corruption enough to bring down President Dilma Rousseff (though Rousseff was impeached as part of the wider backlash to the anti-corruption investigations, the impeachment charges were based on unrelated matters, and she has yet to be convicted of any crimes exposed by the anti-corruption investigation; additionally some evidence suggests her removal was politically motivated by those who sought to evade investigation[108]) but corruption allegations also ensnared her successor, Michel Temer.

President Temer has been implicated in the payoff schemes exposed by Operation Car Wash, however, before he even stepped in as interim president, finishing out the term of the impeached Rousseff, he had already seen himself convicted of violating election laws, and as punishment was barred from running for office for a period of eight years.[109] Just as important however is the fact that Car Wash was catching not just the leading accused politicians but also their accusers; the rich elites which many average Brazilians had always viewed as being above the law; and the legislative and ministerial politicians who had been getting rich off the corruption kickback schemes. In the case of Senator Amaral (a friend of senior Petrobras executive Nestor Cerveró, who has received sentences of five and twelve years from two separate Car Wash cases), this was particularly noteworthy as his arrest was the first time a Brazilian senator had been arrested in thirty years.[110]

It was in this environment of tumult that saw Brazil's 2018 election season (open positions included the presidency, as well as twenty-seven governorships, two-thirds of the Senate, and all 513 seats in the House, as well as state and municipal positions) focus heavily on anti-corruption measures. Jair Bolsonaro, a former army captain, campaigned heavily on toughening the Brazilian government's stance on corruption and even appointed the star judge of many of the Car Wash cases, Sergio Moro, to be justice minister. As part of Moro's crusade against corruption, and in line with Bolsonaro's campaign promises, Moro introduced a sweeping anti-corruption package in early 2019, which would extend federal powers to continue to prosecute the continuing revelations from Operation Car Wash, and Bolsonaro expanded autonomy in the Ministry of Justice, as well as expanded the federal police.[111] The anti-corruption package of laws, which went into effect in the start of 2020 will also clarify aspects of civil non-persecution agreements (plea deals), which were previously subject to differing judicial interpretations under the Administrative Improbity Law.[112] President Bolsonaro has also passed a series of executive decrees to expand the scope of the Clean Record Law (Lei de Ficha Limpa) to include positions of appointment to commissioned or public trust posts, as well as other jobs inside the federal government.[113]

From the start of Operation Car Wash through his appointment as justice minister under President Jair Bolsonaro, Moro was seen as a star ascendant and a hero of the anti-corruption push. Moro was fundamentally altering the way corruption cases would be tried in Brazil, most notably by vastly speeding up the trial process and liberally using the pretrial detention policy to apply extra pressure on the politicians and corporate executives who got caught.[114] Moro also gained notoriety by the people he was trying; under the Brazilian constitution, federal ministers and congressmen are afforded "privileged jurisdiction," which means they can only be tried by the Supreme Court. As a result, Brazil's Supreme Court, and Moro, were front and center for every trial involving the top-tier politicians.

After being appointed justice minister however, questions began to arise about whether Moro was the paragon of justice which he had seemed to be. Only six months into his tenure of his new post, *The Intercept* news source would reveal a potentially major case of prosecutorial misconduct by federal prosecutors and Moro. Based upon a trove of mobile phone text messages which were leaked, purporting to show collaboration between prosecutors and judges, the aura of invincibility around the Car Wash cases has vanished.[115] This revelation has not only raised questions of serious ethics violations but also raised the potential that the conduct of Mora was legally prohibited and would therefore have major impacts on the cases he oversaw, especially the case of former President Lula. Despite being convicted and receiving a sentence of twelve years, and thus being ineligible to run in the 2018 presidential election, the leaked conversations seemed to show holes in case against the former president and reignited allegations that the case was politically motivated.[116] This has also caused speculation that Operation Car Wash could be prematurely ended, or at least severely truncated (which would allow many corrupt politicians to evade justice). More importantly though, it represents a serious setback to the image and public perception of credibility in Brazil's justice system and its ability to tackle the corruption.

Another issue which threatens the anti-corruption successes of Operation Car Wash is the fact that procedural issues could wind up letting numerous convicted persons slip free. In September 2019, the Supreme Court overturned the conviction of Aldemr Bendine, a former president of Petrobras, based on the procedural fact that he should have been allowed to give a closing response after hearing plea-bargain testimony against him.[117] This has potentially opened the doors to 143 other convictions being overturned, based on the same argument. The obvious implications of such a ruling also therefore reflect upon the integrity of the judicial system. While the successes of the operation have undoubtedly produced impressive results and meant the recovery of billions of dollars, the fact that the anti-corruption operation has its own potential corruption has cast a pall over its legacy.

Given the extent of contacts, projects and activities which Odebrecht and Petrobras have throughout South America, it should not have come as any surprise that other politicians and companies in other countries in the region would be implicated. Indeed, fourteen countries have been directly involved so far, as well as former or current heads of states of Argentina, Chile, Colombia, the Dominican Republic, Ecuador, Guatemala, Mexico, Panama, Peru, and Venezuela (former Peruvian President, Alan Garcia, even committed suicide before he could be arrested).[118] Prosecutors from eleven countries (Brasil, Argentina, Chile, Colombia, Ecuador, Mexico, Peru, the Dominican Republic, Venezuela, Panama, and Portugal) joined forces in the creation of a joint task force to continue the investigation and enhance cooperation and information sharing across borders.[119] Additionally, Mexico, Colombia, Argentina, and Peru have all taken extra steps to ramp up anti-corruption enforcement, including passing new anti-corruption legislation.[120]

Another key player which has been heavily involved in the global reach of Operation Car Wash is the US Department of Justice (DOJ). In fact, the far reaching nature of the FCPA, and the manner in which the DOJ has pursued violation claims has almost made it an intermediary for some of the large foreign corporations caught up along with the Brazilian Otebrech and Petrobras, including British Rolls-Royce (which agreed to pay US$800 million for FCPA violations), Singaporean Keppel O&M (with penalties of over US$470 million), and Dutch SBM Offshore (over US$422 million in penalties).[121] In 2019, South Korean corporate giant, Samsung Heavy Industries (SHI, part of the Samsung Group *chaebol*), agreed to pay US$75 million to Brazilian and US authorities to settle a FCPA claim which arose out of an illegal scheme to purchase SHI's ships.[122] Just how far this will stretch, and how many companies will be caught, has yet to be seen.

Megasports as Accidental Accelerator

Brazil's anti-corruption reforms upended norms and practices that had deep roots in Brazilian history and culture. So too did the implementation of these norms, practices, and laws have far-reaching impact. These are not paper reforms; it was no tick-the-box exercise. Concurrent with its hosting of the Olympic Games and FIFA Men's World Cup, Brazil experienced a historic reform movement.

We should be careful not to overstate the role of megasports. They were not the original or even principal catalyst to these reforms. However, a legacy analysis does not require causation; it only requires acceleration. Just as we should not overstate the role of sports, we should not understate or fail to recognize it. There can be little doubt that perceived megasport corruption was an accelerator here, helping to speed up the reform movement.

Brazil is thus the first country to intimate the possibility of a new megasport legacy. Brazil's legacy was a reactive rather than proactive—it emerged only in reaction to scandal. So too was it accidental rather than intentional—the lawmakers never formulated an intention, as far as we know, to use Brazil's two MSEs to create a legacy. Finally, because Brazil's reforms focused on anti-corruption and not, to a meaningful extent, human rights, this book calls Brazil's reforms one-dimensional. Still, the Brazilian experience portends something important, even transformative, for the future of MSEs.

Standing alone, Brazil is a fascinating study. But as the next chapter will show, juxtaposed with South Korea, these two countries create a pattern. The pattern in turn begins to suggest a new possibility: a proactive, intended, and perhaps even two-dimensional megasport legacy.

Notes

1. Paulo Trevisani, *Brazil's Political Drama Grinds on During Olympics*, WALL ST. J. (Aug. 6, 2016), https://www.wsj.com/articles/brazils-political-drama-grinds-on-during-olympics-1470506493; Brad Brooks, *Ex-Brazil Tycoon Batista Handed 30-year Sentence for Corruption*, REUTERS (July 3, 2018), https://www.reuters.com/article/us-brazil-corruption-batista/ex-brazil-tycoon-batista-handed-30-year-sentence-for-corruption-idUSKBN1JT29R.
2. Peter B. Smith et al., *How Distinctive Are Indigenous Ways of Achieving Influence? A Comparative Study of Guanxi, Wasta, Jeitinho, and "Pulling Strings,"* 43 J. CROSS-CULTURAL PSYCH. 135, 137 (2011); Maria Ferreira et al., *Unraveling the Mystery of Brazilian Jeitinho: A Cultural Exploration of Social Norms*, 38 PERSONALITY & SOC. PSYCH. BULL. 331, 331 (2012).
3. Ferreira et al., *supra* note 2, at 331, 332.
4. *See, e.g.*, FEDERAL RESEARCH DIVISION, LIBRARY OF CONGRESS, BRAZIL, A COUNTRY STUDY (Rex A. Hudson ed., 5th ed., 1998); Keith S. Rosenn, *Separation of Powers in Brazil*, 47 DUQ. L. REV. 839, 850–51 (2009).
5. Ferreira et al., *supra* note 2, at 331, 332.
6. *Id.*
7. *Id.* at 332–33.

8. *Id.*
9. *See, e.g.*, Shasta Darlington, *Brazilians Celebrate Olympics Bid in Rio de Janeiro*, CNN (Oct. 2, 2009), http://www.cnn.com/2009/WORLD/americas/10/02/rio.celebration/.
10. Carlos Roberto Osorio, Felipe Monteiro, & Ken Shropshire, *Brazil's Gold: How Rio Won Its Olympic Bid*, KNOWLEDGE@WHARTON (Mar. 3, 2010), https://knowledge.wharton.upenn.edu/article/brazils-gold-how-rio-won-its-olympic-bid/.
11. *See generally Olympic Games Candidature Process*, INT'L OLYMPIC COMM., https://www.olympic.org/all-about-the-candidature-process.
12. *Q&A: Brazil's "Big Monthly" Corruption Trial*, BBC (Nov. 16, 2013), http://www.bbc.com/news/world-latin-america-19081519; *see also* H.J., *The Economist Explains: What Is Brazil's "Mensalao"?*, THE ECONOMIST (Nov. 18, 2013), https://www.economist.com/the-economist-explains/2013/11/18/what-is-brazils-mensalao.
13. *Id.*
14. Simon Romero, *Key Brazilians in Graft Case Must Go to Jail, Court Says*, N.Y. TIMES (Nov. 14, 2013), http://www.nytimes.com/2013/11/15/world/americas/key-brazilians-in-graft-case-must-go-to-jail-court-says.html.
15. *See* Carolina Cardenas, *The Meaning and Implication of the "Mensalão," Brazil's Largest Trial on Political Corruption*, WILSON CTR. (Oct. 4, 2013), https://www.wilsoncenter.org/event/the-meaning-and-implication-the-mensalao-brazils-largest-trial-political-corruption.
16. Christina Majaski, *Brazil, Russia, India, and China (BRIC)*, INVESTOPEDIA (Dec. 10, 2020), http://www.investopedia.com/terms/b/bric.asp (discussing how "China and India will become the world's dominant suppliers of manufactured goods and services . . . while Brazil and Russia will become similarly dominant as suppliers of raw materials.").
17. *See Brazil's Fall*, THE ECONOMIST (Jan. 2, 2016), http://www.economist.com/news/leaders/21684779-disaster-looms-latin-americas-biggest-economy-brazils-fall.
18. Juliana Barbassa, *Brazil Is in Crisis Ahead of 2016 Olympics*, CNBC (Aug. 17, 2015), http://www.cnbc.com/2015/08/17/brazil-is-in-crisis-ahead-of-2016-olympics-in-rio-commentary.html.
19. Simon Romero, *Bus-Fare Protests Hit Brazil's Two Biggest Cities*, N.Y. TIMES (June 13, 2013), http://www.nytimes.com/2013/06/14/world/americas/bus-fare-protests-hit-brazils-two-biggest-cities.html; *see also* Jonathan Watts, *Brazil Protests Erupt Over Public Services and World Cup Costs*, THE GUARDIAN (June 18, 2013), https://www.theguardian.com/world/2013/jun/18/brazil-protests-erupt-huge-scale.
20. *Id.*.
21. *Brazil Unrest: "Million" Join Protests in 100 Cities*, BBC (June 21, 2013), http://www.bbc.com/news/world-latin-america-22992410.
22. *Id.*
23. Law No. 12,462/11; Andy Spalding, *Andy Spalding on Brazil's First Pillar: Procurement Reform*, FCPA BLOG (July 19, 2016), http://www.fcpablog.com/blog/2016/7/19/andy-spalding-on-brazils-first-pillar-procurement-reform.html.
24. Law No. 12,572/11; Jaclyn Belczyk, *Brazil Freedom of Information Law Takes Effect*, JURIST (May 18, 2012), https://www.jurist.org/news/2012/05/brazil-freedom-of-information-law-takes-effect/.

25. Law No. 12,846/13; *Brazilian Clean Company Act*, GAN: Risk & Compliance Portal, http://www.business-anti-corruption.com/anti-corruption-legislation/brazil.
26. Law No. 12,850/13; Antenor Madruga & Luciano Feldens, *Brazil: White-Collar Crime Defense*, Glob. Investigations Rev. (Aug. 8, 2016), http://globalinvestigationsreview.com/insight/the-investigations-review-of-the-americas-2017/1067457/brazil-white-collar-criminal-defence; Andy Spalding, *Andy Spalding on Brazil's Fourth Pillar: The Organized Crime Law*, FCPA Blog (July 28, 2016), fcpablog.com/blog/2016/7/28/andy-spalding-on-brazils-fourth-pillar-the-organized-crime-l.html.
27. *Transparency and Accountability Are the Main Antidotes for Corruption*, Barbados Free Press (Feb. 26, 2008), https://barbadosfreepress.wordpress.com/2008/02/26/transparency-and-accountability-are-the-main-antidotes-for-corruption/.
28. *See The Brazilian Crisis: Lessons from an Emerging Economy*, The One Brief, http://www.theonebrief.com/the-brazilian-crisis-lessons-from-an-emerging-economy/.
29. Funmi Ojo & Allison Everhardt, *Brazilian Infrastructure and Corruption*, Risk Advisory (Oct. 11, 2013), https://www.riskadvisory.com/news/brazilian-infrastructure-and-corruption/.
30. *Id.*
31. Renato Parreira Stetner & Paulo Henrique Spirandeli Dantas, *Public Procurement in Brazil*, Thomson Reuters Prac. L. (Mar. 1, 2013), https://uk.practicallaw.thomsonreuters.com/0-521-5566?__lrTS=20170402065602319&transitionType=Default&contextData=(sc.Default)&firstPage=true&bhcp=1.
32. Mitigating Corruption Risks in the Procurement of Sporting Events, OECD & Int'l P'ship Against Corruption in Sport 20 (2019), https://www.oecd.org/gov/public-procurement/mitigating-corruption-risks-procurement-sporting-events-IPACS.pdf.
33. Allison Green, *Difference in Public v. Private Procurement*, Chron (Jan. 19, 2021), https://work.chron.com/difference-public-vs-private-procurement-28985.html; *see generally* Federal Acquisition Regulation, U.S. Gen. Servs. Admin. (2005), https://www.acquisition.gov/sites/default/files/current/far/pdf/FAR.pdf.
34. As explained earlier, the governing bodies of the 2016 Olympics consist of both public and private entities. *See id.*
35. *See generally* Nathan Munn, *Olympic Procurement: Past, Present, and Future*, SourceSuite, http://www.sourcesuite.com/procurement-learning/purchasing-articles/Olympic-Procurement-Past-Present-and-Future.jsp.
36. *See* Procurement Fraud Handbook, U.S. Gen. Servs. Admin. 13–28 (2012), https://www.gsaig.gov/sites/default/files/misc-reports/ProcurementFraudHandbook_0.pdf.
37. *See* Andy Spalding et al., *3.14 Rio 2016 and the Birth of Brazilian Transparency, in* Global Corruption Report: Sport 276–85 (2016), for more details on the Clean Companies Act.
38. Integrity in Public Procurement: Good Practice from A–Z, OECD at 21–25 (2007), http://www.oecd.org/development/effectiveness/38588964.pdf.
39. *OECD & Int'l P'ship Against Corruption in Sport*, *supra* note 32, at 11.

40. *Id.*
41. *Id.*
42. *See generally* Eduardo Damiao Goncalves et al., *Construction and Projects in Brazil: Overview*, THOMSON REUTERS PRAC. L. (Apr. 1, 2020), https://content.next.westlaw.com/4-502-3377?__lrTS=20170409042129047&transitionType=Default&contextData=(sc.Default)&firstPage=true&bhcp=1.
43. *See generally* Mohd Nasrun Mohd Nawi et al., *Impact of Fragmentation Issue in Construction Industry: An Overview*, 15 MATEC WEB CONFS. 1, 1 (2014).
44. *See generally* OECD, *Integrity, supra* note 38.
45. *C.f.*. Joseph Burns, *Will Price Transparency Drive Up Health Care Costs?*, ASS'N OF HEALTH CARE JOURNALISTS (Dec. 9, 2013), http://healthjournalism.org/blog/2013/12/will-price-transparency-drive-up-health-care-costs/comment-page-1/ (speaking to the debate around driving up costs in health care through price transparency; "'[o]nce lower-paid physicians see what higher-paid doctors are charging, lower-cost doctors will demand higher rates from health insurers,' thereby driving up premiums.") (citing David Pittman, *Transparency: Big Data Sexy and Pricey*, MEDPAGE TODAY (Dec. 3, 2013), http://www.medpagetoday.com/PracticeManagement/Reimbursement/43236).
46. WAGNER ROSA DA SILVA, THE USE OF SEALED BIDDING AND COMPETITIVE NEGOTIATION IN BRAZIL AND WORLDWIDE 36 (Geo. Wash., The Inst. of Brazilian Bus. & Pub. Mgmt. Issues, 2013), https://papers.ssrn.com/sol3/papers.cfm?abstract_id=2340992; *Lei No. 12.462, de 4 de Agosto de 2011*, PRESIDÊNCIA DA REPÚBLICA, http://www.planalto.gov.br/ccivil_03/_ato2011-2014/2011/lei/l12462.htm.
47. Da Silva, *supra* note 46, at 9–10 (stating that the RDC included infrastructural development for the 2014 Olympics, such as public security and sports facilities, in addition to current infrastructural projects, such as engineering services within the public school and unified health systems).
48. *See generally id.*
49. *Id.* at 9.
50. *Lei No. 12.462, supra* note 46.
51. Da Silva, *supra* note 46, at 39 (stating that those who prefer open bidding take into consideration anti-corruption measures—implying that the RDC trades efficiency for transparency).
52. *OECD & Int'l P'ship Against Corruption in Sport, supra* note 32, at 24.
53. *Lei 12.688, de 18 de Julho de 2012*, PRESIDÊNCIA DA REPÚBLICA, http://www.planalto.gov.br/ccivil_03/_ato2011-2014/2012/lei/l12688.htm; THE INTERNATIONALIZATION OF GOVERNMENT PROCUREMENT REGULATION 359 (Aris Georgopoulos et al. eds., 2017).
54. *See* Ilan Goldberg et al., *Performance Bonds in Brazilian Public Works*, FINANCIER WORLDWIDE (June 2018), https://www.financierworldwide.com/performance-bonds-in-brazilian-public-works#.XyLzQy-ZPOQ; *see also* The International Comparative Legal Guide to: Public Procurement 2019, GLOBAL LEGAL GROUP at 27 (11th ed. 2019), https://www.acc.com/sites/default/files/resources/upload/PP19_e-edition.pdf.

55. *Lei 12.527, de 18 de Novembro de 2011*, Presidência da República, http://www.planalto.gov.br/ccivil_03/_ato2011-2014/2011/lei/l12527.htm; Miriam Ventura, *The Law on Access to Information, Privacy, and Health Research in Brazil*, 29 Perspectives 636, 636 (2013).
56. *See Analyzing Brazil's New Freedom of Information Law*, Greg Michener Blog (Dec. 13, 2011), http://www.observingbrazil.com/2011/12/13/analyzing-brazils-new-freedom-of-information-law/; *see also* Marcelo Sarkis, *Access to Public Information in Brazil: What Will Change with Law No. 12.527/2011?*, FreedomInfo.org (May 14, 2012), http://www.freedominfo.org/2012/05/access-to-public-information-in-brazil-what-will-change-with-law-no-12-5272011/.
57. Rachel Glickhouse, *Brazil's Senate Passes Landmark Transparency Laws*, Brazil Portal (Oct. 31, 2011), https://brazilportal.wordpress.com/tag/freedom-of-information-law/.
58. *See* Sarkis, *supra* note 56.
59. *See* Glickhouse, *supra* note 57.
60. Fabrizio Rigout & Camila Cirillo, PLAN, Evaluating Readiness for the Implementation of Open Government Systems: The Brazilian Case in Comparative Perspective 4 (2012), https://www.plan-eval.com/repositorio/arquivo/artigo/Rigout&Cirillo_EvaluatingReadinessForImplementation.pdf.
61. *See* Maria Carolina Marcello & Ricardo Brito, *UPDATE 1-Brazil Weakens Law Aimed at Holding Government to Account*, Reuters (Jan. 24, 2019), https://uk.reuters.com/article/brazil-politics-transparency/update-1-brazil-weakens-law-aimed-at-holding-government-to-account-idUKL1N1ZO1KR.
62. Gregory Michener, *Audit Indicates Weaknesses in Some Brazil Jurisdictions*, FreedomInfo.org (July 18, 2014), http://www.freedominfo.org/2014/07/brazil-must-champion-foi-audit-indicates/.
63. *See generally* Gregory Michener et al., *From Opacity to Transparency? Evaluating Access to Information in Brazil Five Years Later*, 52 Braz. J. Pub. Admin. 610 (2018).
64. Andrew B. Spalding, *Brazil's Olympic-Era Anti-Corruption Reforms*, 32 Md. J. Int'l L. 188, 205 (2017).
65. Z. Scott & Elizabeth Pozolo, *Brazil's New Anti-Corruption Law: What You Need to Know*, Arnold & Porter (Feb. 12. 2014), https://www.arnoldporter.com/en/perspectives/publications/2014/02/20140212_brazil_new_anti_corruption_law__10436 (stating that the implementation of Law No. 12.846 led the development of corporate liability in Brazil).
66. *See* Convention on Combating Bribery of Foreign Public Officials in International Business Transactions, OECD 5–6, 11–14 (2009), https://www.oecd.org/daf/anti-bribery/ConvCombatBribery_ENG.pdf.
67. *See Brazilian Clean Company Act*, GAN: Risk & Compliance Portal, http://www.business-anti-corruption.com/anti-corruption-legislation/brazil.
68. *Lei No. 12.846, de 1 de Agosto de 2013*, Presidência da República, http://www.planalto.gov.br/ccivil_03/_ato2011-2014/2013/lei/l12846.htm (explaining the liability at Chapter 1, Articles 1 and 2).

69. A Resource Guide to the U.S. Foreign Corrupt Practices Act, U.S. DEP'T OF JUST. CRIM. DIV. & U.S. SEC. & EXCH. COMM'N ENF'T DIV. 1, 27 (2012), https://www.justice.gov/criminal-fraud/file/1292051/download.
70. *Lei No. 12.846, supra* note 68 (explaining the liability at Chapter I, Article 2).
71. The Bribery Act of 2010: Guidance, MINISTRY OF JUST. (2011), https://www.justice.gov.uk/downloads/legislation/bribery-act-2010-guidance.pdf; *see also* Geoffrey Gauci & Jessica Fisher-Bristows, *The UK Bribery Act and the US FCPA: The Key Differences*, ASS'N OF CORP. COUNS. (June 1, 2011), http://www.acc.com/legalresources/quickcounsel/UKBAFCPA.cfm?makepdf=1.
72. *Lei No. 12.846, supra* note 68 (explaining the liability at Chapter 2, Article 5).
73. *Id.*
74. *United States v. Esquenazi*, 752 F.3d 912, 931–32 (11th Cir. 2014), *superseded by statute on other grounds*, 18 U.S.C. § 1956(c)(9).
75. Sara Sun Beale, *A Response to the Critics of Corporate Criminal Liability*, 46 AM. CRIM. L. REV. 1481, 1493–94 (2009).
76. *See generally* Convention on Combating Bribery of Foreign Public Officials in International Business Transactions, OECD (2009), http://www.oecd.org/daf/anti-bribery/ConvCombatBribery_ENG.pdf.
77. *Lei No. 12.846, supra* note 68 (describing the penalty at Chapter 3, Article 6.1).
78. A Resource Guide to the U.S. Foreign Corrupt Practices Act, U.S. DEP'T OF JUST. CRIM. DIV. & U.S. SEC. & EXCH. COMM'N ENF'T DIV. 69 (2012), https://www.justice.gov/criminal-fraud/file/1292051/download.
79. *Lei No. 12.846, supra* note 68 (explaining consequences at Chapter 6, Article 19).
80. *Principles of Federal Prosecution of Business Organizations*, U.S. DEP'T OF JUSTICE, https://www.justice.gov/usam/usam-9-28000-principles-federal-prosecution-business-organizations.
81. *See Corporate Bribery: The Anti-Bribery Business*, THE ECONOMIST (May 9, 2015), https://www.economist.com/business/2015/05/09/the-anti-bribery-business (analyzing the costs of FCPA litigation for companies and the number of companies that choose to cooperate with federal authorities).
82. *Id.*
83. *See Principles of Federal Prosecution of Business Organizations*, U.S. DEP'T OF JUSTICE, https://www.justice.gov/usam/usam-9-28000-principles-federal-prosecution-business-organizations.
84. *A Resource Guide to the U.S. Foreign Corrupt Practices Act*, U.S. DEP'T OF JUST. CRIM. DIV. & U.S. SEC. & EXCH. COMM'N ENF'T DIV. 55 (2012), https://www.justice.gov/criminal-fraud/file/1292051/download.
85. Chapter 3, Article 7 lists the factors. *Lei No. 12.846, supra* note 68.
86. *Id.*
87. Chapter 5 covers the leniency agreements. *Id.*
88. *Id.*
89. *Id.*
90. Wearing black disguises, the Black Bloc became more organized and visible in the 2013 anti-corruption protests, engaging in vandalism and theft. *See generally* Lulu

Garcia-Navarro, *Brazil's Black Bloc Activists: Criminals or People Power?*, NPR (Oct. 22, 2013), http://www.npr.org/2013/10/22/239860341/brazils-black-block-activists-criminals-or-people-power.

91. Spalding, *supra* note 26.
92. *Lei No. 12.850, de 2 de Agosto de 2013*, Presidência da República, http://www.planalto.gov.br/ccivil_03/_ato2011-2014/2013/lei/l12850.htm.
93. Robert Delmanto Jr., *Introducing Plea Bargaining: A Uniquely Brazilian Approach*, Int'l L. Off. (Dec. 16, 2013), http://www.internationallawoffice.com/Newsletters/White-Collar-Crime/Brazil/Delmanto-Advocacia-Criminal/Introducing-plea-bargaining-a-uniquely-Brazilian-approach.
94. *Lei No. 12.850*, *supra* note 92.
95. *Id.*
96. Joe Leahy, *What Is the Petrobras Scandal that Is Engulfing Brazil?*, Fin. Times (Mar. 31, 2016), https://www.ft.com/content/6e8b0e28-f728-11e5-803c-d27c7117d132.
97. *Id.*
98. Interview with Brazilian Prosecutors, Public Prosecutor's Office, in Porto Alegre, Brazil (2015). These interviews were conducted by the author. Interview notes on file with author.
99. Interview with Brazilian Prosecutors, Public Prosecutor's Office, in Porto Alegre, Brazil (2015); Lenin Cavalcanti Guerra, *Brazil's Operation Car Wash: A Corruption Investigator Is Accused of His Own Misdeeds*, RiskScreen (July 3, 2019), https://www.riskscreen.com/kyc360/article/brazils-operation-car-wash-a-corruption-investigator-is-accused-of-his-own-misdeeds/.
100. *Delatores da Lava Jato*, Politica (Nov. 1, 2019), http://especiais.g1.globo.com/politica/2015/lava-jato/delatores-da-lava-jato/.
101. Adriano Belisario, *Documento da Lava Jato sugere cartel na Olimpiada*, Publica (Apr. 29, 2016), http://apublica.org/2016/04/documento-da-lava-jato-sugere-cartel-na-olimpiada/.
102. *Delatores da Lava Jato*, *supra* note 100.
103. *Id.*
104. Richard L. Cassin, *DOJ and SEC Take Small Slice of Odebrecht-Braskem $3.5 Billion Global Settlement*, FCPA Blog (Dec. 21, 2016), http://www.fcpablog.com/blog/2016/12/21/doj-and-sec-take-small-slice-of-odebrecht-braskem-35-billion.html.
105. Guilherme Costa & Vinicius Konchinski, *Lava Jato aponta propina em 2ª obra mais cara da Olimpiada*, UOL (Mar. 22, 2016), https://olimpiadas.uol.com.br/noticias/2016/03/22/lava-jato-aponta-propina-em-2-obra-mais-cara-da-olimpiada-de-2016.htm.
106. Paulo Roberto Conde, *Para 63% dos brasileiros, Olimpiada vai trazer mais prejuizos do que beneficios*, UOL (July 19, 2016), http://www1.folha.uol.com.br/esporte/olimpiada-no-rio/2016/07/1793059-para-63-dos-brasileiros-jogos-vao-trazer-mais-prejuizos-do-que-beneficios.shtml.
107. Anna Jean Kaiser, *Legacy of Rio Olympics So Far Is Series of Unkept Promises*, N.Y. Times (Feb. 15, 2017), https://www.nytimes.com/2017/02/15/sports/olympics/rio-stadiums-summer-games.html?_r=0; James McBride, *The Economics of Hosting the*

Olympic Games, COUNCIL ON FOREIGN RELS. (Jan. 19, 2018), https://www.cfr.org/backgrounder/economics-hosting-olympic-games.

108. *See* Jonathan Watts, *Brazil Minister Ousted After Secret Tape Reveals Plot to Topple President Rousseff*, THE GUARDIAN (May 23, 2016), https://www.theguardian.com/world/2016/may/23/brazil-dilma-rousseff-plot-secret-phone-transcript-impeachment; *see also Brazil's Ex President Temer Admits That Rousseff's Impeachment Was a "Coup"*, MERCOPRESS (Sept. 18, 2019), https://en.mercopress.com/2019/09/18/brazil-s-ex-president-temer-admits-that-rousseff-s-impeachment-was-a-coup.
109. *Id.*; Glenn Greenwald, *Credibility of Brazil's Interim President Collapses as He Receives 8-Year Ban on Running for Office*, INTERCEPT (June 3, 2016), https://theintercept.com/2016/06/03/credibility-of-brazils-interim-president-collapses-receives-8-year-ban-on-running/.
110. Jonathan Watts, *Operation Car Wash: Is This the Biggest Corruption Scandal in History?*, THE GUARDIAN (June 1, 2017), https://www.theguardian.com/world/2017/jun/01/brazil-operation-car-wash-is-this-the-biggest-corruption-scandal-in-history; *see also Former Petrobras Exec Sentenced for Samsung Drillship Bribe*, REUTERS (Aug. 17, 2015), https://www.reuters.com/article/petrobras-corruption/former-petrobras-exec-sentenced-for-samsung-drillship-bribe-idUSL1N10S16120150817.
111. *See Lei 13.964, de 24 de Dezembro de 2019*, PRESIDÊNCIA DA REPÚBLICA SECRETARIA-GERAL, http://www.planalto.gov.br/ccivil_03/_ato2019-2022/2019/Lei/L13964.htm; *see also Brazil Annual Review 2019*, TRANSPARENCY INT'L, at 13–14, 20–21 (2020), https://issuu.com/transparencyinternational/docs/brazil_annual_review_2019.
112. *Administrative Corruption—New Law on the Matter Wipes Out Legal Incertaintity in Allowing the Execution of Agreement*, KLA LAW, https://www.klalaw.com.br/en/administrative-corruption-new-law-on-the-matter-wipes-out-legal-incertantity-in-allowing-the-execution-of-agreement/.
113. The Clean Record Law (Lei No. 135/10) prevents political candidates from running for office if they have previously been impeached, convicted of corruption crimes, or have resigned their posts to avoid charges or impeachment. TRANSPARENCY INT'L, BRAZIL ANNUAL REVIEW 2019, at 13 (2020), https://issuu.com/transparencyinternational/docs/brazil_annual_review_2019.
114. Dom Phillips, *Brazil's New Hero Is a Nerdy Judge Who Is Tough on Official Corruption*, WASH. POST (Dec. 23, 2015), https://www.washingtonpost.com/world/the_americas/brazils-new-hero-is-a-nerdy-judge-who-is-tough-on-official-corruption/2015/12/23/54287604-7bf1-11e5-bfb6-65300a5ff562_story.html.
115. Andrew Fishman et al., *BREACH OF ETHICS Exclusive: Leaked Chats Between Brazilian Judge and Prosecutor Who Imprisoned Lula Reveal Prohibited Collaboration and Doubts Over Evidence*, THE INTERCEPT (June 9, 2019), https://theintercept.com/2019/06/09/brazil-lula-operation-car-wash-sergio-moro/.
116. *Id.*
117. Ricardo Brito, *Brazil "Car Wash" Corruption Probe Facing "Worst Moment" as Establishment Fights Back*, REUTERS (Sept. 4, 2019), https://www.reuters.com/arti

cle/us-brazil-corruption-analysis/brazil-car-wash-corruption-probe-facing-worst-moment-as-establishment-fights-back-idUSKCN1VP2SR.

118. Marcos Tourinho, *Brazil in the Global Anticorruption Regime*, 61 Revista Brasilieria Política Internacional 1 (2018).

119. *Latin American Prosecutors Join Forces on Odebrecht bribes*, Reuters (Feb. 17, 2017), https://www.reuters.com/article/us-brazil-corruption-latinamerica/latin-american-prosecutors-join-forces-on-odebrecht-bribes-idUSKBN15W2H7.

120. *Key 2017 Developments in Latin American Anti-Corruption Enforcement*, Gibson Dunn (Mar. 15, 2018), https://www.gibsondunn.com/wp-content/uploads/2018/03/key-2017-developments-in-latin-american-anti-corruption-enforcement.pdf.

121. *See* Jenner & Block LLP, *Operation Car Wash Rolls into the History Books with One of the Largest Global FCPA Resolutions*, Lexology (Oct. 11, 2018), https://www.lexology.com/library/detail.aspx?g=9bc05ca3-dd94-4257-ae9a-0508f3b8038d; *see also* Press Release, U.S. Dep't of Just., Rolls-Royce plc Agrees to Pay $170 Million Criminal Penalty to Resolve Foreign Corrupt Practices Act Case (Jan. 17, 2017) (on file with author).

122. *Id.*

4

A Pattern Emerges: South Korea

Introduction: Two Points Make a Line

As if by script, South Korea's 2018 Pyeongchang Winter Olympics left a mark on the host country that bore a remarkable resemblance to their predecessor in Brazil. Olympics-related corruption scandals were part of a constellation of forces that helped to crystallize a historic anti-corruption moment, in which laws, practices, and public attitudes with deep roots in Korean history and culture changed in profound ways.

Admittedly, the role of megasports was not nearly as salient in South Korea as it had been in Brazil. The Olympics scandals were only a minor part of the events that produced substantial legal reforms and unprecedented levels of accountability for high-level public and private officials. Standing alone, we would not build the case for a human rights and anti-corruption legacy upon the example of South Korea. But following immediately in the wake of Brazil, these two countries' megasports experiences constitute a pattern: countries preparing to host the Games undergoing substantial, enduring reforms. Within that pattern lurks an opportunity to move beyond the accidental reforms occurring only in reaction to scandal and toward an envisioned, planned legacy.

The story of South Korea's reforms starts in the Confucian values that drifted over from China centuries ago. Following the devastation of the Korean War, the country would go about its rebuilding with a combination of strong-armed leadership and family-run business conglomerates known as *chaebol*. This formula would prove astonishingly effective in lifting the tiny peninsula from the ashes of war to the twelfth-largest economy in the world. It also provided a recipe for corruption. As South Korea's economic standards rose, so too would the public's expectation of its governance rise. In this context, the country sought the 2018 Winter Olympics with the relatively modest goal of stimulating economic development in the struggling Pyeongchang region. When a ferry sank in 2014, killing hundreds of students, and an investigation would reveal corruption to be among the causes, South Korea reached its tipping point.

A New Megasport Legacy. Andrew Brady Spalding, Oxford University Press. © Oxford University Press 2022.
DOI: 10.1093/oso/9780197503614.003.0004

The historic anti-corruption law, the Kim Young-ran Act, was passed, followed by credible prosecutions that felled high-profile officials in the public and private sectors. Investigations would uncover corruption related to the Olympics implicating the president, her advisor, and numerous prominent businesses.

The effective prosecution of Olympics-related misconduct accelerated the formation of new anti-corruption norms and practices. As this chapter will show, South Korea's corruption roots extended deep into the country's history, just as they did in Brazil. Likewise, a tipping point would occur during the megasport preparations. As with Brazil, South Korea then passed a landmark anti-corruption law, the Kim Young-ran Act. Though a single statute rather than the four Brazil adopted, the Kim Young-ran Act would reach into diverse sectors of South Korean society, uprooting cultural norms and unsettling long-established practices. In its wake came a historically effective series of enforcement actions that felled top corporate leaders and a sitting president, partly for Olympics-related conduct.

Unlike Brazil, it cannot be said that the megasport scandals led to the passage of new statutes; here, those events occurred in the reverse order. But the well-publicized prosecution of those scandals helped to crystallize new attitudes toward corruption and toward anti-corruption enforcement. Megasports accelerated the formation of new anti-corruption norms, intimating, like Brazil before it, the possibility of a human rights and anti-corruption legacy.

This chapter, like the events it describes, follows the Brazilian example. It first shows how historical events shaped South Korea's contemporary corruption landscape. It then discusses the catalyzing event that produced the landmark Kim Young-ran Act. A detailed discussion of that law's provisions illustrates just how far-reaching the reforms have proven to be. Perhaps predictably, these legal reforms were followed by high-profile prosecutions that exposed Olympics-related misconduct. The chapter concludes with reflections on how the South Korea example, in conjunction with its Brazilian predecessor, points to the possibility that megasports can catalyze enduring governance reform.

The Context: Confucianism, the Korean War, and the *Chaebol*

The corruption that modern South Korea has so effectively addressed may be best understood as the accidental outgrowth of social structures rooted in centuries-old cultural teachings. During the long-standing Joseon Dynasty, which spanned five centuries, rulers adopted neo-Confucianism as the official state ideology.[1] Neo-Confucianism is an ethical system that regulates social relations on all levels of society. From formal, authoritarian relationships between rulers and subjects to relationships between friends and equals, neo-Confucianism in the Joseon Dynasty prescribed the social conduct expected of each member of society, regardless of his or her place in the social hierarchy.[2]

This large-scale hierarchical organization of social relations is rooted in the traditional patriarchal family structure encouraged in Confucianism. According to Confucian ideology, family units were headed by patriarchs who commanded "unquestioning obedience in the household,"[3] but also had a duty to care and provide for their wives and children. Filial piety consequently played an extraordinarily important role in Joseon Dynasty familial relationships. Respect for parents and elders became an absolute requirement. The virtue of filial piety and the patriarchal family structure mirrored characteristics of larger-scale hierarchies in Joseon society. Just as devotion and obedience to a father was expected of a son, submission to and respect for the authority of a ruler was expected of all subjects.[4]

These strict Joseon-era hierarchies were reinforced by practices of reciprocity. While the power of a family patriarch or a ruler was absolute with regard to his respective family or subjects, in order to ensure the continued loyalty of subordinates, he was required to act "righteously," which often meant using his authority to materially provide for the welfare of those subordinates.[5] Consequently, a very basic exchange of respect, loyalty, and support in return for various material favors became commonplace. In this way, the custom of gift-giving was established as a core Korean cultural practice. Giving gifts on the basis of family ties or other close relationships became a natural part of Korean relationships. Today, gifts continue to be exchanged as signs of respect. Occasions on which gifts are given are abundant on the Korean calendar. *Chuseok*, the Lunar New Year, and birthdays are among cultural celebrations on which exchanging tokens and small amounts of money are expected.[6] Ultimately, the traditional hierarchical structure of Korean society systemically encourages giving gifts.

Koreans debate whether the introduction of Confucianism to Korean culture has had more positive or negative ramifications for the Korean people.[7] Some argue the adoption of neo-Confucianism as the Joseon Dynasty's state ideology stagnated Korea's economic growth and left it vulnerable to the foreign oppression that would follow after 1910.[8] Others attribute Korea's fast-paced economic growth and development after the Korean War in large part to Confucian aspects of Korean culture.[9] Strong hierarchical relationships present in the *chaebol*—huge Korean business conglomerates organized according to the Confucian family structure—arguably made the rapid growth of the Korean economy possible.[10] Confucianism in Korean society must therefore be understood as a system that permeates all facets of Korean culture.

After the fall of the Joseon Dynasty, political turmoil formed an interesting cultural landscape in what would later become South Korea. Japan annexed Korea as a colony in 1910. For the next thirty-five years the Japanese sought to suppress Korea's cultural identity as they industrialized the Korean Peninsula.[11] Japan began to build large-scale industries on the peninsula in the 1920s and 30s in an effort to provide economic wealth for the home islands. Japanese colonial rule lasted until August 1945, when Japan's surrender ended World War II and led to the division of the Korean Peninsula into Soviet and American zones of occupation. The United States occupied the southern half of the peninsula until 1948, when a pro-United States government was established in Seoul, and in 1950, USSR-backed North Korea invaded South Korea, sparking the Korean War. After three years of fighting, with devastating consequences for the entire Korean Peninsula, a ceasefire was reached.[12] South Korea, greatly influenced by the United States, underwent a swift and dramatic evolution after the Korean War, beginning with a period of particularly rapid growth in the 1960s.[13]

While the Japanese had spent decades bringing industrialization to the Korean Peninsula, the majority of the heavy industry (including energy sources of hydroelectric dams and coal mines) lay in the northern half of the peninsula, under the control of the Soviets at first, and then the communist regime of Kim Il-sung.[14] When the southern half of the Korean Peninsula held elections for a national assembly in May of 1948 and declared the establishment of the Republic of Korea in August of that year, the communist-controlled north rejected its legitimacy. The official severing of the peninsula was apparent when the north shut off electrical power transmission to the south.[15] As an additional blow to the fledgling nation, the Japanese managers and skilled workers who had operated the higher positions in the few industrial elements located in the south all left following Japanese surrender. Furthermore, the war which would soon engulf the peninsula would destroy of much of what was left. This meant that in many respects the new

South Korean government would have to build the nation almost from scratch. In some cases, industrialists who had managed to create businesses under Japanese occupation were able to expand their businesses, while other companies and corporations rose following the departure of the Japanese and were able to grow due to close relations with First Republic president, Syngman Rhee.[16] Rhee's economic vision for the country however was fairly narrow, and the favoritism which his government showed toward select companies did not translate to much of a boom in the economy. This would change under his successor, Park Chung-hee, who would later describe the state of the country when he took over as "a pilfered household or a bankrupt firm" in a "vicious cycle of poverty and stagnation."[17]

In the early 1960s, economic growth became a top political priority under President Park Chung-hee. President Park's leadership style would be directly influenced by his rural upbringing and key formative experiences under Japanese rule. The Confucian values so central to much of Korean culture were further shaped and refined by his experience as an officer in the Japanese military. In particular, he saw how organization and military power could be combined and adapted according to his personal orderliness and sense of organization. He would conduct his leadership of South Korea in a militaristic style, with his orders to be carried out promptly, and without debate. In fact he considered political systems like the American democracy to be an "inconvenient and unproductive practice."[18] When President Park initially took over, he planned to eliminate the corrupt and inefficient business practices which had existed under Rhee, by removing the business leaders who had been part of the corruption. Park quickly realized, however, that since he and his coterie of advisors did not have the economic knowledge or expertise to achieve the ambitious modernization plans which he envisioned, he would need to cooperate with entrepreneurs and the new Korean corporate establishment.[19]

President Park developed a series of five-year development plans under the auspices of the Economic Planning Council (later renamed the Economic Planning Board), each with a focus toward developing a different set of sectors for the South Korean economy. This system was described as " 'guided capitalism,' in which the principle of free enterprise and respect for freedom and initiative of free enterprise [would] be observed, but in which the government [would] either directly participate in or indirectly render guidance to the basic industries and other important fields."[20] President Park personally directed and monitored the direction and development of the economy without micromanaging each specific sector. He would bring in experts in various fields (usually Americans), instruct the relevant businesses on what plans or projects he wished to achieve, direct necessary funds and loans to them, and expected them to come up with innovative solutions to realize them.[21] This would include both domestic infrastructure expansions as well as expanded industrial capacity to work with and export to nations abroad.

President Park used foreign aid from Japan and the United States, as well as US military offshore procurement contracts, to provide loans and business opportunities to Korean export businesses. These businesses would become the *chaebol*, literally defined as "wealth clan[s]."[22] The government, in order to aid in their development, protected these industries from foreign competition.[23] Under Park's authoritarian rule, the economy flourished, as *chaebol* continued to receive preferential treatment from the government and came to dominate the domestic market. While incredibly effective as far as South Korea's industrialization and modernization went, the *chaebol*-driven industrialization meant capital was kept in the hands of a small number of huge conglomerates. Foreign aid, meant for the general population of South Korea, was funneled into the hands of wealthy *chaebol*-owning families.[24] Those families then expanded their dynastic businesses into all areas of the Korean economy with minimal competition.

These conglomerates were not just large businesses—they were essentially powerful commercial dynasties. Operating much like a Confucian dynasty in terms of structure, *chaebol* were (and remain largely) family-owned. Key managerial positions were almost always given to relatives of the chairman.[25] In short, corporate culture in South Korea was built on the same Confucian patriarchal structure that historically ordered all of Korean society. Owners of *chaebol* "operated their businesses with Confucian top-down authoritarianism and paternalistic leadership."[26] Deference to authority and family loyalty combined with government funding and preferential treatment created a wildly successful corporate phenomenon.

To illustrate just how massive and influential these conglomerates remain today, Samsung, the largest of South Korea's *chaebol*, is responsible for 20 percent of all of South Korea's GDP.[27] *Chaebol* are also extremely diversified companies, with Samsung alone encompassing various industries including gadgets, appliances, engineering, construction, shipbuilding, insurance, and credit cards. LG, another *chaebol*, produces everything from smartphones to fertilizer, and also owns professional South Korean sports teams. Hyundai, well known in the United States as an automobile manufacturer, also owns and operates hotels and department stores in South Korea, but is most famous for its heavy industry sector.

For all their success, these strictly hierarchical and economically insulated businesses have proved a fertile breeding ground for corruption. In the context of South Korea's government-driven economic development and modernization, traditional customs and norms took more nefarious shapes, mutating into bribery and solicitation. Such practices have become widely accepted in South Korea as a natural part of doing business.[28] One writer noted, after "corporate Korea got a jumpstart following the Korean War, corruption has run in its veins."[29] While the *chaebol* were instrumental to South Korea's industrialization and ultimate economic success, they arguably created a culture that "accepts corruption as a natural part of doing business."[30] Economic growth was the highest priority during South Korea's economically formative years, and turning a blind eye to the shadier deals was accepted, as at the time it was beneficial to the economy as a whole. The government was in a unique position to enact economic policies that were favorable to *chaebol*. The *chaebol* in turn submitted to government power and used bribery to both gain favor and demonstrate that submission.[31] Even after South Korea transitioned into a true democracy in the 1980s, the power of the *chaebol* failed to subside. They form the backbone of the Korean economy, and thus politicians relied and continue to rely on their support (both financial and political) to win elections. *Chaebol* have been favored by the government since the end of the Korean War, and their special treatment has become so culturally ingrained that even today courts routinely suspend sentences of officials convicted of corruption so as to minimize negative effects to the country's economy as a whole.[32] Arguments about the "soft treatment" of those accused and convicted of bribery, embezzlement, and tax evasion reflect growing frustration in contemporary Korean society with the way corruption in the *chaebol* is addressed.[33]

If chaebol were one manifestation of traditional Korean culture playing out in postwar Korea in ways that gave rise to corruption, another is gift-giving. Gift-giving as a social custom in Korean culture plays a variety of roles. The exchange of gifts has traditionally served as a common social bonding mechanism, allowing individuals to demonstrate respect, gratitude, and courteousness.[34] While gift-giving could simply be a natural way to show affection between those in a close personal relationship, in the political realm, it was historically also a way for a ruler to secure the loyalty of his subjects.[35]

But neo-Confucianism also mandated that rulers and officials were obligated to look after the welfare of their people, and misuse of power could result in the loss of the right to rule.[36] In fact, traditional Confucian thought expects that a ruler "refrain from seeking to enrich himself,"[37] and rulers were judged by their ability to adhere to high moral standards. While gift-giving was one way to reinforce the social hierarchy, high ethical standards of behavior that seemingly condemned corruption were also essential to the hierarchy's maintenance.[38]

Gift-giving is not an inherently corrupt practice. Exchanges are typically made as tokens of respect and friendship, as in many other cultures. At weddings, birthday celebrations, funerals, and other ritual family celebrations, guests are actually expected to bring a financial offering, and in some occasions, failure to offer cash as a gift would be socially unacceptable. At funerals, friends and family offer "bereavement pay" to help cover the costs of the mourning family. This practice stems directly from the traditional custom of *poomasi*, or offering a helping hand to neighbors. A baby's first birthday celebration is a special occasion in South Korea, and monetary gifts are offered to the parents rather than clothes, books, or toys for the child. Similarly, at weddings in South Korea, a table is often set up at the entrance where guests are expected to leave envelopes of money for the couple.[39] While these practices are not corrupt in and of themselves, they can be problematic when combined with other societal factors or when they overlap with business and politics.

This system of gift-giving in South Korea has been called an "underground economy," describing the extensive network of giving or loaning gifts or money to others.[40] While generosity is undoubtedly an admirable quality, when it occurs in an official capacity, it can look more like bribery. In particular, this "underground economy" is problematic when it comes to borrowing money. Many Koreans borrow money from relatives and friends, completely bypassing banks and other financial institutions.[41] If large transactions of money are carried out through this private lending and borrowing system, essentially no oversight exists, and the perfect scene for corruption has been set. Furthermore, because gifts are not just generously given, but largely expected, the line between a bribe and a gift blurs. Further complicating matters is the common understanding in Korea that payments by businesses to individuals in positions of power or to political parties are simply a part of doing business in general, not a bribe for any particular favor.[42] These payments act to ensure continued good relations between the parties to the exchange.

However, gift-giving has recently come under fire in contemporary South Korean culture as the line between a gift and a bribe has become blurry, particularly in the arenas of business and politics. Some argue that the reciprocal practice of giving and receiving has evolved from a way of showing respect into a means of soliciting favors.[43] Indeed, gift-giving and its derivatives occupy a central place in business and political relationships in contemporary South Korean society.

Consequently, bribery masquerading as gift-giving affects a wide swath of South Korean society, from business and politics to mass media and education. Wealthy individuals and large companies are often expected to pay for the cooperation of civil servants, and government officials often pay journalists for favorable coverage.[44] In these contexts, the traditional act of giving *chonji,* or small gifts, has devolved into bribery. Drivers have also been known to offer *chonji* to avoid paying speeding tickets. Similarly, *ttokkap*, literally "rice cake expenses," are gifts of cash, placed in envelopes and exchanged on holidays. The gifts are meant to be symbolic and small, but on occasion the practice is an excuse to slip a large amount of money, as much as tens of thousands of dollars, to a public official in exchange for favorable treatment.[45] Yet another derivative of the traditional practice of gift-giving is *jeopdae*, a common form of "business entertainment" in South Korean society.[46] *Jeopdae* essentially amounts to entertaining business clients, reporters, and even public officials by treating them to rounds of golf, expensive dinners and drinks, or trips to casinos or nightclubs. Such bribery is often successful regardless of the actual wishes of the recipient, because the deep impulse to repay favors is still so ingrained in Korean culture.

One area the complexity of gift-giving has played out, and where recent prohibitions have produced convulsions, is education. South Korea ranks among the most highly educated countries in the world, and a huge emphasis is placed on education.[47] Bribery has traditionally been common in the education system, from as early as kindergarten all the way to universities, to help students gain favorable opportunities. Grateful parents customarily give their children's teachers *chonji* in the form of food or gift certificates. However, other parents have been known to give as much as KRW 1 million to teachers in exchange for good grades or special treatment.[48] Authorities have likened this practice to "economic corruption of the classroom," while many parents simply consider it a "necessary evil," reflecting the complicated attitudes toward corruption within Korean society.[49] Since a system largely tolerant of bribery provides an inherent advantage to the more socially well-off students, the younger generation has started pushing for anti-corruption measures as a means to ensure fair treatment in the education system and broader society, regardless of economic status.[50] This has caused a clash between the traditional Confucian philosophies, reflected in a governance model based on tradition and deference, and the modern reliance upon codified law prohibiting corruption.[51] Many Koreans today are beginning to oppose some of the gifting aspects of their culture, as the social functions certain traditional norms and practices served in the past are becoming more and more incompatible with contemporary Korean society.

More broadly, intersocial bonds hold a prominent place within Korean culture.[52] Strong relationships exist between individuals from the same region, hometown, or college. For individuals occupying higher positions in government or business, there can be pressure to act on those relationships in material ways. In drafting her anti-corruption legislation, Kim Young-ran sought to uproot that urge from its very beginnings by proscribing certain manifestations of the culture of gift-giving in order to ensure fairness among all individuals, especially those who might lack those important connections to ease their way through life.[53]

These social practices came under increasing pressure as South Korea continued to grow economically. Old ways, while appropriate for a period, needed to give way. When the country's first civilian president, Kim Young-sam, was elected in 1993, one of his primary campaign promises was to rid the country of its chronic "Korean disease" and "the corruption that infested every level of society."[54] At the time, this corruption was so rampant that Korean people referred to their country as the " 'ROTC' or Republic of Total Corruption."[55] Despite that promise, over the years "corruption, bribery, embezzlement and the abuse of power remain indisputable components of official South Korea."[56] In fact, in the presidential sphere alone, every president since the country's shift to a democracy has been involved in a corruption scandal in some capacity.

South Korea began adopting anti-corruption laws before Kim Young-ran, but the laws were poorly enforced. These included the Criminal Act, the Code of Conduct for Public Officials, and the Public Service Ethics Act, all in an attempt to clean up domestic corruption.[57] On December 17, 1997, Korea signed on to the Organisation for Economic Co-operation and Development (OECD)'s Anti-Bribery Convention.[58] As a signatory, Korea pledged to implement legislation that criminalized bribing foreign public officials in international business transactions in the country. In response to the Convention's requirements, Korea enacted its foreign bribery legislation, "The Act on Preventing Bribery of Foreign Public Officials in International Business Transactions" (FBPA), just over a year later.[59] The swift enactment garnered praise from the OECD because, even as one of the later signatories to the Convention, Korea was moving quickly to implement its principles and was one of the first countries to pass corresponding legislation.[60]

However, this momentum declined in later years, with the FBPA existing in "relative obscurity, with little enforcement activity."[61] In fact, the first case to involve the bribery of a foreign official on Korean soil was not until May 2011, when two CEOs were charged with bribing the president of the Korean subsidiary of China Eastern Airlines after he sought favorable freight fees and airline tickets at a reduced price.[62] Other cases primarily focused on the "bribery of foreign military officers stationed in Korea, and not bribery in the commercial context."[63] According to one estimate by the Seoul Central District Prosecutors Office, prosecutors have enforced only thirteen cases since the FBPA's inception.[64]

Global anti-corruption organizations, including Transparency International, took note of Korea's lack of anti-corruption regulation and enforcement. During the past several years, the NGO has placed Korea in the "little or no enforcement" category of their annual *Progress Report on the Enforcement of the OECD Convention*, with the exception of 2015, where it moved up one level to "limited enforcement."[65] At the same time, over the past several years, Korea has routinely scored between 53 and 56 in Transparency International's Corruption Perception Index, with the highest scores typically ranging between 90 and 91.[66] When compared against the other 176 countries Transparency International studies, Korea placed fifty-second in 2016, down 15 spots from its rank in 2015. Against other OECD signatory countries' rankings, Korea's numbers are consistently at the bottom.

Poor enforcement was reflected in public opinion. According to the Anti-Corruption and Civil Rights Commission's 2015 Perceptions Survey, 59.2 percent of Korea's general public feels that Korean society is corrupt.[67] The same study showed that 57.8 percent of the general public views the public sector specifically as corrupt. This sentiment is particularly true within the younger generations. While older generations consider corrupt acts or a lack of transparency simply the way things are traditionally done, increasingly educated younger generations largely do not ascribe to this mindset, resulting in increasing frustration and increasing expression of that frustration. Where before, when something might have been considered just helping out a friend, the same actions are now classified as corrupt or unfair, creating a strong cry for reform of the imbalance of opportunities. The continuation of high-profile scandals and public inquiries into corporate corruption has only highlighted the need for additional reforms.[68]

These issues of generational conflict, cultural self-examination, and legal reform provided the context for the 2018 Winter Olympics. But consciously, South Korea's pursuit of the games was not infused with such was grandiose goals. By all accounts their aspirations were notably more modest, and less grandiose, than Brazil's motives in pursuing the 2016 Rio Summer Games. South Korea had already had its Olympic coming-of-age party, in 1988. When South Korea first hosted the Olympics that summer, it had a more ambitious and visionary goal akin to Brazil's. Specifically, it would be a defining moment for nation and a chance to show the world how far South Korea had come. Inspired by the success and acclaim which the 1964 Tokyo Olympics had brought to Japan, South Korea hoped to realize similar international acclaim and recognition, and of course, the diplomatic relations that went with them.[69] Additionally, the Olympics would be the perfect venue to snub their cousins to the north, by being able to play host to the USSR, East Germany, China, and the other various communist states which always had a prominent presence at the Games and had heretofore shunned South Korea diplomatically. President Park specifically noted his two major objectives for seeking to bring the games to South Korea would be "to demonstrate Korea's economic growth and national power" and "to create favorable conditions for establishing diplomatic relations with both communist and non-aligned nations."[70] So too did South Korea use the 1988 Summer Olympics to highlight its economic success story. The tiny peninsula had come to be regarded as among the Asian Tigers, the small Asian countries with astronomical economic growth. The 1988 Summer Olympics trained the world's eye on the Korean Peninsula, and the newly developed country was afforded an opportunity to showcase its stunning economic and, unintentionally, political growth.[71]

This kind of dramatic narrative was absent in the 2018 Winter Games. While the Pyeongchang Games still represented a national statement of pride for South Korea, there was an added regional component for the area of Gangwon Province. The provincial governor of Gangwon Province, Choi

Gak-gyu, initiated efforts to host the Winter Games as early as the 2010 Games. Choi believed hosting the 2010 Winter Games in Pyeongchang would meaningfully impact the economic development of Gangwon Province.[72] He sent representatives to Nagano, Japan, host of the 1998 Winter Games, to gather information.[73] Choi's successor, Kim Jin-sun, determined hosting the Games in Gangwon was a priority. By 2000, Gangwon Province formed a Winter Olympic Bidding Committee and officially announced its intention to bid for the 2010 Games. The national government was forced to step in when Muju, a county in Jeonbuk Province, also voiced its intention to host the 2010 Games. The Korean Olympic Committee put an end to this rivalry when it selected Pyeongchang to be the sole bidder for South Korea, thus making it clear that, at the national level, a somewhat coherent strategy was being pursued. Gangwon hosted the Winter Asian Games in 1999, and many believed that by hosting another international winter sporting event, it would cement its position as a hub for winter sports. The focus was on economic development and provincial pride.

The hope that a successful bid would lead to reunification of the Korean Peninsula was also on the mind of the bidders. "PyeongChang firmly believed that its attempt to make a significant contribution to national reunification through a 'South/North Korea Joint Winter Olympics' would reverberate within the international community of the IOC, and eventually, would help them to win the bid, even though it was PyeongChang's first attempt."[74] Pyeongchang advanced through the rounds with confidence. Despite its efforts, Pyeongchang was defeated by Vancouver, Canada, which secured the bid by a lead of just three votes.[75]

Despite this loss, Pyeongchang was not finished with its Olympic ambitions. Just four months after Vancouver was selected to host the 2010 Games, the governor of Pyeongchang announced his intention to vie for the Winter Olympic Games in 2014.[76] Again, Jeonbuk Province entered the bidding competition against Pyeongchang.[77] The bidding was so fierce the governor of Jeonbuk Province marched to Gangwon, and the Korean Olympic Committee was again forced to mediate between the two provinces. Pyeongchang eventually won the Korean government's support because it already had infrastructure to support winter Olympic events.[78] After negotiations between Pyeongchang and the national government of South Korea, the national government decided that it should lead the bidding process in order to avoid another unsuccessful bid. The national government also promised nationwide support for the Games.[79]

With greater state backing, the goals enunciated in the 2014 bid went beyond the Gangwon-centered ideals marked by the 2010 bid. Specifically, the 2014 bid was more nationally based and aimed at enhancing Korea's international status and contributing to a balanced national and economic development among the South Korean provinces.[80] Despite the rapid economic growth of Seoul and other industrialized areas, many rural areas, including Gangwon, continue to lag behind. The national government hoped that sports tourism would improve Gangwon's economy, eventually balancing out with the wealthier regions. The bid again stressed reunification of the Koreas, but on more general terms, hoping for the "peace and prosperity of the Korean peninsula."[81] The national government in particular, promised "its full support by mobilizing public and private resources."[82]

Unfortunately for the bid's prospects, the South Korean members of the International Olympic Committee and members of the Korean Sport & Olympic Committee (KOC) were embroiled in scandal.[83] Resignations abounded. Park Young-sung, KOC chairman, was under suspension, and Lee Keon-hee, chairman of the Samsung Group and a member of the IOC, went to trial for illegally trading securities.[84] Pyeongchang experienced yet another failed bid, losing by four votes to Sochi, Russia.

It was not long before Gangwon's Governor Kim Jin-sun announced an intention to bid once more for the 2018 Olympic Games.[85] He saw the past failures as educating experiences that could be used to strengthen future bids. However, with two consecutive failures in the recent past, the people of Gangwon Province were somewhat resistant to their governor's intention to bid yet again. Civic groups called for objective evaluations of the Games, assessing how beneficial they truly would be to the province.[86] This resistance did not stop the Korean government from pursuing the bid. It approved the "Resolution for the 2018 Winter Olympic Bidding" in July 2007 and submitted its completed candidature file by October of the same year.[87]

Public criticism continued even after the bid for the 2018 Games was submitted. Several controversial issues dogged the bidding. Some thought that the notion of equal provincial development was a farce.[88] After all, Gangwon would develop economically, but no other provinces were expected to benefit. Furthermore, critical voices pointed to the burden that the people of Pyeongchang had already faced. The Gangwon Province had accumulated substantial debts during its former bids, and these debts would only increase as preparations for the 2018 Games began. Critics also questioned the true benefits of hosting the Games, suggesting that the national and local governments were exaggerating these potential impacts in order to rally national support. Professor Chung Hee-jun of Donga University opined that "[r]esearch centres run by the central or local governments tend to exaggerate or interpret research results to their benefit. The media publishes the results as they receive them and people just believe them as factual."[89] Such criticism, however, did nothing to deter the bidding process. The government avoided political controversies surrounding the process and pressed on, determined to secure the bid.

Likely for this reason, the notion of reunification did not figure prominently in the bidding for the Games.[90] While the official position of the South Korean government is that reunification is a national goal, perhaps, as Michael Breen observes, it is a goal best left unfulfilled.[91] He references a conversation he had with a now deceased Korean assistant foreign minister about reunification. Off the record, the minister said, "We don't want it."[92] When Breen pressed the official, the official said, "We . . . Do . . . Not . . . Want . . . To . . .Unify . . . With . . . North . . . Korea."[93] On the record, the official stressed that Koreans are a divided people and the goal was to become a united people, and for this South Korea favored a gradual process.[94] Then again off the record: "The longer the better. And, for me personally, never is fine."[95] But perhaps more than just a lack of interest in reunification was at play. The very nature of the dialogue surrounding the bidding for the 2018 Games lacked a political nature.

Despite criticism, the South Korean government and the government of Gangwon were determined to secure the bid. With a majority of the South Korean people behind them, they again preached about the positive impacts of the Games: increasing Korea's international presence and promoting regional economic development. Pyeongchang's official bid talked of "New Horizons," and the official motivation for the Games was to launch a new era of winter sports in South Korea, and indeed, all of Asia.[96] Gangwon had the strong financial support of the national government, 93 percent support from its residents, and perhaps most importantly, the necessary infrastructure to host a winter sporting event, including venues, facilities, lodging, and transportation, built over the course of the last two bidding attempts.[97] In July 2011, Pyeongchang finally secured the bid to host the 2018 Winter Olympic Games.

The Catalyst and the Reforms: Sewol Ferry and the Kim Young-ran Act

As South Korea was preparing for the Olympic Games, with public intolerance of corruption mounting, the catalyzing event would occur. On April 16, 2014, an overloaded ferry capsized off the coast of South Korea's southern island of Jindo. Over three hundred of its passengers drowned, most of them high school students traveling to Jeju Island for a field trip.[98] The Sewol ferry tragedy re-emerged as a central issue in the presidential scandal that broke nearly two years later, engulfing much of Korean society and serving as a catalyst for widespread change.

Families of victims sharply criticized the government in the days following the disaster. Crew members apparently instructed passengers to remain where they were below deck to await rescuers, effectively trapping them in the sinking ship. Many of those same crew members later abandoned ship.[99] The South Korean Coast Guard's efforts in carrying out the rescue operation were likewise criticized, with the captain of the first ship to respond to the disaster eventually being found guilty of negligence and making false statements.

In the aftermath of the sinking, President Park pledged major reforms, dismantled the Coast Guard, and initiated an investigation. As the investigation later revealed, the Sewol "was carrying more than twice its legal limit of cargo on its final voyage, having dumped most of the ballast water that would have helped stabilize it."[100] This became practice for ferry operators because "inspectors had limited themselves to monitoring many ships from shore; so long as vessels did not sit too low in the water, the inspectors raised no questions."[101] Additionally, the owners had made an illegal renovation to the ship, modifying it to allow it to carry more cargo, thus generating more income, which also made it more top-heavy. It was alleged that overloading the Sewol was a common practice for the ferry operator, Chonghaejin Marine. An investigator reported that the Sewol was overloaded in a majority of trips it made between 2013 and 2014, making an additional KRW 70 million each trip, totaling KRW 2.96 billion.[102] On the day of the disaster, the Sewol was loaded with double its capacity, with much of the cargo, large containers on deck, unsecured. Due to the sea conditions that day, the containers shifted on the ship, throwing the ferry off balance. Prosecutors accused officials of turning a blind eye to these types of dangerous problems, citing at least one case in which "officials who declared the ship seaworthy did so after they were flown by the ferry company to a resort island."[103] The Sewol was also allegedly operating under a license earned by fraudulent safety documents.[104]

The accident "united the country in trauma over tragedy" and sparked protests across the country as Koreans rallied for anti-corruption reform and change.[105] President Park's investigation and promised "overhaul" of the system left families of the dead wanting both answers and change, stoking the fire of a growing distrust in the government. The public was unhappy not only with the actions of the captain and the crew of the Sewol on the day of the sinking but also with the lax regulatory system that contributed to the safety violations of ferry regulations that in turn led to the sinking, the way the rescue operations were carried out, and President Park's public mishandling of the situation in general. What many Koreans view as government betrayals were brought to light after the Sewol tragedy. The sinking spurred debate about larger shortcomings in the government and revitalized parliamentary discussion on the bill that would become the Kim Young-ran Act.[106] In March 2015, the Improper Solicitation and Graft Act, now colloquially referred to as the Kim Young-ran Act, was passed and set to enter into effect in September of 2016.

On its face, the Kim Young-ran Act simply prohibits improper solicitation of public officials and acceptance of bribes by public officials. But since its enactment, the law has actually been doing much more. In effect, the Kim Young-ran Act is arguably changing cultural norms strongly rooted in Korean traditions and history. While this law fills preexisting gaps in Korea's anti-corruption framework and could serve as a strong enforcement mechanism against those who are committing corrupt acts, thus far, the law has functioned more as a code of conduct and a cultural modifier. In fact, enforcers of the law acknowledge this outright, stating that this new law was enacted "to establish a more advanced corruption prevention system by setting *codes of conduct* and ethics standards of public officials living up to the global standards such as the OECD guidelines."[107] While the legislation may have been initiated as a means of elevating Korea's status in the global anti-corruption community, or as an enforcement tool to clean up certain behaviors, in practice the law is actually serving as a catalyst for a total cultural shift in the way corruption is understood amongst public officials, corporations, and private citizens. As demonstrated by the law's key provisions and their effect across all levels of Korean society, it is clear that this act is primarily serving as a guide for the Korean population to begin reforming their culture, instead of a mechanism used solely for anti-corruption enforcement.

In 2011, a group of Korean legislators led by former Supreme Court Justice Kim Young-ran, proposed initial legislation on what would eventually become the Improper Solicitation and Graft Act.[108] The law was aimed at strengthening the existing anti-corruption framework, particularly with regard to public officials and overall transparency. When asked about her inspiration for drafting the act, Kim Young-ran noted that she was not being "creative" in her drafting and was merely consolidating and codifying behaviors already present in other Korean laws, such as the Public Service Ethics Act,[109] the Act on Aggravated Punishment of Specific Crimes,[110] the Criminal Law,[111] and the Act on Anti-Corruption and Civil Rights Commission.[112] Furthermore, this law was actually intended as a cultural shifter, as Kim Young-ran herself called it a "code of conduct," targeting small instances of bribery on a day-to-day level, rather than focusing only on addressing big corruption scandals. Kim Young-ran initially proposed that the law have a two-year delay in enforcement after its enactment in order to allow the Korean population to learn about it, begin adapting to its restrictions, and become comfortable with the new way of conducting business. Due to the legislature's hesitancy to enact the bill, however, it sat for years in the Korean Congress, preventing this extended time frame. The Sewol Ferry disaster revitalized parliamentary discussion on the bill and, in March 2015, the Kim Young-ran Act was passed and set to enter into effect in September of 2016.[113]

As previously mentioned, the Kim Young-ran Act as an anti-corruption law was not a wholly new concept. However, when looking at the act's provisions more closely, and examining who and what behaviors are targeted by the act and its penalties, it is clear the Kim Young-ran Act is a much broader law than its Korean predecessors or even some of its foreign counterparts. One of the ways the act is so broad is in how it defines a "public official" subject to the act's provisions. By expanding the scope of the term and proscribing the improper requests of an official by Korean citizens and others in the country in addition, the act targets both "public officials" and "non-public officials," directly covering 9 percent of the Korean workforce, but with the scope to cover all of the Korean population, both at home and abroad.[114]

In a break from previous Korean anti-corruption laws and even other, more popular global anti-corruption laws, the Kim Young-ran Act includes more than just those traditionally implicated by the phrase. While the law does include actors typically considered public officials, like "officials and employees performing public duties" and "civil servants,"[115] the act also expressly reaches employees of some private schools and some employees of media companies.[116] But in the law's application, the act may reach even further. According to the Anti-Corruption and Civil Rights Commission (ACRC)'s handbook on the act, such employees are considered public officials regardless of whether they work under an official employment contract or the duties the employee may perform, so long as there is a connection to a regulated institution. Duties can include a range of projects performed the institution including, in the context of a media company, everything from actively collecting the stories to handling "administrative affairs and simpl[e] labor."[117] Furthermore, the ACRC notes that the act includes representatives of media companies, which means "any person with legal authority to represent the operation of a media company, or one with the same status as that person."[118] The definition could even encompass private individuals outside of teachers and journalists, like doctors or other hospital staff, because of the facility's association with a school.[119]

With this definition, the act targets an estimated four million people and approximately forty thousand organizations across the country.[120] According to one report, adding those employed in media and education shows "how much influence these groups have in Korean culture: politics and economics . . . and how they're almost treated as a government official in what kind of powers they have and what kind of influence they have."[121] In another interview, Kim Young-ran agreed, commenting that their inclusion under the law was fair and constitutional because of the public-minded nature of their work.[122]

Notably, this expanded definition was not initially proposed but added at a later point in the legislative process. The initial 2013 bill limited the Kim Young-ran Act to traditional public institutions, like constitutional institutions, central administrative agencies, local governments, provincial education offices, and public service-related organizations.[123] Under the enacted bill, the legislature modified the proposed law to include the private schools, educational corporations, and media companies described earlier. One theory that is floated, but not confirmed, is that the addition of journalists and teachers was meant as a "poison pill" of sorts to kill the bill. At first, there was strong public support for the bill, largely by journalists and reporters. Members of Congress were largely against the bill and the proposed codified code of conduct that would further restrict their behavior. By adding in two groups of professionals with the power to seriously influence the mindset of the public, they could change the bill's momentum. As new targets, theoretically, journalists would begin covering the bill in a more negative light and teachers would speak less favorably to their students about the bill. However, the public actually appreciated the inclusion of the two groups, adding to the fervent support of the bill and the public pressure to pass it.

Still, just two days after the National Assembly finally passed the law, the Korean Bar Association, the Journalists Association of Korea, and representatives of internet media, private schools, and kindergartens filed petitions in Korea's Constitutional Court to challenge the act's constitutionality.[124] In issuing their challenges, the parties took issue with several pieces of the act, including its vagueness, and alleged restrictions on both the freedom of the press and the freedom of conscience. Ultimately, "one of the most contentious issues was whether it was fair to include journalists and private school teachers and workers as subjects of the Act."[125] Months later, in a seven to two ruling, the Court upheld the act, deciding that

> [e]ducation and media have great influence over the country and society, and their corruption has serious implications, causing widespread, long-term damage . . . Journalists and private school teachers are required to have the transparency and impossibility of influence-buying equal to that of civil servants. Only then will education give righteous values and a sense of community to students and the press can make accurate reports and monitor all-powerful people in politics, the economy and society.[126]

As the Court's decision emphasizes, applying the act's restrictions to public and private teachers helps infuse the anti-corruption ethic in a new generation. Requiring the same standards of journalists allows corruption to be fairly reported and could change the overall tone that corruption has in their society. Even if the intention to add journalists and teachers was not wholly honest, this broad reach helps to further the law's ability to change Korean culture.

While the act primarily targets public officials, it also sweeps in others as well, such as private persons performing public duties.[127] Because it regulates the solicitation of a public official, ordinary Korean citizens and foreigners who improperly solicited or offered any unacceptable advantages to a public official are included under the provisions of the act.[128] If a violation, or the violation's consequence, takes place within the Republic of Korea or on a

Korean vessel, the actor is subject to liability, meaning that even non-Korean citizens could be held liable under the law.[129]

The act addresses corruption within that once-sacred sanctum of Confucian social stability, the family. It creates additional liability for a public official based on his or her spouse's conduct, opening up another part of the population's behavior to scrutiny. Under Article 8 of the act, the spouse of a public official may not accept financial advantages in connection with the public official's duties. If they do, and the public official spouse fails to report it, the public official may be subject to criminal penalties or administrative fines.[130] This provision also evolved during the legislative process. The initial bill proposed any family member of a public official who accepted financial or other advantages would open the door to liability for the public official.[131] During debate, Congress limited the bill to only spouses, fearing that it would create too large a pool of affected groups otherwise. This aspect of the act was another place where the Korean Bar Association pushed back in their petition to the Constitutional Court. They argued that the spousal provisions served as an additional violation of Korean citizen's freedom of conscience and liability without fault.[132] The Constitutional Court disagreed, holding instead that their inclusion was not unconstitutional and not excessive for achieving the ultimate goal of the act.[133]

Probably more important to the overall quality of South Korea's governance are the measures designed to deter the systemic corruption of the chaebol. The Kim Young-ran Act continues to distinguish itself from earlier Korean anti-corruption laws by permitting corporations to be held liable for the actions of their employees and agents. Before the Kim Young-ran Act was enacted, corruption was largely monitored under the Criminal Act, which did not provide for any criminal corporate liability.[134] Individuals were punishable for acts of bribery, while corporations they may have worked for were not, despite the individual's conduct being connected to their work. In contrast, Article 24 of the Kim Young-ran Act states:

> When a representative of a legal person or organization, or an agent, employee or other servant of a legal person, organization or individual commits a violation under [the act] . . . not only shall the violator be punished, but the legal person organization, or individual also shall be punished by a fine or fine for negligence provided by a corresponding provision.[135]

Corporations face this liability unless they fall under the act's safe harbor exception by demonstrating that they have "not been negligent in giving due attention and supervision concerning the relevant duties so as to prevent such a violation."[136] Failing to satisfy this standard opens the corporation up to both criminal and administrative fines, depending on the type of violation. For example, "if an employee is punished under the Kim Young-ran Act for provision of money or thing of value to a public official, the corporation may also incur a criminal liability pursuant to the joint penal provision of the Kim Young-Ran Act."[137] Similarly, "if an employee is imposed an administrative fine under the Kim Young-ran Act for provision of money or thing or value to or improper solicitation of a public official, an administrative fine may also be imposed on the corporation pursuant to the joint penal provision of the Kim Young-Ran Act."[138]

The act aggressively targets the culture of corporate impunity that had emerged during South Korea's postwar development. Aside from being a break from Korea's traditional anti-corruption prosecution, the due care "escape route" helps to prosecute corporations who had previously claimed ignorance as a defense, specifically in the context of *chaebol*. As Professor Sungyong Kang explained, the ignorance defense is "commonly asserted by big organizations, as reflected in the consistent 'I didn't know' testimonies of the *chaebol* executives who have been witnesses at congressional hearings."[139] Now, using the "I didn't know" excuse is detrimental because the act rewards those companies that exercise care and supervision.

Additionally, having a due care provision ensures that this act conforms to South Korea's constitution. In 2009, the Constitutional Court held provisions that confer joint punishment on both an employee and its employer, "without confirming what kind of fault the juridical person is responsible for in relation to the offense of its employee," unconstitutional because they punish the employer irrespective of their actions.[140] By levying punishment on businesses that fulfilled a duty of "appointment and supervision related to the employee's offense," the provisions violated "the principle of liability derived from *nulla poena sine lege*" or no penalty without a law.[141] As a result of the decision, the Korean government began revising joint penal provisions in Korean laws to "immunize the employers from criminal liability if they fully perform their supervisory and managerial duties to prevent their employees from committing crimes," but also began implementing that practice into future laws as well, as evidenced by the Kim Young-ran Act.[142]

Corporate lawyers report that the law is already effectuating a change in Korean corporate culture. Corporations have begun to implement programs to educate their employees on the act's provisions, ensure that the improper behavior is not occurring, and create internal policies to prevent future misconduct. As the ACRC's Anti-Corruption Guideline for Companies says, given the Kim Young-ran Act, "Corporate anti-corruption activities are not a matter of choice, but a requirement."[143] This adds to the idea that the Kim Young-ran Act is not just a law to punish those acting improperly but also to change the behavior of people in Korea across all levels of their community.

With global anti-corruption laws like the FCPA, the UK Bribery Act, and other Korean bribery acts already on the books before the Kim Young-ran Act, formal anti-corruption policies for Korean corporations, or foreign corporations doing business in Korea, are nothing new. However, in practice, Korean companies and even foreign corporation's subsidiaries located in Korea "had a tendency to implement a relatively loose version of the global anti-corruption policies of their parent companies, as a reflection of local business culture."[144] With the new act, these corporations face a "significant need" to establish or update their internal anti-corruption policies, mirroring the cultural shift that the Korean population is making. As one reporter put it, "the law amounts to a revolution in local business culture."[145] As time passes and the corporations continue implementing modifications, clients are asking more sophisticated questions to further clarify is and is not permitted.[146]

Despite being a Korean law, the Kim Young-ran Act has a positive effect on global, multinational corporations (MNCs) doing business in Korea as well. MNCs have historically had (and enforced) far stricter policies on bribery and solicitation than Korean companies' policies. Under the Kim Young-ran Act, MNCs and Korean companies are on equal footing, because Korean companies are forced to have compliant policies as well. Now, each corporation is restricted in how much they may spend or how they may communicate with public officials. As a result of the Kim Young-ran Act, Korean companies must do what MNCs have been doing for a while. For example, local corporations may adjust their limits for how much may be spent at a restaurant when eating with a public official, whereas before, there might not have been a policy. Because an MNC likely had policies or guidelines or codes of conduct reflecting the FCPA or similar legislation in their home countries that prevented spending on the same level as the aforementioned local corporation, they could not compete on the same level. Or, as in the case of a company like BMW, the MNC may have had a policy that completely prevents the employee from giving gifts, privileges, or invitations to a public official, judge, politician, or member of a national assembly.[147] While local corporations are still allowed to give a gift or meal to the public official, there are certainly more rules to comply with that limit the value of the gifts, thereby leveling the playing field a bit more. Again, this change in corporate behavior points to the Kim Young-ran Act's role as a cultural modifier rather than a means of enforcement. Even without any enforcement using the joint penal provision, corporations are seeking guidance on how to implement these new standards.

Like the act's broad coverage of *who* is targeted, the act also has broad coverage in *what* is being targeted. As a supply-and-demand statute, the Kim Young-ran Act regulates both the offer and acceptance of a bribe, as well as the mere requests of public officials in certain situation, even without the promise of a benefit. In regulating those behaviors, the act creates exhaustive lists of various types of solicitations and bribes that now constitute violations, creating a broad range of prohibited behaviors now regulated under the act and a far broader range of prohibited behaviors than other global anti-corruption laws target.

A public official may face criminal liability or administrative fines if the public official receives monetary or other benefits exceeding KRW 1 million in a single occasion, or KRW 3 million in a one-year period from the same person. While these thresholds seem relatively high, there is also a corresponding Enforcement Decree, which sets a lower bar in its 3-5-10 Rule.[148] The Rule lays out limits for food and drink (KRW 30,000), gifts (KRW 50,000), and congratulatory and condolence money (KRW 100,000). If a citizen takes a public official to dinner, the meal shall not exceed KRW 30,000, regardless of the citizen's motive, request, or intention. If it does, both the person who took the official to dinner and the official themselves may be subject to penalties. If two categories are given simultaneously, like a gift in addition to dinner, then the maximum value permitted for all items combined is KRW 80,000, provided that the value of each category does not exceed its respective threshold, and the gifts are directly related to the specified permitted purposes and are in compliance with the limits set by the presidential degree.[149] Unlike the threshold set out in the act itself, the Enforcement Decree's limitations have created something of a cultural shock in the country, given the prevalence and level of gift-giving in social relationships and "the Korean business culture of 'jeopdae' (business entertainment), 'ttokkap' (gift-giving) and 'cheongtak' (solicitations based on existing relationships)."[150]

An important area where statute is a culturally contextualized code of conduct is the Enforcement Decree's regulation of gifts and other monetary expenditures. As noted earlier, in Korean culture, gifts of money, commonly offered for hospitality or gratitude, are considered "essential to maintaining business relationships" and social courtesy, particularly at weddings, funerals, or gift-giving holidays.[151] This poses a problem when addressing corruption because regulators struggle to determine where corruption and bribery begins and social courtesy ends. As one newspaper reported, "[e]xpensive food and drinks, and golf have long been an important part of business in this country."[152] With the Kim Young-ran Act's restrictions, these social courtesies and business dealings will have to change.

Stores are changing their inventory to include gift sets within the required monetary threshold, restaurants are altering their menus for lower priced meals, and other vendors are seeing a decline in sales as Koreans modify their behavior to conform to the law.[153] People are learning to "go dutch" when eating out, rather than the oldest party footing the entire bill. In the context of media, "Up to 20 conferences have been canceled for fear that inviting . . . journalists to attend without charging them the full rate for participation, including the cost of meals, teas and coffees, might result in jail time."[154] Within the employment sector, behaviors are similarly changing. In Korea, it is customary to give an orchid to an employee, coworker, or friend when they receive a promotion. Now, with the new law, people are buying a less expensive flower, an artificial flower, or even refraining from giving a gift altogether so they remain in compliance with the act.[155] Even schools are posting signs warning parents not to bring their children's teachers gifts, as they previously might have. Students themselves are also changing their behaviors. After the act's implementation, professors had conversations with their classes about behaviors that could be considered improper under the new law.

New, widespread awareness of the Kim Young-ran Act is notable because knowledge of an anti-corruption law's provisions has not always been the case for Korean law. As one citizen commented, "South Korean people showed a low level of awareness about not only the existence of the FBPA but also the concept of anti-corruption. People expressed their grievances against corruption only when the media covered big corruption cases."[156] The OECD had a similar observation in its Phase 2 Report, commenting on the Korean population's general awareness of the OECD and prior anti-corruption law. It mentioned that a representative of the National Police Agency had "stated that he is not sure whether individual police officials have an adequate level of awareness of the FBPA."[157] In commenting about large Korean corporations, it said, "of the 113 companies that responded to the survey, 79 had a code of ethics. However, 24 of those with codes of ethics were not aware of the Convention or the FBPA."[158] Lastly, when discussing the general population's awareness, the report stated that "the level of awareness of the [OECD] Convention and the FBPA is believed to be quite low" and that "Representatives of Korean newspapers reported a low level of public knowledge of the Convention and the FBPA."[159] Unlike the FBPA, the Kim Young-ran Act affects not only the public official or private actor under the act's umbrella but also the everyday citizen who interacts with them, forcing citizens to be aware of the law's provisions. Everyone, not just police, public officials, or other government actors, must understand this new a code of conduct and the way it functions in society. Because it mandates awareness to prevent punishment, the law continues to stay relevant.

Under the previous structure, citizens were concerned that corruption was unregulated and unprosecuted because of ongoing "sponsorships," and not necessarily quid pro quo exchanges. These "sponsors" "would wine and dine the recipients, as well as provide them with financial support, not necessarily for any immediate favor but to establish long-term collusive ties," preventing them from being punished because there was no direct link between the two actions.[160] In other words, the "sponsors" were creating "insurance" for future requests. Before the law, there "[had] been a couple of court cases where [prosecutors] thought they had caught this government official for corruption but they could not prove causality that the payment resulted in a favor."[161] A prime example of this came in 2011, when a prosecutor was charged with bribery after receiving a credit card, a car, and other items from a lawyer in exchange for her influence to help him win cases.[162] She was initially convicted, but later released, with the court of appeals determining that these were not bribes, but tokens of love between the two. Still, the case garnered nationwide attention as "an example of a loophole in the current legal system as penalizing someone for bribery and corruption by having to prove an exchange of favors."[163] For cases like this, the Kim Young-ran Act would help establish the necessary "causality" aspect and, if a public official receives a gift in excess of the corresponding threshold, create a presumption of guilt to more easily convict these officials.

This particular provision poses a challenge to the previous way business was conducted and relationships were strengthened in Korean culture. On the other hand, it provides a clear framework to guide a large-scale change in behavior of Korean citizens. This further emphasizes how the law is aimed at changing the culture of Korea and providing a guide to the Korean population in their fight to clean up their country's corruption issue. Given the new requirements under the act, "there is a high chance that some of the government relations work that used to be considered as customary business practices will now be classified as 'unlawful acts.'"[164] As one interviewee put it, this is changing the culture of Korean business, not just the corruption of Korean business.

By design, the act's punishments are milder than other anti-corruption laws, as the act is designed to serve as a code of conduct for the country, helping it through a cultural transition in governance norms. According to the act, an individual's punishment is limited to three years in prison and a fine of KRW 30 million, which equates to roughly US$26,304.00.[165] These fines can either be criminal or administrative in nature, with the administrative fines categorized in the same group as other civil fines, like parking tickets. This is drastically different than other global anti-corruption measures. The UK Bribery Act has the potential to impose unlimited fines on both individuals and corporations as a result of violations.[166] Furthermore, individuals may be subject to ten years in prison. Under the FCPA's anti-bribery provisions, an individual may receive a civil penalty for bribes of up to US$10,000 or a criminal fine up to US$250,000 and five years' imprisonment per violation.[167] Corporations guilty under the same provisions face up to US$2 million per violation. This is vastly different from the Kim Young-ran Act, considering these fines have amounted to US$800 million in some cases.[168]

At this level, the Kim Young-ran Act's penalties may resemble more the cost of doing business than a penalty. However, interviews suggested the real penalty is in the reputational costs, not the monetary fines. Corporations and public officials are truly terrified of being the first to be penalized under the act, due to the reputational costs. Because the public is generally aware of the Kim Young-ran Act, the media is quick to report on any developments. Beyond that, the ACRC publishes an annual report, which would surely document the first corporate case. Even though the penalties themselves are not as severe, the potential consequences that accompany those penalties could be far more detrimental.

Of course, the success of the act's enforcement depends on people actually reporting cases. To help encourage reporting, reporters and whistleblowers are protected in several areas of the act that protect the reporter from coercion or disadvantageous measures and impose both administrative and criminal penalties on those who do interfere with "reporting persons" or "cooperators." These reporters are further encouraged by the provision in the act that allows the ACRC to pay the reporting person a cash reward for their tip if their report "contribute[s] to financially benefitting a public institution or preventing damages thereto, or promoting the public interest" or if their report "directly contribute[s] to recovering or increasing the revenue of a public institution or reducing its expenses."[169]

With reforms this substantial and far-reaching, it comes as little surprise that a major enforcement action would follow. The intricate, far-reaching scandal that engulfed South Korea reached nearly every facet of Korean society. The scandal shone a light on the historically shadowy interactions between the Korean government and the *chaebol.* As the scandal widened, it led to investigations within government agencies, as well as to giant conglomerates including Samsung, and its ties to local and international Olympic organizations.[170] These investigations resulted in the arrests and prosecutions of several top executives of various *chaebol*, as well as the historic impeachment and removal of President Park Geun-hye.

South Korea was plunged into political turmoil in October 2016 when its political corruption scandal broke. Dubbed "Choi-gate," the scandal involved President Park Geun-hye and her close friend, "spiritual mentor," and unofficial advisor, Choi Soon-sil.[171] The scandal implicated not only the presidency but also powerful *chaebol* such as Samsung and Lotte, rocking the political and business sectors of South Korea alike. Allegations of extortion, abuse of power, and bribery swirled around the Blue House, South Korea's presidential residence. These claims mingled with whispers of Choi wielding a cult-like, shamanistic power over President Park.[172] Media coverage has gone so far as to accuse President Park of being a "puppet" of Choi. Choi, in turn, was accused of using her personal connection to Park to pressure companies for millions of dollars in donations to two nonprofit organizations she controlled, Mir and K-Sports.

The scandal emerged when Ko Young-tae, a friend of Choi Soon-sil, decided to expose the depth of Choi's relationship with Park after a heated argument with Choi.[173] Ko, who also allegedly managed the Blue K and Widec Sports, paper companies Choi set up in South Korea and Germany to funnel money away from Choi's two nonprofit organizations, accused Choi of influence peddling. Mir and K-Sports, the nonprofit organizations set up by Choi, were ostensibly created to back presidential policy initiatives. Mir was purportedly aimed at promoting cultural exchanges with other countries, and K-Sports was supposedly established to discover athletic talent and expand participation in sports to underprivileged individuals. However, last March the Constitutional Court found that the nonprofit foundations were actually run for the sake of private interests, namely, that Choi was suspected of sending money from those foundations to her paper companies to maintain slush funds.[174]

Reporters at a cable TV network, JTBC, obtained a tablet computer allegedly belonging to Choi in late 2016.[175] This "smoking gun" contained evidence that Choi had been receiving classified documents and intervening in state matters. The tablet contained marked up drafts of President Park's speeches from 2012 to 2014, along with other confidential government documents.[176] After the discovery of the tablet, over a million outraged South Koreans took to the streets for the next seventeen weekends, braving the bitter cold, holding peaceful candlelight protests calling for President Park to step down.

A special prosecutor was appointed to conduct an investigation into the scandal, focusing on the allegations of bribery, coercion, and abuse of power surrounding the corporate donations to Choi's nonprofit organizations and whether President Park played a role in unduly influencing those donations.[177] South Korea's parliament passed a bill that provided for two candidates for independent counsel to be recommended from political opposition groups, and the president then being permitted to appoint one of them. Concerns that Justice Ministry prosecutors appointed by the Park administration might have a conflict of interest in the investigation led to the appointment of the special prosecution team. During its ninety-day term, the team indicted or arrested numerous individuals linked to the corruption scandal, including Samsung head Jay Y. Lee.[178]

In a landmark ruling, Lee was found guilty of bribing the government. Lee was sentenced to five years in prison for paying bribes in anticipation of favors from Park, hiding assets abroad, embezzlement, and perjury. The court found that Samsung's financial support of Choi Soon-sil's companies constituted bribery (including US$6.4 million in sponsoring the equestrian career of Choi's daughter). In return, Samsung allegedly sought Park's support for the merger of two of its affiliates, Samsung C&T Corporation and Cheil Industries, Inc., which would strengthen Lee's control and management rights of the conglomerate.[179] The significance of Lee's sentencing cannot be understated. Samsung is the unchallenged top *chaebol* in the South Korea, accounting for approximately 15 percent of South Korea's entire economy. Some feel that any significant instability of such a giant conglomerate would have a heavy impact on not just the economic landscape of the country but also its cultural and political setting.[180] Consequently, business leaders in South Korea were traditionally rarely held accountable for shady behavior. Lee's sentencing, however, can be considered a turning point for *chaebol*.

Other *chaebol* were similarly under investigation for corruption related to the President Park scandal. Prosecutors indicted the chairman of Lotte Group, Shin Dong-bin, on bribery charges. Lotte is one of South Korea's largest *chaebol*, operating department stores, duty-free shops, malls, hotels, amusement parks, and more. Shin was accused of giving KRW 7 billion in bribes to one of Choi's foundations in exchange for a government license for Lotte's duty-free business.[181] SK Group, South Korea's third largest *chaebol*, was also under investigation over allegations that its senior executives bribed key political figures for business favors. SK Group has been accused of donating over KRW 11 billion to Choi's foundations between 2015 and 2016 to win the presidential pardon of its chairman, in jail at the time for embezzlement.[182] He was pardoned in 2015 shortly after SK Group's interim head met with President Park.

Chaebol have historically been politically favored, remnants of their role in transforming South Korea's economy after the Korean War. Lee's sentencing seems to reflect a more contemporary view that the *chaebol* are negatively monopolizing the South Korean economy and serving as breeding grounds for corruption. Many *chaebol* executives in the past had been convicted of crimes like bribery, embezzlement, and tax evasion, but were granted presidential pardons or lenient sentences in part due to concerns that strict application of the laws to *chaebol* would negatively impact the country's economy. This case arguably sets a precedent for equal application of the law to those "too big to fail" conglomerates, indicating a shift in Korean societal conceptions of bribery and corruption.[183]

Just as South Korea's business world was undeniably shaken by the presidential scandal, the political arena was likewise turned upside down. Public calls for President Park's impeachment were loud, and while remaining peaceful, proved incredibly forceful. The South Korean constitution outlines the procedure for impeachment. If the president violates the constitution or other laws of official duty, the National Assembly can vote to impeach him or her.[184] To impeach a president, the motion to impeach must be proposed by a majority and approved by two-thirds or more of the total members of the National Assembly. The constitution also provides while a motion for impeachment has been passed, the president must be suspended from exercising presidential powers and carrying out presidential duties until the impeachment has been adjudicated.[185] The constitution states that impeachment does not provide exemption from civil or criminal liability for their offenses. The Constitutional Court has 180 days to decide on the validity of impeachment motions after they are passed by the National Assembly.

On December 3, 2016, South Korea's three opposition parties moved to impeach President Park on the grounds that she had violated the constitution and various other laws by engaging in bribery, coercion, and abuse of power. The parties introduced a bill in parliament to impeach President Park backed by 171 members of the Democratic Party, People's Party, and Justice Party; 234 members of the 300-member National Assembly voted in favor of impeachment and temporary suspension of her presidential powers and duties.[186] President Park was subsequently suspended from the presidency until the Constitutional Court of Korea came to a decision. During this time, President Park continued to live in the presidential Blue House, largely removed from the public eye. On March 10, 2017, the eight justices of the Constitutional Court unanimously upheld the impeachment, deciding to remove Park for acts violating the constitution and betraying the trust of the people.[187]

Scandals continued through the end of the decade. These included the 2019 dismissal of South Korea's ambassador to Vietnam for violating the anti-graft provisions of the Kim Young-ran Act, and the indictment of a former justice minister, Cho Kuk, for alleged Kim Young-ran violations involving family investments and seeking to curry academic favors for his children.[188] The former vice mayor of Busan, Yoo Jae-soo, was also convicted of taking bribes and accepting gifts in exchange for providing favors.[189] The end of 2019 and the start of 2020 also saw South Korea take remarkable strides in raising their foreign anti-corruption legislation and enforcement. The South Korean National Assembly passed a pair of strict changes, covering both how foreign bribery cases can be conducted, as well as substantially increasing the financial penalties for individuals and corporations which are found guilty. This is significant since there were only four cases which were finalized between October 2011 and the end of 2018, and of the dozen investigations which took place since 2013, none were the result of initial investigations by South Korean authorities.[190] Instead, the instigating factors came from business rivals, foreign agencies, or corporate whistleblowers. While there are areas of the legislation which could partly be to blame, either with restrictive definitions or by putting time constraints on prosecutorial action, OECD reports seem to indicate the lack of cases is mostly the cause of lack of appetite.[191] As a result, Korean and foreign businesses are almost always more fearful of foreign legislation than domestic Korean laws. These changes hope to shift that perception.

Of additional note is the controversial bill which the National Assembly also passed at the end of 2019, against vocal protest from the main opposition party, which provided for the establishment of an independent anti-corruption investigation unit. There has long been the perception in South Korea that prosecutors have been too easily subject to various political pressures; the goal of the new unit is to put the investigators of cases involving politicians outside of their influence.[192] Some are concerned this task force will extend greater powers to President Moon Jae-in, despite his staunch platform positions of seeking to root out and terminate corruption in the higher levels of government. The South Korean judiciary and prosecutors have long had vast powers and authorities when it comes to investigations and cases, and the perception of internal corruption has persisted. The new agency would break up the monopolistic control which these groups have and allow for outside oversight.[193]

As the reform movement gained momentum and corruption investigations proliferated, Olympics-related misconduct rose to the fore. Ethical issues were lurking, having previously cropped up as early as the bidding process. At least four leaders involved in promoting South Korea's bid for the 2018 Olympics were convicted in South Korea of political corruption or financial malfeasance.[194] Relatedly, then-president Lee Myung-bak pardoned Lee Kun-hee, the chairman of Samsung at the time (a major sponsor of the Olympics) and a member of the International Olympic Committee (IOC), after he was convicted of tax evasion, with the hope that the pardon would aid Pyeongchang's chances of Olympic success. Further, in late 2010, the IOC actually issued a warning to the Pyeongchang committee after Korean Air, a bid sponsor, signed a sponsorship deal with the International Skating Federation, whose president was eligible to vote the next year on the site of the 2018 Olympics.

Allegations of megasport corruption reached a fevered pitch when President Park was accused of plotting with Choi Soon-sil to pressure businesses into donating tens of millions of dollars to Choi's nonprofit organizations, including K-Sports. K-Sports is involved in a variety of sports related projects, including building facilities and developing talent for the Olympic Games.[195] As investigations into the presidential corruption scandal continued, officials arrested top officials from the Ministry of Culture, Sports, and Tourism, including Cho Yoon-sun. Kim Chong, vice sports minister, was accused of helping Choi's foundations win state contracts and of pressuring a former head of the 2018 Winter Games organizing committee to resign after he refused to award a contract to a firm linked with Choi. Corporate sponsors have also been hesitant to support the Pyeongchang OCOG (POCOG) since the scandal broke, as Choi and her niece were suspected of profiting from various deals related to Olympics preparations.[196]

Police raided then four major companies in early 2016 in response to allegations of corruption involving a high-speed railway linking Seoul to Pyeongchang.[197] Hyundai Engineering, Doosan Engineering, Hanjin Heavy Industries, and KCC Engineering were investigated over allegations of collusion in the awarding of railway contracts. The section of the railway in question would connect the city of Wonju, in central South Korea, with Gangneung, a major hub of the Winter Olympics. Building this section of the railway would link Incheon International Airport to Pyeongchang and Gangwon, allowing visitors to make the journey from the airport to the Olympics in just two hours, cutting in half the previous journey time. Prosecutors allege that the firms worked together to ensure each would win a contract for one of the four sections of the project, a US$3.7 billion endeavor.[198]

President Park allegedly ordered officials to help Nussli, a Swiss construction firm specializing in sports facilities and tied to Choi Soon-sil, win a contract for the Winter Olympics. The suspicious connections emerged as part of a widening investigation into allegations that President Park tried to help Choi win a KRW 300 billion construction contract for the Games.[199] According to media sources, Park's former senior secretary for policy coordination, An Chong-Bum, allegedly received an order from Park to help Nussli win a contract to build Olympic facilities. Nussli, however, signed a business partnership deal in March 2016 with the Blue K, Choi's paper company, which had been set up only two months earlier. The contract between the two essentially gave Choi's company an exclusive license for Nussli's businesses in Korea. While, as discussed earlier, Nussli did not ultimately win the contract; if it had, Choi would have made tens of billions of won in profit. Cho Yang-ho, president of POCOG at the time, disapproved of Nussli's involvement in Olympic projects. As mentioned earlier, President Park allegedly subsequently ordered his dismissal. Cho later stepped down as president of POCOG, first citing a desire to focus on his company, Hanjin, but later admitting to government pressure by former Culture Minister Jong-deok, who apparently delivered Park's order for Cho to resign the day before his resignation.[200]

Samsung, a flagship corporation and high-profile Olympic sponsor, saw its chairman Lee Jae-yong convicted of giving more than US$35 million to two of Choi's foundations, including US$6 million to fund equestrian training for athletes (including Choi's daughter).[201] Despite an initial sentence of five years, an appeals court reduced and suspended his sentence. Media also alleged that Lotte received a new duty-free shop license from the government in exchange for officially partnering with the Pyeongchang Olympics. In March 2016, Lotte's Corporate Social Responsibility team presented a "PyeongChang Winter Olympics Sponsor Agenda" to Shin Dong-bin, a chairman of Lotte.[202] Media alleged that on March 14, President Park then met with Shin Dong-bin. The prosecution team suspected that in that meeting, the two discussed duty-free shops. Two days later, on March 16, Lotte entered a partnership contract with the Pyeongchang OCOG to be an official partner. Then, the following month, Korea Customs Service announced a selection policy for opening four additional duty-free shops in Seoul, and Lotte was awarded the license. Shin Dong-bin was eventually convicted of bribery and sentenced to more than two years in prison, but only served a few months before he secured release.[203]

These myriad Olympics-related corruption prosecutions again exposed the long-standing connection between megasports and corruption. But unlike the corruption scandals of old, and much like South Korea's immediate predecessor in Brazil, these scandals resulted in effective prosecutions, made possible by meaningful reforms. The corruption scandals surrounding the megasport were less about impunity than about a new era of legal accountability.

Megasports as Accidental Accelerator, Redux

The parallels with Brazil are remarkable. Two countries outside the traditional megasport regions, in a moment of economic and political optimism, won their inclusion into the rarefied club of megasport hosts. Both encountered devastating corruption scandals that touched on the megasport and accelerated historic reforms. Neither country sought to build a planned, proactive, or two-dimensional legacy, let alone one that checked all three boxes. But their accidental, reactive, one-dimensional legacies, occurring in consecutive games, together suggest a new possibility.

Brazil's and South Korea's reforms were, in relation to megasports, something of an accident. But what if a country intended, or planned, to use megasports as a kind of lever to effectuate lasting anti-corruption or human rights impacts? So too were Brazil's South Korea's reforms enacted in reaction to scandals of the most conspicuous sort. But is that necessary? Might a country adopt reforms proactively, with a knowledge of risk and an intention to prevent, rather than react to, scandal? What if, in this era of globalization, with increasingly recognized anti-corruption and human rights standards, the megasport movement could undertake to deliberately and preventatively leave a legacy of improved norms, practices, policies, and laws?

These are the questions Brazil and South Korea raise. The remainder of this book attempts to answer them.

Notes

1. Koh Young-jin, *Neo-Confucianism as the Dominant Ideology in Joseon*, 43 Kor. J. 59, 64 (2003).
2. *See* William Shaw & Andrea Matles Savada, Libr. of Cong., South Korea, A Country Study 89 (Frederica M. Bunge ed., 1992).
3. *Id.*
4. *Id.*
5. Bronwen Mary Dalton, *Corruption in Cultural Context: Contradictions within the Korean Tradition*, 43 Crime, L. & Soc. Change 237, 248 (2005).
6. *See* Un-yong Kim et al., A Cross-Cultural Reference of Business Practices in a New Korea 146 (1996).
7. Interview with Yoon & Yang Law Firm (Mar. 6, 2017).
8. *Id.*
9. *Id.*
10. *Id.*
11. Shaw & Savada, *supra* note 2, at 23–24.
12. *Id.* at 32.
13. *Id.* at 43.
14. *Id.* at 29.
15. *Id.* at 31.

16. *See* Jim Glassman & Young-jin Choi, *The* Chaebol *and the US Military-Industrial Complex: Cold War Geopolitical Economy and South Korean Industrialization*, 46 Env't and Plan. 1160, 1164 (2014); *see also* Shaw & Savada, *supra* note 2, at 147.
17. Peter H. Lee et al., Sources of Korean Tradition: From the Sixteenth to the Twentieth Centuries 397 (1997).
18. Don Oberdorfer & Robert Carlin, The Two Koreas: A Contemporary History 25–26 (2013).
19. Shaw & Savada, *supra* note 2, at 147.
20. Oberdorfer & Carlin, *supra* note 18, at 28.
21. *Id.* at 28–29; *see also* Shaw & Savada, *supra* note 2, at 148.
22. *See* Glassman & Choi, *supra* note 16, at 1160, 1168–70; Eleanor Albert, *South Korea's Chaebol Challenge*, Council on Foreign Rels. (May 4, 2018), https://www.cfr.org/backgrounder/south-koreas-chaebol-challenge.
23. Carlos Tejada, *Money, Power, Family: Inside South Korea's Chaebol*, N.Y. Times (Feb. 17, 2017), https://www.nytimes.com/2017/02/17/business/south-korea-chaebol-samsung.html.
24. *Id.*
25. *See* Shaw & Savada, *supra* note 2, at 148.
26. Theresa Youn-ja Shim et al., Changing Korea: Understanding Culture and Communication 10 (2008).
27. *See* Steven Borowiec & Paresh Dave, *South Koreans Live in "the Republic of Samsung," Where the Galaxy Note 7 Crisis Feels Personal*, L.A. Times, (Oct. 11, 2016), https://www.latimes.com/business/technology/la-fi-tn-samsung-note-7-korea-20161011-snap-story.html.
28. David I. Steinberg, *Gift Giving and Politics in South Korea*, Wall St. J. (Sept. 12, 1996), https://www.wsj.com/articles/SB842462563700193500.
29. Kim Ji-hyun, *Corruption, Is It All in the Culture?*, The Korea Herald (Oct. 12, 2016), http://www.koreaherald.com/view.php?ud=20161012000724.
30. *Id.*
31. Young Jong Kim, *The New Paradigm of Anti-corruption Policies in Korea: A Focus on the Lobbying Disclosure Act*, 1 GovNet eJournal 10, 14 (2007).
32. Choe Sang-Hun, *South Korea Targets Executives, Pressed by an Angry Public*, N.Y. Times (July 4, 2016), https://www.nytimes.com/2016/07/05/business/dealbook/south-korea-targets-executives-pressed-by-an-angry-public.html.
33. *Id.*
34. Choe Sang-Hun, *Rethinking Weddings that Come with Cashiers*, N.Y. Times (Nov. 17, 2009), http://www.nytimes.com/2009/11/18/world/asia/18iht-gifts.html.
35. *See* Dalton, *supra* note 5, at 237, 249.
36. *See* Shaw & Savada, *supra* note 2, at 90.
37. *See* Dalton, *supra* note 5, at 237, 251–52.
38. *See id.* at 251.
39. Kim Joo-hyun, *Cash the Ultimate Gift for Koreans*, The Korea Herald (Apr. 30, 2014), http://www.koreaherald.com/view.php?ud=20140430001289.

40. Jon Huer, *Gift-Giving and Bribery Culture in Korea*, The Korea Times (Aug. 23, 2009), http://www.koreatimes.co.kr/www/news/opinon/2010/03/137_50572.html.
41. *Id.*
42. Steinberg, *supra* note 28.
43. *See* Dalton, *supra* note 5, at 237, 248–49.
44. Jon S. T. Quah, Curbing Corruption in Asian Countries: An Impossible Dream? 321 (2011), *see also* Yongho Kim, Social Media and South Korean National Security 84–85 (2017).
45. James G. Tillen & Sonia M. Delaman, *A Bribe by Any Other Name*, Forbes (May 28, 2010), http://www.forbes.com/2010/05/28/bribery-slang-jargon-leadership-managing-compliance.html.
46. *Jeopdae in Jeopardy: Korea Cracks Down on Bribes in Brothels*, The Economist (Oct. 15, 2016), http://www.economist.com/news/asia/21708735-new-law-aims-curb-gifts-officials-korea-cracks-down-bribes-brothels.
47. Interview with Kim Young-ran, Former South Korean Supreme Court Justice (Mar. 5, 2017).
48. Baek Byung-yeul & Kwon Ji-youn, *"Chonji," Bribe or Virtue?*, The Korea Times (May 13, 2014), http://www.koreatimes.co.kr/www/news/culture/2014/05/399_157069.html.
49. John M. Glionna & Ju-min Park, *South Korea Cracks Down on Bribery of Teachers*, L.A. Times (May 13, 2009), http://articles.latimes.com/2009/may/13/world/fg-korea-teacher13.
50. *Id.*
51. Interview with Yoon & Yang, *supra* note 7.
52. *Id.*
53. *Id.*
54. Jinwung Kim, A History of Korea: From "Land of the Morning Calm" to States in Conflict 519 (2012).
55. *Id.*
56. Anna Fifield, *Presidential Scandal Shows That "Korean Disease" of Corruption Is Far from Cured*, Wash. Post (Nov. 16, 2016), https://www.washingtonpost.com/world/asia_pacific/presidential-scandal-shows-that-the-korean-disease-of-corruption-is-far-from-cured/2016/11/16/acf7928e-aa7f-11e6-8f19-21a1c65d2043_story.html?utm_term=.026b7d94bf1b.
57. *See* Handbook of the Improper Solicitation and Graft Act, Anti-Corruption & C.R. Comm'n 9 (2017), https://www.acrc.go.kr/en/board.do?command=searchDetail&method=searchDetailViewInc&menuId=020504&confId=64&conConfId=64&conTabId=0&currPageNo=1&boardNum=62408 [hereinafter *Handbook*]; *see also* Mark S. Cohen et al., *Anti-Corruption Enforcement in Korea: Is an Old Law Coming of Age?*, N.Y. L.J. (Nov. 4, 2013), https://www.cohengresser.com/assets/publications/11-4-2013_Anti-Corruption_Enforcement_in_Korea.pdf.
58. *OECD Convention on Combating Bribery of Foreign Public Officials in International Business Transactions*, OECD, http://www.oecd.org/corruption/oecdantibriberyconvention.htm.

59. Korea: Review of Implementation of the Convention and 1997 Recommendation, OECD 1 (1999), http://www.oecd.org/daf/anti-bribery/anti-briberyconvention/2388296.pdf.
60. *Id.* at 21.
61. Cohen et al., *supra* note 57; *see also* Jung Min-ho, *Korea Faces Major Changes on Anti-Graft Law*, The Korea Times (July 29, 2016), http://www.koreatimes.co.kr/www/news/nation/2016/08/116_210704.html ("The effect of Korea's previous bribery law was long questioned and criticized as 'almost useless' because it could not prosecute those who received gifts unless evidence showed that they are given for specific favors.").
62. *See* Richard L. Cassin, *Breakthrough Enforcement Action in Korea*, FCPA Blog (June 16, 2011), http://www.fcpablog.com/blog/2011/6/16/breakthrough-enforcement-action-in-korea.html; *see also* Cohen et al., *supra* note 57.
63. Cohen et al., *supra* note 57.
64. *See South Korea's Renewed Focus on Anti-Corruption*, Anti-Corruption & Governance Ctr. (Dec. 2, 2016), https://acgc.cipe.org/business-of-integrity-blog/south-koreas-renewed-focus-on-anti-corruption/.
65. *Compare* Exporting Corruption, Progress Report 2015: Assessing Enforcement of the OECD Convention on Combating Foreign Bribery, Transparency Int'l 12–13 (2015), http://www.transparency.org/whatwedo/publication/exporting_corruption_progress_report_2015_assessing_enforcement_of_the_oecd, *with* Exporting Corruption: Progress Report 2014: Assessing Enforcement of the OECD Convention on Combating Foreign Bribery, Transparency Int'l 6–7 (2014), http://www.transparency.org/whatwedo/publication/exporting_corruption_ progress_report_2014_assessing_enforcement_of_the_oecd, *and* Exporting Corruption: Progress Report 2013: Assessing Enforcement of the OECD Convention on Combating Bribery, Transparency Int'l 6–7 (2013), http://www.transparency.org/whatwedo/publication/exporting_corruption_progress_report_2013_assessing_enforcement_of_the_oecd.
66. *Corruption Perceptions Index*, Transparency Int'l, http://www.transparency.org/research/cpi/overview (providing the yearly corruption perceptions index reports).
67. Handbook, *supra* note 57, at 3–4 ("Among the 37 OECD member countries, Korea has remained in the 27th place for the past 5 years.").
68. *See* Lana Rask, *How South Korea's Improper Solicitation and Graft Act (Kim Young-ran Act) Can Help Protect US Trade Secrets*, 8 Cybaris 208, 224–26, nn.102–09 (2017).
69. *See* Aloysius M. O'Neill, *The 1988 Olympics in Seoul: A Triumph of Sport and Diplomacy*, 38North (Feb. 8, 2018), https://www.38north.org/2018/02/aoneill020818/.
70. Oberdorfer & Carlin, *supra* note 18, at 140–41.
71. *See, e.g.*, Clyde Haberman, *Student Protests Growing in Seoul: Demonstrators Adopt Bolder Tactics in Their Efforts to Challenge Authorities*, N.Y. Times (Nov. 26 1984), at A8; Associated Press, *Demonstrators in South Korea Ask Direct Vote: Protest Is Largest Since Chun Came to Power South Korean Opposition Rally Draws Thousands*, N.Y. Times (Mar. 24, 1986), at A1.

72. *See generally* Udo Merkel, *The Politics of Sport Diplomacy on the Divided Korean Peninsula: One Nation, Two Countries and Three Flags*, 3 INT'L REV. SOCIO. SPORT 289 (2008).
73. *See* Udo Merkel & Misuk Kim, *Third Time Lucky!? PyeongChang's Bid to Host the 2018 Winter Olympics-Politics, Policy and Practice*, 28 INT'L J. HIST. SPORT 2365, 2371 (2011).
74. *Id.*
75. Richard Sandomir, *OLYMPICS; Vancouver Wins 2010 Winter Olympics by 3-Vote Margin*, N.Y. TIMES (July 3, 2003), http://www.nytimes.com/2003/07/03/sports/olympics-vancouver-wins-2010-winter-olympics-by-3-vote-margin.html.
76. *See* Merkel & Kim, *supra* note 73, at 2365, 2372.
77. *Id.* at 2371.
78. *Id.* at 2375.
79. *Id.* at 2373.
80. *Id.*
81. *Id.*
82. *Id.*
83. Duncan Mackay, *Top Korean Caught in Bribery Row*, THE GUARDIAN (Jan. 9, 2004), https://www.theguardian.com/sport/2004/jan/10/athletics.duncanmackay.
84. *See id.* According to Michael Breen, corruption has been endemic to Korea's economic rise. MICHAEL BREEN, THE NEW KOREANS: THE STORY OF A NATION 234–40 (2017) (noting prosecutors often focused their energy on prosecuting the few American companies doing business in Korea rather than focusing on internal corporate corruption).
85. Merkel & Kim, *supra* note 73, at 2365, 2375.
86. *Id.* Many countries are wary to host the Olympics in fear of the economic effects. Tony Manfred, *Nobody Wants to Host the 2022 Olympics—And One Example From a College Professor Tells You Why*, BUS. INSIDER (Oct. 16, 2014), http://www.businessinsider.com/economic-benefits-of-hosting-olympics-2014-10 (noting that hosting is costly, and many believe that the supposed economic benefits are greatly overstated).
87. Merkel & Kim, *supra* note 73, at 2375–76.
88. *Id.* at 2376.
89. *Id.*
90. *Id.*
91. BREEN, *supra* note 84, at 50.
92. *Id.*
93. *Id.*
94. *Id.*
95. *Id.*
96. *See Pyeongchang 2018 Looking to "New Horizons,"* OLYMPIC.ORG (July 4, 2014), https://www.olympic.org/news/pyeongchang-2018-looking-to-new-horizons; *see also* Peter Rutherford, *Pyeongchang Marks One-Year Countdown to Winter Games*, REUTERS (Feb. 9, 2017), http://uk.reuters.com/article/uk-olympics-pyeongchang-idUKKBN15O0NS.

97. *See* Merkel & Kim, *supra* note 73, at 2376–77.
98. *See* Jiyeun Lee, *How Korea's Anti-Graft Law Runs Counterculture: Quick Take Q&A*, BLOOMBERG (Sept. 27, 2016), https://www.bloomberg.com/news/articles/2016-09-27/how-korea-s-anti-graft-law-runs-counterculture-quicktake-q-a; Jack H. Park, *Korea Should Keep Original Frame of Anti-Corruption Law for Sustainable Society*, BUSINESSKOREA (Mar. 5, 2015), http://www.businesskorea.co.kr/news/articleView.html?idxno=9431; *Opinion: Pass Anti-Corruption Bill*, KOREAN TIMES (May 22, 2014), http://www.koreatimes.co.kr/www/opinion/2019/09/202_157720.html (discussing the public's hope for the bill's passing in the weeks following the accident).
99. Madison Park & Paula Hancocks, *Sewol Ferry Disaster: One Year On, Grieving Families Demand Answers*, CNN (Apr. 16, 2015), https://www.cnn.com/2015/04/15/asia/sewol-ferry-korea-anniversary/.
100. Choe Sang-Hun, *Legacy of a South Korean Ferry Sinking*, N.Y. TIMES (Apr. 11, 2015), https://www.nytimes.com/2015/04/12/world/asia/legacy-of-south-korea-sewol-ferry-sinking.html?_r=0.
101. *Id.*
102. *Sewol Operator Routinely Overloaded Ferry*, CHOSUNILBO (May 7, 2014), http://english.chosun.com/site/data/html_dir/2014/05/07/2014050701710.html.
103. Choe Sang-Hun, *Ferry Disaster That United South Korea Now Polarizes It*, N.Y. TIMES (Oct. 3, 2014), https://www.nytimes.com/2014/10/03/world/asia/sewol-ferry-disaster-polarizes-south-korea.html.
104. Nash Jenkins, *South Korean Ferry Was Operating Illicitly, State Report Says*, TIME (July 9, 2014), http://time.com/2968886/south-korea-sewol-ferry-license-cargo/.
105. Steven Borowiec, *The South Korean Ferry Tragedy Has Exposed a Bitter Political Divide*, TIME (Oct. 24, 2014), http://time.com/3536337/sewol-south-korea-ferry-political-divide/.
106. *See* Maximilian Ernst, *South Korea's New Anti-Graft Law: A Diplomatic Question*, THE DIPLOMAT (Oct. 13, 2016), https://thediplomat.com/2016/10/south-koreas-new-anti-graft-law-a-diplomatic-question/; *see also Handbook*, *supra* note 57, at 7.
107. Introduction of the Improper Solicitation and Graft Act, ANTI-CORRUPTION & C.R. RIGHTS COMM'N 1 (2016), http://www.acrc.go.kr/en/board.do?command=searchDetail&method=searchDetailViewInc&menuId=020504&confId=64&conConfId=64&conTabId=0&currPageNo=1&boardNum=53365.
108. *Handbook*, *supra* note 57, at 6.
109. Public Service Ethics Act, Act No. 8435, May 17, 2007 (S. Kor.).
110. Act on the Aggravated Punishment, etc. of Specific Crimes, Act No. 1744, Feb. 23, 1966 (S. Kor.).
111. The Criminal Law, Act No. 293, Sept. 18, 1953 (S. Kor.).
112. Act on Anti-Corruption and the Establishment and Operation of the Anti-Corruption and Civil Rights Commission, Act No. 8878, Feb. 29, 2008 (S. Kor.).
113. *See* Ernst, *supra* note 106; *see also Handbook*, *supra* note 57, at 7.
114. *Id.* at 15–19.

115. The Improper Solicitation and Graft Act, Act No. 13278, Mar. 27, 2015, art. 2(2) (S. Kor.).
116. *Id.* at art. 2(1) (making the act applicable to employees of "schools of various levels established under the Elementary and Secondary Education Act, Higher Education Act, Early Childhood Education Act, and other Acts and subordinate statutes, as well as educational corporations incorporated under the Private School Act," and making the act applicable to representatives and employees of media companies as prescribed in the Act on Arbitration and Remedies, etc., for Damages Caused by Press Reports).
117. *See Handbook*, *supra* note 57, at 16.
118. *Id.*
119. *See* Kim Bo-eun, *Kim Young-ran Act Needs Revision*, The Korea Times (Aug. 1, 2016), http://www.koreatimes.co.kr/www/news/nation/2016/07/116_209791.html ("For example, doctors at Severance Hospital would be subject to the regulation because they belong to the Yonsei school foundation.").
120. *See* Choe Sang-Hun, *Antigraft Law Stirs Up Wariness Over South Koreans Bearing Gifts*, N.Y. Times (Sept. 29, 2016), https://www.nytimes.com/2016/09/30/world/asia/south-korea-bribery-law.html; *see also* Hwang Mok Park P.C., Corporate Reponses to the Improper Solicitation and Graft Act of Korea (2016), http://bcck.or.kr/bcck/wp-content/uploads/2016/11/Improper-Solicitation-and-Graft-Act_HMP.pdf.
121. Interview with Jun-Sok Yang, Professor, The Catholic University of Korea (Jan. 5, 2017).
122. *Opinion: Originator Speaks Up*, The Korea Times (Mar. 11, 2015), http://koreatimes.co.kr/www/news/opinon/2015/03/137_174974.html.
123. *Handbook*, *supra* note 57, at 10.
124. *See* Ser Myo-ja, *Constitutional Court Upholds Antigraft Law*, Korea JoongAng Daily (July 28, 2016), http://koreajoongangdaily.joins.com/news/article/article.aspx?aid=3021918&cloc=joongangdaily%7Chome%7Cnewslist1.
125. Bo-eun, *supra* note 119.
126. Ser Myo-ja, *supra* note 124.
127. The Improper Solicitation and Graft Act, Act No. 13278, Mar. 27, 2015, art. 11 (S. Kor.).
128. *Handbook*, *supra* note 57, at 17.
129. *Id.* at 19.
130. *Id.*
131. *Id.* at 10.
132. *See* Sayuri Umeda, *South Korea: Controversial Anti-Corruption Law Promulgated*, Libr. of Cong. (Apr. 16, 2015), http://www.loc.gov/law/foreign-news/article/south-korea-controversial-anti-corruption-law-promulgated/.
133. *See* Myo-ja, *supra* note 124.
134. Shin & Kim, The Kim Young-Ran Act and Criminal Corporate Liability 1 (2017), https://www.shinkim.com/eng/media/newsletter/920.

135. The Improper Solicitation and Graft Act, Act No. 13278, Mar. 27, 2015, art. 24 (S. Kor.).
136. *Id.*
137. Yoon & Yang LLC, Implementation of Kim Young-Ran Act: What Is to Be Done for Corporations? 3 (2016), https://www.lexology.com/library/detail.aspx?g=620a675f-0a3d-45c2-a597-c293907fdd66.
138. *Id.*
139. Sungyong Kang, *Can Korea Ever Clean Up the Chaebol Republic*, FCPA Blog (Jan. 23, 2017), http://www.fcpablog.com/blog/2017/1/23/sungyong-kang-can-korea-ever-clean-up-the-chaebol-republic.html ("This liability overcomes the obstacle of proving corporate knowledge of employers about corruption.").
140. Constitutional Court [Const. Ct.], 2008 Hun-Ka 14 July 30, 2009, 117, 128 (S. Kor.).
141. *Id.* at 117.
142. Byung-Il Im et al., *Measures to Be Taken by Employers in Light of Constitutional Courts Decision on Unconstitutionality of Joint Penal Provisions*, 63 Newsletter 16, 17 (2010).
143. *Anti-Corruption Guidelines for Companies*, Anti-Corruption & C.R. Comm'n 5 (2016), http://www.acrc.go.kr/en/board.do?command= searchDetail&method= searchDetailViewInc&menuId=020504&confId=64&conConfId=64&conTabId= 0&currPageNo=1&boardNum=63806.
144. Shin & Kim, *supra* note 134.
145. *Korea Cracks Down, supra* note 46.
146. *See generally News Focus 2 with Yoori Choi: Evaluation & Outlook for Kim Young-ran Act*, tbs eFM This Morning (Jan. 10, 2017) (downloaded using Podbbang).
147. Hwang Mok Park P.C., Corporate Reponses to the Improper Solicitation and Graft Act of Korea (2016), http://bcck.or.kr/bcck/wp-content/uploads/2016/11/Improper-Solicitation-and-Graft-Act_HMP.pdf.
148. *See* Enforcement Decree of the Improper Solicitation and Graft Act, Presidential Decree No. 27490, Sept. 8, 2016, *amended by* Presidential Decree No. 28590, Jan. 17, 2018 (S. Kor.), http://www.acrc.go.kr/en/data/3.1.Enforcement%20Decree%20of%20the%20Improper%20Solicitation%20and%20Graft%20Act.pdf.
149. *Id.*; *see also* The Improper Solicitation and Graft Act, Act No. 13278, Mar. 27, 2015, art. 8(3)(2) (S. Kor.).
150. Latham & Watkins, Expansive Korean Anti-Corruption Law Comes into Force 3 (2016), https://www.lw.com/thoughtLeadership/LW-korean-anti-corruption-law-comes-into-force.
151. Soo-Mi Rhee et al., *Compliance Alert: Gift-giving, rebates and kickbacks in South Korea*, FCPA Blog (Aug. 11, 2016), http://www.fcpablog.com/blog/2016/8/11/compliance-alert-gift-giving-rebates-and-kickbacks-in-south.html.
152. Jung Min-ho & Choi Ha-young, *Korea Faces Major Changes on Anti-Graft Law*, The Korea Times (July 30, 2016), http://www.koreatimes.co.kr/www/news/nation/2016/08/116_210704.html.
153. *See* Rowan Callick, *Anti-Graft Law Bites into Long Lunch*, Australian (Oct. 1, 2016), http://www.theaustralian.com.au/news/world/south-koreas-anticorruption-law-

bites-into-the-long-lunch/news-story/8671a7f7fcc04f167a031c5674a18632; *Antigraft Law Produces Tears, Smiles, Cynicism*, Korea JoongAng Daily (Jan. 8, 2017), https://koreajoongangdaily.joins.com/news/article/Article.aspx?aid=3028398.

154. *Id.*
155. *See generally News Focus 2 with Yoori Choi: Evaluation & outlook for Kim Young-ran act*, tbs eFM This Morning (Jan. 10, 2017) (downloaded using Podbbang).
156. *South Korea's Renewed Focus, supra* note 64.
157. Korea: Phase 2 Report on the Application of the Convention on Combating Bribery of Foreign Public Officials in International Business Transactions and the 1997 Recommendation on combating Bribery in International Business Transactions, OECD 10 (2004), http://www.oecd.org /investment/anti-bribery/anti-briberyconvention/33910834.pdf.
158. *Id.* at 11.
159. *Id.* at 12.
160. *See* Choe Sang-Hun, *South Korea Tightens Rules Against Gifts to Fight Graft*, N.Y. Times (Mar. 3, 2015), https://www.nytimes.com/2015/03/04/world/asia/south-korea-seeking-to-curb-graft-passes-law-restricting-gifts.html.
161. Interview with Jun-Sok Yang, *supra* note 121.
162. *See* Kim Rahn, *"Benz Prosecutor" Case Fizzles Out*, The Korea Times (Dec. 28, 2011), http://www.koreatimes.co.kr/www/news/nation/2016/01/117_101754.html; Kwon Sang-soo, *Three Cleared in Mercedes Love Triangle Scandal*, Korea JoongAng Daily (Dec. 29, 2011), http://koreajoongangdaily.joins.com/news/article/article.aspx?aid=2946308.
163. *See* Kim Yon-se, *Top Court Clears "Benz Prosecutor" of Bribery*, The Korea Herald (Mar. 12, 2015), http://www.koreaherald.com/view.php?ud=20150312001036.
164. Chris Thomson, *Corruption Clampdown*, Asian Legal Bus. (Sept. 16, 2016), http://www.legalbusinessonline.com/features/corruption-clampdown/73173.
165. The Improper Solicitation and Graft Act, Act No. 13278, Mar. 27, 2015, art. 22(1) (S. Kor.).
166. *See generally* Bribery Act 2010, c. 23, § 11 (Eng.).
167. 15 U.S.C. § 78ff.
168. Richard L. Cassin, *Teva Ranks Fourth on Our New Top Ten List*, FCPA Blog (Dec. 27, 2016), http://www.fcpablog.com/blog/2016/12/27/teva-ranks-fourth-on-our-new-top-ten-list.html.
169. The Improper Solicitation and Graft Act, Act No. 13278, Mar. 27, 2015, art. 15(5) (S. Kor.).
170. *See* Peter Rutherford, *2018 Games Chief Has No Doubts about Samsung Commitment*, Reuters (Feb. 21, 2017), https://www.reuters.com/article/us-olympics-pyeongchang-samsung/2018-games-chief-has-no-doubts-about-samsung-commitment-idUSKBN1600GB.
171. Yoonjung Seo, *Why Are South Koreans So Angry about Presidential "Choi-gate"? Here Are 4 Reasons*, Wash. Post (Nov. 23, 2016), https://www.washingtonpost.com/news/worldviews/wp/2016/11/23/why-are-south-koreans-so-angry-about-presidential-choi-gate-here-are-4-reasons/?utm_term=.187a44c92420.

172. James Griffiths, *South Korea Presidential Scandal: What You Need to Know*, CNN (Mar. 31, 2017), http://www.cnn.com/2016/11/02/asia/south-korea-president-scandal-explained/index.html.
173. Choe Sang-Hun, *Key Figure in South Korean Leader's Troubles: A Puppy*, N.Y. Times (Dec. 9, 2016), https://www.nytimes.com/2016/12/09/world/asia/park-geun-hye-puppy.html.
174. *See* Ju-min Park, *South Korea Closes Foundations at Center of Political Scandal*, Reuters (Mar. 20, 2017), https://www.reuters.com/article/us-southkorea-politics-foundations/south-korea-closes-foundations-at-center-of-political-scandal-idUSKBN16R0PM.
175. James Griffiths, *The Sprawling Corruption Scandal That Rocked South Korea*, CNN (Aug. 25, 2017), http://www.cnn.com/2017/08/25/asia/south-korea-corruption-scandal-park-samsung/index.html.
176. S. Nathan Park, *The Fall of "Corrupt by Competent" Leadership in South Korea*, The Atlantic (Mar. 14, 2017), https://www.theatlantic.com/international/archive/2017/03/south-korea-park-impeach-sewol/519483/.
177. Ju-min Park & Jack Kim, *South Korea to Appoint Special Prosecutor to Probe Park Scandal*, Reuters (Nov. 17, 2016), https://www.reuters.com/article/us-southkorea-politics/south-korea-to-appoint-special-prosecutor-to-probe-park-scandal-idUSKBN13C0RR.
178. Brian Padden, *South Korea Impeachment Drama Enters Final* Act, VOA (Feb. 27, 2017), https://www.voanews.com/a/south-korea-impeachment-drama-enters-final-act/3741307.html.
179. Joyce Lee & Yuna Park, *Samsung Leader Jay Y. Lee Given Five-Year Jail Sentence for Bribery*, Reuters (Aug. 24, 2017), https://www.reuters.com/article/us-samsung-lee/samsung-leader-jay-y-lee-given-five-year-jail-sentence-for-bribery-idUSKCN1B41VC.
180. Matt Burgess, *Samsung Boss Gets Five Years in South Korean Corruption Scandal*, Wired (Aug. 25, 2017), http://www.wired.co.uk/article/samsung-boss-jailed-guilty-corruption-lee-jae-yong.
181. Alec Macfarlane & Taehoon Lee, *South Korea's Corruption Scandal Ensnares 2nd Top Boss*, CNN Money (Apr. 18, 2017), http://money.cnn.com/2017/04/17/news/companies/lotte-chairman-bribery-indictment/index.html.
182. Jung Yeon-jin, *SK Group Executives Questioned in Park Guen-hye Bribery Probe*, Korea IT Times (Mar. 17, 2017), http://www.koreaittimes.com/news/articleView.html?idxno=67029.
183. Lee & Park, *supra* note 179; Shelly Banjo, *Jay Y. Lee's Trial Is About More than Samsung*, Bloomberg (Aug. 24, 2017), https://www.bloomberg.com/gadfly/articles/2017-08-24/jay-y-lee-s-trial-is-about-more-than-samsung.
184. Anna Fifield, *Here's What's Involved in Impeaching a President in South Korea*, Wash. Post (Nov. 24, 2016), https://www.washingtonpost.com/news/worldviews/wp/2016/11/24/heres-whats-involved-in-impeaching-a-president-in-south-korea/?utm_term=.c9731e381a5d.
185. Daehanminkuk Hunbeob Const. art. LXV, §§ 2–4 (S. Kor.).

186. *South Korea's Parliament Votes to Impeach President Park*, DEUTSCHE WELLE (Dec. 9, 2016), https://www.dw.com/en/south-koreas-parliament-votes-to-impeach-president-park/a-36700623.
187. Nyshka Chandran, *South Korean Court Upholds Motion to Impeach President Park Geun-hye*, CNBC (Mar. 10, 2017), https://www.cnbc.com/2017/03/09/south-korean-president-park-geun-hye-impeached-after-court-ruling-south-korean-president-park-geun-hye-avoids-impeachment-after-court-ruling.html.
188. *See* Yonhap, *S. Korea's Ambassador to Vietnam Fired for Violating Anti-Graft Law*, KOREA HERALD (June 6, 2019), http://www.koreaherald.com/view.php?ud=20190606000224 (noting that the former ambassador, Kim Do-hyun, was a former senior executive for Samsung); *see also South Korea Indicts Former Justice Minister Cho Kuk, a Confidant of President Moon Jae-in*, THE STRAITS TIMES (Dec. 31, 2019), https://www.straitstimes.com/asia/east-asia/south-korea-indicts-former-justice-minister-cho-kuk-a-confidant-of-president-moon-jae.
189. JoongAng Ilbo, *A Questionable Ruling*, KOREA JOONGANG DAILY (May 25, 2020), https://koreajoongangdaily.joins.com/2020/05/25/editorials/ruling-irregularities-taking-bribes/20200525203400088.html.
190. Wooyoung Lee, *South Korean Anti-Graft Reforms Alone Won't Resolve Poor Enforcement Record*, MLEX (Jan. 21, 2020), https://mlexmarketinsight.com/insights-center/editors-picks/area-of-expertise/anti-bribery-and-corruption/south-korean-anti-graft-reforms-alone-wont-resolve-poor-enforcement-record.
191. *Id.*
192. Lee Chi-dong, *Moon Orders Speedy Work to Create Special Anti-Corruption Investigation Unit*, YONHAP NEWS AGENCY (Jan. 7, 2020), https://en.yna.co.kr/view/AEN20200107007051315.
193. *Id.*
194. Katie Thomas, *Ethics Issues Don't Deter S. Korea's Olympic Bid*, N.Y. TIMES (Dec. 7, 2010), http://www.nytimes.com/2010/12/08/sports/08olympics.html.
195. *Id.*
196. *See* Bruce Harrison, *In South Korea, Scandal Poses Challenge to Creating Olympic Buzz*, VOA (Dec. 28, 2016), https://www.voanews.com/east-asia-pacific/south-korea-scandal-poses-challenge-creating-olympic-buzz.
197. Dan Palmer, *Four Companies Raided Amid Alleged Corruption Involving Pyeongchang 2018 Railway Line*, INSIDE THE GAMES (Apr. 20, 2016), https://www.insidethegames.biz/articles/1036652/four-companies-raided-amid-alleged-corruption-involving-pyeongchang-2018-railway-line.
198. *Id.*
199. Kang Seung-woo, *Park Attempted to Help Swiss Firm Tied to Choi*, THE KOREA TIMES (Jan. 17, 2017), http://www.koreatimes.co.kr/www/news/nation/2017/01/113_222246.html.
200. *Id.*
201. *South Korea's Presidential Scandal*, BBC (Apr. 6, 2018), https://www.bbc.com/news/world-asia-37971085.

202. *See* Kyo-hyeong Koo & Seung-min Yoon, *Lotte, New Duty Free Shop "Transaction Status" Captured*, KYUNGHYANG SHINMUN (Jan. 14, 2017), http://news.khan.co.kr/kh_news/khan_art_view.html?artid=201701140600035&code=940301.
203. Heekyong Yang, *Lotte Group Chairman Stays out of Jail as South Korea Court Ruling Upheld*, REUTERS (Oct. 17, 2019), https://www.reuters.com/article/us-southkorea-corruption-lotte/lotte-group-chairman-stays-out-of-jail-as-south-korea-court-ruling-upheld-idUSKBN1WW0CT.

PART III
APPROACHING A MODEL

5

The First Intentional Legacy: Qatar

Introduction: The Unlikely Architect of a New Model

FIFA's decision to award the 2022 World Cup to Qatar elicited a crisis-level barrage of global criticism. Corruption allegations and investigations of the 2018/2022 bidding process ensued, touching on Qatar, Russia, and multiple unsuccessful bidders.[1] Civil society and international organizations would then drill down on a different problem: Qatar's failure to protect the internationally recognized labor rights of its migrant workers. Within a couple years of its historic victory, the country was facing international pressure as severe as any modern megasport host.

Few Westerners—armed with prejudices toward the Islamic Middle East and little knowledge of Qatar's distinctive identity—could have expected what happened next. Many will struggle to acknowledge it now. Qatar became the unlikely architect of a new model of megasport host country reform. Even preceding the initial global criticism and legal filings, Qatar had formulated an intention to leave a legacy of human rights reforms. The ensuing cascade of outside criticism and pressure only accelerated that process. The country is indeed now using this mega sporting event (MSE) to catalyze national labor reforms. That is, the country is building the first intentional and proactive human rights legacy. The legacy is one-dimensional, focusing only on the human rights side with no discernible intention to create an anti-corruption legacy. Still, as the first intentional and proactive legacy, this small country is making perhaps the single most significant contribution to the evolution of the human rights and anti-corruption legacy.

The labor reforms Qatar adopted as it prepared to host the 2022 FIFA Men's World Cup now include: a mandatory, nondiscriminatory minimum wage for all workers; a wage protection system to ensure payment; a Minimum Wage Commission; an overhaul of the *kafala* sponsorship system, to include the abolition of no-objection certificates, passport confiscation,

A New Megasport Legacy. Andrew Brady Spalding, Oxford University Press. © Oxford University Press 2022.
DOI: 10.1093/oso/9780197503614.003.0005

and exit permissions; enhanced heat mitigation strategies; various measures to amplify workers' voices and enhance access to justice, including Ministry of Labor committees for resolving labor disputes; enhanced training of labor inspectors to help ensure compliance with these reforms; a workers support and insurance fund; the establishment of visa centers in the migrant workers' home countries; a domestic workers law; and the ratification of two principal international human rights conventions.[2] These reforms are not limited to World Cup projects or even to sports, nor are they temporary measures designed to soon expire. Rather, they are national in scope and indefinite in duration.

At press time the reforms remain fairly new. Substantial work must still be done to make them effective: legislative gaps remain, and enforcement challenges loom. But these are good problems to have. The question Qatar now faces is not whether it will dismiss the criticism, dig in its heels, and refuse to change, as previous megasport hosts did; Qatar has already proven otherwise. Rather, the question is whether Qatar can adequately implement these reforms, whether the implementation will endure beyond 2022, and whether it can resist the already-mounting political pushback.[3] The expected ongoing engagement of the International Labour Organization (ILO) will provide both support and accountability. For this and other reasons, cautious optimism may be in order.

Given the West's long domination of megasport standards and narratives, it is surprising, and yet fitting, that a small, Muslim, Middle Eastern nation would design this new template for megasport host country governance. How did this happen? Why Qatar? While the answer proves complex, two reasons are perhaps most salient. The first is an extraordinary human rights challenge inherent in the country's economic model. The second is an extraordinary initiative from Qatar's principal World Cup organizing body, the Supreme Committee (SC) for Delivery and Legacy.

Owing to the country's explosive economic growth, low native population, and proximity to countries with a surplus of labor, Qatar has the highest ratio of migrant citizens in the world.[4] There are approximately two million migrant workers in this country of less than three million. They hail from Asian countries such as India, Nepal, the Philippines, Bangladesh, and Sri Lanka, and constitute an astonishing 95 percent of Qatar's labor force.[5] Qatar relies particularly heavily on migrant workers in construction and will continue to do so in preparation to host the 2022 FIFA World Cup. Just after this nation won the rights to host the 2022 World Cup, a variety of international organizations and commentators trained their sights on what they knew would become, in the years leading up to 2022, a highly visible human rights issue.

In the face of these challenges, Qatar leaned in. As this chapter will further explain, four moments may have been most critical and most clearly reflect Qatar's uniquely constructive posture. First, as early as the Qatar 2022 Strategic Plan, published in 2011, the embryonic form of a labor rights legacy appears in publication. Even prior to the international criticism, Qatar had conceived of the World Cup as a lever for implementing broader human rights reforms. While Qatar was already under pressure from International Trade Union Confederation (ITUC) and the Building and Wood Workers International (BWI), no scandal had yet erupted. Qatar's legacy is thus both proactive and intentional. Second, it commissioned a credible independent report on its own human rights problems, which largely corroborated the outside criticism. In so doing, Qatar acknowledged rather than minimized the extent of its human rights issues. Third, the SC designed substantial labor reforms that would apply to all World Cup projects. The cornerstone of the SC's reforms was the Workers Welfare Standards (WWS), a comprehensive set of labor protections that are contractually binding on all World Cup contractors and subcontractors. The standards include numerous ethical recruitment procedures; guarantee of a written employment contract; a prohibition on passport confiscation and a guarantee of freedom of movement; paid annual leave; free medical insurance; detailed requirements on accommodations, food, and transportation; and the establishment of Workers Welfare Forums (WWFs), in which elected labor representatives meet with management to discuss workplace concerns. Fourth, the Qatari national government agreed, under pressure, to collaborate with the United Nations' ILO to help convert many of the SC's ideas into national law. The end result was a substantial, though not yet complete, overhaul of Qatar's labor laws.

This chapter explains how the World Cup helped this extraordinary challenge to produce the first intentional human rights legacy. To be clear, it does not purport to comprehensively document Qatar's reforms; that work is done elsewhere. Neither does it attempt to separate out and explain the roles of the many stakeholders—which include national and international government agencies, nongovernmental organizations, and others—in bringing about these reforms; that work is beyond the scope of this project. Rather, this chapter aims to understand how winning the rights to host an MSE catalyzed these reforms.

Following this introduction, this chapter discusses the unique combination of political, social, and economic circumstances that created the environment from which this legacy emerged. It then describes three mechanisms, or what this chapter calls levers, by which the government of Qatar, the SC, and other stakeholders both within and beyond Qatar leveraged the FIFA Men's World Cup to adopt human rights reforms extending well beyond the event. This chapter then acknowledges lingering questions of corruption related to winning the 2022 bid, but reframes that problem in a way that is more accurate, and less hypocritical, than much of the current commentary. The chapter concludes with a brief account of the human rights reforms beyond labor that Qatar is now adopting, and with reflections on Qatar's contribution to the development of intentional, proactive, and two-dimensional human rights and anti-corruption legacies.

What Made This Possible? Enablers of an Unlikely Legacy

To the casual observer, Qatar would seem the least likely country to produce such reforms. It has not been a major global player in either the international football or international human rights spaces. This irony begs the question: What combination of social, economic, and geopolitical factors converged to produce this seemingly unlikely outcome?[6] This section attempts to identify the distinctive domestic and geopolitical conditions that combined to create an environment in which Qatar wrote the template for a megasport human rights legacy. They may fall into three categories: the domestic context; the geopolitical context; and the early leadership of the emir and the SC.

When Qatar won the 2022 World Cup rights in 2010, the country had not yet celebrated its fortieth birthday. Qatar's nascent institutions and political identity would prove a feature rather than a bug. The World Cup arrived in a country uncommonly eager to define its national identity and chart its future development. Historically, the peninsula that is Qatar was quite isolated from Middle Eastern trade routes and therefore the rest of the world. A distinct and autonomous sheikhdom of Qatar would be eventually recognized in the mid-nineteenth century through agreements negotiated with various regional powers, including Turkey and Great Britain.[7] Through the late nineteenth and early twentieth centuries, the sheikhdom's principal industry was pearling, until the Great Depression that began in 1929 decimated global demand and half the country's population left the peninsula.[8] Then in 1939, oil was discovered, and following World War II its exportation began. The United Kingdom, which had been a strong presence since the mid-nineteenth century, withdrew its military forces east of Suez by 1971. Qatar gained full independence as a sovereign state that year, as did neighboring Bahrain and the United Arab Emirates (UAE) the following year.[9] In the late 1970s, petroleum prices soar, bringing a tremendous influx of capital to this brand-new country. That capital would be shared among a mere fifty thousand inhabitants, producing tremendous per capita wealth. Some of this newfound wealth would be invested in infrastructure development and institution building.[10]

With money came infrastructure, and with infrastructure came the need for labor. Qatar's population would explode in the following decades and its growth continues today. Though a mere 50,000 in the late 1970s, by 2006 its population reached 800,000; as if that weren't sufficient growth, the following year it would surge to 1.5 million[11] and today approaches 3 million.[12] This combination of youth and rapid growth created a kind of urgency in molding the country's governance identity. To this end, in 2008, Qatar's Emir, His Highness Sheikh Hamad bin Khalifa Al Thani, developed a strategy for the country's economic, environmental, and social progress. Called the "Qatar National Vision 2030," the document acknowledged Qatar's progress as measured by economic prosperity and increasing standards of living. But the document recognized that despite, or perhaps because of these rapid changes, the country was at a "crossroads," as its wealth created "formidable challenges," requiting Qatar to choose the "best development path."[13] The contours of that path are described later. The document would become the first in a series of documents that laid the conceptual foundation for Qatar's eventual megasport human rights legacy. Qatar's SC would embrace the goal of "accelerat[ing] progress towards achieving national development goals."[14]

Even with this skyrocketing rate of population growth, Qatar remains, relative to other World Cup hosts, quite tiny. Consider a comparison to the last three hosts. The 2010 host South Africa had, at the time of the event, a population of approximately 50 million.[15] Brazil, host of the 2014 Men's World Cup, was at the time about 200 million. The most recent host, Russia, was in 2018 at about 150 million.[16] Qatar is one-fiftieth that number. The estimated 1.5 million visitors for the World Cup will amount to about half the entire country's population.

The FIFA Men's World Cup is a big deal in any country; when the country is small, the event becomes even bigger. The enormity of the event is among the factors that made possible Qatar's unique model for managing the preparations. It created the SC for Delivery and Legacy, a government agency deemed "supreme" because the emir is its nominal head. The SC was established by His Highness Sheikh Hamad Bin Khalifa Al Thani and is now overseen by the new Emir, His Highness Sheikh Tamim Bin Hamad Al Thani. The Board of Directors includes a number of Qatari ministers.[17] In effect, Qatar has created a nearly cabinet-level government agency dedicated exclusively to delivering the proposed tournament venues and host country planning and operations. Bringing to bear this strong, centralized authority on World Cup preparations results in more control over the implementation of new standards.

As indicated earlier, though Qatar is small, it is extraordinarily wealthy. According to World Bank rankings based on purchasing power parity (sometimes called "real GDP"), Qatar is the third wealthiest country in the world, behind Macao and Singapore.[18] Economists use a variety of indicators to compare national wealth, and Qatar is consistently high in almost all of them. The source of Qatar's wealth is the extraction of petroleum and natural gas. Human rights observers will be quick to point out that per capita measurements of Qatar's wealth include only Qatari nationals, and not expat laborers. Nevertheless, with wealth comes means.

Despite this wealth, Qatar has managed to largely avoid the "resource curse." Sometimes called the paradox of plenty or the poverty paradox, this is the phenomenon of countries whose wealth depends heavily on abundant natural resources, particularly fossil fuels and natural minerals, suffering from very weak economic development and, among other problems, very high levels of corruption.[19] Notwithstanding Qatar's difficulties in its interactions with the FIFA Executive Committee (to be explored later), the data shows that Qatar is among the least corrupt countries in the world. Transparency International has been scoring countries based on the global perception of corruption in a country's public sector since 1995[20] and is today one of the most oft-cited measures of corruption. Qatar was added to the index in 2003. It first appeared ranked thirty-two out of roughly two hundred countries, and steadily improved to a peak ranking in 2010 of nineteen, or the top 10 percent. Notably this is the year Qatar won the World Cup, and marked the peak of their corruption perception rankings. They would drop and hover around thirty ever since, or the top 15 percent. A similar pattern appears in the Worldwide Governance Indicators (WGI).[21] Qatar should not be readily equated with its larger and more notoriously corrupt neighbors like Egypt or Iran. In sum, good governance and exceptional wealth, combined with the country's small size and young age, would prove an optimal environment for designing a new approach to megasport governance.

So too would Qatar's geopolitical position and strategies. In foreign policy, Qatar plainly punches well above its weight.[22] Though dwarfed by its neighbors, it had deliberately cultivated, and indeed achieved, a disproportionate prominence on the international stage even before winning the World Cup hosting rights. This prominence is a result of competition among Persian Gulf countries and the country's very effective use of the less obvious instruments of influence.

Power was of course historically thought to be a function of population and wealth.[23] In the early 1990s, Joseph Nye developed an alternative theory of power—"soft power"—in which power is exercised through utilizing resources such as institutions, ideas, values, and culture.[24] Nye would later introduce the concept of "smart power," which is "the combination of the hard power of coercion and payment with the soft power of persuasion and attraction."[25] Qatar might not fit perfectly into either category. A further refinement of Nye's original theory to Qatar lies in the scholarship of Dr. Mehran Kamrava, who developed the concept of "subtle power": a combination of the exercise of influence, the ability to create conditions favourable to one's goals, and the mobilization of bias to shape perceptions of a target.[26] Whatever the framing, Hugh Eagin may have most aptly characterized it as the "strange power of Qatar."[27]

Qatar has needed these more subtle forms of power to survive and excel in an intensely complex and competitive regional environment. Kamrava built a model that helps explain where Qatar fits in. He divides the Middle East into two basic camps: the "status quo states" and the "counter-hegemonic states." He then distinguishes between dominant powers and middle powers, the latter being less influential than the dominant states either due to their size and resources or their strategic decisions. The status quo states perceive themselves as "guardians of the international and regional status quo," and its two dominant powers are Saudi Arabia and Israel. Its middle powers are Bahrain, Egypt, Jordan, and the UAE. The counterhegemonic states' dominant powers are Iran and Turkey. Its middle powers are Algeria, Morocco, Oman, Tunisia, and Qatar. These "pragmatic middle powers," including

Qatar, make decisions based less on ideology and identity than on pragmatic and strategic decisions.[28]

Between the coming need for economic diversification, and the foreign policy shadows cast by larger neighbors, Qatar finds itself in a competition to form a unique identity, role, and influence. In wielding its power, Qatar has developed a foreign policy that in the assessment of one commentator, has Qatar "clearly leaving behind its two giant neighbors—Iran and Saudi Arabia."[29] This approach especially took shape in the mid to late 2000s, in the preparations for and ultimate launch of Qatar Vision 2030 in 2008. This document addressed the concerns of an Arab state seeking to modernize itself to be a more active and prominent member of the global community.

In the years following the 2008 vision, global events accelerated the formation of Qatar's uniquely prominent status.[30] In 2010, the Tunisian street vendor Mohamed Bouazizi committed self-immolation, triggering uprisings across the Middle East called the "Arab Spring," which Qatar saw as an opportunity to further its efforts at foreign policy and branding. "Flush with the success of the 2022 World Cup bid and with its international recognition soaring . . . Qatar seized on the opportunity to mark Qatar as distinct from the troubles afflicting the wider region."[31]

Though conflicts between the Gulf Cooperation Council states were relatively minor prior to the Arab Spring, this would soon change. In early 2011, Emir Hamad bin Khalifa Al Thani and the Prime Minister Hamad bin Jassim Al Thani decided to back the protestors across the majority of the other Arab states and used the media reach of Al Jazeera to spread the messaging.[32] The approach by Qatar also reflected its desire to project itself more fully into the global sphere by riding the wave of "people-led" revolution and showing itself to be current and dynamic in regard to the powerful Western values of political rights and human freedoms.[33] As the state sponsor of the Al Jazeera news network, with reporters live on the ground and through the broadcast of information, pictures, and video from social media, Qatar was also controlling the Arab narrative broadcast both across the Arab world and especially out to the West.[34]

This is especially important to understand in the context of Qatar having just won the 2022 FIFA World Cup bid in December of 2010. This was the latest and largest test display of Qatar on the global stage, and the reaction of Qatar to the Arab Spring would have a profound consequence on the international views of Qatar as World Cup host and as a nation in general.[35] While other nations in the region took a hardline approach to the Arab

Spring, Qatar was actively supporting opposition and dissident groups. The underlying political rift was growing. In 2017, the Qatar News Agency was hacked,[36] revealing a stream of statements which seemed to be from the Qatari emir. In June 2017, the UAE severed diplomatic ties with Qatar, expelled all Qataris within its borders, prohibited Qataris from traveling through the UAE, closed UAE airspace and seaports to Qatari nationals, and shut down local Qatari media outlets, most notably Al Jazeera.[37] Bahrain, Saudi Arabia, and Egypt in a gesture of support imposed land, sea, and air blockades on Qatar. Yemen, the Eastern government of Libya, Maldives, Mauritania, and Comoros then cut diplomatic ties with Qatar.[38] While the goal of the blockading countries was to wreck Qatar's economy, the country's liquidity and large domestic currency reserves resulting from years of high oil prices allowed them to mitigate the effects of the blockade. Additionally, the recently completed Hamad Port and International Airport allowed Qatar to not be paralyzed by an Emirati cession of shipping.[39] In January 2021, the blockade was lifted. Domestically, the blockade seemed to have the effect of unifying the country and generating support for the reform movement. Qatar seemingly invested some of this new social capital in developing its labor reforms, the fruits of which are described later.

In the context of this regional competition and soft power strategy, Qatar carefully formulated a branding strategy to change its global image. Indeed, state branding may have proven to be the most salient component of Qatar's "soft power." Investing in its international profile allowed it to foster a reputation as a "leading, moderate, internationally focused, socially developing, knowledge-led country."[40] The Qatari brand is based on "images of political and media freedom, active diplomatic engagement in the Middle East, economic openness and a willingness to host investment in most sectors, and a desire to globalize and socially adapt to technological and social change."[41] As the United States has struggled to achieve its Middle East goals with the use of hard power, Qatar has far more effectively utilized this alternative tool.

This brand was constructed by carving out a unique niche where Qatar assumed several imperative political and cultural roles that the region was lacking,[42] such as political mediation,[43] hosting sporting events, and hosting cultural and shopping festivals.[44] Components of this strategy included: the founding of Al Jazeera and its relative press freedom; investment in education and cooperation with Western institutions through Qatar Education City; hosting of the Doha film festival; and the hosting World Trade Organization (WTO) negotiations. Perhaps the most visible component of its branding strategy has been sports, to include: Qatar Airways and its sponsoring of sports teams, especially FC Barcelona; the Qatar Investment Authority's partial ownership of Paris St. Germain; the hosting of a number of high-profile sporting events over the last two decades; and, of course, the culmination of this effort in the 2022 FIFA Men's World Cup.

In foreign relations, Qatar has sought to portray itself as a "good citizen" through mediation and conflict resolution.[45] It mediated a conflict between the Yemeni government and the Houthi rebel group in 2008; persuaded the Sunni-led government in Lebanon and the opposition Shiite Hezbollah group to sign the 2008 Doha Agreement; helped negotiate a ceasefire agreement between the Sudanese government and the Darful rebel group in 2019; mediated another Darfur Peace Agreement 2011;[46] and joined NATO's military effort in Libya against Colonel Qaddafi in 2011. Indeed, Qatar's flag "flying atop the ruins of Gaddafi's . . . compound was as rich in symbolism as it was reflective of the country's outsize role in engineering regime change."[47] Additional examples include Qatar's signing of military basing agreements with the United States in 1992,[48] the establishment of an Israeli trade office in Doha in 1996,[49] making regular monetary contributions to the United Nations,[50] paying the wages of Palestinian government officials,[51] and even making a contribution of US$100 million to New Orleans after Hurricane Katrina.[52] In addition, Qatar hosted an array of international conferences such as the 2001 WTO's Ministerial Meeting, known as the "Doha Round," which continues to provide Qatar with name recognition and exposure.[53] The small country served two terms on UN Security Council, 2006–2007, a big step in raising profile.[54] Most recently, Qatar hosted the peace talks between the government of Afghanistan and the Taliban.[55]

Qatar has managed not only to participate in high-profile regional and global events but to influence the way the world understands those events. Its principal instrument has been the Al Jazeera Media Network. In a promise of better freedom of expression, Emir Hamad founded Al Jazeera Media Network, which is the parent company of Al Jazeera Satellite Channel that began broadcasting in 1996.[56] Then in 1998, the emir abolished the Ministry of Information, which was responsible for media censorship and replaced it with it with a new Culture Ministry.

This unprecedented level of freedom of expression in the Middle East quickly made Qatari press, radio, and television more attractive to journalists and audiences alike. The Al Jazeera channel discussed controversial political, social, economic, and religious issues of the region. It also hosted live debates between guests including political pundits, professors, and known dissidents. While the Al Jazeera channel is a privately held company, it is funded by the Qatari government. Though likely started with a narrower vision, Al Jazeera has become a key tool in the soft power arsenal of Qatar. It provides not only a platform for Qatar to showcase itself and interact with the West in a manner which speaks to Western norms (through the press), but it also provides Qatar the growing capability to present a narrative separate from and outside of a larger regional narrative.[57] The origin of Al Jazeera is rooted in the push to modernize and revitalize the image of Qatar at home and abroad.[58] Under his vision, Qatar sought to rebuild itself into something attractive to Western nations, by building a modern news outlet. Qatar also sought to present itself as a forum where outside actors could express differing views; this included persons and groups who espoused ideologies hostile to the West and those who were exiled from other countries in the region.[59] Especially noteworthy was coverage of 2001 Arab Spring, popularity skyrocketed, viewers rising 2500 percent, included in US satellite television packages.[60]

In addition to foreign policy negotiations and news media, Qatar has invested in high-profile educational projects. Hamad invested billions of dollars in Qatar's public education system[61] and US$2 billion in Qatar Education City (QEC).[62] QEC is a twelve-square kilometer campus outside Doha with over eight thousand students, International Baccalaureate accredited K–12 schools, multiple Qatari universities, and many leading Western-based research universities, including Carnegie Mellon, Georgetown, Northwestern, Virginia Commonwealth University, University College London, University of Aberdeen, and others. Each of these universities specialises in a focus area to prevent duplication of curriculum.[63] Each university has its own building on campus and follows admission standards equal to that of its home campus.[64] It also hosts regional offices of research institutions, including RAND-Qatar Policy Institute and the Brookings Doha Center. QEC sponsors debates, which it broadcasts worldwide, called the "Doha Debates."[65] Relatedly, Qatar has invested in culture; it hosted the Doha Tribeca film festival and is home to the Islamic Museum of Art.[66]

As yet another prong of its branding strategy, Qatar developed its own airline, Qatar Airways, which continues to give Qatar name recognition in airports around the world.[67] The airline industry features the competition among regional countries, with an "intensely competitive triangulation" of Doha, Abu Dhabi, and Dubai for business and travel symbolized in the sudden salience of Qatar Airways, Dubai's Emirates Air, and Abu Dhabi's Etihad. Qatar Airways also participates in highly visible commercial sponsorships, such as the sponsorship of shirts of famous football teams in Spain, Italy, and Argentina,[68] and their sponsorship of FIFA 2018 World Cup. Qatar Airways has thus helped Qatar to become not only an effective hub for global travel but a globally recognized brand.[69]

Of course, the most relevant component of this strategy is Qatar's investment in sports, a strategy that far predates the 2022 World Cup. Sponsored events go back to the 1990s, and have included the1995 FIFA Under-20 Football World Championship, Qatar Open tennis tournament in 1998, the 2006 Asian Games, Qatar Masters golf tournament started in 2009,[70] 2011 football's Asian Cup and multi-sport Arab Games, and the 2017 IAAF World Championships.[71] Further examples of sports-related national branding include buying major shares in the 2012 Olympic Athletes' Village, Qatar Airways' sponsorship of FC Barcelona starting in 2010, and the Qatar Investment Authority acquiring a major stake in French football club Paris St. Germain in 2011, same year Al Jazeera acquired broadcasting rights for French football league.[72]

One of the main goals is showcasing Qatar's influence and effectiveness despite its status as a small state with a small population and a Third World Middle Eastern country.[73] Organizing and hosting a successful global event that is being watched and celebrated around the world allows Qatar to emphasize its success, professionalism, and ability to deliver on its promises.[74] This allows Qatar to take better control of its image and actively participate in shaping the global narrative on Qatar. Moreover, hosting MSEs highlights the differences between the sociopolitical reputations of Qatar and other Middle Eastern countries, which reinforces Qatar's effort to set itself apart from countries involved in conflicts in the region. This also supports its goal to associate itself with themes of peace, security, and integrity.[75] MSEs present the Qatari brand to audiences around the world as a fun, attractive and secure destination, which bolsters its pursuit to establish itself as a global tourist destination and a committed business partner.[76]

Organizing MSEs is expensive, requires the use of advanced technologies, and requires additional construction and infrastructure development. This gives Qatar the opportunity to highlight its modern culture and its use of advanced technologies. For example, each of the World Cup stadiums was designed to include artistic expressions in an effort to create a theme of state-of-the-art sporting architecture.[77] In addition to artistic designs, these stadiums use pioneering, environmentally friendly, advanced technologies to reduce the impact of the hot summer climate.[78] Moreover, modular construction technologies are being used to build the stadiums so they can be disassembled after the World Cup and given away to developing countries in Africa, South America, and the Middle East, thus eliminating the anticipated problem of post–World Cup underused sporting facilities.[79] Qatar's use of such advanced sporting architecture and technologies brings to mind the experience of places like Singapore and Kuala Lumpur, where the use of advanced sporting architecture was viewed as a "dramatic symbol" of change and development.[80] Qatar thus used this multipronged branding strategy to distinguish itself within an intensely competitive regional environment.

Qatar's grasp of the power of branding generally, and sports specifically, would then combine with a recognition of the need for social reform. There can be no question that outside pressure greatly contributed to the acceleration of Qatar's movement toward human rights reform. However, this reform did not start from scratch; it did not occur in a vacuum. Qatar's gradual approach to reform might be traced back as early as 1995, when Hamad bin Khalifa Al Thani seized power from his father in a bloodless coup and immediately began implementing a series of forward-thinking initiatives. These included the globalization of Qatari business, establishing Al Jazeera as a dominant and Westward-facing media group, the drafting of a new constitution and in turn holding elections and allowing women to vote, and a variety of related changes.[81]

Against this political backdrop, Qatar would seek the rights to host the World Cup. In so doing both the Qatari national government and the SC published a number of documents evincing a commitment to social reform generally and to labor reforms specifically, as well as an early intuition that the World Cup could advance these goals. These documents include the Qatar National Vision 2030, the Qatar National Development Strategy, the Bid Book, the Qatar 2022 Strategic Plan, and the SC Legacy Framework. A review of these documents shows the steady development of the notion that the country can use the event for lasting social impact, including the improvement of working conditions. Though these documents do not use the terms "labor rights," "human rights," or "human rights legacy," they continue the effort that began with Qatar National Vision 2030 in building the normative foundations for an eventual human rights legacy.

This narrative begins with the emir's 2008 vision for the twenty-plus-year growth trajectory captured in the Qatar National Vision 2030. The vision is organized around several principles: five "major challenges," three "guiding principles," and four "pillars" on which the vision rests. The country's five "major challenges" variously address the difficulties in managing economic and social growth, preserving traditions while modernizing, and recognizing the needs of current and future generations. One of the identified five challenges is "the size and quality of the expatriate labor force and the selected path of development." The document states that Qatar must "weigh the consequences of recruiting expatriate workers in terms of their cultural rights, housing and public service needs as well as the potential negative impact on national identity" against the economic benefits of their presence and productivity. While the implication that these workers pose a cultural threat would not sit well with today's human rights observers, the document acknowledges the needs, and even the rights, of these workers. Notably, the rights mentioned are cultural rights, rather than human rights more broadly or labor rights specifically. Indeed, these latter two phrases do not appear in the document. Qatar's approach to these challenges is to be shaped by the three guiding principles: the protection of "public and personal freedoms," the promotion of "moral and religious values and traditions," and the guarantee of "security, stability, and equal opportunities."[82] The four pillars of the vision are, in turn, human development (the development of "all its people" to allow them to "sustain a prosperous society"), social development (a "just and caring society based on high moral standards"), economic development (which will secure "a high standard of living" for "all its people for the present and the future"), and environmental development (creating "harmony between economic growth, social development and environmental protection").[83] The rising presence of migrant workers is apparent throughout this document, although specifically improving their working conditions is not yet a major focus.

Qatar's SC then took upon itself the goal of "accelerat[ing] progress towards achieving national development goals."[84] Its Bid Book was finalized and submitted in May 2010, two years following release of the Qatar National Vision 2030.[85] The Book provides a vision for the event, a key component of which is "a transformation in attitude." It explains that the games will foster public health, women's participation in sport, and "foster anti-discrimination, social integration, and peace."[86] These are, of course, intimations of human rights, though at a fairly high level of abstraction. Most would read these statements principally as an implied reference to gender and religion, not likely intended as a reference to migrant workers. The Book repeats the four pillars of Qatar National Vision 2030: sustainable human development, social development, environmental development, and economic development.[87] Here, social development discusses "improvement through football," and refers to sports and inclusion of women therein, and creating structured and well-supported football opportunities for migrant workers and refugees.[88] The theme of social and human development emphasizes donations to various global initiatives, and by using football to promote health and social inclusion, especially of women, the disabled, and the expatriate workforce. Drawing on FIFA's Corporate Social Responsibility guidance and the UN Millennium Goals, stakeholders recommended to Qatar that social development include "education on tolerance" and football facilities for refugees. Global Development includes sports development for refugees and disadvantaged youth abroad.[89]

The Bid Book thus includes multiple iterations on the theme of a legacy of social impact. The references to women, the disabled, and the social inclusion of migrant workers and refugees could all be framed as human rights issues, though the Bid Book does not do so. Indeed, it does not yet include a mention of rights, and no mention of working conditions. The concept of workers welfare and the WWS were seemingly not a part of Qatar's initial hosting concept. This would come later.

Just after winning the bid in 2010, the national government published the Qatar National Development Strategy 2011–2016. This document builds on the foundation of the Qatar National Vision 2030 published three years previously.[90] In effect, it is an elaboration of the National Vision's four pillars: human development, social development, economic prosperity, and environmental development. Though containing detailed descriptions of the national commitment to strengthening healthcare and fostering a capable workforce, the document does not focus in much detail on the condition, much less the human rights, of migrant workers. It does briefly mention a goal of increasing the proportion of high-skilled expat laborers, and increasing the number of ILO conventions.[91]

The SC, under the leadership of Hassan Al Thawadi, then drafted two documents that further built out its vision for the social impact of the World Cup. The first, the Qatar 2022 Strategic Plan, is a brief statement issued in 2011 of its three-year plan for getting WC preparations off the ground.[92] The document affirms a commitment that the WC should accelerate the implementation of the broader goals in the Qatar National Vision 2030 and the National Development Strategy 2011–2016. The document recognizes four dimensions of legacy: human, economic, environmental, and social. Here, among the social legacies it specifically mentions is improved construction worker standards.[93] The mention is admittedly brief. Still, it is the first evidence that the SC had begun to understand the World Cup as a catalyst for the long-term improvement of Qatari labor standards.

Then in April 2012, the SC issued its Legacy Framework.[94] This document provides a more fulsome account of the various legacies the SC envisions. It includes a sophisticated explanation of the many facets of megasport legacy and an impressive vision of how Qatar can use the event to become a progressive, Arab, Muslim, nation. Integrating the robust academic commentary on the many kinds of legacies that MSEs can create or have created, it acknowledges that legacies can be both hard and soft; economic, social, human, or environmental; local, national, regional, or global; and tangible or intangible. To that end, it draws upon the Qatar National Vision, the National Development Strategy, the Bid Book, and the Qatar 2022 Strategic Plan to establish the foundation of the event's legacies. Improved construction worker standards again get mentioned, this time with elaboration. The document explains that the event can leave a legacy of "improved enforcement and monitoring of appropriate living and working conditions for construction workers" and can produce an "increase in the level of skills and training provided to workers to enable delivery of high quality facilities and leave a lasting personal legacy."[95] So too do the document's formidable charts suggest that these improved labor conditions will in turn allow Qatar to achieve a number of its Bid Book commitments, however indirectly.

With the Legacy Framework, the notion that the World Cup can leave a legacy of improved living and working conditions for migrant laborers takes a more recognizable and credible shape. Additional pressure would help the idea reach fruition, as the next section shows.

The Levers of Legacy

Although the previous section describes factors that are entirely unique to Qatar, to assume no country could replicate Qatar's successes would be a mistake. Rather, Qatar's unique social conditions served to highlight a number of processes that can occur anywhere.

This section aims to identify those processes. It identifies three "levers" by which the World Cup effectuated governance reforms that can leave a legacy.

The preceding factors created the conditions in which these levers were most visible and worked to greatest effect. This report calls those levers the spotlight, the laboratory, and the ripple effect.

No one person or entity designed or operated the levers. Through a combination of civil society, national governments, intergovernmental organizations, socially mindful companies, and the media these dynamics took effect to produce meaningful reform. These levers constitute the takeaway for future hosts. To varying degrees, they could be replicated anywhere.

First is the spotlight. The widely invoked notion that megasports shine a spotlight on the host country is borderline trite. But expressions are often trite precisely because they are true. In Qatar, this familiar spotlight shone especially brightly. It both exposed problems and left the organizers feeling exposed. What distinguishes Qatar is how it responded to the spotlight. That spotlight exposed problems and pressured actors to respond, in four principal stages. It began to shine in 2011, and its dimmer was turned up substantially with the 2012 report of Human Rights Watch. This spotlight then began exercising its leverage with the publication first of the Qatar Foundations Worker Standards in 2013. The Foundation had thus laid the groundwork, and set the bar, for later reforms.

The year 2014 would prove to be the truly pivotal year for Qatar's eventual megasport human rights legacy. In that year, both the SC and the national government made decisions that would set the country on the road to a human rights legacy. The SC followed the Qatar Foundation's lead and adopted its own WWS. Second, in response to Human Rights Watch and other reports, the national government commissioned an independent report that largely corroborated the concerns voiced by civil society and the media. In so doing, the government signalled its willingness to embrace the criticism and address the problems. Then in 2015, a complaint filed at the ILO would expedite the formation of the institutional arrangement that would support the government in instituting reforms: the Technical Cooperation Programme. So too would a complaint filed with the lesser-known National Contact Point for the Organization for Economic Cooperation and Development pressure FIFA to lend institutional support. This section details these steps.

Perhaps the first organization to direct a spotlight on Qatar was the ITUC, an organization that promotes workers' rights and interests through international cooperation between trade unions and global advocacy.[96] For its work in Qatar, the ITUC collaborated with BWI, itself a global federation of hundreds of unions in the building, building materials, wood, forestry, and allied sectors.[97] As early as 2011, ITUC and BWI were in meetings with the FIFA General Secretary, impressing upon him that without the active protection of labor rights, FIFA and Qatar would face years of active campaigning.[98] Both organizations would continue to exert their influence in the coming years, as the following sections explain.

The watershed moment occurred in June 2012, when the international human rights NGO Human Rights Watch published their report, "Human Rights Watch, Building a Better World Cup."[99] Foreseeing a need of over a million additional workers in the ten years leading up to the World Cup to complete the construction, Qatar's then-existing labor rights framework was a looming social problem of enormous proportions.[100] The report combined a series of interviews with migrant workers in Qatar and a review of Qatari laws and norms to present recommendations that would improve the protection of human rights in the context of Qatar's migrant workers leading up to the World Cup.[101] The report identified several principal problems that in turn presented opportunities for substantive growth toward respecting human rights.

The first issue identified in the report concerned the recruitment and treatment of migrant workers. The migrant worker recruitment system was set out in the Labor Law and Ministerial Decision No. 8 of 2005 (see the second issue following for more on the Labor Law).[102] In relevant part, the Labor Law and Ministerial Decision stated that employers must use licensed recruitment agencies to bring in migrant workers and that the recruitment agents are prohibited from charging workers for costs associated with recruitment. However, Human Rights Watch found that these prohibitions did not stop recruitment agencies from charging migrant workers enormous fees in the recruiting process. Sixty-nine of the seventy-three migrants interviewed for the report described paying recruiting fees between US$726 and US$3,651 (or in some cases had their salary reduced to account for recruiting fees).[103] These fees and subsequent debts became a major impediment to migrant workers' ability to leave when exploited or abused. Further, many migrant workers reported that beyond the debts incurred from the recruiting process itself, the recruiting more often than not was misleading. The report noted that "though workers take on significant debts to fund their employment in Qatar, few of them have accurate or complete information about the jobs that await them, making the migration process a gamble in which workers risk being trapped in jobs that they never agreed to, or receiving salaries far below what they counted upon earning."[104] While the Labor Law allowed workers to terminate employment for an employer's misrepresentations, there was no redress for misrepresentations made by the recruitment agencies.

The second set of issues concerned compensation, leave, and the security of employment.[105] The Labor Law established maximum work hours, one month of annual paid leave, end-of-service payments, conditions employers and employees must meet to obtain a work permit (such as medical exams and a security clearance), and the right of an employee to terminate employment for a limited set of reasons (such as assault or misrepresentation of contract terms). While the Labor Law did at that time contain significant protections, the report described that "many workers fail to benefit from these provisions [of the Labor Law] because of inadequate oversight and implementation,"[106] as well as gaps in protection. The most obvious gaps in the Labor Law included: no minimum wage protections, bans on migrant worker unionization and collective bargaining, and exclusions of domestic workers. The lack of oversight lead to further problems such as heavy recruitment fees (as described earlier), low wages, and inaccurate information or wages or job descriptions when signing contracts.

The report also uncovered a widespread disregard for regulations regarding worker accommodations, as well as health and safety. Despite applicable Qatari regulations, Human Rights Watch observed workers sleeping in rooms that housed as many as twenty-five people, up to thirty people sharing one bathroom, and rooms where the air conditioning had been broken for a year.[107] There also appeared to be an issue with underreporting occupational injuries and deaths on the job. At the request of the Human Rights Watch, the Ministry of Labor stated that there had been no more than six worker deaths from 2009 to 2011, while the embassy of Nepal recorded 191 Nepali worker deaths in 2010 alone.[108] Construction workers in Qatar reported little to no safety training, as well as working during hours in which work is prohibited due to extreme heat.

The third issue, the Immigration Law, is the heart of the *kafala* system and the cornerstone of the reform agenda. The law required migrant workers to be sponsored by their employer for the duration of their expatriation.[109] The law prohibited workers from changing jobs without sponsor's consent, required exit visas to leave the country, and allowed for transfer from sponsor only in very limited scenarios of abuse by employer. Within the first few months of arriving in Qatar, the sponsor had to use the employee's passport to obtain a work permit. In practice, this often results in sponsors confiscating an employee's passport and delaying filing of the work permit, rendering an employee unable to obtain proper identification or move freely through Qatar. These are key indicators of forced labor.[110] While passport confiscation was prohibited under a 2009 Qatari law, workers interviewed for the report "nearly universally reported their employers continued to hold their passports."[111] The difficulty in obtaining an exit visa from sponsors was another common sentiment among workers, leaving them stuck in Qatar and laboring for their sponsor in poor conditions with little ability for redress.

The largest cited impediments to the redress in Qatar focused around access.[112] The system relied heavily on workers filing complaints against their employer. Labor Ministry Officials reported that they had conducted "know your rights" seminars for workers. However, workers stated that despite knowing their rights, there was widespread reluctance to file complaints. Once a complaint had been filed, the Complaints Department of the Labor Ministry would the employer, after which time many workers feared that they would be fired, expelled from living accommodations, and have their visas canceled. Reporting complaints also required overcoming a language barrier, as complaints could only be filed in English or Arabic (neither of which are the dominant language of any country sending migrant workers to Qatar). Thus, the risk of losing their only source of income and living accommodations forces a tolerance of exploitation among the migrant workers.

The Labor Ministry reported labor inspections as a proactive solution to addressing human rights violations against migrant workers. However, at the time the Human Rights Watch Report (HRW Report) was published, there were only 150 inspectors to monitor compliance. The Labor Ministry's Legal Affairs Unit noted that interviews with workers are conducted when inspecting worksites, but also admitted that the inspectors speak Arabic and sometimes English, thereby inhibiting effective interviews. Human Rights Watch stated that "[w]ithout available translators or inspectors who speak languages commonly spoken by migrant workers in Qatar, it remains unclear how this measure is implemented. Without speaking to workers, inspectors have no means to accurately assess whether the workers have possession of their contracts, whether they receive the wages or work the hours recorded, or whether they have faced deception, threats, or conditions of forced labor."[113] Between the risk of employer retaliation and the significant language barriers, there are few practical opportunities for redress when a Qatari sponsor exploits its migrant workers.

With the publication of the HRW Report, the spotlight was shining glaringly. Noting its own exposure, the SC responded with the WWS. Soon after the HRW report, the exposure and pressure of the spotlight seemingly accelerated the implementation of substantive reforms. The SC ultimately designed a comprehensive set of labor standards, called the WWS, that applied to all SC work. A demonstrated commitment to these standards became a precondition for every contractor submitting a bid for SC work, and would then become binding on contractors and subcontractors through legally enforceable contracts. The WWS are the defining achievement of the SC and the foundation of the Qatar 2022 human rights legacy.

As described earlier, the SC was not starting from scratch. The conceptual and normative foundation for the WWS had been laid with the Qatar National Vision 2030, the Qatar National Development Strategy, the Bid Book, the Qatar 2022 Strategic Plan, and the SC Legacy Framework. In addition to these documents, the SC had previously participated in the drafting of labor standards for another Qatari organization. The Qatar Foundation for Education, Science, and Community Development, is a nonprofit organization founded in 1995 by Sheikh Hamad Bin Khalifa Al Thani and Her Highness Sheikha Moza bint Nasser. Its "flagship initiative" is Education City, a twelve-square-kilometer campus described earlier.[114] As a sizable campus with substantial new construction, the foundation, much like the SC, engaged significant numbers of migrant laborers. So too was it called to task by the HRW Report. While the Qatar Foundation has already been in internal discussions about workers welfare, following the HRW Report, it launched a new initiative focusing on "enhanc[ing] its migrant workers' quality of life" and "curb[ing] unfair employment practices." The foundation established a working committee involving a number of stakeholders, including the SC. After signing a Workers Welfare Charter in October of 2012, in April of 2013, it released its Welfare Standards.[115] These standards deal with recruitment standards; employment and contract requirements; accommodations; communal and recreational facilities; food requirements; fire safety; construction standards; and establishing a reporting mechanism. The standards became mandatory and incorporated into agreements between the foundation and all its contractors. While detailed comparisons of the foundation's standards with the SC's Standards exist, experts interviewed for this research view the two sets of standards as essentially similar.[116] The foundation aimed to create an "exemplary model for the ethical treatment of workers," setting a "benchmark for the rest of the country."[117]

That benchmark would be honored, and well exceeded, by the SC. The SC adopted the Workers Welfare Charter in 2013 and the First Edition of the Workers Welfare Standards in early 2014. This document is significant in at least three ways. First, it moves well beyond the SC's prior documents in providing a comprehensive statement of leading workers welfare standards. While the Bid Book, Strategic Plan, and Legacy Framework included more general statements of a commitment to workers welfare, the standards operationalized these commitments with extensive, specific, enforceable requirements. Second, the WWS include a commitment to embedding these standards in contracts with third parties. Consistent with broader human rights principles, the SC is no longer merely preventing its own violations, but is now taking measures to ensure that the third parties with whom it does business will likewise take measures. Implementation of the WWS has become a prerequisite (along with all other relevant Qatari laws) for contractors and subcontractors hired in connection with World Cup projects. The WWS also place responsibility on contractors for ensuring that their subcontractors are in compliance. Third, the standards specifically use the concept of legacy in connection with workers welfare. At this moment, the notion that a megasport could produce a human rights legacy was born.

The WWS are aimed at addressing ten principles: health and safety, employment standards, equality, dignity, unlawful practices, working and living conditions, wages, grievances, access to information, and training.[118] Upon consideration for a contract, the applying contractor must "demonstrate their commitment to the Welfare of Workers in accordance with the Workers Charter and these WW Standards."[119] This commitment is shown through a proposal with a Commitment Statement, documents that help show compliance, an inspection, and a technical evaluation report. If selected by the SC, all parties enter into a contract that implements the WWS. The WWS document then details how these principles will be implemented into each step within the worker's employment from recruitment through repatriation, which are each described in detail later.[120]

Two of the most impactful features of the WWS are the various provisions concerning the ethical recruitment of workers, and the WWFs. The WWS require all contractors to use only validly registered recruitment agencies that have entered into a contract with the contractors. That contract must prohibit either party from charging the worker with recruitment fees or retaining their personal documents, provide that the contractor will pay all recruitment and processing fees, and stipulate that the worker will be informed of the job in their native language, among other provisions. The recruitment section also sets out affirmative duties for the contractor to report the recruitment agency upon breach of contract and reimburse the worker for recruitment fees if there is substantiating proof that the worker paid any such fees. Finally, the contractor must complete a checklist within the first month of the worker's employment that contains information on the worker's recruitment process.[121] To implement these ethical recruitment standards, the SC implemented in 2017 the Universal Reimbursement Scheme, which shifts the burden of proof to contractors to show workers had been hired ethically. The SC reports that to date, over 250 contractors have paid nearly US$30 million to roughly 50,000 workers for their recruitment fees.[122]

Similarly, the WWS require each contractor to establish a WWF for each accommodation site. At least once a month, a WWF must be held for worker representatives to raise concerns without fear of retaliation.[123] Any grievances brought to light during the WWF must be captured anonymously in the meeting minutes, and then recorded again in the meeting minutes when the grievance is resolved.[124] The SC reports that at its peak, over 110 WWFs were operating, covering more than 23,000 workers. Over fifty elections for worker representatives have been conducted at nearly thirty accommodation sites with voter turnout in excess of 80 percent.[125] Notably, at least a dozen contractors are providing forums for non-SC workers, adding protections to an additional 12,000 workers beyond the World Cup.[126]

To address the many concerns surrounding employment offers, the standards require that the workers receive their offer of employment in their home country with the following information included: the nature of the work to be performed; the worker's duties and responsibilities; the worker's rights and expectations regarding hours, wages, and off days; and employment benefits such as accommodations, food, and medical care. In addition to dictating the information contained within the contract, the WWS also dictates standards for delivery of the offer. The offer must be in writing and explained to the worker in their language, the signatures must be witnessed, and after the offer is signed, the employer is responsible for all relocation costs such as airfare and visa costs. Examples of acceptable employment offers are appended at the end of the WWS.[127] Migrant workers sign an employment contract that complies with the minimum requirements set out by Qatari law and other applicable standards, and clarifies the employee's terms and benefits (which "must be no less favourable than the Original Offer of Employment").[128]

A section dedicated to employment conditions puts many of the aspirational principles into practice by requiring the contractor to develop written policies providing for: equal opportunity; prohibition of compulsory labor, additional work, or financial penalties as a means to discipline workers; prohibition of violence, threats, intimidation, exploitation, or similar behavior against workers; and disciplinary procedures if employees violate the WWS. The contractor must also ensure that their workers retain their passports or other identification documents and obtain valid work visas, requirements that push back against the previous norms among Qatari contractors.

Contractors must ensure freedom of movement within Qatar and outside of Qatar through granting their entitled annual leave, rest periods, and other leave, and may take this leave without penalty or threat. If a worker's immediate family member dies or suffers a serious debilitating injury, the worker is entitled to fourteen days of unpaid leave.

Workers are also entitled to medical insurance provided and paid for by the contractor, medical treatment paid for by the contractor if the injury or disease is work related, and payment of wages if injury prevents the worker from performing their job. Notably, medical professional counseling services must also be provided for free to the workers by contractors if treatment is necessary for emotional, traumatic, or mental illness issues.[129]

The section on payment of workers enumerates standards opposite the employer norms as documented by various human rights reports. First and foremost, contractors must ensure that their workers (and subcontractors' workers) get paid on time, in accordance with the Qatari Labor Law, and without deductions (except those in accordance with the law). Impermissible deductions are those for recruitment fees, visa processing, accommodations, transportation, training, and medical insurance. Each contractor must keep a wage register and provide workers with a pay slip for each pay period.[130]

At the end of the employment, a contractor is responsible for the worker's repatriation travel expenses, as well as making sure that all wages and end of service gratuity is paid as soon as reasonably practicable. Employment contracts must state that a worker is entitled to terminate the contract, receive end of service gratuity, and repatriation at the contractor's expense in certain circumstances.[131] Contractors must give all workers an induction to the accommodation site (in a language the worker understands) upon arrival and must keep documents as evidence of induction. Additionally, the WWS enumerates the type of information that must be provided during the induction, including: emergency evacuation procedures, medical care procedures, key personnel, the WWF and Program Welfare Forum roles and procedures, the accommodation's health and safety rules, a summary of the worker's rights and responsibilities.[132]

Appended to the WWS are also a series of accommodation and food standards. Contained within the appendix are the minimum requirements that ensure building and infrastructure safety, suitable bedroom and bathroom accommodations, social and recreational facilities, and laundry services. Additionally, there are requirements for food and onsite catering, access to clean drinking water, prayer rooms, and medical care.[133] Also appended to the WWS are a series of transportation requirements, which include the requirement that contractors provide free transportation to workers to the construction sites and other services such as medical care.[134]

Facilities management programs at each accommodation must be prepared through the contractor and made available to the SC upon request. The program must include a daily cleaning plan, a monthly cleaning plan, fire safety procedures, a menu plan, a Security and Emergency Management Plan, and a Workers Induction Plan.[135]

Appendix D of the WWS contains the specific requirements with which all contractors must comply. The included provisions relate to air conditioning; drinking water; maintenance, features, and number of adequate sanitary facilities; mess areas; and medical facilities and required supplies.[136]

The contractor must also designate a Workers' Welfare Officer (WWO). The WWO is responsible for coordinating employee relations relating to the issues between workers and the contractor, must be qualified in human resources management and first aid training, is appointed by a contractor, and is required at all accommodation sites.[137] One of the tasks the WWO is required to undertake is the contractor's reporting requirements. Each month, the contractor (via the WWO) must submit a report on the accommodation site's medical records, the wage register, new employment checklists, and information on each worker—such as nationality, start date, contract expiry date, identification numbers, position, and construction site. The contractor is also responsible for this information for each subcontractor. If the WWO has evidence of suspected or actual breach of law or the WWS, there is an affirmative duty to report to the SC, who will further investigate the matter.[138]

Auditing is the main compliance and enforcement mechanism for the SC to monitor the adherence to the WWS and other relevant Qatari law. If a contractor is noncompliant, the SC may use contractual remedies, including but not limited to: suspension of payment, blacklisting, reporting to the Ministry of Labor or the State of Qatar Central Tenders Committee, or contract termination.[139] The WWS sets out a four-tier auditing system: Self-Audits, SC Audits, Independent Monitor Audits, and Ministry of Labour Audits. The contractor is to perform a self-audit every month using the WWS self-audit checklist, require its contractors to also perform a self-audit, and report the results with a rectification plan for any partial compliance or noncompliance.[140]

Finally, the WWS sets out procedures for entities that choose to voluntarily adopt the WWS. For any entity that wishes to adopt the WWS and utilize the SC's services in an advisory capacity, the entity must notify the SC of its intentions in writing. This final section especially reflects the SC's desire for these standards and the 2022 FIFA World Cup more broadly to have a lasting positive impact on Qatar's labor practices.[141]

With these detailed standards, the SC had put in place measures that would reduce incidences of labor rights violations during the preparations for the World Cup. However, a legacy lies not merely in prevention. Rather, it consists of reforms that extend beyond the event itself and endure after the event is over. Following WWS publication, a number of additional events and decisions would allow the labor reform movement to spread beyond the sporting event and become integrated into national law. The spotlight would become a floodlight. In the wake of the HRW Report, a wide variety of public- and private-sector institutions released reports on the need for labor reforms in Qatar.

In June 2013, the US Department of State issued a report on a variety of human rights issues in Qatar.[142] Some of those issues, such as the failure to criminalize spousal rape or restrictions on free association and expression, may reflect more universal norms, while others, such as restrictions on freedom of religion or the ability to vote the emir out of office, might be construed as a rejection of Qatar's governance model—an Islamic hereditary monarchy. Still, the report dedicated the last several pages to workers' rights. It emphasized the "pervasive denial of noncitizen workers' rights," the inability of foreign laborers to freely travel abroad, inadequate protections on the freedom to collectively bargain, lack of a minimum wage, failure to implement safety and health standards, and human trafficking in the domestic work and other sectors.[143] While not particularly in-depth or otherwise likely to galvanize the public's attention, the report served to presage the coming flood.

The floodgates would open with the report issued by the British newspaper *The Guardian*. Published in September of 2013,[144] the report put faces and stories to the migrant worker's allegations previously documented. In the report, the workers voiced their mounting frustrations with Qatar's state sponsorship program, which binds migrant workers to a single employee for the duration of their stay. Migrant workers find themselves forced to take out loans to come to Qatar for work, and then find that their contracts vary drastically in terms of job description and salary upon arrival. However, many are unable to leave because they need the money to pay off their debts, they need permission from their employer to leave the country. Further, because employers have the clear upper hand in this relationship, there are widespread allegations of employers preventing their workers from running away by refusing to pay workers for months at a time, confiscating their passports, or refusing to process the workers' identification cards (making the workers illegal aliens without proper documentation of sponsorship if they tried to leave). In effect, the workers are at the mercy of their employers.

The video report goes inside a Qatari migrant worker camp to show living conditions and interview Nepalese migrant workers. The video showed cramped living quarters, unsanitary bathrooms, and kitchens infested with bugs, which the workers described as very typical for their living accommodations. Most concerning was the video footage shot at a sixteen-year-old's funeral in Nepal. His family took out a loan to send him to Qatar for work, only for him to die of cardiac arrest only months later. Now his family is at risk of losing their home because of the outstanding loan that they are unable to pay. This report compiled a wide range of evidence that Qatari employers are engaging in abusive and exploitative practices that constitute modern-day slavery, as defined by the ILO, despite assurances that workers' rights would be respected. When the report was published in September 2013, the SC made it clear that construction specific to the 2022 World Cup had not yet begun, but that the allegations against contractors and subcontractors were "deeply concerning."

More reports followed. Amnesty International released "Qatar: The Dark Side of Migration" in November 2013 and would continue to observe and report on issues in Qatar.[145] Five months later, in February of 2014, the UN Human Rights Council released its second cycle periodic review of Qatar's human rights record (the first cycle review occurred in 2010 and the third cycle in 2019).[146] In April of 2014, the UN Special Rapporteur on Human

Rights of Migrants released a report on the human rights of migrants, which implicated Qatar.[147]

However, perhaps the most important subsequent report would be the one the Qatari government commissioned, as the next section explains. Now under a barrage of international criticism, Qatar could make either of two choices. It could go into denial: rejecting the criticism, denying the facts, clamping down on dissidents, restricting free speech, prohibit entry by journalists and civil society advocates, and commission a specious report that was little more than a snow job. Qatar could have done these things, but it did not. What it did instead would set the country on the course toward a human rights legacy.

One year following the HRW Report, in November of 2013, the Qatari national government commissioned the international law firm DLA Piper to perform an independent review of Qatar's legislative and enforcement framework for its labor laws.[148] Notably, Qatar elected to conduct an independent, rather than an internal, report, evincing a genuine interest in understanding the full scope of its labor issues. Published in 2014, the report substantially corroborates, and indeed relies on, the prior outside reports. Qatar does not attempt here to conceal those issues the spotlight exposed, or distance itself from the issues. Rather, Qatar embraces the critique, and leans in to the reform movement.

To complete the independent review, DLA Piper reviewed reports, national and international legislation, treaties, and internationally recognized best practices, and consulted with the relevant Qatari government agencies and stakeholders. DLA Piper also considered the HRW Report and the Amnesty International Report findings in making recommendations. The report identifies nine key issues for examination: recruitment agents and fees; *kafala* sponsorship system; contract misrepresentation and substitution; wages; health and safety; accommodation; labor inspections; freedom of association and collective bargaining; and access to justice.[149]

The report did not try to sugarcoat the labor situation in Qatar, noting a number of problems previously documented. Recruitment agencies are a common way that migrant workers connect with Qatari employers. However, these agencies often collect fees—averaging US$1,250—that migrants take out loans to pay, resulting in "indebtedness caused by the payment of these fees [that] significantly burdens the migrant workers arriving into Qatar."[150] While Qatari law prohibits recruitment fees, it only reaches Qatari employees and Qatari recruitment agencies, not recruitment agencies that operate outside of Qatar. These migrant workers typically incur the recruitment fees to agents in their home countries.[151]

The report similarly acknowledged the *kafala* problem. Designed to control migration to Qatar, the *kafala* sponsorship system has in effect created a system of forced migrant labor for many.[152] Migrant workers must be sponsored by their employer for the duration of their time in Qatar. The sponsors are legally responsible for the migrant workers, are charged with obtaining the necessary documents and identification for the migrant worker, and must issue an exit visa to the migrant worker upon departure. The ILO described this system as "disproportionately restrictive," while DLA Piper notes that "there are plainly circumstances in which the *kalafa* system could be abused, with potential detrimental effect." The sponsorship system enables Qatari employers to retain employees, despite substandard living conditions, low (or sometimes altogether withheld) wages, and abuse by confiscating passports and refusing to grant exit visas. Further, it is extremely difficult for migrant workers to obtain a sponsorship transfer, even when there is evidence of abuse due to the possibility of employer retaliation when a migrant worker files a complaint. The final barrier to migrant workers in the sponsorship system is the threat of being accused of absconding, in which an employer can report a migrant worker for a potential violation, issue a fine, and strip them of legal residence in Qatar. The report concluded, "these factors can result in a situation where migrant workers are 'trapped' in Qatar, with an abusive employer, and without means of exit or the ability to legally transfer to another employer for months." Notably, some of these common practices, such as passport confiscation, are prohibited by the Qatari Sponsorship Law. Despite this, there are still problems with the law being too narrowly focused and ineffectively enforced.[153]

The report similarly acknowledged problems with contract misrepresentation and substitution.[154] As was earlier reported by Amnesty and the Human Rights Watch, migrant workers alleged that the contracts they signed in their home countries were substantially more favorable than the contracts the migrants actually received once arriving in Qatar. This occurred in three ways. DLA Piper noted that "there is active deception in the State of Origin such that the migrant workers only become aware of the true terms of their employment upon arrival in Qatar," that there is coercion among recruitment agencies for migrant workers to sign the contracts before arriving in Qatar—only to find terms or entire contracts to be substituted upon arrival, and that "by reason of illiteracy,"[155] or by virtue of the contract not being in their native language, many migrant workers are unaware of the agreement to which they are signing.[156]

The report further acknowledged problems with worker payment. Despite provisions in the Labor Law requiring that workers must be paid at least once every month if employed on a yearly or monthly basis, and once every two weeks for all other workers,[157] nonpayment of wages was the most common complaint reported from migrant workers to embassy representatives. Other common wage-related complaints included: wage deductions, threat of employers reporting the workers as absconders "as leverage to reduce wages unilaterally,"[158] withholding for months at a time, and wages received in cash (making governmental monitoring more difficult). These complaints amount to many migrant workers performing forced labor.[159]

Health and safety received attention as well.[160] Among the allegations were stories of denied medical treatment, working through prohibited hours of day (i.e., when it has been deemed too hot for work in the summer months), and not providing proper training or equipment for workers. When requested, the data on workplace accidents and deaths varied significantly between records from labor-sending countries and records from the State of Qatar.[161]

While Qatari law set out conditions of suitable housing—which includes provisions relating to bedroom supplies and maximum capacities, bathroom capacities, kitchen specifications, air conditioning, and maintenance provisions—migrant workers reported that these standards are frequently disregarded. The disregard was generally attributed to ineffective monitoring and enforcement by the Labor Inspection Department and that (similar to described earlier) the complaint mechanism is ineffective. Other concerns include: insufficient space designated for contractors to build accommodations and that there is not enough storage for personal items (such as passports). These problems are exacerbated by Law No. 15 of 2010, which prohibited migrant worker accommodations from being built in residential areas.[162]

The report found that due to insufficient departmental resources and insufficient time allocated to carrying out inspections, recognizing and addressing violations was inadequate. Another recognized shortcoming of the inspections is the lack of interaction with migrant workers (language barriers are cited as the most common impediment to migrant worker interaction). Without this interaction, inspectors cannot properly ascertain the ongoing living accommodations and general treatment of workers by their employers.[163]

Under Qatari law, migrant workers are prohibited from unionizing and from collective bargaining.[164] Most notably, the absence of these rights exacerbates problems with the rest of the migrant worker system in Qatar by severely inhibiting migrant workers' ability to "respon[ed] in an organized manner to exploitative practices and other abuses by their employers."[165] Both the United Nations and the ILO have numerous provisions aimed at protecting freedom of association and collective bargaining for migrant workers, but Qatar has not ratified any such Conventions.[166]

The final area of focus, access to justice, reiterates what the other reports have found: Qatar has the legislation in place to assist migrant workers who have been abused or exploited, but there are impediments in securing access to this assistance.[167] Access problems stem from lack of knowledge on available redress, literacy and language barriers, the complaint system being overly burdensome, and the remedies not always being enforced.[168]

The DLA Piper report seemingly pulled no punches. Instead, it seemed to presage the government's constructive response to the international criticism. That constructive response would be further induced by legal action. International pressure would come not merely in the form of NGO reports and unfavorable media coverage, but through formal legal action as well. Indeed, a distinctive institutional framework that would prove essential in building Qatar's new labor regime resulted directly from such legal action. A complaint in the ILO against Qatar would produce the ILO's Technical Cooperation Programme, described later. So too would a filing with the OECD's National Contact Point in Switzerland put pressure on FIFA to further address host-country labor issues.

Two formal complaints were filed with the ILO against Qatar alleging Qatar's nonobservance of the Forced Labour Convention and the Labour Inspection Convention: the first, in January 2013, by the International Trade Union Confederation and the International Federation of Building and Wood Workers, and then in June 2014 by delegates of twelve member states.[169] The initial complaints noted that the problem of forced labor affected a migrant worker population of nearly 1.5 million workers.[170] They described working conditions under *kafala* in Qatar as exploitive, which enabled employers to exact forced labor. More specifically, the complaint identified main practices at the root of the problem: contract substitution, recruitment fees, and passport confiscation. It also advised that the Qatari government did not maintain a legal framework sufficient to protect the rights of migrant workers consistent with international law and raised particular concern for the *kafala* system, identifying it as one of the most restrictive sponsorship laws in the region.[171] The complaints further explained that Qatar's labor inspection and justice system failed to enforce the limited rights migrant workers do have under Qatari law, especially because of the small size of the inspectorate (roughly two hundred inspectors), lack of interpreters, insufficiency of fines, and inspectors' lack of power to enforce findings. Grievance mechanisms were also identified as ineffective because migrant workers have virtually no access to these mechanisms due to the absence of information, inaccessible legal aid, unavailable interpreters, and fear of retaliation. Migrant workers who filed claims did not have accommodation and did not receive their wages during the usually lengthy process. The grievance department's limited working hours were identified as one of the reasons migrant workers working outside of Doha were barred from accessing the grievance mechanisms. Moreover, the complaint indicated that Qatari authorities enabled trafficking for forced labor by arresting, detaining, and deporting potential trafficking victims who escaped from their employers or sponsors. Some of these migrant workers spent extended periods of time in detention centres because of debts or false charges of theft filed by their employers.[172]

In January 2015, the government of Qatar submitted a detailed reply to the governing body, providing information on measures taken to combat forms of forced labor and human trafficking. The ILO Governing Body then recommended that a high-level tripartite mission be taken to Qatar before June 2015.[173] In November 2016, the governing body gave Qatar an ultimatum to either begin to cooperate on labor issues or sit through a Commission of Inquiry, which is the ILO's highest level of investigative procedure.[174] Qatar began addressing labor issues to the level the governing body was demanding.[175] In October 2017, the ILO governing body decided to close the complaint and not set up a commission for the inquiry.[176] Instead, the governing body endorsed the establishment of a Technical Cooperation Programme between the government of Qatar and the ILO.[177] This program was launched to ensure accurate compliance with ratified labor conventions and to apply fundamental principles and rights at work in Qatar in a gradual manner for the duration of the program beginning in 2018 and ending in 2020.[178] The ILO set up a project office in Doha to lend local support to the Qatari government's labor reform agenda. A governance structure was also created to foster collaboration between the ILO and the Ministry of Administrative Development, Labor, and Social Affairs (hereinafter the Ministry of Labor), the entity responsible for labor and employment affairs related to Qatari citizens and foreign residents.[179] The key focus areas of the technical cooperation program have included the dismantlement of the *kafala* sponsorship system with a contractual scheme, improvements in wage payments and labor recruitment, increased accountability regarding forced labor, enhanced labor inspection and safety protocols, and the promotion of workers' voices through complaint and dispute settlement mechanisms.[180]

Interviews conducted in writing report praised both sides of this cooperative program. Both the ILO and the Qatari government apparently worked to foster an effective working relationship, without which far less progress would have been made.

A second legal filing would prove less impactful on Qatar than on FIFA. Still, it provides another example of how the World Cup spotlight can leverage change. The Organisation for Economic Co-operation and Development (OECD) member states are required to adhere to the OECD Guidelines for Multinational Enterprises (Guidelines).[181] The Guidelines come in a nonbinding annex to the OECD Declaration on International Investment and Multinational Enterprises. They are meant to provide governments with a recommended framework to address multinational enterprises. The Guidelines are standards and principles for conducting responsible business in a global context consistent with applicable laws and internationally recognised standards. The Guidelines are the only multilaterally agreed comprehensive code of responsible business conduct governments have committed to promoting.

Multinational enterprises in countries that bind themselves to the Guidelines are required to perform risk-based due diligence depending on the circumstances of a situation.[182] In addition, these enterprises are expected to avoid adverse impacts on human and labor rights through their own activities and to prevent or mitigate an adverse impact where the enterprise itself has not contributed to the impact but is directly linked to the operations, products, or services by a business relationship. Such business relationships encompass relationships with business partners, entities in the supply chain, and any other non-state or state entities directly linked to its business operations, products or services.[183] Furthermore, the Guidelines highlight that "contributing to" an adverse impact is interpreted as a "a substantial contribution, meaning an activity that causes, facilitates or incentivises another entity to cause an adverse impact and does not include minor or trivial contributions." In effect, the Guidelines are like the UN Guiding Principles on Business and Human Rights, but with an enforcement mechanism.

Governments that bind themselves to the Guidelines are required to set up a local National Contact Point (NCP).[184] NCPs facilitate the application of the Guidelines mainly through providing a platform for mediation and conciliation to resolve issues that arise from alleged non-observance of the Guidelines through the procedure of a Specific Instance.[185]

In May 2015, the BWI—the same labor union that had been instrumental in filing the ILO complaint—presented a written submission to the Swiss NCP regarding FIFA in relation to human rights violations of migrant workers involved in the construction of the FIFA 2022 World Cup facilities in Qatar.[186] The BWI alleged that FIFA, as an association incorporated in Switzerland, a country that binds itself to the Guidelines, violated the Guidelines when it awarded the FIFA 2022 World Cup to Qatar knowing of the well-documented preexisting labor rights violations.[187] The BWI further argued that FIFA violated the guidelines by its failure to conduct adequate and ongoing human rights due diligence, to prevent its own contribution to the human rights violations of migrant workers in Qatar, or to use its leverage to develop and reinforce necessary labor rights reforms to mitigate additional human rights violations. BWI hoped the mediation would result in implementation and publicization of FIFA's human rights due diligence policy; creation of the Human Rights Advisory Board, including trade union representatives as members; addresses FIFA's responsibility to utilize its leverage with the Qatari government to accelerate labor and other human rights–related reform; ensure commitment and application to international conventions, guidelines, and principles related to human and labor rights; adopt the existing FIFA policy on Decent Work Stadium and Infrastructure Standards; amend FIFA policies to include binding provisions for health and safety and independent labor inspections; and agree to conduct joint labor inspections with the BWI.[188]

In response, FIFA questioned whether the Guidelines were applicable to FIFA considering its status as an association organized under Swiss Civil Code.[189] FIFA also questioned the validity of the BWI's claim of FIFA's leverage over the government of Qatar and emphasized that its direct counterparty is not the government of Qatar but the member association—which is the Qatar Football Association, the Bid Committee, and the Local Organising Committee, which are all independent from the Qatari government. They emphasized their 2011 announcement that all future biddings will adhere to the UN Guiding Principles on Business and Human Rights (UNGP).[190]

The threshold question was whether FIFA was a multinational enterprise for purposes of the OECD Guidelines. An NCP must determine, on a case-by-case basis, whether an entity has commercial activities.[191] The Swiss NCP found that the contract between FIFA and counterparts in Qatar includes a number of commercial elements such as insurance, finance, and marketing rights.[192] Within the scope of this contractual relationship, the activities of this agreement can be interpreted to be of a commercial nature, to which the Guidelines apply.[193]

The proceedings lasted for approximately two years, during which six mediation meetings took place at the Swiss NCP premises in Bern and included representatives from the BWI, FIFA, the Swiss NCP, International Labour Affairs of the State Secretariat for Economic Affairs, and a mediator. In May 2017, the NCP announced that the parties had reached agreements in several areas.

First, even though FIFA is not in violation of domestic law, it is responsible to mitigate risks by aiming to build and use its leverage when applicable with actors in Qatar to ensure decent and safe working conditions on 2022 World Cup facilities. In relation to the bidding requirements, FIFA will base its future bidding approach on strengthening the due diligence process. FIFA also agreed to strengthen its cooperation with the BWI and reach out to relevant stakeholders to maximize efforts for improving working and accommodation conditions on 2022 World Cup facilities.[194]

Second, FIFA agreed that stakeholders, including the BWI, would be included in the development of FIFA Human Rights Policy.[195] FIFA also confirmed its commitment to integrate human rights in existing mechanisms and relationships with other stakeholders. The parties agreed on the importance of securing human rights compliance of subcontractors throughout the supply chain and raised special concern about the payment of migrant workers. On the issue of labor inspections, the parties emphasised the importance of establishing a better process to monitor labor conditions including migrant workers' participation and representation. In addition, the parties recognized that an effective grievance mechanism is greatly needed and scheduled a meeting in Doha between FIFA, the BWI, and the Qatari SC to examine this issue. The parties emphasized the important role of the new Human Rights Advisory Board in the implementation of FIFA's human rights commitment. The BWI was invited to appoint a member to this oversight body.[196]

In the wake of this process, FIFA developed new bidding requirements that include binding human rights commitments for governments and host cites, which shall be made public before the selection of a host country. FIFA established a new Human Rights Policy emanating from the newly amended Article 3 of the FIFA statutes. A memorandum of understanding was signed between the BWI and the SC allowing for joint labor inspections, in addition to the SC's own new monitoring process. The FIFA Human Rights Advisory Board was established, though its mandate expired in 2021.[197]

These legal filings were but one component of a larger mechanism by which international pressure resulted in national reforms. The sequence is clear. Qatar wins the rights to host the World Cup. International organizations that might work on any of a number of countries with labor issues suddenly turn their focus to Qatar. Reports are published, and problems are exposed. Under this exposure, the SC and then the national government adopted a number of reforms that are likely to remain in place after the World Cup is over. The spotlight thus becomes a principal lever of legacy.

A second lever may be called the laboratory. The US Supreme Court Justice Louis Brandeis famously articulated the idea that smaller units of government may "choose [to] serve as a laboratory; and try novel social and economic experiments without risk to the rest of the country."[198] In a different intellectual tradition, the Italian political philosopher Giorgio Agamben wrote of the "state of exception" as a zone within which a government introduce new laws "to cope with exceptional circumstances of necessity" and which can remain in place after the circumstances return to normal.[199]

If the Qatar 2022 FIFA Men's World Cup created a state of exception, the SC became the laboratory. The SC experimented with systemic labor reforms in the form of the WWS. The ILO and Ministry of Labor would participate in shaping the SC's reforms and then collaborate to fashion similar reforms nationwide. This laboratory function was not part of the SC's original design and may never be officially acknowledged. The intention to use the SC as a laboratory or incubator for national reforms is not articulated in the Bid Book, Legacy Framework, or any Ministry of Labor publication. However, multiple interviews suggested that this dynamic was in effect occurring. So too does the timing of the national reforms in relation to the SC standards strongly suggest a laboratory effect.

Though the laboratory metaphor helps to understand certain dynamics at work in Qatar, the metaphor should not be taken too far. To the extent the metaphor suggests that the SC's reforms were nothing more than an experiment, it becomes misleading. The SC's reforms were no mere means to some other end; the many workers on World Cup projects were not lab rats. The SC undertook the reforms for their own sake. Still, the SC's work had the effect of providing reliable data that informed the national government's reforms.

The three places where this "laboratory effect" is most prominent are wages, accommodations, and the WWFs.

Withholding of wages addressed in the first version of the SC's WWS by requiring contractors to open bank accounts for workers.[200] Additionally, the standards specified that workers must be paid at regular intervals that cannot exceed one month between payments. As a backstop, the first version of the WWS stated that the contractor is strictly prohibited from deferring, delaying, or withholding wages, and further specified that contractors may not deduct expenses such as accommodation or recruitment fees from a worker's wages.

This system of contractors opening Qatari bank accounts to pay their workers in regular intervals, which came to be known as the Wage Protection System, was implemented into Qatari law in February 2015 as Law No. 1 of 2015. The Wage Protection System (WPS) codified the requirements that contractors must set up bank accounts for workers' wage deposits and that workers must be paid at least monthly if employed on a monthly or yearly basis. Additionally, the law imposes penalties such as fines and imprisonment for contractors found to be in violation of the WPS.[201] Subsequently, the 2016 edition of the WWS provided less substance for wage requirements, but simply stated that contractors must be in compliance with the WPS—and ensure that its subcontractors are in compliance with the WPS—and enumerates the same series of prohibited wage deductions found in the first version of the WWS.[202]

The ILO emphasized its continuing work to improve the WPS throughout the 2018, 2019, and 2020 progress reports. In particular, the 2019 progress report cited a strengthened WPS as one of the technical cooperation program's achievements. The report stated that an assessment of the WPS led to a series of recommendations that the ILO will assist the Ministry of Labor in implementing, leading to extending coverage, ensuring identification of noncompliance, and reducing prolonged nonpayment for workers.[203] The 2020 progress report highlighted that many of the recommendations mentioned in the 2019 report were successfully implemented. The Wage Protection System Unit has implemented real time technology to detect and track violations, analyze trends, and guide compliance. With this change, coverage of the wage protection system increased from 75 percent to 96 percent of eligible workers, and from 78 percent to 94 percent of companies. This allowed for less obvious wage-related violations such as "payment below the basic minimum wage and non-compliance with the newly introduced thresholds for food and accommodation allowances" to be detected.[204] Further, companies considered "high risk" are automatically blocked from certain government services until they fall into compliance. Notably, the ILO is assisting Qatar to continue the momentum started by the WWS. For example, the 2020 progress report notes that the Ministry of Labor is also adopting measures that extend these protections to domestic workers, and that the newly established Workers' Support and Insurance Fund has been facilitating payment of previously withheld wages to migrant workers.

Worker accommodations is another area where observers can clearly see the laboratory effect of the World Cup on Qatar's labor practices. Among the accommodation standards in the WWS were specifics on requirements for worker accommodations, such as the condition of bedrooms and furnishings for all living accommodations, necessities for kitchen accommodations, and numerous safety provisions relating to emergency training, evacuation plans, and onsite medical personnel.[205] In November 2014, the Qatari Ministry of Labor and Social Affairs issued Ministerial Decision No. 18 of 2014, titled "Setting the Conditions and Specifications of the Workers' Accommodations." Here we see the exact specifications from the WWS implemented into Qatari law so to bind all employers with accommodation sites for migrant workers, not just those under contract in connection with construction for the 2022 World Cup. Like the 2013 version of the WWS, Ministerial Decision No. 14 of 2018 states that certain requirements must be met. Among these similarities are the requirement that each employer shall provide accommodations with enumerated basic furnishings for bedrooms and kitchens, fire extinguishers, smoke detectors, alarm systems, health and safety emergency plans, safety and evacuation training, and an appointed resident nurse for accommodations hosting one hundred to five hundred workers, an appointed doctor for accommodations with over five hundred workers, and a resident doctor for accommodations hosting over five thousand workers.[206] These specifics were reiterated in the most recent version of the WWS.[207]

There has been less overt work done in conjunction with the ILO on accommodations than with the WPS. One of the main objectives of the technical cooperation program is to promote the workers' voice, which is where the headway on improving accommodations becomes apparent. In the 2018 progress report, the only mention of accommodations was in the election of worker representatives who can bring forth workers' concerns on matters including but not limited to accommodations.[208] The 2019 report noted that labor inspectors would be receiving enhanced training throughout 2019 and 2020 to ferret out violations relating to working and living conditions, that there would be a forthcoming assessment of best practices legislation—including the regulation of accommodations.[209] The 2020 report stated that all labor inspectors had undergone training on the labor law and labor inspection skills, and that there is ongoing work to promote workers voice through programs such as explanatory guides, webinars, and "Know your rights campaigns" on Qatar's labor law.[210] Working and living conditions were improved for workers in the hospitality industry, potentially pointing toward a shift of improved working conditions across all employment sectors, not just those in the construction sector under contract with the SC where the WWS originated.[211]

The final place is the WWFs themselves and their impact in developing the national Joint Committees. The SC's WWFs were launched in 2014. The SC collaborated with contractors to establish WWFs at each of its twenty-four main contractor accommodation locations and at seventy subcontractor accommodation sites. It also developed guidelines, reviewed and endorsed by the BWI, to help contractors hold worker representative elections. The ILO and Ministry of Labor conducted a review of these forums and adopted what they believed were the most successful practices for its own committee initiative. The two entities have collaborated on a number of sustainability and capacity-building events to catalyze the joint committee and workers' welfare programs.[212]

The third lever may be called the ripple effect. While the laboratory effect focuses on legally mandated reforms, additional practices were adopted above and beyond legal requirements. Of course, a great many companies are doing work for the SC in preparation for the World Cup. While working on SC projects, they are contractually obligated to comply with the WWS. However, these companies are often not working exclusively for the SC. They will have World Cup projects and non-WC projects occurring at the same time. Where the WWS afford greater worker protections than current Qatari law, such companies face an ethical question: whether to treat their employees on non-WC work more poorly than their concurrent WC workers.

The SC provided information on select companies that have applied the SC standards across their non-SC operations. This report acknowledges the inherent limitations on this data. Still, to the extent it accurately reflects the behavior of at least some companies, the data suggests yet a third mechanism for the effectuating of a human rights legacy. Certain companies have affirmatively implemented select SC standards across their non-SC operations. The SC's standards thus "ripple" across these companies' operations, providing labor protections even to workers not employed on World Cup projects. Three such companies serve to illustrate this dynamic.

Nakheel Landscape Company is a main contractor on a number of World Cup projects including the training sites and Al Bayt Stadium. The company employs over five thousand workers, but at press time only about 10 percent worked on SC projects. Nonetheless, Nakheel is providing certain of the SC benefits and protections to its non-SC workers, even in the absence of any statutory or contractual obligation. These include: monthly recruitment fees for twenty-four months; a return air ticket to each worker's home country each year; and an overall commitment to providing equal benefits to SC and non-SC workers.

Similarly, Pigeon Engineering is a Qatar-based construction firm working on several stadiums as well as on Education City. Like Nakheel, Pigeon employs several thousand workers though only a fraction work on SC projects. Nonetheless, for SC and non-SC workers alike Pigeon has begun providing twenty-four months of recruitment fees. The company also provides a monthly air ticket allowance in the first year of employment and a return ticket in the second year.

A third example is Teyseer Security Services. Teyseer is a private security company based on Qatar. It has reportedly modeled its hiring practices after the SC standards even for non-SC employees. Specifically, it has provided life insurance and a monthly airfare allowance for both categories of workers.[213]

The phenomenon of the higher World Cup standards rippling across the corporate sector has important implications for the potential human rights legacy of megasports. Once their World Cup preparations are over, it is of course possible that these companies will revert to the minimum labor rights required by law. Some certainly would. And yet it is difficult to imagine that all companies would unwind all such heightened protections immediately following the event. Employees will have been introduced to higher standards. Companies will have to compete for these employees. So too will those companies have learned, presumably, how to operate at a profit under these standards. Outside observers, including but not limited to the ILO, will be monitoring their behavior. To the extent any companies continue to abide by the SC standards after their SC work is done, even when national law does not require it, this too becomes a facet of Qatar's legacy. Finally, these heightened practices may make future national reforms easier, as leading companies are already accustomed to them. Norms, like practices, can constitute a legacy.

Of course, the ripple effect would not occur without the spotlight. Private companies, much like the SC and the national government, do not wish to see substandard business practices exposed to the world. Just as the ripple effect depends on the spotlight, so too did the laboratory. Ultimately, what this report calls "levers" have overlap and synergy. The point is to identify the different dynamics by which these changes occur.

The Elephant That Won't Leave the Room: Corruption Allegations, Properly Framed

In the global movement to improve megasport governance, human rights reform is closely related to anti-corruption reform. Because they are kindred reform movements, and because of overlapping interest in these issues among global commentators and fans, a report describing Qatar's exceptional human rights successes would lack credibility if it failed to acknowledge lingering corruption issues. These suspicions have three primary and interrelated touch points: the Garcia Report; FIFA's expulsion of Mohammed Bin Hammam; and the ensuing government investigations of multiple jurisdictions, most visibly the United States. The latter yielded credible allegations, which as of press time had not been fully adjudicated, due in part to the inability to extradite certain suspects and the deaths of others.

Though unanswered questions remain, global commentary has largely failed to place these questions in a proper perspective. Without that perspective, reports on these allegations smack of what the scholar Edward Said called "Orientalism": the tendency of Western commentators to characterize Eastern and particularly Islamic countries and ideas with an unjustified attitude of superiority, constituting a residual form of colonialism.[214]

The facts supporting the corruption allegations are briefly described later. Placing these facts in a proper perspective requires a number of qualifications. First, it must be understood that Qatar is not a systemically corrupt country. It should not be carelessly lumped together with its notoriously corrupt neighbors such as Egypt or Yemen or Iraq. As noted earlier, Qatar is among the top 15 to 20 percent of all countries in the world for controlling corruption. More suitable comparisons might be France, South Korea, or the United States. Notably, the corruption allegations here relate exclusively to Qatar's dealings with select individuals at FIFA. Qatar's corruption problem lies in its nexus with the FIFA Executive Committee.

Second, as will be detailed later, the Garcia Report identified a number of improper acts. However, those acts were generally allowed under FIFA's rules. To the extent this is true, Qatar may bear less responsibility than FIFA itself. Admittedly, a country arguing that it is no more corrupt than FIFA will earn scant sympathy. Still, the corruption allegations surrounding the Qatar's hosting of the FIFA World Cup are, again, a problem in the Qatar-FIFA nexus.

Third, such problems are hardly unique to Qatar. Entities from a wide variety of countries that the Western press would be far less inclined to characterize as systemically corrupt, such as Germany or Japan, have also been implicated in megasport bribery scandals, even recently. Qatar did not write the rules by which all countries, Eastern and Western, have historically interacted with certain FIFA individuals and with megasport bodies generally. Qatar may have been no better than the rest of the world, but it was also no worse.

Fourth, even if bribes occurred, we should be careful not to assume that all persons involved in the World Cup preparations were involved and that their work is therefore inescapably tainted. Almost certainly, the SC personnel now leading the charge on labor rights, or even on anti-corruption compliance, were not involved. They may be unwilling to talk about it now, but we can hardly blame them: some may simply wish to put those events, now over ten years old, behind them; some may feel they should not be asked to answer for the potential misdeeds of others whose work is only indirectly connected to their own; some may regret that allegations for which they are in no way responsible can tarnish the public's perception of their life's work; some may feel that whatever they say, it will be used against them and construed in the worst conceivable light. Each of these concerns is understandable. Although the present research project found the SC categorically unwilling to talk about the corruption allegations or about any anti-corruption reforms since adopted, we should read little into it. In sum, the corruption allegedly occurred over ten years ago, the SC does not want to discuss it, and the unanswered questions should not taint an unprecedented labor rights effort undertaken in good faith.

Finally, the world should not presume that Qatar's unexpected success in winning the 2022 is, by itself, evidence of unprecedented bribery. This may itself be the most egregious form of Orientalism. Western academics, NGOs, and journalists writing on these remaining unanswered questions should be very careful not to perpetuate colonial attitudes that, in the context of megasport governance, are plainly hypocritical. To the extent the global press is vigilant of any form of racial, religious, or ethnic prejudice, it should comment on these allegations with care.

Having said all this, the allegations of bribery and corruption that surfaced soon after the selection of Qatar to host the World Cup were not surprising.[215] For years before the decision to award the 2022 World Cup to Qatar, FIFA's reputation was already tarnished for its involvement in an array of scandals including money laundering, game fixing, commercial bribery, and gambling.[216] Following several media reports of bribery and corruption during the voting process, FIFA had no option but to develop a set of correcting steps including an investigation in the 2022 bidding process.[217] FIFA established an Independent Governance Committee that included independent international corporate governance experts. FIFA amended its statutes to allow FIFA Congress Member Associations instead of the Executive Committee to vote and determine hosts of future World Cup tournaments.[218]

FIFA also revised its Ethics Code and restructured its Ethics Committee to establish a new Investigatory Chamber chaired by an independent former US Attorney, Michael Garcia, and an Adjudicatory Chamber chaired by a German judge, Hans Eckert.[219] Some of the first substantive allegations came from *The Sunday Times*, in which articles were alleging that the Qatar bid team paid US$1 million to Samson Adamu, who was the son of FIFA Executive Committee member Amos Adamu, to sponsor an African Football Legends Dinner.[220] *The Sunday Times* handed over some of this information to FIFA, which passed it to the Investigatory Chamber as a starting point for the investigation. In 2012, FIFA appointed Garcia as the Chairman of the Ethics Committee's adjudication chamber. Shortly thereafter, Garcia announced that he would be investigating accusations of bribery and corruption the bidding process. The investigation was expanded beyond the initial *Sunday Times* incident to include the 2018 and 2022 bid processes.[221] In September 2014, the investigation was concluded and Garcia submitted the Garcia Report to the Adjudicatory Chamber. In November 2014, the Adjudicatory Chamber published a summary of the Garcia Report, drafted by Eckert, announcing that even though there is a "prima facie case that serious violations of bidding rules and the FIFA Code of Ethics" occurred, the Ethics Committee concluded that the selection of Qatar to host the World Cup was not induced by bribery and corruption. Garcia objected to Eckert's summary and conclusion asserting that it was "materially incomplete and erroneous" and demanded the release of the full report. Eckert refused, and Garcia resigned.[222] On June 24, 2017, a German newspaper received a leaked copy of the report.[223] The following day FIFA published the full report.[224]

Garcia's report covered over four hundred pages and examined all nine bids and eleven member associations (there were two joint bids—Belgium/Holland and Spain/Portugal) for 2018 and 2022.[225] The report exposed an array of rule breaches committed by almost all of the countries that submitted bids for 2018 and 2022 World Cup tournaments.[226] Among the most damaging concerned the Qatari Mohammed Bin Hammam, who from 2002 until 2011 was president of the Asian Football Confederation, one of six continental confederations that constitute FIFA. Bin Hammam challenged Sepp Blatter for the FIFA presidency in 2011, but suddenly withdrew in response to FIFA allegations that he had bribed Caribbean officials with the help of Jack Warner, who was at that time a member of the FIFA Executive Committee. Media reports later alleged that Warner had been bribed upward of US$2 million by individuals representing Qatar. They further reported that payments were made from Mohammed Bin Hammam, and by extension the Qatar 2022 bid team, to OFC Executive Committee Member Reynald Temarii.[227] The investigation did not uncover a direct link between Qatar 2022 and the payments to Temarii.[228] In July 2012, FIFA banned Bin Hammam for life, though the Court for Arbitration in Sport reversed the decision. Then in December of 2012, following the Garcia Report's findings that Bin Hammam had committed "repeated violations" of the FIFA ethics code concerning conflicts of interest between 2008 and 2011, he was banned for life a second time.[229]

The Garcia Report also became the basis for criminal complaints in multiple jurisdictions over money laundering, racketeering, fraud, corruption within FIFA, and an FBI investigation. During testimony in 2014, one official testified that Julio Grondona—former FIFA Senior VP—told the official that

Grondona had taken money (at least US$1 million) for his vote for Qatar.[230] While Grondona did not tell him the exact amount or the source of the bribe, this was considered the strongest evidence that the 2022 vote was tarnished by bribery. In April 2020, the US DOJ took action with an indictment that, among other FIFA corruption allegations, accused three senior FIFA officials of receiving bribes to vote for Qatar.[231] These three officials were Nicolas Leoz, Ricardo Teixiera, and Grondona (listed as Co-Conspirator #1). Because Leoz and Grondona have both recently passed away, and Teixeira has not been extradited, a trial remains unlikely. Notably, in this same indictment, DOJ charged two former 21st Century Fox executives with bribery for the 2018 and 2022 broadcasting rights.[232]

In sum, the global commentariat is right to acknowledge unanswered corruption issues, and it is right to take offense at persistent megasport bribery. It is wrong to wag a finger at Qatar as if it were the first country to face these allegations. So too would it be wrong to allow those allegations to dwarf its substantial human rights achievements.

A Changing Qatar, a Template for Future Events

This final section acknowledges Qatar's legacy beyond its own labor law regime. That legacy includes protecting the rights of the disabled, increased human rights training for its security forces, and FIFA-level reforms. It then concludes with observations on the future of Qatar's reforms.

Qatar's likely domestic World Cup human rights legacy is not limited to labor rights. Two additional areas are accessibility and security training. With an estimated eight hundred wheelchair users expected to be present at any one moment of the World Cup, the SC aspires to create a signified, safe, and independent experience for all persons with accessibility needs. As with labor rights, the World Cup has become a launching pad to ongoing discussions with the national government on how Qatar might create a legacy of accessibility that extends well beyond the football stadiums. This legacy will require a combination of physical infrastructure and governance infrastructure.

To this end, in 2016 the SC created the Accessibility Forum, a group of Qatari residents with disabilities and of organizations serving the needs of the disabled. Participants include the Ministry of Transportation & Communications, Hamad International Airport, Qatar Tourism Authority,

Ministry of Municipality & Environment, Katara Cultural Village, Qatar Museums, and the Ministry of Culture & Sport. The forum is both a think tank and a lobbying group, holding workshops and engaging in dialogue with stakeholders to develop plans that will ensure the best outcome for people with disabilities.

At press time, the SC had already achieved a number of successes. These include dropped curbs and raised crossings; wider footpaths; fewer pedestrian and footpath obstructions; better surfaces; controlled parking; tactile paving; and improved signage. New Metro by Qatar Rail already functioning with thirty-five stations. Include tactile routes for visually impaired people, level access boarding onto the trains; designated wheelchair spaces; lift access throughout the station and the availability of assistance at the station. All eight football stadiums have been built in accordance with international standards on accessibility, to include: lift access; dedicated seating with quality sightlines for wheelchair users; easy access seats; accessible toilets and baby change facilities; and accessible prayer rooms and concession areas. They intend to include sensory rooms and adult changing facilities. These are all permanent changes.

The work is ongoing. The SC aims to ensure adequate wheelchair accessible rooms with easy access and adapted bathrooms, as well as adaptations for people with hearing or visual impairments. It is developing an extensive program of awareness and training to assist and support disabled people will be provided to stadium, hotel, and transport staff. For the World Cup, it intends to bring in an appropriate number of new buses equipped with ramped access and a designated wheelchair space. The taxi fleet will be greatly expanded to include a number of wheelchair-accessible vehicles. These taxis will be dedicated to wheelchair users during the World Cup, and thereafter will become part of the standard fleet.

Qatar's unique demographics make this commitment to an accessibility legacy all the more remarkable. Given the exceptional levels of wealth per capital, Qatari nationals typically do not use public transportation. Rather, it is generally for migrants who, having come to Qatar to engage in various forms of physical labor, rarely come with preexisting accessibility needs.

A second potential human rights legacy of Qatar 2022 lies in the human rights training of security personnel. Security for an MSE is of two types: government security forces, who are typically full-time police, wearing uniform, located long-term in the host country; and private security, who may be temporary hires and may come from outside the host country. Because Qatar has a negligible market of surplus labor, and due to the size of the country vis-à-vis the event, it is estimated that as much of 90 percent of the World Cup security personnel will be private personnel brought in temporarily from abroad. Qatar will likely rely heavily on large international private security companies to supply these personnel.

All must be trained, and the exercise of police authority obviously brings human rights risks. While the host country retains substantial discretion to set its human rights standards training security personnel, FIFA actively consults the host country. Interviews suggested that due to Qatar's history of hosting international sporting events, its human rights protocols were already relatively good. Still, for the World Cup, Qatar established an independent government entity, called the Safety and Security Operations Committee, devoted exclusively to delivering security operations. Interviews suggested the committee was fully aware of the international scrutiny its conduct will face, and that it is focused on the human rights training of these personnel.

The potential legacy of heightened human rights awareness exists both domestically and internationally. Domestically, Qatar's existing forces may undergo more advanced training, though as of press time it is too early to tell. Internationally, the large international private security companies on which Qatar must rely will be required to abide by SC standards and Qatari law during the World Cup. These standards will likely be higher than in many of the countries in which these companies operate. To the extent those companies leave Qatar with even an awareness of the potential to operate their companies by higher human rights standards, a legacy of human rights norms exists.

No one is naïve about the human rights risks inherent in World Cup security or about the potential of one event to upend what is globally a notoriously abusive business. Still, opportunities for progress also exist and observers should look at these issues carefully.

Qatar's labor reforms may also be creating a labor rights legacy beyond Qatar. As one example, Building Responsibly is a global group of engineering and construction companies collaborating to raise global standards for the treatment of workers. The organization launched in 2017 and, according to interviews, was influenced heavily by the work in Qatar in anticipation of the World Cup. Indeed, Building Responsibly developed its own Worker Welfare Principles that mirror the SC's WWS in a number of respects, focusing on recruitment, freedom to change employment, workplace health and safety, living conditions, access to documentation and unrestricted mobility, wage and benefits, worker representation, and the availability of grievance mechanisms.[233] Members, signatories, and supporters now include major multinational corporations from around the world. It may be credibly said that the Qatar World Cup accelerated the formation of this organization and their standards.

Labor rights have not turned out to be Qatar's only export. Qatar's election as 2022 FIFA Men's World Cup host, the ensuing scrutiny, and the resolution of the dispute with the OECD National Contact Point quickened FIFA's human rights awareness.[234] FIFA hired John Ruggie, principal author of the UNGPs, to evaluate FIFA's policies and practices. The ensuing report, "For the Game. For the World. FIFA and Human Rights," included a number of recommendations.[235] Based on the report, FIFA adopted a human rights policy in May 2017 that commits to respecting human rights in accordance with the UNGPs. So too did FIFA overhaul its bidding process.

That new process was apparent in the bids for the 2026 Men's World Cup. The 2026 World Cup was the first bidding process after FIFA integrated the UNGPs into the bid documents[236] and made compliance with them required for both contractual partners as well as parties in the supply chain.[237] Key principles of FIFA's reformed bidding process include commitments to human rights and sustainability as well as transparency. Transparency informs accountability, which in turn holds FIFA answerable to its commitments. With regard to transparency, the whole bidding process was open to the public.[238] On its website, FIFA published the Bid Books, hosting requirements, and subsequent reports, making them readily accessible for all interested parties. This transparency extends to FIFA's evaluation reports for each bid, and for the first time an independent audit company evaluated the bidding process.

What now is the path ahead? There is no question that Qatar has implemented a remarkable set of reforms. A legacy, by definition, endures for several years beyond the mega event. As this book goes to press, the looming questions are whether Qatar can adequately implement these reforms, and whether that implementation endures significantly beyond the event. The ILO's commitment to remain present in Qatar beyond the World Cup bodes well. Similarly, as Qatar continues its tradition of hosting sporting events, civil society organizations will remain on the watch. A number of organizations are now, and will likely in the future, publish reports on the work that remains to be done.

The first is the SC itself, which provides Workers' Welfare Progress Reports. The most recent as of press time noted the need for stronger audits of corporate compliance, and observed that contractors still need assistance in implementing new policies for recruitment fees, life insurance, minimum wage, and annual air ticket allowance.[239] Concerning worker engagement and empowerment, the report noted ongoing progress in raising workers' awareness of their rights. The report also described the SC's future objectives of integrating the existing framework into new sectors and projects, improving worker empowerment and remuneration, and additional health and safety training.[240]

The SC also issues co-authored reviews with BWI. The two organizations formed a Joint Working Group (JWG) in 2016 focusing on workers' rights. The JWG publishes a yearly overview of the inspections at construction sites and accommodation sites to monitor progress and identify areas for growth.[241] As of press time, the most recent report focused both on construction sites and accommodations. The construction sites needed training to create a proactive—rather than the current reactive—medical clinic operation, further training in topics related to occupational health hazards, more expansive signage around sites in languages native to the migrant workers, and more engagement with senior site management during the JWG inspections. The main challenges concerning accommodation sites were a need for more dining and restroom facilities, a need for more cool rooms, and the presence of black mold on sites.[242] Of note, Education City Stadium was the only site that had a number of unresolved noncompliances or observations. The report attributes this to a "rapid increase in workforce" in a short period of time.[243] For this reason, the JWG conducted two follow-up inspections at Education City Stadium, after which the noncompliances and observations were reported as "Addressed by the Contractor."[244]

Yet another source of ongoing evaluation is the reports issued by Impactt, an ethical trade consultancy that the SC retained to serve as an external labor rights auditor.[245] Impactt is strongly committed to the principle of a labor rights legacy but, as an auditor, is constructively critical in identifying remaining steps to be taken. Impactt's most recent report focuses on five identified areas of concern. The first is ethical recruitment, where Impactt finds a lack of adequate policies to check for whether recruitment fees were paid and to verify receipts and reimbursement.[246] Wages, the second area of concern, have increased steadily due to the national temporary minimum wage that eventually became codified as a nondiscriminatory minimum wage.

However, the full effect of the minimum wage has not yet been realized because of the recency of its implementation. Additionally, while compliance overall is at 78 percent, there remain some challenges with timely and accurate payment.[247] With respect to the third area, working areas, the Impactt observes that security contractors (or construction contractors with a small security team) had lower compliance scores compared to purely construction contractors regarding working hours. However, there was an overall increase in working hour compliance across audited contractors.[248] On worker health and safety, the percentage of workers feeling safe at work has increased from 70 percent in 2018 to 98 percent in 2020, there were no critical issues raised in this safety in 2020, and workers at SC sites reported higher safety standards than those working at non-SC sites.[249] Finally, regarding health, access to mental health resources, and payment for medical fees, as workers are not aware of procedures that exist for reimbursement of medical fees.[250]

One remaining source of ongoing evaluation is Amnesty International, author of one of the early reports exposing Qatar's labor challenges. Amnesty's most recent evaluation, titled "Reality Check 2020: Countdown to the 2022 World Cup," acknowledges a variety of notable legislative changes, including the Domestic Workers Law, the Labor Committees, the state support funds to address nonpayment of wages, the nondiscriminatory minimum wage, repealing the No-Objection Certificate, and the ratification of the International Covenant on Civil and Political Rights (ICCPR) and the International Covenant on Economic, Social and Cultural Rights (ICESCR).[251] However, they find that some of the concerning labor practices continue due to poor enforcement mechanisms, threats of employer retaliation, and loopholes. The two main retaliatory measures that employers are turning to in order to continue their labor practices are: reporting (or threatening to report) employees as absconding—which comes with criminal consequences for the workers that could result in arrest or deportation, and passport confiscation. Two areas of particular note in the Amnesty report were the failure to adequately address pay grievances and the remaining prohibition on the workers' right to organize. With respect to pay grievances, although 588 companies (according to the ILO) were blocked from accessing government services because of wage violations, the government often failed to take effective remedial action on behalf of the workers. The Wage Protection System has made significant progress in detecting and confirming wage violations, but little progress in remedying these issues. One such remedy is the Workers' Support and Insurance Fund, which pays successful claimants who take their grievances to the Labor Committees and leaves the government to recover those costs from the employer. However, the Amnesty report noted that this fund has been operational for less than a year; at present it lacks transparency on workers' eligibility criteria for collecting money from the fund and is underfunded generally.[252] On the right to organize, Qatar ratified the ICCPR and ICESCR, and has worked with the ILO on initiatives to promote workers' voices especially through the WWFs, but migrant workers in Qatar are still prohibited from forming trade unions and freely associating. The Amnesty report notes that this is a "fundamental right" and other initiatives fall short of extending that right to migrant workers.[253] Ultimately, Qatar's reforms require proper implementation, heightened enforcement and monitoring, and potential updates to ensure effectiveness and deter abuses.

Beyond these reports, additional issues include corruption in worker recruitment generally. The work of Professor Rajai Ray Jureidini is especially trenchant on this point.[254] So too will the commentariat pay much attention to the estimates of worker deaths in Qatar generally and on SC projects specifically. The methodologies used to calculate these estimated are hotly disputed, and this report takes no position on the issue. As this book goes to press, investigative journalists are in Qatar. As the tournament approaches, there will surely be no shortage of allegations. Doha, once called "possibly the most boring place on Earth" by *Lonely Planet*,[255] is in 2022 anything but.

The global commentariat must therefore decide: How shall we use Qatar? Which narrative should we construct? To what end is the Qatari experience best put? The world's default position will likely prove to be the affirmation of cynicism; by this account Qatar is just another example of an MSE imperfectly governed. This narrative is lacking both in imagination and in facts. While there have been, and will be, human rights and anti-corruption issues surrounding Qatar 2022, so too is something else there. Qatar is building the first intentional and proactive human rights legacy. To the extent the world wishes to see change in megasports, we must acknowledge, and support, the changes in Qatar. The remaining chapters in this book explore how to build on Qatar's precedent.

Notes

1. Mikhail Reider-Gordon, *Money Laundering, Corruption, and the World Cup: In the Wake of Brazil 2014*, 21 Sw. J. Int'l L. 97, 104 (2014).

2. *In Focus: Labour Reform*, State of Qatar Government Communications Office, https://www.gco.gov.qa/en/focus/labour-reform/.
3. *Shura Council Makes Recommendations on Change of Employer and Expat Worker's Exit*, The Peninsula (Feb. 22, 2021), https://www.thepeninsulaqatar.com/article/22/02/2021/Shura-Council-makes-recommendations-on-change-of-employer-and-expat-worker%E2%80%99s-exit.
4. DLA Piper, Migrant Labour in the Construction Sector in the State of Qatar 2 (Apr. 2014).
5. *Qatar Events of 2020*, Human Rights Watch World Report 2021, https://www.hrw.org/world-report/2021/country-chapters/qatar#b94615.
6. *See, e.g.*, Kristian Coates Ulrichsen, Qatar and the Arab Spring: Policy Drivers and Regional Implications (Sept. 1, 2014) Allen Fromherz, Qatar: A Modern History (2012); Matthew Gray, Qatar: Politics and the Challenges of Development (2013); Mehran Kamrava, Qatar: Small State, Big Politics (2015); David Roberts, Qatar: Securing the Global Ambitions of a City-State (2017)(all cited in Ulrichsen, at 6).
7. Ulrichsen, *supra* note 6, at 17.
8. *Id.* at 18.
9. *Id.* at 19.
10. *Id.* at 21–26.
11. *Id.* at 42.
12. *Qatar Population*, Worldometers, https://www.worldometers.info/world-population/qatar-population/#:~:text=Qatar%202020%20population%20is%20estimated,643%20people%20per%20mi2).
13. *Qatar National Vision 2030*, Qatar General Secretariat for Development Planning, https://www.psa.gov.qa/en/qnv1/Documents/QNV2030_English_v2.pdf (July 2008).
14. Qatar Supreme Committee for Diversity & Legacy, LinkedIn, https://www.linkedin.com/company/supreme-committee-for-delivery-&-legacy/about/.
15. Statistics South Africa, *Mid-year Population Estimates 2010*, Statistical release P0302 (July 20, 2010), at 3, https://www.statssa.gov.za/publications/P0302/P03022010.pdf.
16. *Russia: Total Population 2016 to 2026*, Statista, https://www.statista.com/statistics/263767/total-population-of-russia/.
17. Qatar2022 Supreme Committee, *Qatar 2022 Strategic Plan 2012–2015*, on file with author.
18. World Bank, *Gross National Income Per Capita 2019, Atlas Method and PPP* (Feb. 12, 2021), https://databank.worldbank.org/data/download/GNIPC.pdf.
19. Syed Mansoob Murshed, The Resource Curse (2018).
20. Transparency International, *Corruptions Perception Index*, Transparency.org, https://www.transparency.org/research/cpi.
21. Worldwide Governance Indicators, World Bank, http://info.worldbank.org/governance/wgi/#doc.
22. Neil Ford, *Qatar Punches Above Its Weight*, 343 The Middle East 49 (2004).

23. *See, e.g.*, JOHN J. MEARSHEIMER, THE TRAGEDY OF GREAT POWER POLITICS (updated ed. 2014); ROBERT KEOHANE, AFTER HEGEMONY: COOPERATION AND DISCORD IN THE WORLD POLITICAL ECONOMY (rev. ed. 2005).
24. JOSEPH S. NYE, JR., THE FUTURE OF POWER (reprint ed. 2011).
25. *Id.*
26. KAMRAVA, *supra* note 6, at 93.
27. Hugh Eakin, *The Strange Power of Qatar*, THE NEW YORK REVIEW OF BOOKS, Oct. 27, 2011, at 43–45.
28. Mehran Kamrava, *Multipolarity and Instability in the Middle East*, 62 ORBIS 598, 615–16 (2018).
29. Mohammed Nuruzzaman, *Qatar and the Arab Spring: Down the Foreign Policy Slope*, 8 CONTEMP. ARAB AFFS. 1 (2015).
30. Kristian Coates Ulrichsen, *Perceptions and Divisions in Security and Defense Structures in Arab Gulf States*, *in* DIVIDED GULF: THE ANATOMY OF A CRISIS 29 (Andreas Krieg ed., 2019).
31. *Id.* at 105.
32. ULRICHSEN, *supra* note 6, at 26–27.
33. *Id.* at 27.
34. *Id.* at 26.
35. *Id.* at 28.
36. *Qatar Says State News Agency Hacked After Report Cites Emir Criticising US*, BBC.COM (May 24, 2017), https://www.bbc.com/news/world-middle-east-40026822.
37. Christopher Rossi, *Game of Thrones: The Qatar Crisis, Forced Expulsions on the Arabian Peninsula*, 7 PENN ST. J. L. & INT. AFFS. 1, 4–5 (2019).
38. *Id.* at 9.
39. Steven Wright, *The Political Economy of the Gulf Divide*, *in* DIVIDED GULF: THE ANATOMY OF A CRISIS 152–53 (Andreas Krieg ed., 2019).
40. David B. Roberts, *Understanding Qatar's Foreign Policy Objectives*, 17, MEDITERRANEAN POLITICS 233, 234–35 (2012).
41. GRAY, *supra* note 6, at 161.
42. J. E. Peterson, *Qatar and the World: Branding for a Micro-State*, 60, THE MIDDLE EAST JOURNAL 732, 748 (2006).
43. ROBERTS, *supra* note 6, at 236.
44. Peterson, *supra* note 42, at 748.
45. Kamrava, *supra* note 28, at 116.
46. Nuruzzaman, *supra* note 29.
47. ULRICHSEN, *supra* note 6, at 2.
48. *Id.* at 235.
49. Steven Wright, *Foreign Policies with International Reach: The Case of Qatar*, *in* THE TRANSFORMATION OF THE GULF: POLITICS, ECONOMICS AND THE GLOBAL ORDER 299 (David Held et al. eds., 2011).
50. *Id.*
51. *Id.*
52. Peterson, *supra* note 42, at 733.

53. *Id.* at 741.
54. Ulrichsen, *supra* note 6, at 37.
55. Mujib Mashal, *Afghanistan Peace Talks Open in Qatar, Seeking End to Decades of War*, N.Y. Times (Sept. 12, 2020), https://www.nytimes.com/2020/09/12/world/asia/afghanistan-taliban.html.
56. Louay Bahry, *The New Arab Media Phenomenon: Qatar's Al-Jazeera*, Middle E. Pol'y, 8, 88–89 (2001).
57. Tal Samual-Azran, *Al-Jazeera, Qatar, and New Tactics in State-Sponsored Media Diplomacy*, 57 Am. Behavioral Scientist 1293, 1307 (2013), https://www.researchgate.net/publication/258122794_Al-Jazeera_Qatar_and_New_Tactics_in_State-Sponsored_Media_Diplomacy. *See also* Han Shin, *Al Jazeera as a Qatari Public Diplomacy Tool: Focusing on Egypt During and the Aftermath of the Arab Uprising* (Sept. 15, 2016) (unpublished MSc dissertation, University of London), https://www.academia.edu/36067492/Al_Jazeera_as_a_Qatari_Public_Diplomacy_Tool_Focusing_on_Egypt_During_and_the_Aftermath_of_the_Arab_Uprising.
58. Andreas Krieg, *The Weaponization of Narratives in the Gulf Crisis*, *in* Divided Gulf: The Anatomy of a Crisis 93–94 (Andreas Krieg ed., 2019).
59. *Id.* at 94, 96–97.
60. Ulrichsen, *supra* note 6, at 48–50.
61. David B. Roberts, *The Four Eras of Qatar's Foreign Policy*, 5 Comillas J. Int'l Rels. 1, 7 (2016).
62. Jane Knight, *Education Hubs: A Fad, a Brand, an Innovation?*, 15 J. Stud. Int'l Educ. 221, 231 (2011).
63. *Id.* at 23.
64. *Id.*
65. Ulrichsen, *supra* note 6, at 53.
66. Roberts, *supra* note 61, at 236.
67. Peterson, *supra* note 42, at 747.
68. Paul Michael Brannagan & Richard Giulianotti, *Soft Power and Soft Disempowerment: Qatar, Global Sport and Football's 2022 World Cup finals*, 34 Leisure Studies 703, 704 (2014).
69. Ulrichsen, *supra* note 6, at 3.
70. *Id.* at 60.
71. *Id.* at 58.
72. *Id.* at 60.
73. Peterson, *supra* note 42, at 710.
74. *Id.* at 711.
75. *Id.* at 714.
76. *Id.*
77. *Id.* at 711.
78. *Id.* at 713.
79. *Id.* at 712.
80. *Id.* at 711.
81. Matthew Gray, Qatar: Politics and the Challenges of Development 47–48 (2013).

82. *Id.*
83. *Id.*
84. Supreme Committee, *supra* note 14.
85. Qatar Bid Book, on file with the author.
86. *Id.* at 59
87. *Id. at* 68.
88. *Id.* at 90.
89. *Id.* at 114–118.
90. *Qatar National Development Strategy 2011-2016: Summary of Programmes*, QATAR GENERAL SECRETARIAT FOR DEVELOPMENT PLANNING (2011), https://www.psa.gov.qa/en/nds1/Documents/NDS_ENGLISH_SUMMARY.pdf.
91. *Id.* at 26.
92. *Qatar 2022 Strategic Plan*, *supra* note 17.
93. *Id.* at 42.
94. "Qatar 2022: A framework for Legacy," on file with the author.
95. *Id.* at. 40.
96. International Trade Union Confederation, *About Us*, ITUC-CSI, https://www.ituc-csi.org/about-us.
97. BWI Building and Wood Workers International, *About*, https://www.bwint.org/cms/about-2.
98. International Trade Union Confederation, *Qatar: No World Cup Without Labour Rights*, ITUC-CSI (Nov. 17, 2011), https://www.ituc-csi.org/qatar-no-world-cup-without-labour.
99. *Building a Better World Cup: Protecting Migrant Workers in Qatar Ahead of FIFA 2022*, HUMAN RIGHTS WATCH 1 (June 12, 2012), https://www.hrw.org/report/2012/06/12/building-better-world-cup/protecting-migrant-workers-qatar-ahead-fifa-2022.
100. *Id.*
101. *See id.* at 28.
102. *See generally id.* at 51.
103. *Id.* at 52.
104. *Id.* at 57.
105. *See generally id.* at 61.
106. *Id.* at 41.
107. *Id.* at 66.
108. *Id.* at 68.
109. *See generally id.* at 69.
110. *Id.* at 71.
111. *Id.* at 73.
112. *See generally id.* at 77.
113. *Id.* at 78–79.
114. Qatar Foundation, *About*, QF.ORG.QA, https://www.qf.org.qa/about.
115. Qatar Foundation, QF MANDATORY STANDARDS OF MIGRANT WORKERS' WELFARE FOR CONTRACTORS & SUB-CONTRACTORS (Apr. 20, 2013), https://www.migrant-rights.org/wp-content/uploads/2018/01/QFMandatoryStandards_Rev0_20April20131.pdf.

116. MIGRANT WORKERS WELFARE STANDARDS, MIGRANT-RIGHTS.ORG, (Apr. 2018), https://www.migrant-rights.org/wp-content/uploads/2018/04/MR-Comparison-of-Workers-Welfare-Standards-Qatar.pdf.
117. Qatar Foundation, *Qatar Foundation Implements Welfare Standards to Guarantee Human Rights*, QF.ORG.QA/MEDIA CENTER (Apr. 23, 2013), https://www.qf.org.qa/media-center/qatar-foundation-implements-welfare-standards-to-guarantee-workers-rights.
118. QATAR SUPREME COMMITTEE FOR DELIVERY & LEGACY, WORKERS' WELFARE STANDARDS 2 (2d ed. 2016), https://www.qatar2022.qa/sites/default/files/documents/Workers-Welfare-Standards-Qatar-2022-EN.pdf [hereinafter WORKERS' WELFARE STANDARDS].
119. *Id.* at 12.
120. *Id.* at 11–14.
121. *Id.* at 15–17.
122. Information provided by SC to author.
123. *See supra* note 2 and accompanying text.
124. WORKERS' WELFARE STANDARDS, *supra* note 118, at 39–40.
125. Information provided by SC to author.
126. Qatar2022, WORKERS' WELFARE, https://www.qatar2022.qa/en/opportunities/workers-welfare.
127. *Id.* at 18.
128. *Id.* at 20–21.
129. *Id.* at 22–25.
130. *Id.* at 26–27.
131. *Id.* at 28–29.
132. *Id.* at 30–31.
133. *Id.* at 51–64.
134. *Id.* at 65–67.
135. *Id.* at 68–69.
136. *Id.* at 70–74.
137. *Id.* at 34–36.
138. *Id.* at 37–38.
139. *Id.* at 47–48.
140. *Id.* at 45–46.
141. *Id.* at 49–50.
142. Qatar 2013 Human Rights Report, U.S. Dep't of State, Bureau of Democracy, Human Rights and Labor (2013), https://2009-2017.state.gov/documents/organization/220583.pdf.
143. *Id.* at 1.
144. Pete Pattison, *Revealed: Qatar's Work Cup "Slaves,"* GUARDIAN (Sept. 25, 2013), https://www.theguardian.com/world/2013/sep/25/revealed-qatars-world-cup-slaves.
145. *Qatar: The Dark Side of Migration: Spotlight on Qatar's Construction Sector Ahead of the World Cup, MDE 22/010/2013*, AMNESTY INTERNATIONAL (Nov. 18, 2013), https://www.amnesty.org/en/documents/MDE22/010/2013/en/.

146. *Universal Periodic Review Second Cycle—Qatar*, United Nations Human Rights Council, https://www.ohchr.org/EN/HRBodies/UPR/Pages/QAindex.aspx.
147. François Crépeau (Special Rapporteur on the Human Rights of Migrants), *Addendum: Mission to Qatar*, U.N. Doc. A/HRC/26/35/Add.1 (Apr. 23, 2014), http://undocs.org/A/HRC/26/35/Add.1.
148. DLA Piper, *supra* note 4, at 2.
149. *See generally id.*
150. *See generally id.* at 27–43.
151. *Id.* at 36–42.
152. *Id.* at 43–60.
153. *Id.* 56–59.
154. *See generally id.* at 43–69.
155. *Id.* at 61.
156. *Id.* at 64–68.
157. *See generally id.* at 69–76.
158. *Id.* at 71.
159. *Id.* at 74–75.
160. *See generally id.* at 76–96.
161. *Id.* at 92.
162. *Id.* at 96.
163. *Id.* at 110–13.
164. *See generally id.* at 114–28.
165. *Id.* at 114.
166. *Id.* at 126–27.
167. *See generally id.* at 128–35.
168. *Id.* at 132–34.
169. Complaint alleging non-observance by Qatar of the Forced Labour Convention, 1930 (No. 29), and the Labour Inspection Convention, 1947 (No. 81), made by delegates to the 103rd Session (2014) of the International Labour Conference under Article 26 of the ILO Constitution, International Labour Standards Department, 323rd Session, Mar. 12–27, 2015, 3, GB.323/INS/8(Rev.1) (Mar. 16, 2015), https://www.ilo.org/wcmsp5/groups/public/---ed_norm/---relconf/documents/meetingdocument/wcms_348745.pdf.
170. *Id.* at 4.
171. *Id.*
172. *Id.*
173. *Id.* at 2.
174. Interview with Giovanni Di Cola, Special Adviser, Office of the Deputy Director General ILO, Geneva, Switzerland (Oct. 18, 2018) (notes on file with the author).
175. *Id.*
176. Beryl Ph. ter Haar, *The FIFA 2022 World Cup and Labour Rights—Seizing the Moment for Labour Law Reforms in Qatar*, 5 Kutafin U. L. Rev. 139, 150 (2018).
177. *Id.*
178. Follow-Up to the Decision Adopted by the Governing Body at its 331st Session to Support the Technical Cooperation Programme Agreed Between the Government

of Qatar and the ILO and its Implementation Modalities, International Labour Office, 3334th Session, Oct. 25–Nov. 8, 2018, 1, GB.334/INS/8 (Oct. 24, 2018), https://www.ilo.org/wcmsp5/groups/public/---ed_norm/---relconf/documents/meetingdocument/wcms_647832.pdf.

179. *See Project Office for the State of Qatar*, ILO https://www.ilo.org/wcmsp5/groups/public/---arabstates/---ro-beirut/documents/briefingnote/wcms_648005.pdf; *About Us*, MADLSA, https://www.adlsa.gov.qa/en/site/the-ministry/about-us.
180. *Id.*
181. *See* OECD, OECD Guidelines for Multinational Enterprises: Revision 2000, 12 (2000).
182. *Id.* at 23.
183. *Id.* at 23.
184. *Id.* at 30.
185. *Id.*
186. National Contact Point of Switzerland, Initial Assessment Specific Instance regarding the Fédération Internationale de Football Association (FIFA) submitted by the Building and Wood Workers' International (BWI), 1 (Oct. 13, 2015), https://mneguidelines.oecd.org/database/instances/ch0013.htm.
187. *Id.* at 8.
188. *Id.*
189. *Id.* at 4.
190. *Id.*
191. Interview with Nicolas Hachez, OECD, Paris, France (Oct. 17, 2018) (notes on file with the author).
192. *Id.*
193. *Id.*
194. *Id.* at 3
195. *Id.* at 4.
196. *Id.* at 5.
197. *Id.* at 2.
198. *New State Ice Co. v. Liebmann*, 285 U.S. 262, 311 (1932) (Brandeis, J., dissenting).
199. Giorgio Agamben & Kevin Attell, State of Exception 7 (2005).
200. Supreme Committee for Delivery & Legacy, Workers' Welfare Standards 14 (1st ed. 2014), https://www.sc.qa/workerswelfare [hereinafter WWS 1st ed.].
201. NATLEX-ILO, Qatar: Law No. 1 of 2015 amending certain provisions of the Labour Code promulgated by Act No. 14 of 2004 (2015), https://www.ilo.org/dyn/natlex/natlex4.detail?p_lang=en&p_isn=99861.
202. Supreme Committee for Delivery & Legacy, Workers' Welfare Standards 27 (2d ed. 2018), https://www.sc.qa/workerswelfare [hereinafter WWS 2d ed.].
203. *Annual Progress Report on the Technical Cooperation Programme Agreed Between the Government of Qatar and the ILO*, International Labour Office 1–2 (Oct. 7, 2019), https://www.ilo.org/wcmsp5/groups/public/---ed_norm/---relconf/documents/meetingdocument/wcms_723203.pdf.
204. *Progress Report on the Technical Cooperation Programme Agreed Between the Government of Qatar and the ILO*, International Labour Office 3 (Oct. 9, 2020),

https://www.ilo.org/wcmsp5/groups/public/---ed_norm/---relconf/documents/meetingdocument/wcms_757599.pdf.

205. WWS 1st ed., *supra* note 200, at 27–39.
206. Gulf Labor Markets, Migration, & population Programme, Qatar: Ministerial Decision No. 18 of 2014 Setting the Conditions and Specifications for Workers' Accommodations (Nov. 5, 2014), https://gulfmigration.org/qatar-ministerial-decision-no-18-of-2014setting-the-conditions-and-specifications-for-workers-accommodations/.
207. WWS 2d ed., *supra* note 202, at 51–64.
208. International Labour Office, *supra* note 1, at 4.
209. International Labour Office, *supra* note 2, at 2–8.
210. International Labour Office, *supra* note 3, at 8–11.
211. *Id.* at 7.
212. *Id.* paras. 38–45.
213. All information on these corporate practices was provided by the Supreme Committee and is on file with the author.
214. Edward W. Said, Orientalism (1979).
215. Kate Youd, *The Winter's Tale of Corruption: The 2022 FIFA World Cup in Qatar, the Impending Shift to Winter, and Potential Legal Actions against FIFA*, 35 Nw. J. Int'l L. & Bus. 167, 169 (2014).
216. Bruce W. Bean, *An Interim Essay on FIFA's World Cup of Corruption: The Desperate Need for International Corporate Governance Standards at FIFA*, 22 ILSA J. Int'l & CompAR. L. 367, 371 (2016).
217. *Id.* at 377.
218. *Id.*
219. *Id.* at 378.
220. *Qatari World Cup Bidders in $1m Offer to Fund Stars' Gala*, Sunday Times (Nov. 18, 2012), https://www.thetimes.co.uk/article/qatari-world-cup-bidders-in-dollar1m-offer-to-fund-stars-gala-ldsh7qn7vmk.
221. *Garcia Report*, at 6.
222. Aaron Gordon, *What FIFA Whitewashed from the Garcia Report*, Vice (June 28, 2017), https://www.vice.com/en/article/padejn/what-fifa-whitewashed-from-the-garcia-report.
223. Ben Rumsby, *Garcia Report Q&A: What Are the Findings and What Do They Mean for Russia 2018 and Qatar 2022?*, The Telegraph (June 27, 2017), https://www.telegraph.co.uk/football/2017/06/27/garcia-report-qa-findings-do-mean-russia-2018-qatar-2022/.
224. *Id.*
225. *See generally id.*
226. *Id.*
227. *Id.* at 247.
228. *See generally id.* at 230–49.
229. *Rise and Fall of Mohamed Bin Hammam—Timeline*, The Guardian (June 1, 2014) https://www.theguardian.com/football/2014/jun/01/mohamed-bin-hammam-timeline.

230. David Conn, *Fifa Trial Leaves Questions over 2022 Qatar World Cup*, GUARDIAN (Dec. 23, 2017), https://www.theguardian.com/football/2017/dec/23/fifa-trial-questions-2022-qatar-world-cup.
231. Indictment, *United States v. Full Play Group, et al.*, No. 15-CR-252, para. 92 (E.D.N.Y. 2020).
232. *Indictment, supra* note 12.
233. *Worker Welfare Principles*, BUILDING RESPONSIBLY, https://www.building-responsibly.org/worker-welfare-principles.
234. *See, e.g.*, A. Duval & D. Heerdt, *FIFA and Human Rights—A Research Agenda* 25 TILBURG L. REV. 1 (2020), http://doi.org/10.5334/tilr.189.
235. *See* JOHN G. RUGGIE, HARVARD UNIV. CORPORATE RESPONSIBILITY INITIATIVE, FOR THE GAME. FOR THE WORLD, FIFA AND HUMAN RIGHTS 8–9 (2016), https://www.hks.harvard.edu/sites/default/files/Ruggie_humanrightsFIFA_ reportApril2016.pdf.
236. *Id.*
237. *See FIFA Executive Committee Sets Presidential Election for 26 February 2016 and Fully Supports Roadmap for Report*, FIFA (July 20, 2015), http://www.fifa.com/about-fifa/news/y=2015/m=7/news=fifa-executive-committee-sets-presidential-electionfor-26-february-2–666448.html.
238. FIFA, GUIDE TO THE BIDDING PROCESS FOR THE 2026 FIFA WORLD CUP 5, https://img.fifa.com/image/upload/hgopypqftviladnm7q90.pdf.
239. *Id.* at 24–25.
240. *Id.* at 54–55.
241. THE SUPREME COMMITTEE FOR DELIVERY AND LEGACY AND BUILDING AND WOOD WORKERS' INTERNATIONAL, JOINT WORKING GROUP 2019 REPORT 10 (Mar. 3, 2020), https://www.qatar2022.qa/sites/default/files/SC-Building-and-Wood-Workers'-International-Report-2019.pdf.
242. *Id.* at 19.
243. *Id.* at 10.
244. *Id.* at 33.
245. IMPACTT, ANNUAL EXTERNAL COMPLIANCE REPORT OF THE SUPREME COMMITTEE FOR DELIVERY AND LEGACY'S WORKERS' WELFARE STANDARDS Page (Feb. 2020), https://impacttlimited.com/wp-content/uploads/2020/07/IMPA09-2020-Qatar-Annual-Report-v12-Digital.pdf.
246. *Id.* at 6–7.
247. *Id.* at 7.
248. *Id.* at 7–8.
249. *Id.* at 40–41.
250. *Id.* at 41.
251. REALITY CHECK 2020: COUNTDOWN TO THE 2022 WORLD CUP, AMNESTY INTERNATIONAL (Nov. 2020), https://www.amnesty.org/download/Documents/MDE2232972020ENGLISH.PDF.
252. *Id.*

253. *Id.* at 25–26.
254. *See, e.g.*, "Transnational Culture of Corruption in Migrant Labour Recruitment," report of the International Organization for Migration, https://migrationnetwork.un.org/resources/transnational-culture-corruption-migrant-labour-recruitment.
255. ULRICHSEN, *supra* note 6, at 3.

6

A Latent Legacy: France

Introduction

In the evolution of the idea that megasports can leave a human rights and anti-corruption legacy, France is a key player for two reasons. As this chapter will explain in detail, the country presents an exceptionally promising opportunity to leave a proactive, intentional, and two-dimensional legacy. Globalized anti-corruption and human rights reforms intersected in France with the hosting of a mega sporting event about as dramatically as one could imagine. And yet, as of press time, stakeholders to the Paris 2024 Summer Olympics largely seem not to have noticed. France thus illustrates what we might achieve, and yet at the same time underscores what remains to be done if we are to achieve it.

France's opportunity lies in the unprecedented confluence of four distinct events in a single year: 2017. First, France adopted a landmark anti-corruption law, called Sapin II, requiring large French companies to adopt anti-corruption compliance programs. Though previously thought something of an anti-corruption laggard relative to the United Kingdom, Germany, and other European peers, Sapin II is an innovative anti-corruption statute that positions France as something of a global anti-corruption thought leader.

Second, that same year, France adopted a similarly pathbreaking law imposing human rights obligations on corporations. In contrast to the anti-corruption arena, France has a proud human rights heritage dating back more than two hundred years. Building on that heritage, the new Duty of Vigilance Law requires larger French companies to identify and prevent human rights and environmental impacts companies among themselves, the companies they control, and their subcontractors and suppliers. The Duty of Vigilance Law places France at the very forefront of the movement to make companies more cognizant of the human rights risks in their global business practices.

As prior chapters explained, the year the Duty of Vigilance Law and Sapin II took effect is also the year the International Olympic Committee (IOC) awarded France the rights to host the 2024 Summer Olympics. This was the

A New Megasport Legacy. Andrew Brady Spalding, Oxford University Press. © Oxford University Press 2022.
DOI: 10.1093/oso/9780197503614.003.0006

third major event of 2017. And as Chapter 8 will explain in much greater detail, 2017 was likewise the same year of a fourth remarkable event: the IOC introduced the new anti-corruption and human rights provisions into the host-city contract. Thus a country already immersed in a domestic anti-corruption and human rights movement would be tasked with designing the original precedent for operationalizing the new host-city contract provisions.

This is a human rights and anti-corruption legacy opportunity if ever there were. The megasport came to France at precisely the moment the country needed to implement its new laws. The laws included both anti-corruption and human rights dimensions. There had not yet been a major anti-corruption or human rights scandal, raising the possibility of a proactive rather than reactive legacy. It might even be fitting that the country which gave birth to modern megasports in the late nineteenth century could now create the first complete anti-corruption and human rights legacy. The only remaining piece, of course, is intentionality: megasport organizers, or other stakeholders, would need to recognize, as Qatar did, the opportunity to create a legacy and formulate an intention to build it.

That intention seems not to have formed. A research grant from the IOC's Olympic Studies Centre financed multiple in-person interviews conducted over two years. Those interviews illustrated a commitment among many to adopt meaningful preventative anti-corruption and human rights measures. These efforts should be lauded. So too may these efforts leave an accidental legacy—lasting impacts on norms, policies, and practices that no one intended but that nonetheless occurred. But through no fault of those stakeholders, the notion that these preventative measures could leave a legacy—that Paris, and France, could have a lasting, positive anti-corruption and human rights impact as a direct result of the event, and that we could reasonably say describe Paris and France as stronger, not weaker, because they hosted the Olympics—had not yet taken hold. The broader patterns captured in this book, and the opportunities they create, are not yet integrated into our megasport discourse, policies, and expectations.

In the context of past legacies, Brazil and South Korea intimate a possibility, which Qatar moves forward. But France illustrates both the opportunities that will arise and the work that needs to be done if the megasport movement can fully leverage these events to create legacies.

The following section details the extent of the reforms France adopted at the moment it won the rights to host the 2024 Games. The chapter then explores a variety of policies that relevant French organizations have adopted or, as the case may be, not adopted, and their legacy implications. The chapter concludes with reflections on the juxtaposition of France and Qatar and what it means for the development of the human rights and anti-corruption legacy.

France's Anti-Corruption and Human Rights Moment

France emerged in 2017 as a global anti-corruption and human rights reform hot spot. At least in the human rights space, this was not surprising. Since the 1789 Declaration of the Rights of Man, France has been widely associated with the notion that governments had human rights obligations. But in 2017, France brought its human rights leadership to a new domain: the obligations of business.

France's roots as a global human rights leader extend back to the Declaration of the Rights of Man and of the Citizen, written at the peak of the revolution in 1789.[1] The basic idea of the document is encapsulated in its First Article that all "men are born and remain free and equal in rights."[2] These rights included the principle of personal liberty, inviolability of the person, resistance to oppression, equality before the law, and freedom of religion and speech.[3] While it was written in the same years as the US Bill of Rights, the Declaration had the added moral credibility of not tacitly condoning slavery.[4]

However, the full legal impact of this document would not be felt until quite recently. Though the French constitution did not historically allow oversight of legislative decisions with regard to human rights, this changed as late as 1971 when the French Constitutional Council in a landmark decision established the principle of the "constitutional block."[5] This principle enables the Constitutional Council to vacate any law violating the French constitution itself or the Declaration of the Rights of Man and of the Citizen, the preambles of the constitution of 1946, and the Charter of the Environment of 2004.[6] The preambles of the constitution of 1946 includes social rights, such as the equality of men and women.[7] France has ratified both human rights conventions discussed in Chapter 2. Other notable human rights treaties ratified or ascended to by France include the International Convention on the Elimination of All Forms of Racial Discrimination; the Convention on the Elimination of All Forms of Discrimination against Women and its optional protocol; the Convention on the Rights of the Child and its amendment; and the Convention on the Rights of Persons with Disabilities and its optional protocol.[8] Notably, France, like most other developed countries, has not signed or ratified the Convention on the Right of Migrant Workers. France has also ratified or signed conventions relating to refugees. These include the Convention Relating to the Status of Refugees and its protocol, and the Convention Relating to the Status of Stateless Persons.[9] Lastly, France is a member of the International Labour Organization, which provides further human rights related obligations. As a member state, the International Labour Organization Declaration on Fundamental Principles and Rights at Work is binding upon France.[10] France also adheres to the European Convention on Human Rights.[11]

With the government's obligation to protect human rights thus firmly embedded, the extension of similar obligations to corporations would take place following a catalyzing event in 2013. A poorly constructed complex of garment factories in Bangladesh collapsed, killing over a thousand people and injuring thousands more.[12] Western retailers were profiting from the factories concerned, including big French retailers such as Auchan and Carrefour.[13] Human rights groups, as well as the general public, in France demanded better supply chain management regarding human rights. The French legislature responded with the Duty of Vigilance Law.

The Duty of Vigilance law requires the following:

> [A]ny company that employs, for a period of two consecutive financial years, at least five thousand employees itself and in its direct or indirect subsidiaries whose registered office is located within French territory, or at least ten thousand employees itself and in its direct or indirect subsidiaries whose registered office is located within French territory or abroad, shall establish and implement a vigilance plan in an effective manner.[14]

The law applies only to the largest French companies. Parent companies must comply with the law if their number of employees exceeds five thousand, including direct or indirect subsidiaries with a registered office in France, for a period of two consecutive fiscal years. Furthermore, parent companies must comply with the law if their number of employees exceeds ten thousand, including direct or indirect subsidiaries with a registered office in France or abroad, for a period of two consecutive fiscal years. For a group of companies, the relevant procedure is counting the employees individually for each company and then checking if any exemptions exist. An exemption is in place for companies that are controlled by another company which already satisfies the requirements of the law.[15] After an interpretation by the Constitutional Council, the law is only applicable if a parent company is registered in France.[16] The explanatory memorandum to the law explicitly references the UN Guiding Principles on Business and Human Rights as one of the reasons the law was drafted and these principles are broadly construing the scope of business obligations.[17]

Any company subject to the law must establish, implement, and publish a vigilance plan. The plan must "identify the risks and prevent severe impacts on human rights and fundamental freedoms, health and safety of persons and on the environment."[18] The vigilance plan of a company must include more than just the company itself. It must include all activities of the "companies that it controls . . . as well as the activities of subcontractors or suppliers with whom they have an established commercial relationship, when these activities are related to this relationship."[19] Supplying can potentially be interpreted as "any provision of goods and services to a company by operators," which would significantly increase the scope of the law.[20] Accordingly, a vigilance plan should include the parent company, the controlled companies, and subcontractors and suppliers of both the parent and the controlled entities.

The law does not provide a definite, exhaustive list of covered human rights. The French legislature and government purposefully rejected including a list because the international conventions ratified by France are sufficiently precise to establish the legal norms.[21] Moreover, the evolving nature of human rights can better be captured without referencing an exhaustive list. However, the preparatory work mentions the International Bill of Rights, the Preamble of the French Constitution of 1946, and the European Convention for the Protection of Human Rights and Fundamental Freedoms.[22] Furthermore, the French legislature in its preparatory work mentioned the inclusion of first-generation rights, referencing political rights, second-generation rights, meaning social, economic, and cultural rights, and third-generation rights, such as environmental rights.

Vigilance plans are different from traditional risk assessments. Where traditional compliance measures involve risks for the company, the vigilance plan focuses on the rights of individuals. Thus, a company must consider all possible impacts on individuals rather than any risks to itself. The vigilance plan must be dynamic, process-based on specific instances, and tailored to the affected individuals.[23] A vigilance plan must have five components: (1) risk mapping, (2) processes for a regular assessment, (3) tailored measures to prevent severe impacts, (4) an alert mechanism established with trade unions, and (5) an implementation monitoring system.[24]

A comparison to other countries' corporate human rights statutes in place in 2017 underscores the cutting-edge character of the Duty of Vigilance law. The Modern Slavery Act of the United Kingdom requires companies with an annual turnover of more than £36 million to publish a slavery and human trafficking statement.[25] A company can either choose to report the steps taken to prevent slavery and human trafficking in its supply chain or report that no steps were taken. There are no penalties or fines for a lack of due diligence. The government of the United Kingdom presumes that the public and nongovernmental organizations will pressure companies to implement due diligence plans. Similarly, the California Transparency in Supply Chains Act requires a company with annual worldwide gross receipts of over US$100 million to disclose the steps taken to prevent human trafficking and slavery in its supply chain.[26] If there were no steps taken, there is no responsibility to report anything. The Duty of Vigilance Law is different from the laws in the United Kingdom and California because it requires that companies have due diligence plans.

Following enactment of the Duty of Vigilance, other countries followed France's lead. In 2020, the Dutch Senate voted to adopt the Child Labour Due Diligence Bill to combat child labor in global supply chains. This law is similar to France's Duty of Vigilance Law, in that companies must determine whether child labor occurs in their supply chains and, if so, establish a plan of action to address this, as well as a statement on their investigation and plan of action.[27] However, it only covers child labor and not human rights violations in their entirety.[28] Switzerland took up legislation on the same issue. In 2019, Switzerland's Council of States voted to adopt a government proposal that was limited to reporting, and issue-specific due diligence, without liability rules. Switzerland's due diligence law has been criticized for not having adequate provisions that would give the law enforceability, nor provisions that properly hold corporations accountable.[29] Also in 2020, the European Commission announced it would develop legislation requiring EU companies to carry out environmental and human rights due diligence.[30]

France is thus clearly on the front end of a burgeoning movement to bring human rights obligations to the private sector. So too does it have leading ideas in the anti-corruption space, though it took some time to get there. France has typically been viewed as an anti-corruption laggard in both enforcement and compliance,[31] as reflected in nonenforcement of prior French anti-corruption legislation.[32] Some commentators observe that the French have traditionally tolerated corruption, particularly in the political sphere, if it meant that political ends were being accomplished.[33] Corruption has been found outside politics as well, including business. The GAN French Corruption Report highlighted corruption as a particular problem in public procurement and when "business and politics overlap."[34] GAN also reported that illegal political funding was common in many French politicians' careers.[35] The public historically viewed corruption and bribery in politics as tolerable so long as the politician is acting on behalf of their interests.[36] Many companies admit to taking kickbacks.[37] Previous to Sapin II, corporate compliance and corporate anti-bribery rules were a "nonobject" in French criminal law.[38] The OECD Working Group was "seriously concerned" with the number of foreign bribery proceedings in France.[39]

However, several recent scandals illustrate the public's recent shift in perspective. Jacques Chirac, France's president from 1995 to 2007,[40] and Nicolas Sarkozy, France's president from 2007 to 2012,[41] have faced corruption charges. The prosecutor leading Chirac's case, Eric Halphen, discussed the problem of corruption in politics lay partly with French voters, who accept this behavior if their interests are pursued.[42] The pushback against corrupt practices in politics appears to have begun with Sarkozy as his "political ends" did not always align with French voters.[43] The French did not agree with Sarkozy's policies in Libya and, thus, may have been less tolerant of his behavior.[44] This lack of tolerance was demonstrated in the past year when Francis Fillon, a presidential candidate, dropped out from the race after facing several corruption scandals, including giving his wife an apparently sham position as an administrator and funneling 900,000 euros into her private bank account.[45] Recent surveys also illustrate that the French are rejecting corruption in favor of more transparency from their government.[46]

The primary catalyst for Sapin II was the US Department of Justice's (DOJ's) enforcement of the Foreign Corrupt Practices Act (FCPA) against several French companies, which the French viewed as harsh and overreaching.[47] Four corporations, including Alcatel-Lucent, Alstom, Technip and Total, have entered deferred prosecution agreements with the DOJ.[48] At one point in time, each of these settlements landed in the top ten largest FCPA settlements.[49] These agreements coupled with criticism from groups such as the OECD and Transparency International pushed the French legislature to enact Sapin II.[50] There is a perception that fines from a French enforcement agency are more palatable than fines imposed by the DOJ.[51]

In December of 2016, France passed Sapin II, which went into effect in June of 2017.[52] The requirements of Sapin II are laid out in the text of the law and clarified through guidelines released by AFA, a national government service.[53] The guidelines are not binding but provide companies and public sector organizations guidance on how to comply effectively.[54] Most importantly, Sapin II places requirements on those in both the public and private sector to implement compliance programs aimed at preventing corruption.[55] Those covered include:

> Companies headquartered in France that employ over 500 employees and have an annual revenue of at least [100 million euros] or, companies belonging to a group headquartered in France that employ over 500 employees and a consolidated annual revenue of at least [100 million euros]. In the case of a group, the parent company must implement a compliance program in all its subsidiaries (including their foreign subsidiaries). Conversely, subsidiaries whose parent company has a Sapin II compliance program are deemed to comply with Sapin II.[56]

Failure to implement offense could lead to a maximum of two years of imprisonment and/or a fine of 50,000 euros.[57] Moreover, the law applies to all public entities.[58]

Though seemingly straightforward, this requirement that companies adopt anti-corruption compliance programs is actually quite novel. While the United States and the United Kingdom are widely perceived as global leaders in the anti-corruption compliance movement, few realize that neither country requires companies to adopt compliance programs. That is, failure to adopt a compliance program is not itself punishable in either the United States or the United Kingdom. Rather, both jurisdictions provide various kinds of rewards in the course of a corruption investigation, but neither actually requires a compliance program.[59] With Sapin II, France became the first major country to do so, thrusting itself into the forefront of anti-corruption policy debates.

To help implement the newly required compliance programs, Sapin II established the Agence Française Anticorruption (AFA).[60] Notably, AFA is not a criminal prosecutor. Rather, AFA is a dedicated anti-corruption compliance regulator. AFA's responsibilities include helping both the private and public sector to prevent and detect corruption, reviewing companies' compliance programs, reporting potential violations to prosecutors, and overseeing company monitorships.[61] It is subject to the French Ministry of Justice and the Minister for the Budget and will be led by a judge who will serve a six-year term.[62] Its enforcement powers include conducting off- and on-site reviews of company procedures required under Sapin II.[63] AFA has compliance and assistance missions and control missions,[64] comprised of both the Sanctions Committee and a Strategic Council.[65] The Sanctions Committee imposes injunctions and penalties on noncompliant companies, while the Strategic Council works with investigations and helps corporations implement compliance programs.[66] The agency has authority over private sector companies, subject to the limits discussed earlier, and all public sector entities, including state administrative and local agencies and public hospitals.[67] This too represents an innovation, as neither the United States nor the United Kingdom has dedicated compliance agencies; for both countries, the criminal prosecutors double as compliance regulators. Again, in this respect, Sapin II brings new ideas to global anti-corruption discussions.

Sapin II lists what is required of both private companies and the public sector. They must implement a compliance program, which are mandated to include the following: code of conduct, internal whistleblower system, risk mapping for risk of bribery, assessments of clients based on risk mapping, accounting controls to prevent bribery and influence peddling, training for managers and employees on bribery and influence peddling, disciplinary actions for breaking the code of conduct, and control procedures to ensure the program is working effectively.[68] The guidelines provide direction on how companies and governments can effectively establish these requirements.[69]

The sanctions associated with not implementing the law's requirements are discretionary but are capped at 1 million euros for legal entities and 200,000 euros for individuals.[70] These sanctions are administrative in nature and modest in size.[71] If AFA decides not to sanction the organization for any violations, it can request the company to take steps to comply.[72] To date, AFA's actions have been more educative than punitive, helping companies to implement best practices rather than punishing them for failure to do so.

Among the most culturally radical features of Sapin II are those concerning enforcement. Breaking from traditional French law enforcement, Sapin II established a process for deferred prosecution agreements similar to the Brazilian Leniency Agreement called the Judicial Agreement in the Public Interest (CJIP).[73] CJIPs are available to French legal persons who are suspected to have committed an act of corruption.[74] In the settlement, the company may be required to acknowledge the facts and their legal consequences.[75] Although not considered an admission of guilt, it may have a similar effect.[76] CJIPs must be approved by a judge and must specify the specific requirements of the company, which can include fines as well as oversight of the AFA in implementing changes to its compliance code.[77] CJIPs represent a change in French criminal prosecution culture.[78] Previously, France's federal prosecutor had conducted long investigations rather than using an expedited process.[79] CJIPs encourage cooperation among the companies, the federal prosecutor, and other authorities.[80] Still, the stripped-down judicial process raises just concerns for many observers. Sapin II is pushing the cultural envelope.

After a series of minor enforcement actions, France's defining post–Sapin II enforcement action was against Airbus. The case symbolized the advent of a new season of anti-corruption enforcement as well as France's arrival on the global enforcement scene. Airbus agreed to a €3.6 billion settlement. This settlement was unique in that it was the first settlement between a company and three countries. Airbus entered into a settlement with French, UK, and US prosecutors, having to pay €2.1 billion, €1 billion, and €530 million, respectively.[81] Airbus was found guilty of more than a decade of corruption involving bribes, fraudulent contracts, fake invoices, and the use of code names by executives to cover up discussions of illicit payments. Executives were found to have been using medication names, dosage amounts, and famous art as code names in emails. One commentator noted, "France's role in the Airbus settlement signaled a new phase for the country on a global stage."[82]

With these reforms, France had entered a new phase of corporate accountability for corruption and for human rights abuses. The globalized anti-corruption and human rights standards described in Chapters 1 and 2 descended on France quite forcefully. But have the preparations for the 2024 Olympics seized upon this opportunity? Perhaps not as much as one might hope.

Olympics as Accelerator?

After three failed attempts over the previous twenty-five years—1992, 2008, and 2012—Paris finally won the rights to host the 2024 Summer Olympics.[83] Awarded in 2017, and with new host-city contract anti-corruption and human rights obligations in place, Paris seemed to present the perfect confluence of events for building a proactive, intentional, and two-dimensional legacy. The country had two new laws, with substantial public support, waiting to be implemented.

But interviews with stakeholders suggested that an intention to build a human rights and anti-corruption legacy simply had not taken root. No one expected it, and no one knew even to imagine it. The concept was not yet embedded in IOC policy or the public's consciousness. Of course, the Paris bid was prepared and submitted before these laws took effect. We would not expect the bid documents to make reference to a human rights or anti-corruption legacy. Indeed, they don't. The Paris candidature file emphasizes environmental legacy (framed as "sustainability," a most ambiguous and problematic word in megasport governance, as Chapter 8 will explain). Another, and more closely related, theme is social inclusion, meaning inclusion in economy and in the cultural life of the city.[84] But the documents pay scant attention to anti-corruption and human rights preventative measures, let alone legacy.

We might therefore look to policy statements or new initiatives adopted by any of the key host-country players. As Chapters 8 and 9 will explain further, these include the National Olympic Committee (NOC), the host city, the national government, and the Organizing Committee. Each of these entities could conceivably adopt reforms that would eventually become legacies.

Starting with the NOC, multiple interviews revealed that the entity does not view the Olympics as a catalyst and is in fact not adopting any new policies at this time. The host city municipality—the City of Paris—has not yet announced any new initiatives. However, multiple sources suggested that the city was exploring ways to use the Olympics as a lever to improve their anti-corruption compliance system. These interviews further suggested the city may actually exceed the provisions of Sapin II and adopt stronger measures than the law requires. Though yet to be seen, if the city were to do so it would in fact constitute a significant anti-corruption legacy.

The national government has produced two Olympics-related anti-corruption initiatives. Though neither is framed in terms of legacy, both could and likely will leave accidental legacies. Shortly after its creation, AFA was tasked with drafting a "National Multi-Year Plan to Fight Corruption."[85] Immediately following sections on anti-corruption in all ministries, and in local governments, the plan notably contains a section entitled "Promoting integrity in sport organizations and events." That section articulates meaningful goals concerning the Olympics, but then applies those same goals to other events and organizations.[86] To the extent the Olympics accelerated the implementation of new norms, practices, or policies in organizations that will operate after the 2024 Games are over, they become a legacy. Similarly, AFA's 2020 annual report explains that, consistent with its mission to help companies build compliance programs, AFA has conducted nonpunitive audits of over twenty entities engaged in Olympics preparations.[87] These audits have the effect of strengthening these entities' compliance programs. To the extent those enhancements remain in place after the Olympics, they too become legacy. While AFA has not framed these initiatives with an explicit intention to leave an anti-corruption legacy, they can nonetheless constitute what this book calls an accidental legacy.

Similarly, the Paris 2024 Organizing Committee for the Olympic Games (OCOG) is, with the help of AFA, adopting preventative measures that are likely to produce accidental legacies. The OCOG and its closely related Olympic Venue Delivery Authority (SOLIDEO) would not normally fall under Sapin II: the OCOG is an association, a hybrid between a private and public firm, and SOLIDEO is a private corporation that will not reach five hundred employees.[88] However, France's the Olympic laws placed both of these organizations under Sapin II and AFA's inspection authority.[89]

The OCOG's executive board, which includes a representative from AFA, has adopted the Paris 2024 Code of Ethics (sometimes called the Ethics Charter).[90] The Code is made up of eighteen articles that apply to members, employees, and volunteers. It protects individual rights and forbids harassment abuse and discrimination, as well as corruption, bribery, and conflicts of interest, also setting up a whistleblower alert system. It also includes loyalty and noncompete clauses, a provision on sport manipulation, doping, gambling, fraud, and data protection. So too has the OCOG adopted a Good Practices Guide, which creates anti-corruption (and anti-discrimination) standards for the OCOG's conduct, including in relation to third parties.[91] Neither the Code of Ethics nor the Good Practices Guides seems intended to leave an anti-corruption legacy, but both can and likely will do so accidentally. OCOG personnel, as well as the companies with which it does business, will be introduced to new norms, practices, policies, and laws.

Unfortunately, neither of these documents contains a robust third-party policy. One can imagine a requirement that any contractor or supplier seeking a contract to perform Olympics-related work should, as a condition of submitting its bid, have a reasonable and tailored anti-corruption compliance program in place. Such a requirement would greatly strengthen a private-sector anti-corruption legacy. Interviews revealed a common perception that EU laws prohibit such a requirement.

That position may need examination. The applicable legislation is Directive 2014/24/EU of the European Parliament and of the Council on public procurement. Article 58 limits the requirements. Permitted selection criteria may relate to: suitability to pursue the professional activity; economic and financial standing; and technical and professional ability.[92] Contracting authorities shall limit any requirements to those that are appropriate to ensure that a candidate or tenderer has the legal and financial capacities and the technical and professional abilities to perform the contract to be awarded. A review of the directive suggests that the first two permitted bases would not reasonably include compliance or due diligence programs. However, the third—"technical and professional ability"—might. The directive provides that contracting authorities may impose requirements to ensure that companies "possess the necessary human and technical resources and experience to perform the contract to an appropriate quality standard."[93] It would seem by no means a stretch, given the rapidly evolving best practices related to anti-corruption compliance and human rights due diligence, that these could be included among the "human and technical resources" necessary to "perform the contract to a quality standard." Indeed, it seems far more likely than not that a contractor which had no compliance program in place and then became embroiled in a corruption scandal during its work would be deemed to have performed that contract to a quality standard.

The COJO's human rights policy, called the Social Charter, is much stronger in this regard.[94] Following the Qatari example, the Social Charter pays special attention to labor rights, though framed in terms of inclusion—companies and workers gaining inclusion into the economic, legal, and cultural community. The Social Charter announces three goals: give all companies access to contracts; contribute to the occupational integration of vulnerable groups; and ensure decent working conditions. The charter will be automatically applied to contractors in their operations, and an integral part of contracts signed with both contractors and subcontractors. Project managers will have to incorporate into their projects detailed measures to conform to the principles in the charter. They will also have to anticipate sanctions in case of noncompliance with the principles. While not a condition of a bid, it does become a requirement following a bid award.

With the Social Charter, the OCOG is certain to expose numerous companies to international labor standards, leaving a legacy that is accidental but still substantial. Its Code of Ethics and Good Practices Guide will likely do the same. But France may not get to the point of building an intentional human rights or anti-corruption legacy, as its predecessor megasport host, Qatar, has done.

To Be Outdone by Qatar?

The juxtaposition is tantalizing. France, a prominent country with a long and proud human rights tradition but a notorious intolerance for public displays of the Muslim faith,[95] follows Qatar, a small, Muslim country with a very short history and well-publicized human rights challenges. And yet Qatar built the first intentional megasport human rights legacy, and in so doing set a standard that France does not yet seem poised to meet. France could still do so, and more: it could build a legacy that is intentional, proactive, and two-dimensional.

Yet France seems largely unaware of both the standard Qatar has set and its own opportunity to meet or exceed it. We should not fault the OCOG, which continues to do pathbreaking work in adopting effective preventative policies. Rather, France exposes the absence of a conspicuous public discourse surrounding the capacity of megasports to leave human rights and anti-corruption legacies. Kickstarting that conversation is the purpose of this book.

Notes

1. *See* LEO GERSHOY, THE FRENCH REVOLUTION AND NAPOLEON (1964), at 141–44.
2. *Id.* at 142.
3. *See id.* at 142–44; U.S. CONST. amend. I, II, III, IV, V, VI, VII, VIII, IX, X.
4. GERSHOY, *supra* note 1, at 141; *Bill of Rights*, BILL OF RIGHTS INSTITUTE, https://billofrightsinstitute.org/founding-documents/bill-of-rights/.
5. Alec Stone Sweet, *The Politics of Constitutional Review in France and Europe*, 5 INT'L J. CONST. L. 69, 80–81 (2007).
6. *France's Constitution of 1958 with Amendments through 2008*, CONSTITUTE PROJECT, https://www.constituteproject.org/constitution/France_2008.pdf?lang=en.
7. *Constitution de 1946, IVe République*, CONSEIL CONSTITUTIONNEL, https://www.conseil-constitutionnel.fr/les-constitutions-dans-l-histoire/constitution-de-1946-ive-republique.
8. *See Status of Treaties*, UNITED NATIONS TREATY SERIES, https://treaties.un.org/pages/Tre aties.aspx?id=4&subid=A&clang=_en.

9. *See id.*
10. *The Text of the Declaration and Its Follow-up*, INTERNATIONAL LABOUR ORGANIZATION, https://www.ilo.org/declaration/thedeclaration/textdeclaration/lang--en/index.htm.
11. *European Convention on Human Rights*, EUROPEAN COURT OF HUMAN RIGHTS, https://www.echr.coe.int/Documents/Convention_ENG.pdf; European Convention for the Protection of Human Rights and Fundamental Freedoms, Nov. 4, 1950, 213 U.N.T.S. 221.
12. Jim Yardley, *Report on Deadly Factory Collapse in Bangladesh Finds Widespread Blame*, N.Y. TIMES (May 22, 2013), https://www.nytimes.com/2013/05/23/world/asia/report-on-bangladesh-building-collapse-finds-widespread-blame.html.
13. *Auchan Lawsuit (Re Garment Factories in Bangladesh)*, BUSINESS & HUMAN RIGHTS RESOURCE CENTRE, https://www.business-humanrights.org/en/auchan-lawsuit-re-garment-factories-in-bangladesh; *Bangladesh: Factory Deaths Could Have Been Prevented*, HUMAN RIGHTS WATCH (Nov. 14, 2013), https://www.hrw.org/news/2013/11/14/bangladesh-factory-deaths-could-have-been-prevented#.
14. Loi 2017–399 du 27 mars 2017 relative au devoir de vigilance des sociétés mères et des entreprises donneuses d'ordre [Law 2017-399 of Mar. 27, 2017 on the duty of care of parent companies and subsidiary companies], JOURNAL OFFICIEL DE LA RÉPUBLIQUE FRANÇAIS [J.O.] [OFFICIAL GAZETTE OF FRANCE], Mar. 28, 2017.
15. Stéphane Brabant & Elsa Savourey, *Scope of the Law on the Corporate Duty of Vigilance*, INT'L REV. OF COMPLIANCE AND BUS. ETHICS (Dec. 14, 2017), at 92, 7.
16. *Id.* at 2.
17. *Id.* at 6.
18. Stephane Brabant, Charlotte Michon, & Elsa Savourey, *The Vigilance Plan*, INT'L REV. OF COMPLIANCE AND BUS. ETHICS (Dec. 14, 2017), at 93, 1 (quoting CODE DE COMMERCE [C. COM.] [COMMERCIAL CODE] art. L. 225-102-4, para. 3).
19. *Id.* at 2 (quoting CODE DE COMMERCE [C. COM.] [COMMERCIAL CODE] art. L. 225-102-4, para. 3).
20. *Id.*
21. *See id.* at 6.
22. *Id.* at 7.
23. *See* Brabant, *supra* 18, at 9.
24. *Id.* at 10.
25. Modern Slavery Act 2015, c. 30, § 54; *Modern Slavery and the Modern Slavery Act of 2015*, BAKERMCKENZIE, https://www.bakermckenzie.com/en/insight/publications/2017/10/modern-slavery-act.
26. CAL. CIVIL CODE § 1714.43 (West 2018).
27. Anneloes Hoff, *Dutch Child Labour Due Diligence Law: A Step Towards Mandatory Human Rights Due Diligence*, BUSINESS & HUMAN RIGHTS RESOURCE CENTRE (June 10, 2019), http://business-humanrights.org/en/dutch-companies-issue-open-letter-in-support-of-child-labour-regulation.
28. *The Netherlands Takes a Historic Step by Adopting Child Labour Due Diligence Law*, MVO NEWS, AMSTERDAM (May 14, 2019), http://mvoplatform.nl/en/the-netherla nds-takes-a-historic-step-by-adopting-child-labour-due-diligence-law.

29. SDA, National Press Agency of Switzerland, *Swiss Parliament Adopts Reporting Focused Proposal*, BUSINESS & HUMAN RIGHTS RESOURCE CENTRE (June 9, 2020), http://buisness-humanrights.org/en/switzerland-ngo-coalition-launches-responsible-buisness-initiative.
30. Sam Eastwood et. al., *Mandatory Human Rights Due Diligence—European Commission to Introduce a Legislative Initiative by 2021*, MAYER BROWN, BUSINESS AND HUMAN RIGHTS BLOG (May 19, 2020).
31. REED SMITH, *Anti-Corruption & Bribery in France*, LEXOLOGY (Oct. 5, 2018), https://www.lexology.com/library/detail.aspx?g=0c71067e-04b1-4a57-8731-fc141be57c2d.
32. *Id.*
33. Henry Samuel, *Corruption Is Still Rife at Top Level of French Government*, TELEGRAPH (Mar. 27, 2005), https://www.telegraph.co.uk/news/worldnews/europe/france/1486547/Corruption-is-still-rife-at-top-level-of-French-government.html.
34. *France Corruption Report*, GAN BUSINESS ANTI-CORRUPTION PORTAL (Oct. 2017), https://www.business-anti-corruption.com/country-profiles/france/.
35. *Id.*
36. Catherine Martens, *Nicolas Sarkozy Corruption Charges Reveal France's Loose Campaign Finance Practices*, DW (Mar. 21, 2018), https://www.dw.com/en/nicolas-sarkozy-corruption-charges-reveal-frances-loose-campaign-finance-practices/a-43075459.
37. Samuel, *supra* note 33.
38. *Id.* at 478.
39. OECD, PHASE 3 REPORT ON IMPLEMENTING THE OECD ANTI-BRIBERY CONVENTION IN FRANCE 5 (Oct. 2012).
40. *Jacques Chirac*, ENCYCLOPAEDIA BRITANNICA, https://www.britannica.com/biography/Jacques-Chirac.
41. *Nicolas Sarkozy*, ENCYCLOPAEDIA BRITANNICA, https://www.britannica.com/biography/Nicolas-Sarkozy.
42. Samuel, *supra* note 33.
43. Robert Zaretsky, *Le roi Sarkozy*, LE MONDE (July 13, 2010), https://mondediplo.com/outsidein/le-roi-sarkozy; Catherine Martens, *Nicholas Sarkozy Corruption Charges Reveal France's Loose Campaign Finance Practices*, DEUTSCHE WELLE (Mar. 3, 2018), https://www.dw.com/en/nicolas-sarkozy-corruption-charges-reveal-frances-loose-campaign-finance-practices/a-43075459.
44. Martens, *supra* note 43.
45. Rodrigo Amaral, *Sapin II Aims to Challenge France's Culture of Corruption*, COMPLIANCE WEEK (Feb. 28, 2017), https://www.complianceweek.com/news/news-article/sapin-ii-aims-to-challenge-frances-culture-of-corruption#.W9oNcS-ZO1s.
46. *Id.*; Thibaud Vadjoux, *The French Are Demanding Change in the Face of Corruption*, EQUAL TIMES (June 9, 2017), https://www.equaltimes.org/the-french-are-demanding-change-in#.W9oOIi-ZO1s.
47. Nicholas Tollet, *Nicholas Tollet on the New French Anti-Corruption Law: Shall We Be Scared of France Now?*, FCPA BLOG (Sept. 30, 2016), https://fcpablog.com/2016/09/30/nicolas-tollet-on-the-new-french-anti-corruption-law-shall-w/. An unease

toward foreign intervention in prosecution of French companies is illustrated in France's blocking statute, which prohibits companies from sharing information with foreign prosecution agencies. Pierre Grosdidier, *The French Blocking Statute, the Hague Convention and the Case Law: Lessons for French Parties Responding to American Discovery*, HAYNES BOONE (Sept. 15, 2014), http://www.haynesboone.com/Publications/the-french-blocking-statute-the-hague-evidence-convention-and-the-case-law-lessons-for-french-parties-responding-to-american-discovery. However, there has only been one conviction in forty years and is viewed as not having much teeth (last updated Aug. 31, 2014). Ela Barda & Thomas Rouhette, *The French Blocking Statute and Cross-Border Discovery*, 84 DEFENSE COUNSEL J. (2017), https://www.iadclaw.org/publications-news/defensecounseljournal/the-french-blocking-statute-and-cross-border-discovery/. Sapin II references compliance with the blocking statute in Article 3, but it is unclear if this will be effective. *Id.*

48. Johann le Frapper, *Sapin 2 Act: A Patchwork of Reforms but a Clear Progress (Part 1)*, ABOUT GOVERNANCE, ETHICS AND RISK BLOG (Nov. 26, 2016), http://Iohannlefrapper.com/?p=34.
49. Richard L. Cassin, *With Alstom, Three French Companies Are Now in the FCPA Top Ten*, FCPA BLOG (Dec. 23, 2014), http://www.fcpablog.com/blog/2014/12/23/with-alstom-three-french-companies-are-now-in-the-fcpa-top-t.html; Richard L. Cassin, *Alcatel-Lucent Settles Bribery Case*, FCPA BLOG (Dec. 28, 2010), http://www.fcpablog.com/blog/2010/12/28/alcatel-lucent-settles-bribery-case.html.
50. Margo Sève & Michel Perez, *International Financial and White Collar Crime, Corporate Malfeasance and Compliance*, CHRONIQUE (2017), at 3, https://www.kramerlevin.com/images/content/2/3/v2/23527/1701-RTDF-Dill-Aliz-e-Framework-to-implementing-an-effective-co.pdf; Rodrigo Amaral, *Sapin II Aims to Challenge France's Culture of Corruption*, COMPLIANCE WEEK (Feb. 28, 2017), https://www.complianceweek.com/news/news-article/sapin-ii-aims-to-challenge-frances-culture-of-corruption#.W_V_1S3MyCQ; Sarah Krys, *France's Failure to Fight Foreign Bribery: The Problem is Procedure*, GAB: THE GLOBAL ANTICORRUPTION BLOG (Dec. 14, 2015), https://globalanticorruptionblog.com/2015/12/14/frances-failure-to-fight-foreign-bribery-the-problem-is-procedure/.
51. *See generally* Samuel, *supra* note 33 (discussing how DOJ fines are an embarrassment because it implies the French system is too weak to sanction corporations).
52. *Anti-Corruption Legislation*, GAN BUSINESS ANTI-CORRUPTION PORTAL, https://www.business-anti-corruption.com/anti-corruption-legislation/sapin-ii-law/.
53. Loi 2016-1691 du 9 décembre 2016 relative à la transparence, à la lutte contre la corruption et à la modernisation de la vie économique [Law 2016-1691 of December 9, 2016 relating to the transparency, the fight against corruption and the modernization of the economic life] [hereinafter Law 2016-1691], https://www.legifrance.gouv.fr/affichTexte.do?cidTexte=JORFTEXT000033558528&categorieLien=id; Philippe Bouchez El Ghozi & Morgan A. Heavener, *French Anticorruption Agency Issues Detailed New Guidelines for Compliance with Sapin II*, PAUL HASTINGS (Apr. 16, 2018), https://www.paulhastings.com/publications-items/details?id=4c43866a-2334-6428-811c-ff00004cbded.

54. Agence Française Anticorruption, French Anticorruption Agency Guidelines 4 (2017) [hereinafter AFA Guidelines].
55. Ludovic Malgrain et al., *Corporate-led Internal Investigations Become a Prerequisite to Enter into a French DPA*, Lexology (July 23, 2019), https://www.lexology.com/library/detail.aspx?g=1fceb930-ca8b-4505-8190-621d66bb29f7.
56. Antonin Levy et al., *The Emergence of Compliance in France*, Hogan Lovells (Mar. 16, 2018), https://www.expertguides.com/articles/the-emergence-of-compliance-in-france/AROFNYFM; Law 2016-1691, *supra* note 53. The Special Investigative Commission of the National Assembly has created a report that suggests AFA expand its jurisdiction to include foreign subsidiaries of companies not headquartered in France. Xavier Oustalniol, *Xavier Oustalniol: Will France Expand the Scope and Reach of its Anti-Corruption Agency?*, FCPA Blog (May 8, 2018), http://www.fcpablog.com/blog/2018/5/8/xavier-oustalniol-will-france-expand-the-scope-and-reach-of.html.
57. Quinton Newcomb & Olivier Lopez, *Sapin I to II—French Anti-Bribery Law, an Evolution*, Fraud Intelligence, http://www.fulcrumchambers.com/wp-content/uploads/2017/05/sapin-french-anti-bribery-law.pdf.
58. AFA Guidelines, *supra* note 54.
59. Those subject to Sapin II must implement a compliance program and are subject to sanctions by AFA if not properly implemented. Law 2016-1691, *supra* note 53. This differs from the UK Bribery Act, which allows a compliance program as a defense for not preventing an act of bribery. UK Bribery Act 2010, c. 23, § 7. Under the FCPA, companies have implemented corporate compliance programs to prevent violations, but it is not a violation in itself to not implement a compliance program. Foreign Corrupt Practices Act, 15 U.S.C. § 78dd-1 (2012); Philip H. Hilder, *FCPA Compliance Requirements: A Guide for Global Companies*, Hilder & Associates, https://www.hilderlaw.com/Publications/Understanding-FCPA-Compliance-Requirements-A-Guide-for-Global-Companies.shtml.
60. Malgrain et al., *supra* note 55; *Sapin 2—France Strengthens Anti-Corruption Law*, FRA Blog (Dec. 7, 2016), https://www.forensicrisk.com/sapin-2/.
61. Newcomb & Lopez, *supra* note 57; Saskia Zandieh & Leah Moushey, *France's Game-Changing New Anti-Corruption Law*, Miller & Chevalier (Oct. 11, 2016) https://www.millerchevalier.com/published-article/frances-game-changing-new-anti-corruption-law.
62. Newcomb & Lopez, *supra* note 57.
63. *Id.*
64. *The Agency: Missions*, AFA, https://www.economie.gouv.fr/afa/missions.
65. *The Agency: Organization*, AFA, https://www.economie.gouv.fr/afa/organisation.
66. *Sapin II Compliance Guide*, GAN Business Anti-Corruption Portal, https://www.business-anti-corruption.com/anti-corruption-legislation/sapin-ii-law/.
67. *Id.*
68. Law 2016-1691, *supra* note 53; Malgrain et al., *supra* note 55.
69. Some companies have responded more positively to the guidelines than others. Some have found the guidance helpful, while others find that its specificity does not apply

to their business. Many companies had these compliance programs in place due to needed compliance with the FCPA. AFA Meeting, October 16, 2018.

70. Sève & Perez, *supra* note 50, at 4.
71. *See generally The Agency*, AFA, https://www.economie.gouv.fr/afa/lagence (explaining AFA is an administrative agent).
72. *Id.*
73. Sève & Perez, *supra* note 50, at 5–6; Elizabeth Loftus, *Laissez-nous Faire: France Is Forgoing an Opportunity to Fight Corruption, but Maybe It Is the Wrong One*, GAB: The Global Anticorruption Blog (May 9, 2016), https://globalanticorruptionblog.com/2016/05/09/laissez-nous-faire-france-is-foregoing-an-opportunity-to-fight-corruption-but-maybe-it-is-the-wrong-one/.
74. *Id.* at 6.
75. *Id.*
76. *Id.*
77. Jamie L. Boucher et al., *France Announces Its First Deferred Prosecution Agreement*, Skadden, Arps, Slate, Meagher & Flom (Dec. 8, 2017), https://www.skadden.com/insights/publications/2017/12/france-announces-deferred-prosecution-agreement.
78. *Id.*; Loftus, *supra* note 73.
79. Boucher et al., *supra* note 77.
80. *Id.*
81. Kate Beioley, *Airbus Case Shows France's New-Found Anti-Corruption Drive*, Fin. Times (Feb. 17, 2020), http//:ft.com/content/fe71368e-11ea-95a0-43d18ec715f5.
82. *Id.*
83. Elian Peltier, *Paris Won the 2024 Olympics by Learning From Its Mistakes*, N.Y. Times (Sept. 17, 2017).
84. *Canditature File: Paris Candidate City Olympic Games 2024*, Olympic World Library, 36–40, https://library.olympics.com/Default/doc/SYRACUSE/171681/candidature-file-paris-candidate-city-olympic-games-2024.
85. *National Multi-Year Plan to Fight Corruption 2020–2022*, AFA (2020), https://www.agence-francaise-anticorruption.gouv.fr/files/files/PlanVAnglais.pdf.
86. *Id.* 7.
87. *Annual Report*, AFA, 26–27 (2020), https://www.agence-francaise-anticorruption.gouv.fr/files/2021-05/RA_AFA_2020_ENG_Version_Finale.pdf.
88. AFA meeting, October 16, 2018. *See id.* (describing the OCOG as a privately funded organization).
89. Loi 2018-202 du 26 mars 2018 relative à l'organisation des jeux Olympiques et Paralympiques de 2024 [Law 2018-202 of March 4, 2018 relating to the organization of the Olympic and Paralympic Games of 2024], https://www.legifrance.gouv.fr/eli/loi/2018/3/26/SPOV1729269L/jo/texte.
90. Paris 2024, *Le Comite D'Ethique*, https://www.paris2024.org/fr/heritage-integrite-et-transparence/.
91. *Id.*

92. Article 58, § 1 https://eur-lex.europa.eu/legal-content/EN/TXT/PDF/?uri=CELEX:32014L0024.
93. Article 58, § 4.
94. Paris 2024, *A Social Charter for Responsible Games*, https://www.paris2024.org/en/a-social-charter-for-responsible-games/.
95. Alan Cowell, *French Ban on Face Veils Upheld by European Rights Court*, N.Y. Times (July 1, 2014), http://nytimes.com/2014/07/02/world/europe/european-rights-court-upholds-frances-ban-on-full-face-veils.html.

7
Future Legacy Opportunities

Introduction

As explained in Chapter 1, the human rights and anti-corruption legacy is not invented so much as it is discovered. Various geopolitical factors have combined to create an environment in which a pattern naturally emerged: mega sporting events (MSEs) accelerating the implementation of host-country anti-corruption and human rights reforms that seem likely to endure beyond the event. Past chapters have documented this pattern across Brazil, South Korea, Qatar, and France. So too does the pattern have an organic future trajectory. As this book went to press, although the pattern appeared to largely bypass the Tokyo 2020 Summer Olympics and Beijing 2022 Winter Olympics (for a variety of reasons beyond the scope of this book) it passes directly through several subsequent hosts: Australia and New Zealand, as it prepares to host the 2023 FIFA Women's World Cup; Italy, host to the 2026 Winter Olympics in Milan and Cortina d'Ampezzo; and ultimately the United States, Canada, and Mexico, who as the United Bid will collectively host the 2026 FIFA Men's World Cup.

As with the countries discussed in Chapters 3, 4, 5, and 6, the MSE meets the host country or countries in their distinctive legal and cultural landscapes. Their intersection presents distinctive legacy opportunities. This chapter looks at these subsequent hosts to determine where the legacy opportunities might lie, and how stakeholders may better support and encourage them. It could not possibly be exhaustive; it is merely representative, expressed here with the hope that other stakeholders will see further opportunities.

Each host's set of bid documents clearly evinces a commitment to prevention: to implementing measures that will reduce the likelihood of substantial corruption or human rights problems arising in the course of preparations. This alone is an important step for the megasport movement. So too can preventative measures produce accidental legacies. But where a host intends to leave a human rights and anti-corruption legacy, that legacy will of course tend to be stronger.

A New Megasport Legacy. Andrew Brady Spalding, Oxford University Press. © Oxford University Press 2022.
DOI: 10.1093/oso/9780197503614.003.0007

Generally, no organizing committee is yet aspiring to anything resembling Qatar's legacy of systemic national reforms. This is hardly surprising; Qatar's combination of social and economic factors described in Chapter 5 is absolutely unique and will not soon be replicated. Still, each country can contribute to the steady building of precedents and expectations concerning the long-term anti-corruption and human rights impacts of hosting an event.

Australia and New Zealand mark a significant step forward in their commitment to the prevention of human rights abuses. They conducted an independent human rights assessment and developed a robust human rights strategy. However, the bid documents reveal a couple of limitations: the explicit human rights legacy aspirations relate almost exclusively to participation in sports, and the bid pays little attention to anti-corruption. As Chapter 8 will discuss, this is hardly the organizing committee's fault; it is more reflective of limitations in FIFA policies. Despite those limitations, at press time the Australian and New Zealand national human rights commissions were actively exploring how to further develop their human rights legacy.

In Italy, the Milan/Cortina bid shows intimations of Organizing Committee for the Olympic Games (OCOG) policies that can set a leave a legacy in Italy and set a vital precedent for future games. Milan/Cortina thus advances the ball in two important respects. First, Milan/Cortina is imposing significant requirements on third parties. Because Milan/Cortina is the second Olympic host, following Paris, that is bound to the new host-city contractual provisions described in Chapters 1, 6, and 8, they thus present an implied interpretation of the host-city contract that can have precedential value for future hosts. Second, Milan/Cortina' nascent policies pay attention to both anti-corruption and human rights. Though thus far (and in contrast to Australia/New Zealand) far stronger on corruption than on human rights, this presents a realistic opportunity to leave a two-dimensional legacy. Still, any human rights or anti-corruption legacy thus far seems likely to be accidental; the bid contains no express anti-corruption or human rights legacy aspirations.

In the United Bid, we see the high-water mark in post-Qatar megasports. That bid takes three significant steps beyond past hosts. First, it shows an integration of both corruption and human rights, roughly equally rigorous on these two dimensions. Second, it imposes significant requirements on third parties, which, as Chapters 9 and 10 explain, is where so much of the legacy opportunity exists. Third, the bid shows an express intention that these efforts leave a legacy. Accordingly, the United Bid is at least poised to produce the first proactive, intentional, and two-dimensional legacy.

This chapter discusses each event in turn.

Australia and New Zealand: The 2023 FIFA Women's World Cup

The FIFA Women's World Cup is inherently a human rights event. Its existence, not to mention its popularity, is itself a symbol of progress in respecting the rights of women. But though the event's popularity has skyrocketed in recent years, it has remained peripheral to discussions about megasport governance. This too should change.

The hosts conducted a sophisticated, independent human rights assessment and, to their credit, devised certain preventative measures that can leave a legacy of norms and knowledge. But the scope of their anti-corruption and human rights legacy, as revealed in the bid documents, is limited by three factors. First, they pay very little attention to the anti-corruption side, with the balance tilting very heavily toward human rights. Second, the hosts are imposing limited requirements on third parties. Though they develop Ethical Sourcing Principles, these don't quite match the rigor of the UN Guiding Principles on Business and Human Rights (UNGPs). Finally, their talk of legacy focuses almost exclusively on women's participation in soccer. While this theme has a human rights flavor, it could certainly go further. Indeed, at press time, the two countries' national human rights commissions were engaging stakeholders how to take it further. But the bid itself is rather constrained, and ultimately reflects shortcomings in the FIFA policies in place at the time.

Australia in particular may leave an additional legacy on women's soccer globally: the country is a prominent example of achieving equal pay for its women's national team. Equal pay is a global issue, but becomes especially salient where, as in Australia and, even more obviously, the United States, the women's national team is vastly more successful than the men's. But a careful analysis shows that what Australia means by equal pay, and what the US Women's National Team means, are not the same. Accordingly, the takeaways from the Australian model for other countries are harder to identify than one might hope or expect; the Australian model may or may not provide the solution to unequal pay problems elsewhere. At press time, the

US women were fighting for a compensation package entirely different from the Australian women. Still, Australia can, and should, hold itself up as a country that has worked hard to achieve what it considers to be equal pay. Australia's example can at very least help motivate other countries to achieve their own definitions of equality.

For their World Cup bid, Australia and New Zealand commissioned Professor Susan Harris Rimmer from Griffith University to conduct an independent human rights risk assessment.[1] FIFA required the assessment to consider how Australia and New Zealand's national practice may "impede or enable" the joint bid's ability to host the 2023 FIFA Women's World Cup ("FWWC") "in a manner that respects internationally recognized human rights," and also identifies "adverse human rights impacts" that come from hosting the event.[2] The assessment outlined three key areas of human rights risk associated with the FWWC 2023: security, rights of athletes, and rights of local communities.[3] The assessment identifies that freedom of expression and peaceful assemblies in public places are the most salient security risks associated with hosting the FWWC. The proposed mitigation strategy that the Assessment offers is for Australia and New Zealand to host "scenario-based training" on human rights issues, and to "recommend to relevant police to place an emphasis on community policing skills."[4] For the risks associated to the rights of athletes, the assessment identifies sexual orientation and gender identity, homophobic or racists chants in stadiums, access to stadiums for the disabled, gender discrimination, asylum claims, and victims of crimes are the relevant potential human rights risks. Some of the proposed mitigation strategies include offering trainings on incident management, mental health resources to all athletes during the FWWC, and a hotline for antisocial behavior within the hosting venues.[5] Identified human rights risks to the local community include the homeless population, volunteers, and local workers that may be mistreated or underpaid. Proposed mitigation strategies there are to partner with broadcasters to run a "human rights for broadcasters" initiative for the media; ensure that the Organizing Entity ensures that the homeless are treated respectfully and are not discriminated against; and generate a complaints process and coordinate with the relevant Anti-Discrimination Commissions on how to handle complaints.[6]

Based on the human rights assessment, Australia and New Zealand developed a *Sustainability Concept and Human Rights Strategy*.[7] This document is in effect a set of answers to a questionnaire that FIFA provides. The bidding countries' answers address the risks presented in the human rights assessment and develops concrete strategies to mitigate those risks. It proposes an impressive set of measures addressing potential risks in supply chains, security, and rights of athletes and local communities. They include: supply chain oversight through Ethical Sourcing Principles; a risk management framework; a Spectator Code of Behaviour and Disciplinary Code to ensure spectator accountability; human rights training for security forces; a policy to protect children and vulnerable adults; and effective grievance mechanisms.[8]

This is an impressive list, and sets an important precedent for megasport governance. FIFA's strategy template has elicited the design of meaningful preventative human rights measures. However, notice a few limitations. First, only the first measure, concerning the Ethical Sourcing Principles, imposes significant requirements on third parties. As Chapter 9 explains, third-party requirements are not only an effective preventative measure but a critical legacy tool. The more rigorous the third-party requirements, the greater exposure companies will have to leading human rights principles and practices. The exposure to these principles and practices can leave a legacy of norms and knowledge. Additionally, to the extent any of these corporations integrate these new practices into their non-World Cup work, they can become a legacy of corporate policies. While Australia and New Zealand's proposed ethical sourcing principles will do some of this work, they are unlikely to match the rigor of the UNGPs; though the UNGPs are briefly mentioned twice in the strategy document,[9] their specific requirements are not. Most conspicuously absent is Guiding Principle 13's requirement that an entity must "seek to prevent or mitigate adverse human rights impacts that are directly linked to business operations, products or services by their [business] relationships, even if they have not contributed to those impacts."[10] As Chapter 8 and 9 discuss, this requirement extends an entity's human rights responsibilities deep into their webs of third-party relationships. It is unclear why the Australia and New Zealand strategy does not rely on the UNGPs here, and its substitute, the Ethical Sourcing Principles, is unlikely to match the rigor of the UNGPs.

Second, throughout the strategy's otherwise remarkable discussion of human rights measures, there is no mention of legacy. While the bid book contains explicit legacy aspirations, they are in turn unrelated to the above preventative measures.[11] The bid book identifies four ways that Australia and New Zealand can leave a lasting legacy: (1) more women and girls playing football; (2) more pathway opportunities for women and girls;

(3) more female participation in football governance bodies; and (4) more investments in Australia and New Zealand's facilities to increase the number women and girls playing football overall. Australia's *Gender Equality Action Plan* encourages equality across "all aspects of the game," to encourage more women and girls to play football and achieve a 50–50 split in registered players in Australia by 2027.[12] New Zealand's *Map to Success Strategy* aims to increase the number of female coaches and referees to participate in sport.[13] While this theme has a human rights element to it, it falls fall short of aspiring to leave a legacy of human rights norms, practices, or policies in the host country.

Finally, anti-corruption gets short shrift. Throughout the strategy document, anti-corruption is subsumed under the term "sustainability." But as Chapter 8 discusses in detail, sustainability is an ambiguous word that, even within FIFA policies, means different things in different contexts. It does not always include anti-corruption measures, and when it does, becomes a cryptic way to refer to them. The Australia and New Zealand strategy document follows FIFA's approach, detailed in Chapter 8, of relying on ISO 20121 and GRI Standards.[14] But as that chapter also explains, neither of these is an anti-corruption compliance program. Absent from the Australia and New Zealand strategy is a freestanding, explicit, sustained commitment to adopting anti-corruption compliance measures. As the following discussion shows, the United Bid will remedy this problem.

A distinct potential legacy lies in the issue of compensating female players. Australia has accomplished something few countries can claim: it has implemented what it calls equal pay. This is properly styled a human rights achievement. Many women's national teams—most prominently at press time, the US Women's National Team—now seek equal pay. But the phrase means different things to different women's national teams. The issue turns out to involve economic valuations, legal arguments, and rhetoric that often create more heat than light. The following pages offer a few details to help frame the debates that will likely arise in discussions around the time of the 2023 Women's World Cup.

To sort through the sound bites, rhetoric, and legal posturing, it may be helpful to think about:

1. *The nature and value of the benefits.* These can include guaranteed salaries, performance-based bonuses, tournament prize money, and various other benefits to include field quality, travel reimbursement,

sponsorship appearances, parental leave, health insurance, and so forth. The benefits are negotiated together, with trade-offs between the various pieces. In the US litigation between the women's team and US Soccer, each side marshaled its expert-witness economists with competing calculations of the overall value of each team's compensation. This issue can become very difficult to dissect.

2. *Sources of funding.* National soccer federations pay the athletes. The federations' funding derives from various sources: sponsorships; the revenue generated by soccer matches (broadcasting contracts, ticket sales, etc.); and tournament prize money. Different countries use these various sources of funds in different ways to pay their athletes. For example, the Australian Women's National Team players are compensated in part based on a revenue-sharing agreement; at press time, the US women's compensation was not tied to revenue, and they did not wish it to be. Tournament prize money presents a particularly sticky problem. If the revenue source is grossly unequal does equality mean equal percentages of that revenue, or equal payout to each player? For example, if the men and women from a single country both participate in a tournament, and both are guaranteed the same percentage of the prize money, but the amount of total prize money is extremely unequal such that the men would get several times more than the women for achieving the same degree of success in the tournament, do we call this equal? The Australian women do; the US women do not.
3. *Back pay versus the negotiation of future contracts.* The US women have asked for back pay, raising the thorny legal issue of whether the collective bargaining agreement they negotiated several years ago should remain enforceable until it expires in 2022. The distinction between what the women ought equitably to be paid now versus what the women are entitled to receive based on their own collective bargaining agreement becomes easily confused, as seen in the federal district court opinion.

With these distinctions in mind, what does equal pay mean in Australia, and how did they achieve it? It means that on commercial and sponsor revenue, the men and women receive an equal payout, but in relation to tournament prize money, the men and women receive an equal percentage of the available prize money available respectively to the men and women.

The Australian Men's National Team, the Caltex Socceroos, and the Women's National Team, the Westfield Matildas, are represented for the purposes of collective bargaining by the same union, Professional Footballers Australia (PFA).[15] This is not universally the case; in the United States, for example, the men's and women's teams are represented by separate unions and separately negotiate their collective bargaining agreements ("CBAs"). In November 2019, Football Federation Australia ("FFA") and PFA signed a CBA that created pay parity between the national men's and women's team.[16] After the signing, the FFA released a statement, representing that "the new agreement reflects football's determination to address issues of gender equity in all facets of the game and build a sustainable financial model."[17]

When entering negotiations with the FFA, PFA aimed to elevate the Matildas without bringing the Socceroos down. One way the Australian teams were able to achieve this goal was to create a revenue sharing agreement, the first enacted by any major federation. PFA also sought to guarantee in both CBAs that the Matildas and the Socceroos would have the same resourcing, such as on field and off field staff, accommodation, and travel.[18] In broad strokes, the CBA provides that the men's and women's teams "will receive equal shares of total player revenue as part of a four-year deal between the Football Federation Australia and the Union, Professional Footballers Australia."[19] Specifically, the Matildas and the Socceroos will receive a 24 percent share of an aggregate of generated revenue in 2019–2029, rising by 1 percent each year as their salaries.[20] Basically, the FFA pools together the total revenue from both teams, then gives 50 percent of the total 24 percent to either team.[21] Not all teams want this; at press time, the US women's team was not asking for a revenue-sharing agreement.

The greatest challenge for achieving equal pay may lie in tournament prize money. Disparity in World Cup bonuses is presently a source of substantial pay inequality. For example, the US Soccer Federation received US$9 million when the men's team advanced to the second round of the 2014 World Cup. However, when the women's team won the entire event in Canada in 2015, US Soccer only received US$2 million.[22] When a national team wins the FIFA World Cup, FIFA awards the prize money to the winning country's federation. The Federation then distributes prize money to its players based on each team's collective bargaining agreement.[23] When the Socceroos or Matildas qualify for the World Cup, the players are entitled to 40 percent of the prize money, and their share increases to 50 percent if the team advances to the knockout rounds.[24] Meanwhile, in the Asian Football Federation Asian Cup, either national team is entitled to 33 percent for qualifying and 40 percent for advancing to the final match.[25] However, despite the CBA creating parity in the percentage that either national team would take home in prize money, a pay gap persists because the prize money varies drastically for the men and women's tournaments. For example, the prize money for the 2019 Women's World Cup was US$30 million, while the prize money for 2018 men's World Cup was US$400 million.[26] For this reason, some have argued that rather than fighting for pay parity, women's national teams should lobby FIFA to increase tournament prize money.[27] On prize money, when Australians say they have pay parity, they mean equal percentage of a base number of total prize money.

At press time, the US women mean, and were asking for, something different: an equal total payout. Their attorneys argue that the US Soccer Federation ("USSF") cannot pass on discrimination in the forms of unequal awards by FIFA to the team members.[28] It would be different if FIFA paid the teams directly, but as discussed earlier, FIFA pays the federations who distribute the prize money.[29] Consequently, the players through their attorneys argue that the unions and US Soccer cannot extinguish the rights of the players on the women's team under federal law.[30] Instead, according to the USWNT and its attorneys, the USSF should be lobbying to equalize the FIFA prize money.[31]

The main difference between the goals of Australia and the WNT in creating pay parity can be considered in terms of the difference between equity and complete equality. Where the Australian teams created pay parity with equity in mind, the available FIFA prize money is still the elephant in the room. Meanwhile, the WNT continue to demand equality—the equal payment of the players beyond an equal cut of the unequal prize money. Despite the excruciating nuances, there can be little doubt that Australia's achievement of equal pay, however defined, will support worldwide efforts to bring better compensation to women's teams.

Additional human rights initiatives may yet emerge. In mid 2021, FIFA announced a collaboration with the Australian and New Zealand Human Rights Commissions to further identify human rights "risks and opportunities."[32] Though the announcements do not explicitly invoke the concept of a human rights legacy, interviews with participants in that collaboration suggested legacy strategies might result. In sum, Australia and New Zealand have solid human rights preventative measures in place that could in turn leave accidental legacies. Whether any substantial human rights legacies become intentional remains to be seen. Though the hosts are not yet showing comparable interest in the anti-corruption dimension, subsequent hosts seem poised to recalibrate that balance.

Italy: The 2026 Milan/Cortina Winter Olympics

Italy (Milan/Cortina) will be the second country subject to the new anti-corruption and human rights provisions of the host-city contract discussed in Chapter 7. Any measures the OCOG, National Olympic Committee (NOC), or host city adopts will constitute an implied interpretation of the new host city contract provisions. At press time, the event remains six years away, and the OCOG's policies are not yet published. Much can change. However, interviews with multiple stakeholders revealed a consistent expectation that the Milan/Cortina OCOG will integrate an existing Italian compliance program—known as the 231 Model—into its policies and will require all partners to do the same. As the following discussion will show, the 231 Model is both an anti-corruption and human rights compliance requirement, though at present a bit more robust on the anti-corruption than on the human rights side. Still, if Milan/Cortina were to formally implement this requirement, not just for the OCOG but for all third parties, it would mark a significant step forward the anti-corruption and human rights legacy.

Italy presents a particular anti-corruption challenge, and opportunity. In 2020, Transparency International ranked Italy twentieth out of twenty-seven European countries for corruption,[33] owing in part to its long-standing problem with organized crime. A GRECO (Europe's Group of States Against Corruption) evaluation report acknowledged the close connection between corruption and organized crime in Italy, specifically in the southern regions.[34] This problem was manifest in 2015, when Italy hosted its most recent international event, the Universal Exposition (Expo). Though Italy wanted to use the Expo to demonstrate to the world that it was getting handle on mafia-related corruption, multiple scandals "undermined Italy's efforts to distance itself from a past in which the Mafia held sway over business and politics."[35] Several politicians and corporate officials were arrested for their involvement in a "criminal ring aimed at influencing procurement" and were charged with suspected criminal association, money laundering, and tax fraud.[36]

The IOC has tacitly expressed concern about mafia-related risks in the 2026 Winter Games. In early 2021, the IOC threatened to impose sanctions against Italy, including stripping Italy of its 2026 hosting rights, because the country had violated a provision in the Olympic Charter.[37] Under the Olympic Charter, Olympic committees are required to be neutral and thus must be operated separately and independently from the country's government.[38] However, the Italian government had a direct role in the finances of the Italian National Olympic Committee ("CONI"), including determining how much money went to the Olympic committee and how the money should be used.[39] In a last minute effort to avoid sanctions, Italy passed a decree that provides more autonomy and independence for the Italian Olympic committee in compliance with IOC requirements.[40] While the Italian CONI's strengthened autonomy is a huge success in combating corruption, the episode illustrates the risks unique to Italy's hosting of the Olympics.

Similar concern then manifested in the host-city contract.[41] In addition to the anti-corruption and human rights amendments of 2017, the IOC added a fourth, novel provision to the Milan/Cortina host-city contract. This fourth provision requires the host city's National Olympic Committee and its OCOG to "operate in conformity with, and promote, internationally recognized standards of governance applicable in the Host Country."[42] We do not yet know whether this fourth provision will apply to future host cities. Nor is it clear what the provision adds to the existing anti-corruption provision. Still, the amendment appears to signify the IOC's concern with mafia activities in Italy.

On the human rights side, Italy adopted its own Italian National Action Plan, which was amended in 2018 after a midterm review.[43] The plan describes the country's expectations of businesses, specifically the crossover between business conduct and human rights. Accordingly, the plan focuses on six priority areas, including promoting human rights due diligence processes; remedying forced labor issues; addressing labor rights; strengthening Italy's role in human rights based international development; opposing discrimination, specifically gender discrimination; and promoting environmental and sustainability protection.[44] Under the plan, there are several measures that the Italian government plans to implement to increase corporate promotion and protection of human rights. These measures include promoting human rights in the public procurement process, encouraging business entities to promote an anti-discriminatory culture within the business itself, and provide victims of corporate human rights violations access to remedies.[45] While the plan only extends through 2021, the plan itself is demonstrative of the Italian government's commitment to addressing human rights within the corporate context.

The Olympics thus come to Italy at a moment in which corporate human rights due diligence is gaining support, and the need for anti-corruption compliance is at the forefront of Italy's consciousness. Meanwhile, Italy has in place a novel corporate governance approach that can work very well in relation to corruption, but still has its limitations in relation to human rights. The 2026 Olympics can help Italy strengthen this approach.

This approach is popularly known as the 231 Model. Decree 231 holds corporations liable for certain crimes committed in the interest or to the advantage of that business entity.[46] The original purpose of this decree was to comply with the OECD Anti-Bribery Convention, and is originally an anti-corruption compliance model. However, the decree has been amended to add abuses of certain human rights, including slavery, human trafficking, and forced labor, as well as racism and xenophobia.[47] Because it was not created with the intent to address human rights violations, the amended version fails to cover all possible human rights risks entities face or that Italy otherwise recognizes. Although Decree 231 provides a strong anti-corruption legal framework, the human rights component of Decree 231 remains underdeveloped.

Although Italian law does not create a legal obligation for business entities to adopt due diligence and compliance programs, Decree 231 creates a strong incentive for business entities to adopt a program designed specifically to prevent to crimes listed in the decree.[48] The existence and enforcement of a 231 Model or another adequate compliance program can exonerate a company from corporate administrative liability or mitigate its liability.[49] Practitioners have explained that the 231 Model is the primary method by which a business entity can mitigate liability under Decree 231. In contrast, under Decree 231, a business entity without a 231 Model may be held directly liable for the alleged crime. Thus, if a business entity has a 231 Model, the business entity itself, though not the individual accused of the crime, may be exempt from liability.[50] To be effective, a 231 Model should identify risks, create specific protocols for preventing future crimes, appoint a monitoring body, provide for employee training, and provide for disciplinary sanctions for misconduct.[51] Decree 231 has resulted in corporate compliance programs becoming increasingly common within both domestic and foreign companies doing business in Italy. Not only do the majority of domestic companies have 231 Models, but many foreign companies exposed to compliance risks in Italy also have 231 models.

Interviews with local stakeholders further confirmed two key points. First, the Italian OCOG, the Milano Cortina 2026 Foundation, will have a 231 Model. While the OCOG's 231 Model will exclude the foundation from potential corporate liability, the implementation of the 231 Model ensures that there is a compliance program in place to prevent corrupt practices within the foundation itself. Second, these same practitioners have suggested that the Italian OCOG will require all business entities conducting business in Italy for the Olympic Games to adopt compliance programs. That is, in order to do business with the Italian OCOG, domestic and foreign companies will be required to have a 231 Model.

Were this to happen, it will leave anti-corruption and human rights legacies both for the broader megasport governance movement and for Italy specifically. For megasports, were this robust third-party requirement to become binding precedent on future hosts as an implied interpretation of the host-city contractual provisions, Italy would have created a significant precedent for future hosts to follow. Within Italy, such a requirement can further promote 231 programs and the resulting anti-corruption and human norms, skills, knowledge, and policies across the corporate sector. One amendment could help the effort. The OCOG might explore expanding the human rights that it and its third parties must respect through their 231 Models beyond those currently legally required. It might consider incorporating the rights mentioned in the National Action Plan. Such an amendment could significantly the human rights legacy for Italy.

Ultimately, Italy seems presently on track to leave a two-dimensional legacy, though it may well prove accidental. One can hope it does not become reactive to scandal. Building on the precedents of Australia and New Zealand, as well as France, this would constitute a modest step forward. However, the prospect of a proactive, intentional, and two-dimensional legacy seems most promising with the subsequent FIFA Men's World Cup hosts.

The United States, Canada, and Mexico: The United Bid's FIFA 2026 Men's World Cup

The United Bid is the joint—and winning—bid by Canada, Mexico, and the United States to host the 2026 FIFA Men's World Cup. The games will be staged across sixteen existing stadiums throughout the three countries, with ten matches in Canada, ten matches in Mexico, and sixty matches in the

United States.[52] Each match will be played at an existing stadium, reducing infrastructure costs and freeing up resources.

The United Bid's Bid Book contains three remarkable and unique features that move the anti-corruption and human rights legacy forward in a significant way. First, the bid incorporates rigorous risk assessments and compliance measures on both the human rights and anti-corruption sides. Second, it imposes exacting anti-corruption and human rights requirements not just on its own entities but on all third parties. Third, and most unique, it explicitly states an intention to leave legacies in regard to both human rights and anti-corruption. The United Bid thus raises the bar the highest of any megasport host, post-Qatar, effectively promising a proactive, intentional, and two-dimensional legacy.

The United 2026 strategy to address human rights and anti-corruption (as well as environmental and other sustainability issues) is called Sustainability+ .[53] Its goal is to embed sustainability into all aspects of its hosting vision and strategy.[54] Here sustainability takes on a broader meaning—respect for human rights, anti-corruption, and environmental protection, and ethical behavior—that Chapter 9 will further examine, and critique. The Bid Committee designed this approach by looking at international and domestic regulatory requirements, the UNGPs, the human rights risk assessment, as well as stakeholder engagement.[55]

As Australia and New Zealand before it, and in accordance with the FIFA bid requirements, United 2026 commissioned an independent human rights risk assessment.[56] United 2026 included the assessment as part of its bid documents and used the study to develop its Proposed United Human Rights Strategy.[57] As will be discussed further in Chapter 8, the 2026 World Cup was the first bidding process to occur after FIFA integrated the UNGPs into the bid documents[58] and made compliance with them required for both contractual partners as well as parties in the supply chain.[59] United 2026 not only commits itself to respecting internationally recognized human rights and labor standards but also intends for that commitment to be "shared with contractors, suppliers and workers, as well as potentially affected groups people, communities, fans, and consumers."[60] This will include embedding protections into operational policies and procedures, both for internal activities as well as those with its business partners.[61] Additionally, they plan to have grievance mechanisms to address negative impacts to human rights, publicly report any adverse impacts and how they were redressed, and monitor behavior to ensure compliance.[62] It will work with FIFA to publish Human Rights Reports that will assess and measure progress throughout the lifecycle of the World Cup.[63] The details of the United 2026 Human Rights Strategy are built into a supplemental document that, like the Bid Book, has also been made public.[64] They plan to get quantifiable data through the use of a scorecard that helps "assess Candidate Host City performance on human rights and measure progress throughout the lifecycle of the event."[65] The scorecard, which stakeholders are working with United 2026 to develop, will provide a baseline against which to assess each city's performance.[66]

United 2026 shows a similar commitment on the anti-corruption side. For the bidding process, United Bid retained an independent compliance and ethics firm.[67] The firm is designing a program that includes: "(1) a Culture of Compliance and Ethics; (2) Governance and Oversight; (3) Risk Assessments and Due Diligence; (4) Codes, Policies, and Procedures; (5) Training and Communications; (6) Speaking Up Program; (7) Case Management and Investigations; (8) Auditing and Monitoring; (9) Third Party Risk Management; and (10) Continual Improvement."[68] Furthermore, to ensure compliance United 2026 intends to develop and implement training programs for involved parties, whistleblower mechanisms for individuals to use to raise concerns and track issues, and a monitoring program to assess effectiveness of compliance activities. United 2026's approach not only governs internal affairs but extends to supply chains and associated third parties. They too will be "informed, monitored, and managed to ensure compliance."[69] All stakeholders involved with the 2026 World Cup are automatically incorporated into the Compliance and Ethics Program.[70] The Bid Book goes even further to set out specific sourcing compliance measures by way of contract drafting, sustainable purchasing, and performance reviews of third-party transactions.[71] These measures are titled the "Stakeholder Engagement Plan."[72]

As an additional anti-corruption measure, United 2026 plans to have a sustainable procurement process, which aligns with regionally and internationally trusted sourcing standards, all FIFA rules, and the UN Office on Drugs and Crime Strategy for Safeguarding Against Corruption handbook.[73] United 2026 outsourced a sustainability report from the Global Reporting Initiative (GRI) while preparing its bid.[74] This particular GRI report details the United Bid's organizational strategy, governance structure, and organizational requirements to ensure good governance including ethical conduct, compliance, and stakeholder engagement.[75] The three host countries for

United 2026 plan to publish additional GRI reports throughout the World Cup lifecycle.[76]

Ultimately, the bid commits to "measuring and communicating the social and environmental returns on the United 2026 sustainability legacies" with "the same rigor, transparency, and clarity used to measure financial outcomes."[77] Note here the invocation of an anti-corruption and human rights legacy. The specific contours of this legacy—and the mechanisms by which the preventative measures will produce the legacy—is a level of detail remaining to be developed. Still, United 2026's present policies carry the potential to significantly advance the effort to allow, or even require, megasports to leave lasting, positive, human rights and anti-corruption impacts.

United 2026 thus aspires to the first complete human rights and anti-corruption legacy: proactive, intentional, and two-dimensional. It represents, at least potentially, the apex in a trajectory that begins with Brazil and South Korea and moves roughly through Qatar, France, Australia and New Zealand, and Italy. Two questions of course remain. The first is what the United Bid organizing committee and stakeholders can do to deliver on these promises. The second is whether subsequent hosts will make, and then fulfill, similar promises. Part IV of this book explores these questions.

Notes

1. *Independent Human Rights Context Assessment Australia and New Zealand*, GRIFFITH UNIVERSITY (Dec. 2019), https://resources.fifa.com/image/upload/human-rights-assessment-report-australia-and-new-zealand.pdf?cloudid=kl8xzu1uqojlhmdir5qm.
2. *Id.*
3. *Id.* at 6.
4. *Id.*
5. *Id.* at 7.
6. *Id.* at 8.
7. *FIFA Women's World Cup 2023 FWWC 2023 Bid Sustainability Concept and Human Rights Strategy*, FOOTBALL FED'N AUSTL. & N.Z., https://img.fifa.com/image/upload/pmi88swvazmvi3dqrmkl.pdf [hereinafter *Sustainability document*].
8. *Id.* at 16.
9. *Sustainability document*, *supra* note 7, at 1–2.
10. *Guiding Principles on Business and Human Rights*, Guiding Principle 13, U.N. HUMAN RIGHTS OFFICE OF THE HIGH COMMISSIONER (2011), https://www.ohchr.org/Documents/Publications/GuidingPrinciplesBusinessHR_EN.pdf.

11. *As One Australia and New Zealand Bidding to Host the FIFA Women's World Cup 2023*, FIFA, https://img.fifa.com/image/upload/fwtyuwa9pb3encyeqlwc.pdf [hereinafter *Bid Book*].
12. *Id.* at 16.
13. *Id.*
14. *Sustainability document*, *supra* note 7, at 2.
15. *Collective Bargaining*, Professional Footballers Australia, http://pfa.net.au/collective-bargaining/.
16. *Bid Book*, *supra* note 11.
17. Karen Zraick, *Australian Women and Men's Soccer Teams Reach Deal to Close Pay Gap*, N.Y. Times (Nov. 6, 2019), https://www.nytimes.com/2019/11/06/sports/soccer/australia-soccer-matildas-equal-pay.html.
18. *Id.*
19. *Id.*
20. *Historic CBA to Close Football's Gender Pay Gap*, Football Australia (Nov. 5, 2019), https://www.footballaustralia.com.au/news/historic-cba-close-footballs-gender-pay-gap; Alana Glass, *Australian Soccer Deal Closes Gender Pay Gap*, Forbes (Nov. 7, 2019), https://www.forbes.com/sites/alanaglass/2019/11/07/australian-soccer-deal-closes-gender-pay-gap/?sh=2f8f4fbf4486.
21. *Id.*
22. *Id.*
23. Meg Kelly, *Are U.S. Women's Soccer Players Really Earning Less Than Men?*, Wash. Post (July 8, 2019), https://www.washingtonpost.com/politics/2019/07/08/are-us-womens-soccer-players-really-earning-less-than-men/.
24. Glass, *supra* note 20.
25. *Id.*; *Historic CBA*, *supra* note 20.
26. Zraick, *supra* note 17.
27. Mahita Gajanan, *The USWNT Seeks Nearly $67 Million in Damages In Equal Pay Lawsuit Against U.S. Soccer. Here's What to Know About the Case*, Time (Feb. 21, 2020), https://time.com/5653250/uswnt-equal-pay-lawsuit/. *See also* Graham Dunbar, *FIFA to Upgrade Flights, Raise Prize Money for Women's WCup* (Sept. 20, 2018), https://apnews.com/article/e78eb030fd9347adb449f7e2e607493a.
28. Gajanan, *supra* note 27.
29. *Id.*
30. *Id.*
31. *Id.*
32. *FIFA Announces Collaboration with Australia and New Zealand Human Rights Commissions*, FIFA (July 16, 2021), https://www.fifa.com/tournaments/womens/womensworldcup/australia-new-zealand2023/news/fifa-announces-collaboration-with-australian-and-new-zealand-human-rights.
33. *Corruptions Perceptions Index*, Transparency Int'l (2020), https://www.transparency.org/en/cpi/2020/index/nzl.
34. *Id.*

35. Sabrina Pisu, *Expo Exposed: Corruption at Milan's Global Food Event Leaves Sour Taste*, EURONEWS (May 29, 2015), https://www.euronews.com/2015/05/29/expo-exposed-corruption-at-milan-s-global-food-event-leaves-a-sour-taste.
36. Emilio Parodi, *Arrests, Corruption Probe, Cast Cloud over Italy's Expo 2015*, REUTERS (May 9, 2014), https://www.reuters.com/article/us-italy-corruption-expo/arrests-corruption-probe-cast-cloud-over-italys-expo-2015-idUSBREA480DW20140509; *Italy Mafia Arrests Linked to Milan Expo*, BBC (July 6, 2016), https://www.bbc.com/news/world-europe-36722906.
37. Karolos Grohmann, *Italy Staves Off Threat of Olympic Sanctions with Decree*, REUTERS (Jan. 26, 2021), https://www.reuters.com/article/us-olympics-ioc-italy/italy-staves-off-threat-of-olympic-sanctions-with-decree-idUSKBN29V159.
38. *See* Nicole Miller, *Italian Flag Will Be Allowed at Tokyo 2021 Olympics, CONI Autonomy Restored*, SWIMSWAM (Jan. 26, 2021), https://swimswam.com/italian-flag-will-be-allowed-at-tokyo-2021-olympics-coni-autonomy-restored/ ("In the letter, the IOC raised several doubts pertaining to the decree, including concerns about the anatomy of CONI. As a participant in the Olympic movement, all sports organizations must remain neutral."); *see also Olympic Charter*, IOC, https://stillmed.olympic.org/media/Document%20Library/OlympicOrg/General/EN-Olympic-Charter.pdf.
39. Grohmann, *supra* note 37.
40. *See id.*
41. *Host City Contract: XXV Olympic Winter Games 2026*, IOC, https://stillmedab.olympic.org/media/Document%20Library/OlympicOrg/Documents/Host-City-Elections/XXV-OWG-2026/Host-City-Contract-2026-Principles.pdf.
42. *Id.*
43. *Italian National Action Plan on Business and Human Rights 2016–2021*, https://negocioresponsable.org/wp-content/uploads/2018/02/ITALIA2016-2021-NuevoBorradorINGL%C3%89S.pdf.
44. *Human Rights Intergovernmental Cooperation*, COUNCIL EUR. PORTAL, https://www.coe.int/en/web/human-rights-intergovernmental-cooperation/-/italy-nap.
45. *Italian National Action Plan*, *supra* note 43.
46. *Italian Legislative Decree No. 231/2001: A Model for Mandatory Human Rights Due Diligence Legislation?*, INT'L FED'N HUM. RTS. (Nov. 2019), https://media.business-humanrights.org/media/documents/files/documents/report_231_2001_ENG.pdf.
47. *See id.*
48. *See id.*
49. *See id.*
50. *See id.*
51. Aurelio Giovannelli & Roberto Cursano, *Corporate Liability in Italy*, GLOBAL COMPLIANCE NEWS, https://www.globalcompliancenews.com/white-collar-crime/corporate-liability-in-italy/.
52. UNITED 2026, UNITY. CANADA, MEXICO, AND THE UNITED STATES UNITED BID TO HOST THE 2026 FIFA WORLD CUP 4, https://img.fifa.com/image/upload/w3yjeu7dadt5erw26wmu.pdf [hereinafter UNITED 2026 BID BOOK].
53. *Id.* at 9.

54. *Id.* at 446.
55. *Id.*
56. Independent Report: Human Rights in Canada, Mexico and the USA in the Context of a Potential FIFA 2026 World Cup Competition, Ergon Associates, Ltd. (Mar. 18, 2018), https://resources.fifa.com/image/upload/independent-human-rights-assessment-united-2026-bid.pdf?cloudid=ywklipdfwenjx8kwfunj, at 16.
57. *See generally* United 2026, Proposal for a United Human Rights Strategy (Mar. 16, 2018), https://resources.fifa.com/image/upload/proposal-for-a-united-human-rights-strategy-united-2026-bid.pdf?cloudid=s2xnrvfjg9kp0zelhxnt [hereinafter Proposal for a United Human Rights Strategy].
58. *See* John G. Ruggie, Harvard Univ. Corporate Responsibility Initiative, For the Game. For the World, FIFA and Human Rights 8–9 (2016), https://www.hks.harvard.edu/centers/mrcbg/programs/cri/research/reports/report68.
59. *See FIFA Executive Committee Sets Presidential Election for 26 February 2016 and Fully Supports Roadmap for Report*, FIFA (July 20, 2015), http://www.fifa.com/about-fifa/news/y=2015/m=7/news=fifa-executive-committee-sets-presidential-election for-26-february-20-2666448.html.
60. Proposal for a United Human Rights Strategy, *supra* note 57, at 16.
61. United 2026 Bid Book, *supra* note 52, at 460.
62. *Id.*; Proposal for a United Human Rights Strategy, *supra* note 57, at 16–18.
63. *Id* at 457–58.
64. Proposal for a United Human Rights Strategy, *supra* note 57.
65. *Id.* at 23.
66. *See* Amy Farkas Karageorgos, *Advancing the Human Rights Agenda in the Lead Up to the 2026 World Cup* (Mar. 10, 2020), https://www.sporthumanrights.org/library/advancing-the-human-rights-agenda-in-the-lead-up-to-the-2026-world-cup/.
67. United 2026, United Bid 2026: GRI Reference Report 8 (Mar. 16, 2016), https://resources.fifa.com/image/upload/gri-referenced-report-united-bid.pdf?cloudid=msbdtfolv8bozcnvxlda.
68. *Id.*
69. *Id.*
70. United 2026 Bid Book, *supra* note 52, at 452.
71. *Id.*
72. *Id.* at 453.
73. *Id.* at 450.
74. *Id.* Note: there is also a supplement available on the GRI report commissioned for the bid—the reports during the actual preparations for United 2026 will likely prove even more useful.
75. *Id.*
76. *Id.*
77. *Id.* at 454.

PART IV
BUILDING A FRAMEWORK

8

The Legal Foundation

Introduction

Creating a legacy of improved human rights and anti-corruption norms and practices in the host city or country begins with imposing meaningful requirements: on its governments, organizing committees, and companies. In the wake of the host-country anti-corruption and human rights scandals that erupted in the 2010s across Brazil, Russia, and Qatar, both the International Olympic Committee (IOC) and FIFA took substantial steps to impose heightened human rights and anti-corruption standards. The reforms of these respective organizations took different shapes.

As referenced throughout this book, the IOC amended its host city contract in 2017 to impose human rights and anti-corruption requirements on the host city. The first host country subject to these requirements will be Paris, host of the 2024 Summer Olympics. Though the IOC does not make public the actual 2024 host-city contract, it does make public a model host-city contract with operational requirements.[1] FIFA takes a different approach. It does not publish a model contract (or what FIFA calls a "hosting agreement"). FIFA cites "commercial considerations" as the reason for these contracts' privacy, which is understandable.[2] Of course, the IOC publishes a model contract with all relevant language and then assures the public that the actual contract contains these model provisions, a practice FIFA has elected not to follow. Still, despite the absence of a model hosting agreement, host-country obligations can be roughly inferred from various other documents. To their credit, so too have FIFA personnel, especially on the human rights side, been accessible and supportive in relation to the research contained in this chapter.

A review of IOC and FIFA documents reveals a common theme. Both organizations are substantially stronger on human rights than on anti-corruption. Both provide reasonable, clear, practical, and impactful guidance to host countries or cities on how to reduce human rights violations and, by implication, leave a lasting imprint of improved human rights governance.

A New Megasport Legacy. Andrew Brady Spalding, Oxford University Press. © Oxford University Press 2022.
DOI: 10.1093/oso/9780197503614.003.0008

However, neither organization has quite managed to do the same with anti-corruption compliance. The host-country anti-corruption requirements, at least insofar as they became available for review, are not quite as well developed. As presently formulated, for both the IOC and FIFA, they are quite likely to prove far less impactful than their human rights counterparts. As the following analysis will show, this is true to different degrees, and in different ways, for the IOC and FIFA, respectively. Although the problem is shared, it may be easily remedied.

The disparity between the human rights and anti-corruption requirements is in part due to differences between the international legal landscapes in these two fields. As described in Chapter 2, on the human rights side there exists a single, authoritative guidance document for the obligations related to private entities: the UN Guiding Principles on Business and Human Rights (UNGPs). The UNGPs provide specific requirements for identifying, preventing, and mitigating adverse human rights impacts that entities may commit in the course of their operations. Formally endorsed by the Human Rights Council in June of 2011, the UNGPs are internationally recognized and essentially unrivaled. Both the IOC and FIFA have, to their great credit, woven the UNGPs into the legal obligations a host country or city undertakes. As Chapter 9 further explains, the adoption of the UNGPs into the legal obligations of host countries or cities is a powerful tool for creating a human rights legacy.[3]

By contrast, the field of anti-corruption compliance is far more diverse. No analogue to the UNGPs exists. As discussed further later, anti-corruption compliance standards come from a variety of sources, including national governments, intergovernmental organizations, and private entities. This is not to say that anti-corruption compliance globally is less dynamic, or less transformative of corporate behavior. As Chapters 1 and 2 explain, the last two or three decades have seen a global sea change in norms, laws, and practices in relation to corruption. However, that movement is not dependent on, or captured in, a single document. It therefore becomes far more difficult for an organization like the IOC or FIFA to point to a single, authoritative set of standards and integrate those standards into clear, specific, legally binding agreements with host-country entities that compliance professionals can easily operationalize.

Perhaps unsurprisingly, both the IOC and FIFA are struggling to fill this void. In stark contrast to their human rights guidance, the resulting anti-corruption guidance is hazy, and likely to prove far less impactful. A private conversation with an individual working closely on the anti-corruption compliance standards for the Paris 2024 Olympics proved telling. When asked about the work the IOC's new anti-corruption compliance requirement in the Host City Contract (discussed later) is now doing, the individual replied, "none." When asked why, the interviewee explained, "because no one knows what it means."[4] Until the IOC and FIFA can clarify their host-country anti-corruption requirements, this will remain the case. This chapter and Chapter 10 aim to help remedy this problem.

Because the IOC model Host City Contract is publicly available but the FIFA hosting agreement is not, the following discussions have different characters. This chapter first provides a careful, detailed analysis of the IOC's Host City Contract's anti-corruption and human rights provision. In so doing, it explicates the UNGPs as they apply to an Organizing Committee for the Olympic Games (OCOG). The analysis aims to provide practical guidance to any organization trying to operationalize this contractual language. As of press time, it was the first such detailed analysis of the new Host City Contract provisions. The chapter then looks at a wide variety of FIFA documents to understand the legal obligations a World Cup host undertakes. That section necessarily provides less detail than the IOC section. Still, it shows how the FIFA host-country requirements have a strong footing in the UNGPs but are still searching for an analogous anti-corruption foundational document.

The IOC's Host City Contract

Any host city will be bound by national and international anti-corruption and human rights already in effect in that country. But the IOC has seemingly recognized that relying on existing laws, and enforcement levels in the host country may or may not prove effective in bringing the Games up to international standards. Accordingly, the IOC has recently augmented those legal obligations with a new set of contractual obligations. These clauses in the omnibus Host City Contract have the potential to create meaningful legal obligations for the parties to adopt appropriate and effective anti-corruption and human rights compliance systems. As Chapter 8 explains, those systems can in turn produce significant improvements in

Host Country anti-corruption and human rights governance that endure after the event is over.

This section is written in conjunction with the Olympics Compliance Task Force—a group of fourteen anti-corruption and human rights professionals and academics from nine countries.[5] The Task Force was convened at the request of Compliance 2024,[6] a working group of French compliance professionals created within France's leading compliance association, Le Cercle de la Compliance.[7] These organizations are collaborating to make the contractual clauses meaningful for the first Host City to be bound by them: Paris, host of the 2024 Summer Games. The following interpretation of the clauses therefore represents the consensus view of experts with no conflicts of interest.

The Human Rights Clause provides a solid and workable starting point for compliance officers as they implement measures to prevent violations. The Anti-Corruption Clause is structured similarly to the Human Rights Clause but, owing to differences in how anti-corruption standards are promulgated internationally, is far less clear on its face.

The Anti-Discrimination and Human Rights Clauses

For as long as the idea of human rights has existed, it has been understood that governments have the principal obligation to protect those rights. In recent years, there has been a rising awareness that in addition to governments, certain private-sector organizations, particularly corporations and other businesses, wield substantial power over the lives of individuals. If rights are to be meaningful in practice, the law must ensure that both state and non-state actors do not infringe upon widely recognized human rights. This fundamental principle is formalized in the UNGPs. Because many of the key Olympics players, particularly OCOGs, are often constituted as private-sector entities, the notion that such entities also have human rights obligations is potentially transformative for the Olympic Movement.

The new contractual provisions require each of the Host City, the Host City's National Olympic Committee (NOC), and its OCOG to:

> prohibit any form of discrimination with regard to a country or a person on grounds of race, colour, sex, sexual orientation, language, religion, political

> or other opinion, national or social origin, property, birth or other status; [and] protect and respect human rights and ensure any violation of human rights is remedied in a manner consistent with international agreements, laws and regulations applicable in the Host Country and in a manner consistent with all internationally-recognised human rights standards and principles, including the United Nations Guiding Principles on Business and Human Rights, applicable in the Host Country.[8]

This book calls the first clause "the Anti-Discrimination Clause" and the second "the Human Rights Clause." (The Anti-Corruption Clause is discussed further later.) While this book examines both clauses, the Anti-Discrimination Clause is fairly straightforward and receives relatively brief treatment here. This subsection devotes the bulk of its attention to the Human Rights Clause, both because it is more complex and novel, and because it carries greater potential impact.

The UNGPs are historic in their description of the human rights responsibilities of businesses. Of course, the responsibilities of businesses cannot be the same as the responsibilities of governments. The UNGPs capture these differences with the careful use of terminology. First, while businesses have a responsibility to "respect" human rights (the meaning of that word and others will be clarified below), governments have a duty to both "respect" and "protect" human rights. Access to effective "remedy" must be ensured by both governments and businesses, though the respective roles of these actors must be different.

In considering the requirements of the contract's "protect, respect, and remedy" framework, it should be kept in mind that this obligation extends to activities of the Host City, the NOC, and the OCOG that are "related to the organization of the Games."[9] This includes activities related to the preparations for the Games, the conduct of the Games, and the eventual winding down of the Games. While all of the OCOG's activities are of course related to the organization of the Games, the NOC undertakes many responsibilities not related to hosting the Games, and this is of course true for the Host City, albeit to a far greater degree. Although many stakeholders and observers might like to see human rights measures adopted across all of the operations of the three entities, the Contract only requires those measures to be adopted in activities related to organizing the 2024 Games.

This subsection discusses the Anti-Discrimination and Human Rights Clauses in turn.

1. The Anti-Discrimination Clause

The Anti-Discrimination Clause requires the Host City, NOC, and OCOG to "prohibit any form of discrimination with regard to a country or a person on grounds of race, colour, sex, sexual orientation, language, religion, political or other opinion, national or social origin, property, birth or other status." The Anti-Discrimination Clause precedes the human rights provision, thus mirroring the structure of the three key human rights instruments that collectively constitute the "International Bill of Human Rights:" the 1948 Universal Declaration of Human Rights,[10] the 1966 International Covenant on Economic, Social, and Cultural Rights,[11] and the 1966 International Covenant on Civil and Political Rights.[12] The sequence matters. It means that all measures to protect and respect human rights must be consistent with the principle of nondiscrimination: nondiscrimination is a cross-cutting right that is applied in conjunction with all other substantive human rights.

The structure of the Anti-Discrimination Clause is notably different from both the Human Rights Clause and the Anti-Corruption Clause. While these latter two clauses both refer to international laws or standards applicable in the Host Country, the Anti-Discrimination Clause makes no such reference. This is significant, and it means that the Host City must abide by the nondiscrimination principle irrespective of any international agreements it may have joined or any domestic laws that may have been enacted. The nondiscrimination principle cannot vary with the different legal or cultural contexts of various Olympic hosts.

The first word of the Anti-Discrimination Clause—"prohibit"—seems to derive from the anti-discrimination principles in the International Covenant on Civil and Political Rights. In that Covenant, Article 26 provides that "the law shall prohibit any discrimination" on various enumerated grounds.[13] This term requires parties to take affirmative steps to diminish or eliminate conditions which cause or perpetuate discrimination within their spheres of competence. It means that the parties will take steps to ensure that discrimination does not occur in the course of activities connected with the operation of the Games, as they affect—for example—athletes, audience members, workers, and communities. This protection should extend to activities carried out by the parties, and by agents contracted by the parties, such as contractors and subcontractors, suppliers, franchisees, and other business partners.

The Anti-Discrimination Clause adds two terms that do not appear in the International Bill of Human Rights. First, unlike those instruments, the Host-City contractual clause explicitly makes sexual orientation a protected attribute. Sexual orientation has been interpreted in international law as part of the human rights prohibition against discrimination "as to sex," and on the ground of "other status," but the host-city contract makes this explicit. The inclusion of sexual orientation in the Anti-Discrimination Clause carries powerful symbolic value. It underscores the particular relevance of this category to the Games, for athletes and fans alike, and gives effect to the Sixth Fundamental Principle of Olympism—which the IOC amended by unanimous vote in 2014 to include sexual orientation.

Second, unlike the International Bill of Human Rights, which prohibits discrimination with regard to *persons*, the contract's Anti-Discrimination Clause prohibits discrimination with regard to "*a country or* a person." The extension of this clause to prohibit discrimination against countries reflects an important feature of Olympic history. Although Olympic competition occurs between individuals or teams rather than between countries, modern Olympic history contains numerous examples of a country's categorical exclusion from the Games. As Chapter 1 mentions, countries have been banned or have withdrawn from the Games based on military conflicts, political disagreements, or violations of the norms of competition. Today, the Olympic Games can highlight differences in culture, religion, or government, raising the specter of potential discrimination against a country. Although it can sometimes be difficult to imagine how discrimination against a country would not be discrimination against persons, prohibiting discrimination against a country is a notable feature of this Contract.

An interpretive question arises concerning the bases on which the Contract prohibits discrimination against countries. Again, consider the structure of the clause: "prohibit any form of discrimination with regard to a country or a person on grounds of race, colour, sex, sexual orientation, language, religion, political or other opinion, national or social origin, property, birth or other status." This clause admits of two potential readings of the grounds on which discriminating against countries is prohibited. The first is that the clause prohibits discrimination against both countries and persons on each of the enumerated bases. That is, discrimination against persons on the grounds of race, color, sex, and so forth is prohibited, and discrimination against countries on the basis of those same categories—race, color, sex, and so forth—is also prohibited. The second interpretation is that "country" should stand alone, as an object of discrimination, separately from the bases of discrimination enumerated in the Contract that apply only to discrimination against persons. Under this latter reading, the Contract prohibits discrimination against persons only on the enumerated bases, while discrimination against countries is simply prohibited.

There may be unresolved alternative views on this question. There are compelling reasons to recommend either reading. There may be two reasons to support of separating "country" from the enumerated bases. First, attaching the enumerated bases to "country" is awkward because many of the enumerated bases would not seem to apply to countries; while discrimination against a country on the basis of religion, for example, is easy to imagine, discrimination against countries on many of the other grounds, such as color, sex, or sexual orientation, is more difficult to contemplate. Second, there are potential bases of discrimination against countries that do not apply to individuals, such as diplomatic relations with the Host Country or certain forms of government.

However, there may be a problem in detaching "country" from the enumerated bases. The Contract would be left with little guidance on the prohibited bases of discrimination against countries. Because anti-discrimination law globally is generally focused on discrimination against individuals, there exists scant guidance on how to interpret a clause prohibiting discrimination against countries. If the established principles regarding discrimination in international human rights law were to apply, it would likely be necessary to consider, for example, General Comment 18 of the UN Human Rights Committee, which (among other things) allows reasonable and objective distinctions that are designed to achieve a legitimate aim.[14] The issue merits further consideration.

In short, the clause establishes a fundamental principle of nondiscrimination that should apply to the implementation of both clauses discussed in the following.

2. The Human Rights Clause

The Contract's Human Rights Clause requires the Host City, NOC, and OCOG to:

> protect and respect human rights and ensure any violation of human rights is remedied in a manner consistent with international agreements, laws

> and regulations applicable in the Host Country and in a manner consistent with all internationally-recognised human rights standards and principles, including the United Nations Guiding Principles on Business and Human Rights, applicable in the Host Country.

As indicated earlier, the Contract establishes three principal obligations: to "protect" human rights, to "respect" human rights, and to "ensure any violation of human rights is remedied." The content of these obligations is derived from two sources: the first is "international agreements, laws, and regulations" applicable in the Host Country, and the second is "internationally-recognized human rights standards and principles" applicable in the Host Country. Each of these three key phrases is examined separately in the following.

The "protect, respect, and remedy" terminology originates in the International Bill of Human Rights and is fundamental to the UNGPs. Importantly, state actors typically have an obligation under international human rights law to both "protect" and "respect" human rights. Non-state actors (in particular businesses) have the responsibility to "respect" human rights, with this duty being most fully articulated under the UNGPs. The responsibilities of state and non-state actors therefore vary significantly. The Host City Contract Operational Requirements[15] dedicate an entire section—Section 27—to protecting and respecting human rights. These requirements track the UNGPs, essentially providing a synopsis of the "protect" and "respect" framework.

A threshold question arises concerning whether the Human Rights Clause treats the OCOG as a public-sector or a private-sector entity. As drafted, the clause could be read to require all parties to "protect and respect," in which case the OCOG has the responsibilities of a state actor. Alternatively, the phrase "consistent with international agreements" might modify the prior "protect and respect" clause to mean that entities shall either "protect and respect" or merely "respect" depending on their legal status; in this case, the OCOG might be deemed a nongovernmental actor and be held only to the lower "respect" standard. While the former reading seems more natural, the IOC seemingly intends the clause to treat the OCOG as a business and to impose on the OCOG only the responsibility to respect. This is apparent from various operational requirements as well as from meetings with the IOC. The Task Force believes that the clause could plausibly be read either way. In practice, as applied specifically to the OCOG, the difference ultimately proves slight. Still, should a future OCOG be constituted in such a way that the obligation to protect seems fitting, no modification of the clause would be required.

a. Protect Human Rights

Protecting against human rights violations is a duty that international law typically assigns to state actors. The duty to protect requires states to take measures to protect the human rights of individuals from the conduct of third parties, such as other individuals and corporations. States must do more than simply refrain from engaging in human rights abuses; they must take affirmative measures to prevent, investigate, punish, and provide remedy for third party abuses within their jurisdiction.

So too should the parties implement formal human rights laws or policies and issue guidance on how third parties should implement those laws and policies. For the city, these measures must apply to all persons within their territory and jurisdiction.

Of the counterparties, only the Host City is clearly a state actor and therefore subject to the duty to protect. While it is unclear whether the IOC typically regards an NOC as a state or non-state actor, the IOC clearly deems the OCOG a non-state actor. Because the key compliance questions concern the conduct of the OCOG, and the OCOG is deemed a non-state actor, this book focuses at much greater depth on what it means to respect human rights.

b. Respect Human Rights

The Human Rights Clause requires the counterparties to respect human rights, subject to their legal authority and institutional capacities. Most fundamentally, the responsibility to respect requires parties to refrain from acts or omissions that harm the human rights of a person or people.

To this end, the UNGPs impose on businesses a responsibility to reduce both their own violations and the violations of the third parties with whom they do business. Guiding Principle 13, in particular, describes the corporate responsibility to protect human rights as entailing a responsibility to "avoid causing or contributing to adverse human rights impacts" within its operations.[16] "Causing adverse human rights impacts" occurs when the harm results from the business's own acts. "Contributing to adverse human rights impacts" occurs when a third party has caused the harm, but the business has contributed by, for example, imposing unreasonable contractual conditions regarding cost or speed of delivery. The responsibility to take positive action to "avoid causing or contributing" is an integral part of the responsibility to "respect" under the UNGPs.

Additionally, there is also a responsibility, according to Guiding Principle 13, to "seek to prevent or mitigate adverse human rights impacts that are directly linked to business operations, products or services by their [business] relationships, even if they have not contributed to those impacts." All work that suppliers perform in relation to preparing for the Olympics will, of course, be directly linked to the OCOG's operations. For this reason, in relation to OCOGs in particular, the practical difference between "protect" and "respect" may ultimately be slight. While in the context of broader human rights law the difference between protect and respect can be quite significant, under the UNGPs, specifically in relation to the OCOG, that difference becomes more limited. "Protect" might extend and deepen the expectations upon businesses, particularly in relation to providing remediation measures where human rights impacts are directly linked to their operations through supply chain relationships but are not impacts that OCOG can be said to have itself contributed to or caused. However, in this early stage in the process of establishing a credible and practical human rights framework for the OCOG, this subtle difference may not be of immediate concern.

Focusing then on the responsibility to respect, the UNGPs provide two conceptual links between a business and the third parties with whom it does business. First, the business must "avoid causing or contributing to" human rights violations of third parties. Second, the business must "seek to prevent" (or, where the harm has already occurred, "seek to mitigate") third-party abuses. The UNGPs thus envision an active, ongoing relationship between a business and its third parties.

Translated to the Olympics context, the responsibility to respect imposes a number of requirements on the counterparties. First, the responsibility to respect human rights requires the counterparties to adopt a meaningful and meaningfully enforced human rights policy. The operational requirements allude to this responsibility by requiring a "policy commitment" from the contractual parties concerning human rights.[17] Under the UNGPs, that policy should have several features. It should be approved at the most senior level of the organization. It should clearly state the human rights expectations of personnel, business partners, and other parties directly linked to its operations. It should be publicly available and communicated both internally and externally to all personnel, partners, and other parties. The policy should then be embedded in all the entity's policies and procedures. Ultimately, the human rights policy must be enforced and breaches in operations must be responded to effectively, including by making any necessary revisions to the policy.

This policy must concern not only the entity's own operations, but the operations of third parties. This is among the most impactful implications of the Human Rights Clause for the Host Country: it provides the strongest opportunity for the Olympics to leave a legacy of improved governance among entities that will continue to operate after the Games are over. These implications for third parties are captured in the operational requirements, which provide that the counterparties (as well as certain other parties) must develop a human rights strategy to address the risks that arise from these entities' own activities as well as the activities of third parties. In particular, the operational requirements require the counterparties to "seek to prevent or mitigate adverse human rights impacts" by third parties.[18]

Second, after formulating a policy, respecting human rights requires the counterparties to conduct human rights due diligence. This involves assessing actual and potential human rights impacts, acting upon findings, tracking responses, and communicating how these impacts are being addressed. Due diligence should involve meaningful consultation with human rights experts and affected stakeholders. So too does due diligence require the mitigation of adverse effects, including by third parties whom the entity can control or influence.

Notably, the phrase "due diligence" has a broader and deeper meaning under the UNGPs than it does in anti-corruption compliance. For the latter, due diligence simply means determining whether the third party presents a risk to the principal company—for example, conducting due diligence to determine whether a third party may be paying bribes that create legal liability for the company. Whether the company seeks to prevent further misconduct, or instead severs the relationship, is essentially a business decision; in anti-corruption due diligence there is no expectation or encouragement to reform third parties. Moreover, mitigating the harm is generally not contemplated as part of anti-corruption due diligence.

By contrast, the UNGPs imbue businesses with a strong sense of responsibility for the conduct of their third parties. They envision an ongoing relationship of engagement with third parties, actively preventing and mitigating those parties' human rights violations. This relationship is evident in multiple sections of the UNGPs. As referenced earlier, Section 13 explains that the responsibility to respect means companies should "seek to prevent or mitigate adverse human rights impacts that are directly linked to their operations, products or services by their business relationships, even if they have not contributed to those impacts."[19] Companies thus assume responsibility for both the prevention, and mitigation, of violations even where the company did not itself contribute to them. As long as the abuse is linked to the principal company's operations, the UNGPs hold the company responsible.

The UNGPs provide helpful guidance on what these abstract terms—"prevent" and "mitigate"—look like in practice. The document provides that "if the business enterprise has leverage to prevent or mitigate the adverse impact, it should exercise it."[20] The UNGPs thus contemplate the principal company affirmatively reforming the third parties' business practices; merely severing the business relationship would not quite fulfill the UNGP's human rights objectives. Where companies do not quite possess the needed leverage, "the enterprise should increase" that leverage. Recommendations for increasing leverage over a third party include "offering capacity-building or other incentives" to the third party and "collaborating with other actors." In cases where the third party is difficult to reform, the principal company should demonstrate "ongoing efforts to mitigate the impact." This degree of responsibility for the conduct of third parties should begin with the company's code of conduct or, to use the UNGPs' alternative phrasing, its "policy commitment." That document should stipulate "the enterprise's human rights expectations of personnel, business partners and other parties directly linked to its operations, products, or services."[21]

By explicitly incorporating the UNGPs into the Host City Contract, the IOC has conveyed an expectation that the counterparties build a relationship of ongoing engagement with third parties to ensure their compliance with applicable human rights laws and standards. Indeed, an example of such an ongoing relationship of preventing violations by third parties is present in the IOC's own supplier code.[22] This code, like the Human Rights Clause of the Host City Contract, is explicitly linked to the UNGPs. It therefore provides an example of the reasonable expectations of an Olympic entity in relation to third parties under existing human rights standards. The supplier code specifically requires the IOC's suppliers, as well as the suppliers to the suppliers, to actively comply with the code's detailed human rights standards.[23] The IOC has here illustrated that "respecting" human rights includes requiring third parties to adopt human rights compliance.

This responsibility for third party conduct is among the most impactful provisions of the UNGPs. It has the potential to create a legacy of improved human rights governance with companies engaged in the work of preparing to host the Olympics. As we explain further in the following, the Anti-Corruption Clause should incorporate a similar responsibility.

c. Ensure Access to Remedy

Under the UNGPs, remedies must be provided to victims of business-related human rights abuses. Appropriate grievance mechanisms must therefore be established. The UNGPs assign to the states the principal responsibility to make grievance mechanisms available. However, Article 29 of the UNGPs provides that "business enterprises should establish or participate in effective operational-level grievance mechanisms" to complement the state-based mechanisms.[24] The responsibility to make grievance mechanisms available to victims of human rights abuses is thus shared by public- and private-sector entities.

Grievance mechanisms may be judicial or nonjudicial. They can include civil or criminal courts, arbitration or other alternative dispute resolution methods, labor tribunals, national human rights institutions, OECD National Contact Points, and various government-sponsored mechanisms like ombudsperson offices and government-run complaints offices. The UNGPs also specify the attributes of effective operational-level grievance mechanisms.[25] Such mechanisms should exist in addition to, not instead of, more formal national or international (judicial or nonjudicial) mechanisms. Remedies can include apologies, restitution, rehabilitation, financial or non-financial compensation, and punitive sanctions.

The operational requirements require the counterparties to make remedies available, but provide no guidance on how to do so. Elaboration in the operational requirements of what "remedy" should look like in practice would help to make that contractual duty more meaningful. Under the UNGPs, the Host City, NOC, and OCOG have a shared duty to make available grievance mechanisms, to participate in those mechanisms, and to ensure that their laws, policies, and agreements do not limit access to other mechanisms and remedies. Specifically, the NOC and OCOG should adopt operational level (nonjudicial and non-state) grievance mechanisms. This could involve the more liberal use of the Court for Arbitration in Sport for the resolution of human rights grievances, or the creation of alternative mechanisms specific to human rights. The Host City, NOC, and OCOG should require similar mechanisms of all business partners.

Under the language of the Human Rights Clause, the counterparties' contractual obligation to implement the UNGP framework is informed by two additional phrases: (1) "in a manner consistent with international agreements, laws and regulations applicable in the Host Country," and (2) "in a manner consistent with all internationally-recognized human rights standards and principles, including the United Nations Guiding Principles on Business and Human Rights, applicable in the Host Country." Each of these phrases is further explicated in the following.

d. ". . . in a manner consistent with international agreements, laws and regulations applicable in the Host Country . . ."

This clause, in conjunction with the Contract's subsequent clause, provides parameters for implementing the "protect, respect, and remedy" framework. The clause immediately presents two questions of interpretation.

The most fundamental question concerns the reach of the term "international." In this regard, the clause admits of two possible readings. The first is that "international" extends not only to "agreements" but also to "laws and regulations." Read this way, the clause references international agreements, international laws, and international regulations. Alternatively, "international" might extend only to "agreements," such that the "laws and regulations" referenced here are non-international (that is, domestic). This distinction, though seemingly technical, has important implications for the human rights obligations of the counterparties.

The second interpretation is stronger. The clause is best read to refer to international agreements, to domestic laws, and to domestic regulations. The most compelling reason is that while the terms "international human rights agreements" and "international human rights laws" are cognizable to human rights experts, the term "international human rights regulations" is not. Put another way, there is simply no such thing as an international human rights regulation. Grammatically, if the adjective "international" does not extend to "regulations," it cannot extend to "laws" either. Additionally, any international human rights law that is not an international agreement is customary law, which is probably covered by the Contract's subsequent "international standards" clause. In conclusion, we find that the Human Rights Clause should be read to reference international human rights agreements, domestic human rights laws, and domestic human rights regulations applicable in the Host Country.

The second interpretive question concerns the phrase, "in a manner consistent with . . ." The Host City, NOC, and OCOG do not have the legal authority to ensure full compliance with every international agreement, domestic law, and domestic regulation relevant to human rights applicable in the Host Country. Accordingly, rather than demanding strict compliance, the contract obligates the counterparties to adopt measures *consistent with* these agreements, laws, and regulations. Though leaving substantial room for interpretation, and making compliance with (or breach of) the contractual clause more difficult to determine, this clause is necessary given the institutional capacities and legal authority of the Host City, NOC, and OCOG.

Accordingly, implementation of this contractual obligation requires a two-step process. First, the parties must identify the international human rights agreements, domestic human rights laws, and domestic human rights regulations that apply in their country. This first step will vary among host countries depending on the international human rights agreements, including regional treaties such as the European Convention on Human Rights, to which the country is a party. For example, the international human rights agreements applicable to the 2024 Host, France, are different from those applicable to the 2028 Host, the United States. In some cases, the Host Country may already have official pronouncements that can aid in this process; France's "National Action Plan" for the implementation of the UNGPs[26] would help in this regard. Similarly, domestic laws and regulations will obviously differ substantially; again, for example, France's domestic human rights regime is substantially different from the United States' own regime, especially following France's adoption of the Duty of Vigilance Law.

Second, the parties must design measures that are "consistent with" these agreements, laws, and regulations, but are adapted to their respective institutional capacities and legal authority. This process is likely to require extensive consultation with the IOC and other stakeholders and will evolve based on the precedents set by successive Olympic hosts. France's implementation of this contractual clause will likely prove quite influential, underscoring the need for rigorous implementation, supported by multiple stakeholders, in Paris 2024.

e. ". . . and in a manner consistent with all internationally-recognized human rights standards and principles, including the United Nations Guiding Principles on Business and Human Rights, applicable in the Host Country . . ."

As with the previous clause, this one recognizes that the counterparties may not be in a position to require strict compliance with all applicable standards and principles. Instead, it requires the counterparties to adopt measures "in a manner consistent with" those standards and principles.

As noted throughout this memo, the clause explicitly references the UNGPs and treats them as foundational to the application of human rights principles to the Olympic Games. However, as the word "including" plainly suggests, the UNGPs are not the only standards or principles that apply. There are others. Though human rights due diligence standards and principles are myriad, the contract carefully limits the domain of applicable standards and principles. Specifically, they must satisfy two requirements: they must be "internationally-recognized" and they must be "applicable in the host country."

The standards and principles that most readily satisfy both these requirements are those promulgated by intergovernmental organizations to which the Host Country is a member. For all foreseeable future hosts—France, the United States, and Italy—there are three such sources: (1) the United Nations, including the Human Rights Council[27] and the UN Working Group on Business and Human Rights;[28] (2) the International Labour Organization, which has published several documents concerning the practical implementation of the Declaration on Fundamental Principles and Rights at Work;[29] and (3) the Organisation for Economic Co-operation and Development, which has published the Guidelines for Multinational Enterprises and may issue future publications concerning megasports governance in particular. Other sources may also issue from regional bodies. As noted, this reference to international standards and principles can be read as incorporating human rights principles arising from customary international law.

Ultimately, the Human Rights Clause and its operational requirements provide a sound framework for the counterparties as they implement the reforms that can produce Governance Legacies. It provides a helpful comparison to the Anti-Corruption Clause, which, as the next section shows, might need reinforcement.

The Anti-Corruption Clause

This clause, like the Human Rights Clause, represents a substantial step for the Olympic Movement and for the global anti-corruption effort. The clause obligates the Host City, NOC, and OCOG to

> refrain from any act involving fraud or corruption, in a manner consistent with any international agreements, laws and regulations applicable in the Host Country and all internationally-recognised anti-corruption standards applicable in the Host Country, including by establishing and maintaining effective reporting and compliance.

This phrase is strikingly similar to the Human Rights Clause, and would seem plainly intended to have a similar effect: to bring Olympic preparations up to leading standards and best practices. However, the human rights and anti-corruption spaces function very differently; the processes that produce the most respected and recognized standards are quite different.

Due to these differences, the Anti-Corruption Clause requires further revision and clarification if it is to provide an effective guide to OCOG compliance officers. Specifically, the Anti-Corruption Clause as now written suffers from three significant problems. First, the phrase "internationally-recognised anti-corruption standards applicable in the Host Country" is not meaningful. There is no analogue to the UNGPs in the anti-corruption space. Second, the Anti-Corruption Clause does not presently have sufficient Operational Principles. The above two problems, taken together, make this clause unlikely to be a meaningfully guide compliance officers seeking to implement it. Third, again in contrast to the Human Rights Clause, the Anti-Corruption Clause as presently written does not imply an obligation to monitor in an ongoing way the compliance efforts of third parties. From an anti-corruption compliance standpoint, this omission becomes problematic in at least three respects: (1) it leaves untouched a significant source of bribery and related forms of corruption in the preparations for the Games, insofar as it creates compliance obligations for the potential recipients of bribes (namely, the OCOG), but not for the potential suppliers of bribes (the third parties); (2) it lags behind global best practices; and (3) it misses an opportunity to leave a legacy of improved anti-corruption compliance in the Host Country. This section explicates the clause, identifies these problems, and proposes revisions to address them.

The Anti-Corruption Clause operates within a preexisting framework of Olympic anti-corruption policies. Prior to amending the Host City Contract, the IOC had in place a Code of Ethics,[30] and the Basic Universal Principles of Good Governance of the Olympic and Sports Movement.[31] These two documents, combined with the new Host City Contract amendments, create the anti-corruption framework for hosting the Olympic Games.

The Code of Ethics provides fundamental corruption prohibitions, while the Basic Universal Principles are a set of compliance guidelines. Because the Code of Ethics and the Basic Universal Principles precede the new contractual provisions, the new Anti-Corruption Clause in the Host City Contract is presumably intended to provide significant new substance to the existing IOC anti-corruption framework. It is likely not intended, and should not be read, to be merely duplicative of existing provisions in the IOC Code of Ethics and Basic Universal Principles of Good Governance. The question then becomes what the Contract is intended to add, and what it does in fact add as presently worded.

The Code of Ethics applies to all "Olympic parties," a term defined to include, inter alia, the NOC, the OCOG, and "the cities and their officials taking part in any type of candidature procedures of the IOC."[32] Although it is not entirely clear whether the Host City is an "Olympic party," once the candidature process has ended and preparations have begun, it seems much clearer that suppliers to the OCOG are not Olympic parties and plainly not subject to the Code's requirements.

The Code provides a number of basic substantive compliance principles. Article 2 uses the phrase that became incorporated in the Host City contractual clause: "refrain from any act involving fraud or corruption."[33] Article 3 prohibits bribery, and Articles 4 and 5 provide limits on gift-giving and hospitality. These are not compliance principles; they are standards with which the parties must comply rather than guidelines on how to comply.

The compliance principles are then referenced in Article 11, which requires the Olympic parties to abide by the Basic Universal Principles of Good Governance of the Olympic and Sports Movement. This document provides extensive compliance guidance, providing that Olympic parties must incorporate the following:

1. *Risk management:* a clear and adequate risk-management process that includes identification of potential risks for the sports organizations; evaluation of risks; control of risks; monitoring of risks; and disclosure/transparency.
2. *Code of Ethics:* parties must develop, adapt, and implement ethical principles and rules inspired by the Code of Ethics, and monitor their implementation.
3. *Accountability:* all bodies, whether elected or appointed, shall be accountable to the members of the organization and, in certain cases, to their stakeholders.

4. *Processes and mechanisms:* adequate standards and processes for accountability should be in place and available to all organizations, and consistently applied and monitored; clear and measurable objectives and targets must be set for the organization, its boards, management, and staff, including also appropriate tools for assessment.
5. *Transparency and communication:* financial information should be disclosed gradually and in appropriate form to members, stakeholders, and the public; disclosure of financial information should be done on an annual basis; the financial statements of sports organizations should be presented in a consistent way in order to be easily understood.
6. *Financial matters:* Applicable laws, rules, procedures, and standards: accounts should be established in accordance with the applicable laws and "True and fair view" principle; the application of internationally recognized standards should be strongly encouraged in all sports organizations and required for an international body; for all organizations, annual financial statements are to be audited by independent and qualified auditors; accountability and financial reports should be produced on a regular basis; information about remuneration and financial arrangements of the governing bodies' members should be part of the annual accounts.
7. *Internal control system:* internal control of the financial processes and operations should be established within the sports organizations; the adoption of a compliance system, document retention system, and information security system should be encouraged; the structure of the internal control system should depend on the size and importance of the organization; audit committees should be appointed for large sports organizations.
8. *Education and training:* there should be an induction program for all new members of staff, volunteer officers, and all board members; ongoing education and training of executives, volunteers, and employees should be integral to operations; the promotion of self-education and regular training within the sport organizations should be encouraged.
9. *Reporting obligation:* Article 18 requires that the Olympic parties must inform the IOC Chief Ethics and Compliance Officer confidentially, particularly by use of IOC Ethics and Compliance Hotline, of any information related to violations of the Code of Ethics, with a view to possible referral to the IOC Ethics Commission.[34]

These create an adequately thorough set of foundational compliance principles, comparable in rigor to the leading standards of governmental and nongovernmental bodies that compliance professionals around the world recognize. The IOC Code of Ethics and the Basic Universal Principles thus create a reasonably strong compliance framework. In the context of these two documents, the IOC has amended the Host City Contract to impose what we presume are additional obligations. The three documents, taken together, should create a reasonable and effective anti-corruption compliance framework for Olympic preparations.

Again, the new contractual clause obligates the Host City, NOC, and OCOG to:

> refrain from any act involving fraud or corruption, in a manner consistent with any international agreements, laws and regulations applicable in the Host Country and all internationally-recognised anti-corruption standards applicable in the Host Country, including by establishing and maintaining effective reporting and compliance.

This section explicates these various clauses.

a. "Refrain from"

This phrase originates in Article 2 of the IOC's Code of Ethics. To our knowledge, the IOC has not provided guidance on its meaning.

The word "refrain" stands in contrast to comparable verbs used in the Human Rights Clauses, particularly "prohibit" or "protect and respect." The latter terms tend to imply an obligation to prevent not merely one's own violations but also violations of the parties with whom one does business. "Refrain," by contrast, tends to imply an obligation only to prevent one's own violations; multiple compliance professionals we have spoken to interpret the word this way. While not too much should be made of subtle semantics, this interpretation is consistent with what this chapter previously called the gaping hole in the clause. "Refrain" may provide the first hint that the contractual parties' compliance requirements do not extend to the point of requiring suppliers to adopt compliance programs.

b. "Any act involving fraud or corruption"

The clause references not merely "corruption" but "fraud or corruption." In contrast to the more limited scope of FIFA's Anti-Corruption Directives, which focus only on corruption, the IOC Host City Contract requires the contractual parties to refrain (to use the wording of the Contract) from both corruption and fraud. These terms, taken in combination, encompass quite a broad array of conduct, much of which is at risk in megasports.

Corruption is often defined as the abuse of public office for private gain. Notably, the international anti-corruption instruments generally avoid defining the term. Instead, they enumerate various forms of corruption and require signatories to prohibit those specific forms. These will include bribery, embezzlement, extortion, money laundering, trading in influence, and the like. Certainly, the most authoritative international source for definitions of specific acts of corruption is the UN Convention Against Corruption (UNCAC).[35] Any country considering a bid to host a mega sporting event would have joined this Convention. The Task Force therefore does not consider the word "corruption" to be problematic or in need of further explication in the Host City Contract.

However, in the compliance community the difference between fraud and corruption is substantial. "Fraud" can have either of two meanings in this context:

1. While corruption typically refers to the way a business interacts with either the government or with customers, "fraud" can often refer to business-to-business dealings. In the context of the host city contract, fraud might be construed to suggest that the OCOG/NOC/Host City have an obligation to prevent their suppliers, sponsors, and other partners from engaging in illicit dealings with other firms.
2. The compliance community can define "fraud" to include a great many forms of conduct not typically included under the rubric of corruption, including anti-competition law, intellectual property, data security, and others. It is not clear whether the IOC intends that the contractual clause encompass so broad a swath of conduct. If so, it would present a formidable compliance challenge.

At any rate, the clause should not be read to require a laundry list of distinct fraud and corruption compliance systems. This would prove utterly unworkable for a contractual party already overwhelmed with the Games' preparations. Rather, the clause may be best read as calling for a single compliance system and a set of standards that applies to all risk areas.

c. "In a manner consistent with any international agreements, laws and regulations applicable in the Host Country"

This clause, as with the Human Rights Clause presents a tricky interpretive question. International anti-corruption agreements frequently distinguish between the obligations of public-sector entities and those of private-sector entities. While host cities are of course public-sector entities, they are not national governments and therefore do not possess all of the attributes or authority that international agreements, which are written with national governments in mind, will assume. NOCs might have attributes of both public- and private-sector entities; their composition and authority can differ among countries. OCOGs are now regarded as nongovernmental actors. International anti-corruption compliance standards must be adapted to the legal authority and institutional capacities of each of the contractual parties.

The phrase "international agreements" could refer to global or regional agreements. Globally, the relevant anti-corruption agreement is the UNCAC. Though the OECD's Anti-Bribery Convention[36] is salient in international anti-corruption compliance, it applies only to extraterritorial bribery and therefore has limited relevance to Olympics preparations (neither the NOC, OCOG, nor Host City would typically be tasked with monitoring bribery that occurs outside the Host Country). Some host cities may be in countries that have joined regional anti-corruption agreements, such as Europe's Group of States Against Corruption (GRECO).[37] Certainly, the preeminent document in this context will always be UNCAC. We recommend basing further guidance on the meaning of this contract on UNCAC.

As with the Human Rights Clause, a key interpretive question concerns whether the adjective "international" in the phrase "international agreements, laws, and regulations" extends to "laws and regulations." In other words, the clause might be read to apply to international agreements, international laws, and international regulations, or instead, to international agreements, domestic laws, and domestic regulations. The Task Force finds the latter interpretation stronger for two reasons. First, there is no such thing as an international anti-corruption regulation; that phrase simply has no meaning in international anti-corruption compliance. Second, though there are international anti-corruption laws ("international" meaning joined by more than one country, as opposed to a "national" or "domestic" law), all such laws are also agreements; there is no international anti-corruption law that is not already encompassed by the word "agreement." Extending the application of "international" in this clause to "laws" and "regulations," therefore, does not make sense. This clause can only be read to reference international agreements, domestic laws, and domestic agreements. Accordingly, the laws referenced in this clause may vary significantly with those of the Host Country. Though international agreements may not yield significant differences between countries, domestic laws and regulations obviously will.

This clause may contain one minor deficiency. Much of international anti-corruption compliance guidance is issued by governments in a form that is neither an agreement, a law, nor a regulation. Rather, enforcement agencies will typically issue guidance documents that facially have no binding legal authority but are in practice the authoritative statements of the enforcement agencies' interpretation of applicable statutes. This is true of the US Foreign Corrupt Practices Act, the UK Bribery Act, and France's Sapin II. A more fulsome clause might include a phrase such as "laws, regulations, and guidance."

While the preceding is provided merely as guidance and not as criticism, the following discussion reveals what the Task Force believes to be one of three principal problems with the Anti-Corruption Clause.

d. "And all internationally-recognised anti-corruption standards applicable in the host country"

International recognition tends to refer to a formal process in which a representative body recognizes a standard through established legal channels. The UNGPs, for example, gained international recognition when endorsed by the UN Human Rights Council.

In the field of anti-corruption compliance, there is no mechanism in place, analogous to the procedures of the UN Human Rights Council, to formally recognize anti-corruption compliance standards. The standards that command the most respect among compliance professionals are not internationally recognized. These standards might fall into three categories. The first category is the compliance guidance promulgated by national enforcement agencies, such as the US Department of Justice,[38] the UK Ministry of Justice,[39] or France's Agence Française.[40] The second is the guidance developed by nongovernmental associations such as the International Organization for Standardization (ISO)[41] or the Committee of Sponsoring Organizations of the Treadway Commission (COSO).[42] The third may be the nonbinding guidance provided by intergovernmental organizations, such as the UN Global Compact.[43]

Though compliance experts of various nationalities might deem any of these standards important or authoritative, none of these standards could be properly be described as "internationally recognised." Anti-corruption compliance thus stands in marked contrast to human rights due diligence in this respect. The parallel phrasing of the anti-corruption and Human Rights Clauses may thus unintentionally carry different meanings.

Confusion between the internationally recognized standards in human rights and the anti-corruption compliance standards which are not internationally recognized is also apparent in the IOC Supplier Code.[44] This code uses the UNGPs to impose relatively rigorous human rights requirements on suppliers to the IOC (as distinguished from suppliers to the OCOG). The code further suggests UNGPs can provide standards for anti-corruption compliance. They do not. No anti-corruption compliance professional would interpret the UNGPs to provide meaningful and coherent guidance on anti-corruption compliance. The IOC Supplier Code, like the Host City Contract, may suggest a lack of appreciation for the difference between human rights due diligence and anti-corruption compliance.

e. "Including by establishing and maintaining effective reporting and compliance"

Effective reporting and compliance standards certainly exist. However, they cannot be "included" among the internationally recognized standards because compliance standards are not internationally recognized. This clause would seem to underscore the core difficulty of the anti-corruption contractual clause: the apparent aim of the clause is to bring Olympics preparations in line with international best practices from the compliance field, but the clause is not worded to have that effect.

While the phrase "internationally-recognised standards" is the first area (as explained earlier) where the Anti-Corruption Clause might be clarified and strengthened, there are two additional areas in need of support. First, while the human rights protect-and-respect framework is the topic of an entire section in the operational requirements, there is no similar focus on corruption and fraud. Indeed, the word "corruption" only appears once in the operational requirements. This occurs in Section 32, which concerns "Sourcing and Resource Management."[45] Because the section discusses both procurement and waste disposal, corruption gets relatively short shrift. The introduction to that section generally provides that the OCOG should have a "successful procurement programme" that supports the OCOG's "organizational objectives and operational requirements." The section's discussion of substantive operational requirements provides that there should be effective oversight, to include the development of a Sustainable Sourcing Code. Subsection 07 then contains the sole reference to corruption, where it provides that the OCOG's Sustainable Sourcing Code must "respect the OCOG's commitments" concerning the "prohibition of any act involving fraud or corruption."[46]

These cursory references to compliance do not equip a compliance officer with the tools necessary to operate a meaningful compliance program. An adequate compliance program would not require excessive resources and would produce a substantial return on investment. Draft operational requirements are provided in the following.

The second area of potential improvement concerns the responsibilities of the OCOG to reduce the corruption risks of third parties. Partners, suppliers, sponsors, and other third parties are of course not parties to the Contract. Neither are they Olympic Parties, therefore falling outside the IOC's Code of Ethics and Basic Universal Principles. Though the IOC has found it appropriate and necessary to adopt a Supplier Code for suppliers to the IOC, the Anti-Corruption Clause of the Host City Contract implies no such code for suppliers to the OCOG. The furthest the Host City Contract might now reach is requiring the contractual counterparties to conduct due diligence on their suppliers. But conducting due diligence on a supplier is a significant step short of requiring suppliers to adopt preventative measures. The Human Rights Clause creates an active, ongoing relationship of engagement between the counterparties and third parties; the Anti-Corruption Clause, as presently worded, does not have this effect.

Within compliance circles, it is well known that the majority of corruption violations involve the conduct of third parties: agents, partners, suppliers, and so forth. A corruption clause that does not involve robust third-party management is therefore unlikely to prove effective. In the Olympics context, inadequate third-party management will inevitably result in the very corruption scandals the contract seems designed to reduce.

As the Paris OCOG works toward requiring suppliers to adopt compliance programs, the Host City Contract is falling behind emerging best practices. So too does the clause and its operational requirements fall behind the standard set in the Human Rights Clause, which contemplates an ongoing relationship with third parties designed to prevent and mitigate abuses. The Host City Contract should therefore be amended to include a requirement that OCOGs require compliance programs among all third parties.

The FIFA Host Country Requirements

The FIFA analysis necessarily looks at a variety of documents rather than a single contract. On the human rights side, these documents evince a reasonably clear and effective framework. Built upon the UNGPs, that framework has three basic mechanisms. First, various documents impose human rights requirements not just on the FIFA parent entity but by extension on FIFA's host-country subsidiary, the organizing committee. This extends FIFA's human rights policy into the host country. Second, the UNGPs also reach any entity "directly linked" to FIFA operations in the host country. Such provisions will tend to leave legacies of improved norms, knowledge, and skills in the corporate sector among third parties. Third, FIFA requires a number of guarantees from national governments, city governments, and other local authorities, which will in turn introduce new norms and practices into these entities. Collectively, the human rights framework seems well poised to leave a host country human rights legacy.

The anti-corruption framework is harder to discern. Indeed, teasing out the design requires some detective work, and the work proves somewhat inconclusive. As the following discussion will show, the absence of an internationally recognized anti-corruption compliance document analogous to the UNGPs, combined with some terminological confusion in the FIFA documents, fails to bring the host-country anti-corruption compliance guidance to nearly the degree of clarity and thoroughness seen in the

FIFA human rights policies. In the absence of clear requirements, prospects for a host-country anti-corruption legacy seem somewhat dimmer. This section analyzes FIFA's host-country human rights and anti-corruption requirements in turn.

FIFA's Human Rights Provisions

FIFA now addresses human rights in a variety of documents and locations. We might put these various sources into three buckets. The first is the general FIFA governance documents. These include the FIFA Statutes, the FIFA Code of Conduct, the Code of Conduct for Third Parties, the Code of Ethics, and most importantly, the Human Rights Policy. The second bucket consists of the documents written specifically for prospective host countries. These include the "Guide to the Bidding Process for the 2026 FIFA World Cup," the "FIFA Regulations for the selection of venue for the final competition of the 2026 FIFA World Cup," and the inelegantly titled, "Structure, Content, Presentation, Format and Delivery of Bid Book." The third is what FIFA calls guarantees. These are detailed in a document that FIFA supplied to this author called the "Human Rights Overview," with assurances that the language of the host country contract largely tracks the language in this document. This section discusses each in turn.

The FIFA Statutes provide foundational, albeit cursory, human rights principles. Article 3 of the General Provisions provides a commitment to respecting internationally recognized human rights, and Article 4 prohibits discrimination on a number of bases.[47] The FIFA Code of Conduct affirms this human rights commitment and then begins the work extending it to the host country. The Code of Conduct applies to officers and employees of FIFA and, critically, to FIFA subsidiaries. Subsidiaries will include the host country organizational body. In Qatar, for example, the host country FIFA subsidiary is called Qatar 2022 and works alongside the Supreme Committee to meet FIFA's obligations related to the organization of the event; in future events, the FIFA subsidiary will likely play a more salient role. The Code of Conduct provides that FIFA, implicitly to include its host country subsidiary, will respect all international recognized human rights.[48]

The general FIFA document with the richest implications for a host-country human rights legacy is the Human Rights Policy. Various provisions of the policy establish four key principles that provide a solid foundation for leaving a positive lasting human rights impact on the host country. First, FIFA expressly adopts the UNGPs as the definitive, authoritative source of guidance for designing its human rights policies and practices. There can be no doubt: the UNGPs are the standard. Second, FIFA embraces all "internationally recognised" rights, including but not limited to the Universal Declaration of Human Rights, the International Covenant on Civil and Political Rights, the International Covenant on Economic, Social, and Cultural Rights, and the ILO's Declaration on Fundamental Principles and Rights at Work. Third, FIFA recognizes that its human rights responsibilities extend into host country operations. Consistent with the UNGPs, FIFA pledges to avoid causing or contributing to adverse human rights impacts not just in its own activities but those that are "directly linked to its operations, products or services by its business relationships, even if FIFA has not contributed to those impacts." Those links will plainly reach into host-country operations, particularly through the host-country FIFA subsidiary and the entities doing business with it. FIFA indeed recognizes, and repeatedly affirms, that its human rights issues are most likely to arise "through its relationships with other entities" and mentions governments and businesses specifically. This is a critical foundational principle. Finally, FIFA will move beyond the responsibility to respect and take measures to "promote the protection of human rights and positively contribute to their enjoyment" especially in or through football.[49] The promotion of these human rights can also lead to a significant legacy of norms, knowledge, or even policies or laws.

The extension of human rights obligations into the host country continues with the Code of Conduct for Third Parties.[50] This applies to "everyone who does business with FIFA," to include suppliers, business partners, and freelance workers. Prohibited conduct includes violations of human rights. This document is not a detailed code but perhaps a pamphlet designed for public consumption. Nevertheless, through FIFA subsidiaries, this policy reaches into third-party relationships within host countries.

As one moves from the general FIFA governance documents to the guidance written specifically for prospective host countries, the human rights legacy implications rise into full relief. FIFA provides an accessible summary of its most recent bidding requirements in its pamphlet, "Guide to the Bidding Process for the 2026 FIFA World Cup."[51] However, the full depth and breadth of the bidding requirements are found in the "FIFA Regulations for the selection of venue for the final competition of the 2026 FIFA World

Cup,"[52] which are turn summarized and fleshed out in FIFA's online document entitled "Structure, Content, Presentation, Format and Delivery of Bid Book."[53]

The Regulations, and the appended "Bidding Registration," provide detailed requirements. Any bidding country must sign and initial every page of the registration. In the selection criteria, the bidding country must develop a vision and strategy for a "meaningful legacy" in the host country or countries and city or cities that includes the "social effects" of the event.[54] Here, FIFA is not just permitting but affirmatively requiring a social legacy, a category into which a human rights legacy fits quite nicely.

The member association must specifically design a "hosting vision and strategy," which includes a "contribution" to what FIFA calls "sustainable development." The meaning of this term turns out to shift substantially in the course of the FIFA documents. That ambiguity does no harm to the human rights effort but does substantial harm on the anti-corruption side. Here, sustainability is defined quite broadly. It includes human rights and closely related labor standards and antidiscrimination principle. Notably, it also includes anti-corruption, environmental protection, and health and infrastructure. Just two pages later, in the subsection entitled "sustainable event management, human rights and environmental protection," sustainability is defined in the narrower sense of environmental sustainability, and human rights are expressly and separately mentioned.[55] This shift has two implications: first, sustainability is defined in the narrower and more conventional sense of environmental protection; and second, anti-corruption falls away. The shift leaves the impression that human rights and environmental sustainability are selection criteria, and anti-corruption is not. That same pattern continues in Section 8 of the Appendix Bidding Registration, entitled "Sustainable Event Management and Human Rights." The "General Principles" provide that FIFA is committed to environmental sustainability and to human rights. Again, a narrower definition of sustainability is seemingly contemplated, one that does not include human rights or anti-corruption measures. Nevertheless, the human rights foundation here provided is quite solid.

The Regulations further require the member association to respect human rights in accordance with the UNGPs related to hosting the competition. As such, it must not only avoid causing or contributing to adverse human rights impacts but must seek to prevent or mitigate such impacts "directly linked to its/their operations, products or services by its/their business relationships even if the Member Association(s) has/have not caused or contributed to such impacts, because a significant part of human rights risk may be associated with the activities of third parties."[56] This is a critical phrase for the prospect of a human rights legacy, in two ways. First, it extends well into host-country operations. Second, it in effect imposes human rights requirements on the business entities that will remain in operation after the World Cup is over. These entities' World Cup work will expose them to new norms, practices, and laws related to human rights. Some companies will comply with these heightened standards only in relation to World Cup work, and only as long as that work continues. Others will slowly incorporate heightened human rights awareness into their broader operations. Chapter 5 contains a detailed description of this phenomenon as it is occurring in Qatar.

The Regulations' requirements for host countries are fleshed out—and indeed expanded—in the "Structure, Content, Presentation, Format and Delivery of Bid Book."[57] This document again defines legacy to include "positive social, environmental and economic effects targeted to be achieved."[58] This document affirms the member association's obligation to avoid causing or contributing to adverse human rights through its own activities. Even more importantly for a legacy analysis, the document further affirms that "a significant part of human rights risk may be associated with the activities of third parties." For this reason, the member association must "identify and take adequate measures to seek to prevent or mitigate adverse human rights impacts that are directly linked to its operations, products or services by its business relationships." This remains true "even if the Member Association has not caused or contributed to such impacts." The operations requiring particular attention include the provision of security, potential resettlement and eviction, labor rights, rights of children, gender and other forms of discrimination, and freedom of expression and peaceful assembly.[59]

Further, the member association must develop a proposal for a human rights strategy to respect all internationally recognized human rights. Tracking the preceding language, the report must identify human rights risks in which the member association may be involved "either through its own activities or as a result of its business relationships." These risks should pay particular attention to the aforementioned rights: security, resettlement and eviction, labor rights, the rights of children, gender and other forms of discrimination, and freedom of expression and peaceful assembly.

However, this document imposes additional significant requirements on the report. It should include an independent study of the country's legal landscape, focusing on whether gaps may exist between the country's laws and enforcement practices and the internationally recognized human rights. The report should be informed by internal or independent external expertise on human rights and consultations with stakeholders. Further, it should identify "relevant international standards and best practices" that the country should adopt to prevent, mitigate, or remediate these risks. Those standards should at least include: the Performance Standards of the International Finance Corporation (part of the World Bank Group); several documents from the International Federation of Consulting Engineers (a Swiss organization that develops construction engineering and construction contract templates); the International Code of Conduct for Private Security Service Providers; the ILO's Code of Practice on Safety and Health in Construction; UNICEF's Children's Rights and Business Principles; and UN Women's Empowerment Principles.[60]

So too must the proposal provide detailed information on the measures it will take to prevent and mitigate its own adverse impacts, to "embed its commitment to respect all Internationally Recognised Human Rights" in its own operational policies as procedures as well in the activities of its business relationships, and to implement "ongoing due diligence" to identify, prevent, and mitigate adverse impacts.[61] The principle of embedding human rights measures into third-party relationships is, again, likely to leave a legacy across the business sector. So too should the report include stakeholder engagement and grievance mechanisms.

The third mechanism consists of the declarations and agreements that the host country, host city, and host country authorities over stadiums, training sites, airports, and hotels.[62] These declarations and agreements obligate the signatories to respect human rights within their respective jurisdictions. Unlike the IOC Host City Contract, which the hosts sign after winning the bid, these are signed in anticipation of winning a bid. The national government declaration includes commitments to: fully support the member association in avoiding adverse human rights impacts; uphold its international law obligations to respect, protect, and fulfill human rights, particularly in relation to security, potential resettlement and eviction, labor rights, rights of children, gender and other forms of discrimination, and freedom of expression and peaceful assembly; make effective judicial or nonjudicial remedies available; protect the labor rights of game-related workers; and train security forces in accordance with various international standards.[63] The host city declaration requires each host city hosting World Cup events to make the same commitments. The stadium, training sites, airport, and hotel authorities must each execute an agreement pledging to conduct all competition-related activities in accordance with the UNGPs.[64] The national government declaration template[65] and host-city declaration templates[66] are publicly available. These requirements have the potential to leave legacies within these various public-sector entities, as well as with the companies subject to their jurisdiction.

FIFA's Anti-Corruption Guidance

FIFA's host-country human rights guidance is thus clear, consistent, and thoroughly woven throughout FIFA's various policy documents. FIFA has taken a single, authoritative source—the UNGPs—and built its policies around it. The anti-corruption framework is harder to piece together. There is no single external set of standards that is consistently integrated into FIFA's myriad policy documents in the manner of the UNGPs. The absence of a single, authoritative, internationally recognized anti-corruption compliance standard is hardly FIFA's fault. But until FIFA finds a way to more fully fill that void, its host-country anti-corruption compliance guidance will suffer.

To determine what the host-country anti-corruption compliance guidance does and does not consist of, one must sift through two kinds of documents: some that are written for FIFA generally, and others that are drafted specifically with prospective host countries in mind. The general FIFA documents include the FIFA's Statutes, Code of Conduct, Code of Conduct for Third Parties, Anti-Corruption Directives, Code of Ethics, and the Compliance Program. The documents designed specifically for bidding countries are the Bidding Regulations and appended Bidding Registration, the Guide to the Bidding Process, the "Structure, Content, Presentation, Format and Delivery of Bid Book," and the Compliance Handbook.

Anti-corruption policies that are likely to leave a legacy of improved anti-corruption governance in the host country will have to meet three criteria: (1) they would have to apply not just to FIFA entities and their third parties but also to host-country entities who may not be in a direct third-party relationship with FIFA (the most obvious example being a company doing work for Qatar's Supreme Committee); (2) they would have to consist of not a mere abstract commitment to a vague anti-corruption principle, but instead be a set of practical guidelines that anti-corruption compliance officers could operationalize; and (3) the guidance should cover myriad forms of corruption—bribery, embezzlement, money laundering, abuse of influence, and the like—that can arise in the course of preparing to host an event.

On the human rights side, the clear and consistent incorporation of the UNGPs into FIFA policies clearly satisfies similar criteria. The "directly linked to operations" provision of the UNGPs has the effect of requiring host-country third-party entities to adopt human rights measures. The UNGPs provide practical guidelines concerning policies and procedures that an entity can operationalize. So too do the UNGPs reference a variety of human rights, as opposed, for example, to a policy focusing on a single human rights violation such as slave labor.

On the anti-corruption side, a document satisfying these criteria does not appear to exist in any one place. Interviews with FIFA compliance personnel suggested such a document may exist, but it is not public, and FIFA declined to share the document with the author. The public documents contain elements that satisfy these criteria. Various of these documents mentioned here contain components of an effective host-country anti-corruption strategy and carry with them the potential to leave a significant anti-corruption legacy.

In particular, two candidate documents emerge, though the legal status of either is entirely unclear. As will be discussed in the following, FIFA's Compliance Handbook could do much of the above-mentioned: it is designed for local stakeholders, includes practical guidance, and applies to myriad forms of corruption a host country might face. However, it is not referenced in the Bidding Regulations, the Guide to the Bidding Process, or any other document imposing requirements on prospective host cities. It is available for anyone who may be interested, but it is not integrated into FIFA's host-country requirements. The second document is the UN Office on Drugs and Crime's (UNODC's) *Strategy for Safeguarding Against Corruption in Major Public Events*. It is expressly referenced in the "Structure, Content, Presentation, Format and Delivery of Bid Book," but nowhere else—not in the Bidding Regulations, or in the Guide to the Bidding Process, or in any other document. It is simply not clear whether FIFA fully intends to require a host country to comply with it. The documents in tandem, were they required, would go a long way toward doing the work the UNGPs do on the human rights side. FIFA does not appear to have yet taken that step.

The references to anti-corruption compliance suffer from an additional problem. FIFA will sometimes shoehorn anti-corruption under the term "sustainability." But this is not a consistent practice, even within single documents. In some parts of some documents, sustainability takes on a broader meaning, to include anti-corruption, human rights, environmental protection, and other norms. This would be fine, were it consistent. However, elsewhere sustainability refers more narrowly to environmental protection only. One might for that reason expect anti-corruption compliance to get short shrift in these policies. In fact it does, as the following discussion explains.

For all the preceding reasons, FIFA's policies struggle mightily to impose specific, clear, enforceable anti-corruption compliance requirements on host countries. This chapter seeks to identify those shortcomings. Chapter 10 will propose reforms.

The review of FIFA's policies begins with those documents seemingly written for FIFA operations and entities generally, rather than for bidding countries specifically. Whatever requirements FIFA will eventually impose on the host country do not find their origin in the FIFA statutes. Though those statutes contain foundational commitments to human rights generally and to anti-discrimination specifically, they make no mention of an anti-corruption principle. The word "corruption" appears only once in the ninety-six-page document, in relation to doping and match-fixing.[67] The principle that the host country must adopt anti-corruption measures related to risks that arise during the preparations for the event is simply not present.

A foundational commitment to preventing host-country corruption is found in numerous other documents. FIFA's Code of Conduct reflects compliance responsibilities of everyone in the organization. In the new Code of Conduct, there is heavy emphasis on FIFA's zero-tolerance stance on corruption, a prohibition on money laundering, and basic guidelines on gifts, meals, and entertainment.[68] So too does it apply to the host-country FIFA subsidiary, thus reaching at least this far into host-country operations.[69] However, carefully comparing the Code of Conduct to the Human Rights Policy reveals a critical difference: FIFA does not take responsibility for the corruption risk posed by other entities "linked to its operations." Put another way, there is no principled commitment to reform the practices of the host-country public and private entities involved with hosting an event. Additionally, the Code of Conduct does not contain specific guidance on what this anti-corruption principle means in practice. In both these respects, the absence of an anti-corruption document analogous to the UNGPs is felt.

The Code of Conduct for Third Parties is a bit better.[70] It applies to "everyone who does business with FIFA," to include suppliers, business partners, and freelance workers. This would seemingly apply to host-country companies doing business with the host-country FIFA subsidiary; whether companies working for Qatar's Supreme Committee, for example, would be included is less clear. Prohibited conduct includes bribery and money laundering, in addition to violations of intellectual property rights, political neutrality, environmental sustainability, and human rights. The document is not a detailed code, being more in the style of a pamphlet for public consumption, and is not at all designed to give firms operational guidance. Still, an anti-corruption ethic begins extending into the host country.

Two FIFA documents are more operational in focus but apply to limited forms of potential misconduct with only marginal relevance to the host-country corruption risks arising in preparing to host an event. FIFA's Anti-Corruption Directives[71] are far more narrowly focused on bribery than the Code of Conduct for Third Parties, providing detailed guidelines on various forms of bribery, and explicitly referencing the well-known international anti-bribery statutes from the United Kingdom (the UK Bribery Act) and the United States (the Foreign Corrupt Practices Act). They do not appear to be written with host countries in mind; rather, the document concerns the interaction between bribery risks that arise in interactions between FIFA and various confederations and member associations (presumably in the process of winning bids to host events, to broadcast the events, etc.). Officials of these confederations and member associations have of course figured prominently in bribery scandals surrounding the winning of the rights to host events, broadcast rights, and so forth, and this is the apparent focus of the document. Similarly, FIFA's Code of Ethics[72] is an anti-corruption code that encompasses bribery, conflicts of interest, gifts, abuse of position, forgery, embezzlement, and others. It applies to officials, players, and "match agents and their intermediaries." This latter phrase refers to event promoters and associated individuals.[73] The Code of Ethics also details procedures for investigating misconduct. The document's focus appears to be protecting the competitive integrity of the game rather than reducing corruption in the preparations for the game. The Code of Ethics becomes applicable to the member associations via the bidding guidance discussed below, but again, would seem to apply to a limited swath of potential misconduct.

Ultimately, the document providing the most practical, concrete guidance on preventing various forms of corruption is FIFA's Compliance Program.[74]

Its aim is to help "build transparency, foster ethical behaviour, identify risks, define policies and create procedures." The program contains many of the familiar hallmarks of a legitimate compliance program: tone at the top; risk assessment; monitoring and review; third-party due diligence; policies, procedures, and controls; and training and communication.[75] So too has FIFA created a Compliance Handbook that is plainly designed for use by member associations and other stakeholders, outlining "basic principles and benefits of implementing compliance guidelines."[76] The handbook is remarkably accessible, user-friendly, and practical, covering numerous topics in corruption and in anti-corruption compliance. From a legacy standpoint, the question is whether any host-country entity is required to implement this compliance program or its equivalent. At present, it may not be.

Turning then to the FIFA policies designed specifically for prospective hosts, one might look first to the Bidding Regulations and the appended Bidding Registration. But these documents reveal a strange absence of host-country anti-corruption requirements. As mentioned earlier, the Bidding Regulations' selection criteria require the bidding country to develop a "hosting vision and strategy," which includes a "contribution" to what FIFA calls "sustainable development" in the host country or countries and city or cities. Sustainability is here defined to encompass human rights, labor standards, anti-corruption, anti-discrimination, environmental protection, and health and infrastructure. Sustainability thus has a broad definition that encompasses anti-corruption; sustainability measures would then, at least in part, include anti-corruption measures. However, in the subsection entitled "Sustainable event management, human rights and environmental protection," sustainability is defined in the narrower sense of environmental sustainability, and human rights are expressly and separately mentioned.[77] Notably, anti-corruption is not. This phrasing leaves the impression that human rights and environmental sustainability are selection criteria, and anti-corruption is not. That same pattern continues in Section 8 of the Appendix Bidding Registration, entitled "Sustainable Event Management and Human Rights." The "General Principles" provide that FIFA is committed to environmental sustainability and to human rights. Again, a narrower definition of sustainability is seemingly contemplated, one that does not include anti-corruption measures.

FIFA's Guide to the Bidding Process contains various guidelines for bidding associations on venues and other requirements. Section 5 deals together with host-country human rights and anti-corruption requirements and again uses the phrase "sustainability and human rights."[78] Here, sustainability seemingly does not encompass human rights. What the term "sustainability" encompasses beyond environmental protection becomes the question.

To wit, the section requires the bidding association to develop a strategy for a "sustainable-event-management system" in accordance with three sets of standards: ISO 20121, AA1000SES, and GRI. If these were anti-corruption compliance standards, corruption might be adequately addressed in this document. They are not. ISO 20121 is a sustainable events standard that defines sustainability in the narrower and more conventional way: environmental sustainability. It is promulgated by the International Organization for Standardization, which publishes standards on a remarkably wide variety of organizational governance issues. By ISO's own description, 20121 is devoted to "sustainable events." Without defining sustainability, ISO explains that ISO 20120 "promot[es] more responsible consumption" and "relieve[s] the strain on local infrastructure and utilities."[79] Ultimately, it is about depleting resources in the conduct of major events. AA1000SES is, as the final three letters in the name suggest, a "stakeholder engagement standard." Its purpose is to "outline[] how to rethink an organization's approach to engagement." The contemplated engagement may touch on corruption issues insofar as the engagement relates to "governance, strategy, and operations." Still, AA1000SES remains a standard for talking to stakeholders; it is not an anti-corruption compliance program.[80] Finally, GRI Standards concern "reporting publicly on a range of economic, environmental and social impacts." Just as AA1000SES focuses on stakeholder engagement, GRI Standards focus on reporting. That reporting concerns a wide variety of economic, environmental, and social impacts. Indeed, the Standards include roughly forty topics on which a company would report, including economic performance, energy, biodiversity, and tax. One, and only one, of these is anti-corruption. GRI 205 is an anti-corruption disclosure standard that helps companies disclose their practices concerning various aspects of anti-corruption compliance, including risk assessments, training, and investigations.[81] This is something. However, it conspicuously is not a set of compliance standards. It is not an anti-corruption compliance program. It does not tell companies how to reduce corruption; rather, it tells them how to talk about whether they have implemented anti-corruption measures.

Compounding the problem, neither the Government Declaration nor the Host City Declaration mention anti-corruption measures. As discussed earlier, both include human rights provisions, and the latter includes a detailed provision on environmental sustainability.[82] That FIFA would expressly include an environmental sustainability provision, but not make require the city to make an anti-corruption pledge of any kind, is telling, and troubling.

However, the document entitled "Structure, Content, Presentation, Format and Delivery of Bid Book"[83]—specifically the chapter entitled—"Sustainable Event Management, Human Rights and Environmental Protection," provides anti-corruption provisions not seen or even alluded to in any other document, including the Bidding Regulations. Immediately preceding the human rights provisions from Section 23 summarized earlier, Section 22 is entitled "Sustainable Event Management." However, here sustainability is not understood in the narrow environmental sense; indeed, "Environmental Protection" is the title of Section 24. Rather, Section 22 is devoted to the broader concept of sustainability. This proves a bit awkward, given that human rights and environmental protection are elsewhere treated. Indeed, even in this section, the lack of clarity on the meaning of the word "sustainable" is glaring. The section begins with an emphasis on the importance of sustainable development without ever defining the term; in a context in which environmental protection and human rights are elsewhere treated, this proves especially confusing. It then requires the member association to develop a sustainability strategy in line with ISO 20201 (discussed earlier). So far, the section has virtually nothing to do with anti-corruption (nor with human rights).

However, it then pivots sharply to a focus on anti-corruption measures. Here, finally, the host country must agree to adopting meaningful anti-corruption measures. The member association strategy should include a comprehensive anti-corruption risk assessment that includes bribery, collusion, embezzlement, fraud, patronage, nepotism, and weak rule of law. It should include an "appropriate and transparent compliance and procurement process" for all goods and services the member association will source.

The document further requires the member association to devise a strategy for "sustainable procurement" in line with two key documents: the FIFA Code of Ethics and the UNODC's handbook entitled, "A Strategy for Safeguarding against Corruption in Major Public Events." The UNODC handbook is a comprehensive guide on the anti-corruption risks associated with hosting mega sporting events and the elements of an anti-corruption compliance that can reduce these risks. Risk areas the handbook discusses at length include procurement, security, infrastructure and construction, recruitment, financial management, conflicts of interest, sponsorship, and others. Specific anti-corruption compliance measures that can help to reduce these risks include risk assessment, risk mitigation, monitoring, reporting, codes of conduct, disciplinary measures, and so forth.[84]

These anti-corruption requirements expressly touch third parties. The member association must develop a "concrete plan and strategy" for ensuring that other "stakeholders involved in the preparation, hosting and staging" of the event apply "ethical and effective business practices." Similarly, the member association must develop a plan for ensuring that "sub-contractors and further third parties" that form part of the supply chain for the event comply with the preceding principles. Here, FIFA has finally set its sights on host-country anti-corruption measures that reach the conduct of third parties. However, FIFA's Compliance Handbook is nowhere mentioned.

Ultimately FIFA, like the IOC, would do well to bring its anti-corruption framework to a level of rigor and impact comparable to the human rights framework. Both organizations have made huge strides in developing host-country human rights frameworks, and for both organizations, anti-corruption lags behind. This need not be resource intensive. Chapter 10 provides some ideas on how to do so. However, Chapter 9 first explains how the various measures that a host city or country might adopt pursuant to these contractual obligations can produce legacies.

Notes

1. *See generally Host City Contract Operational Requirements*, Int'l Olympic Comm. (2018), https://stillmed.olympic.org/media/Document%20Library/OlympicOrg/Documents/Host-City-Elections/XXXIII-Olympiad-2024/Host-City-Contract-2024-Operational-Requirements.pdf [hereinafter *Host City Operational Requirements*].
2. Private Conversation with FIFA personnel.
3. U.N. Off. of the High Comm'r for Hum. Rts., *Guiding Principles on Business and Human Rights: Implementing the United Nations "Protect, Respect, and Remedy" Framework*, U.N. Doc. HR/PUB/11/04 (2011), https://www.ohchr.org/documents/publications/guidingprinciplesbusinesshr_en.pdf [hereinafter *UNGP Framework*].
4. Private conversation with Paris 2024 personnel.
5. See *Olympics Compliance Task Force*, Richmond Blog, https://blog.richmond.edu/olympicscompliance/, for a full account of the Task Force's membership. This section owes particular thanks to Cecilia Fellouse-Guenkel, Tom Fox, and Sungyong Kang on the Anti-Corruption Team, and on the Human Rights Team, Sarah Joseph, Joanna Kyriakakis, Simon Rice, and Jose-Miguel Bello y Villarino.
6. *See Compliance 24*, Le Cercle De la Compliance, https://www.lecercledelacompliance.com/en/compliance-2024-2/.

7. *See* Catherine Delhaye, *The Organization for Compliance Professionals*, Le Cercle de la Compliance, https://www.lecercledelacompliance.com/en/association-2/.
8. *Host City Contract Principles*, *supra* note 1, at 16.
9. *Id.*
10. G.A. Res. 217 (III) A, Universal Declaration of Human Rights (Dec. 10, 1948), https://www.un.org/en/universal-declaration-human-rights/.
11. *International Covenant on Economic, Social and Cultural Rights*, United Nations Off. of the High Comm'r for Hum. Rts., https://www.ohchr.org/en/professionalinterest/pages/cescr.aspx.
12. *International Covenant on Civil and Political Rights*, United Nations Off. of the High Comm'r for Hum. Rts., https://www.ohchr.org/en/professionalinterest/pages/ccpr.aspx.
13. *Id.*
14. *CCPR General Comment No. 18: Non-discrimination*, United Nations Off. of the High Comm'r for Hum. Rts., https://www.refworld.org/docid/453883fa8.html.
15. *Host City Operational Requirements*, *supra* note 2, at 127–28.
16. *UNGP Framework*, *supra* note 4, at 14.
17. *Host City Operational Requirements*, *supra* note 2, at 128.
18. *Id.*
19. *UNGP Framework*, *supra* note 4, at 14.
20. *Id.* at 22.
21. *Id.*
22. *IOC Supplier Code*, Int'l Olympic Comm. (2018), https://www.olympic.org/sustainability/ioc-supplier-code.
23. *Id.* at 3.
24. *UNGP Framework*, *supra* note 4, at 31.
25. *Id.* at 31–32.
26. *France*, Nat'l Action Plans on Bus. & Hum. Rts., https://globalnaps.org/country/france/.
27. *United Nations Human Rights Council*, United Nations Off. of the High Comm'r for Hum. Rts., https://www.ohchr.org/EN/HRBodies/HRC/Pages/Home.aspx.
28. *Working Group on the issue of human rights and transnational corporations and other business enterprises*, United Nations Off. of the High Comm'r for Hum. Rts., https://www.ohchr.org/en/issues/business/pages/wghrandtransnationalcorporationsandotherbusiness.aspx.
29. *ILO Declaration on Fundamental Principles and Rights at Work*, Int'l Labour Org., https://www.ilo.org/declaration/lang--en/index.htm.
30. *Ethics*, Int'l Olympic Comm. (2020), https://www.olympic.org/code-of-ethics.
31. *Basic Universal Principles of Good Governance of the Olympic and Sports Movement*, Int'l Olympic Comm. (2008), https://stillmed.olympic.org/Documents/Conferences_Forums_and_Events/2008_seminar_autonomy/Basic_Universal_Principles_of_Good_Governance.pdf.
32. *IOC Code of Ethics*, Int'l Olympic Comm. 12 (2016), https://stillmed.olympic.org/Documents/Commissions_PDFfiles/Ethics/2016_ioc_code_of_ethics-book-en.pdf.
33. *Id.* at 14.

34. *Id.* at 16 (providing the text of Article 11 of the Code of Ethics).
35. United Nations Convention Against Corruption, Oct. 31, 2003, 2349 U.N.T.S. 41, https://www.unodc.org/unodc/en/treaties/CAC/.
36. *OECD Anti-Bribery Convention*, OECD, http://www.oecd.org/corruption-integrity/explore/oecd-standards/anti-bribery-convention/.
37. *What Is GRECO?*, Council of Eur., https://www.coe.int/en/web/greco/about-greco/what-is-greco.
38. *A Resource Guide to the U.S. Foreign Corrupt Practices Act*, U.S. Dep't of Just. & U.S. Sec & Exch. Comm'n (2020), https://www.justice.gov/criminal-fraud/file/1292051/download.
39. *The Bribery Act of 2010: Guidance*, Ministry of Just. (2011), https://www.justice.gov.uk/downloads/legislation/bribery-act-2010-guidance.pdf.
40. *Sapin II Compliance Guide*, Risk & Compliance Portal, https://www.ganintegrity.com/portal/compliance-quick-guides/sapin-ii-compliance-guide/.
41. *ISO 37001: Anti-Bribery Management Systems*, ISO, https://www.iso.org/iso-37001-anti-bribery-management.html.
42. Lawrence J. Trautman & Joanna Kimbell, *Bribery and Corruption: The COSO Framework, FCPA, and U.K. Bribery Act*, 30 Fla. J. Int'l L. 191, 191 (2018).
43. Lise Kingo, *The UN Global Compact: Finding Solutions to Global Challenges*, United Nations: UN Chron., https://www.un.org/en/un-chronicle/un-global-compact-finding-solutions-global-challenges.
44. *IOC Supplier Code*, Int'l Olympic Comm. (2018), https://www.olympic.org/sustainability/ioc-supplier-code.
45. *Host City Operational Requirements*, *supra* note 2, at 150–51.
46. *Id.* at 151.
47. FIFA Statutes Articles 3 and 4 of the General Provisions, at 11 (May 2021), https://digitalhub.fifa.com/m/7e791c0890282277/original/FIFA-Statutes-2021.pdf [hereinafter FIFA Statutes].
48. *Code of Conduct: Playing by the Rules*, FIFA (2019), https://www.icsf.ca/wp-content/uploads/sites/5/2019/01/FIFA-CODE-OF-CONDUCT.pdf [hereinafter FIFA, Code of Conduct].
49. *FIFA's Human Rights Policy*, FIFA, at 5 (May 2017), https://img.fifa.com/image/upload/kr05dqyhwr1uhqy2lh6r.pdf.
50. *FIFA Code of Conduct for Third Parties*, FIFA (Oct. 2020), https://digitalhub.fifa.com/m/6734cf98cbeaa070/original/i0mtve5d0zapbtzws1wt-pdf.pdf [hereinafter FIFA, *Third Parties*].
51. *Guide to the Bidding Process for the 2026 FIFA World Cup*, FIFA, https://img.fifa.com/image/upload/hgopypqftviladnm7q90.pdf [hereinafter FIFA, *Guide to Bidding Process*].
52. *FIFA Regulations for the Selection of the Venue for the Final Competition for the 2026 FIFA World Cup*, FIFA, https://digitalhub.fifa.com/m/4ab6dd02a42e838d/original/stwvxqphxp3o96jxwqor-pdf.pdf [hereinafter *Venue Regulations*].
53. *Structure, Content, Presentation, Format and Delivery of Bid Book*, FIFA, https://digitalhub.fifa.com/m/2634208645dbf8e4/original/lkcsjfoaovuyptlxrtmm-pdf.pdf [hereinafter *Bid Book Structure*].
54. *Venue Regulations*, *supra* note 53, at 38.
55. *Id.* at 40–41.

56. *Id.* at 55.
57. *Bid Book Structure*, *supra* note 54.
58. *Id.* at 3.
59. *Id.* at 26.
60. *Id.* at 27.
61. *Id.* at 28.
62. FIFA Human Rights Overview, document on file with the author, at 5.
63. *Id.* at 4.
64. *Id.* at 5.
65. *Draft Host Country Declaration Re 2026 FIFA World Cup Tests*, FIFA, https://digitalhub.fifa.com/m/256bbd4681077136/original/ntnx2xcf8hwzwxn2xn3e-pdf.pdf.
66. *Template Host City Declaration*, FIFA, https://digitalhub.fifa.com/m/4eca4118f912ef52/original/o9gqrxii4x3rdijr8auy-pdf.pdf [hereinafter *Template Host City Declaration*].
67. FIFA Statutes, *supra* note 48, at 12.
68. FIFA, *Code of Conduct*, *supra* note 49.
69. *Id.*
70. FIFA, *Third Parties*, *supra* note 51.
71. *Anti-Corruption Directives*, FIFA, https://digitalhub.fifa.com/m/7895e17ae0642f31/original/t8m7wdzgxmerctqienol-pdf.pdf.
72. FIFA Code of Ethics § 5(2)–(4) (Aug. 12, 2018), https://resources.fifa.com/image/upload/fifa-code-of-ethics-2018-version-takes-effect-12-08-18.pdf?cloudid=uemlkcy8wwdtlll6sy3j.
73. *See, e.g.*, U.S. Soccer Federation, *Operating Procedures for International Matches and Tournaments*, USSoccer.com, https://www.ussoccer.com/federation-services/international-games/operating-procedures.
74. *Compliance Programme*, FIFA, https://www.fifa.com/who-we-are/legal/compliance/compliance-program/.
75. *Id.*
76. *FIFA Compliance Handbook*, FIFA (Oct. 2020), https://digitalhub.fifa.com/m/4a1daee06e72f0c6/original/lp015yxfdqesvrleo6ii-pdf.pdf
77. FIFA, *Guide to the Bidding Process*, *supra* note 52, at 40–41.
78. *Id.*
79. *ISO 20121: Sustainable Events*, ISO.org (2012), https://www.iso.org/iso-20121-sustainable-events.html.
80. *AA1000 Stakeholder Engagement Standard*, AccountAbility.org (2015), https://www.accountability.org/standards/aa1000-stakeholder-engagement-standard/.
81. *GRI 205: Anti-Corruption 2016*, GRI (2016), https://www.globalreporting.org/standards/media/1006/gri-205-anti-corruption-2016.pdf.
82. *Template Host City Declaration*, *supra* note 67.
83. *Bid Book Structure*, *supra* note 54, at 23.
84. *The United Nations Convention Against Corruption: A Strategy for Safeguarding Against Corruption in Major Public Events*, U.N. Office on Drugs and Crime (Sept. 2013), https://www.unodc.org/documents/corruption/Publications/2013/13-84527_Ebook.pdf.

9

From Reforms To Legacies

Introduction

Anti-corruption and human rights measures are, of course, in the first instance preventative. Their original and most important purpose is to reduce the risk that violations of these norms will occur. But how can preventative measures produce legacies? How do the various human rights and anti-corruption measures that various host-city/country actors might adopt result in positive impacts that endure years after the event is over?

As explained in Chapter 1, a human rights and anti-corruption legacy consists of norms, policies, practices, or laws that have application beyond the event, will endure after the event is over, and the implementation of which is accelerated by hosting the event. This chapter builds a conceptual model to illustrate how human rights and anti-corruption measures can produce a legacy. It was made possible in large part by a research grant from the International Olympic Committee's (IOC's) Olympic Studies Centre, which yielded two benefits. First, it enabled interviews with multiple stakeholders to the Paris 2024 Games, conducted over two years. Those interviews generated a number of specific examples of policies that are being adopted or might be adopted in the future. Accordingly, the examples in this model are largely a mixture of reforms already adopted in Paris, reforms that were under consideration at the time, and others here imagined. Second, the grant enabled several in-person meetings with IOC personnel in which the dynamics captured in this model were discussed. For both these reasons, the model relies almost exclusively on the Olympic Games. However, it adapts easily to the FIFA Women's and Men's World Cups, as the final section briefly explains.

The model begins from the premise that there are typically four principal organizations implementing the reforms that can eventually produce human rights and anti-corruption legacies. This model will refer to them, for convenience, as "actors." The actors first include the three counterparties to the Host City Contract—the Organizing Committee for the Olympic Games (OCOG), the National Olympic Committee (NOC), and the Host City. An

A New Megasport Legacy. Andrew Brady Spalding, Oxford University Press. © Oxford University Press 2022.
DOI: 10.1093/oso/9780197503614.003.0009

additional actor is the Host City's national government, which enacts laws and policies and provides other forms of support and guidance related to the preparations for the Games.

Each version of the Olympic Games will present a subtle variation on this structure. For Paris 2024, and as described in Chapter 6, France has created an entity separate from the OCOG, called SOLIDEO, to oversee the financing and delivery of Olympic facilities. The 2026 Milan/Cortina Games are, of course, hosted in two entirely separate and unrelated municipalities. The 2028 Los Angeles Games are hosted by a single city, but one situated in a unique government framework: in the US system, states hold significant power, and many of the laws and policies a national government would otherwise adopt related to hosting the Olympics may be adopted by the state of California. Despite these minor variations, these four categories of actors remain useful for purposes of building a model.

Each of these actors may, in the course of preparing to host the Olympics, adopt laws, policies, or practices related to anti-corruption and human rights governance. Some of these laws, policies, or practices will have principal effect within the organization. For example, the Host City may adopt an anti-discrimination law applicable to all municipal employees and officials, or an OCOG might adopt a code of conduct specifically concerning bribes and conflicts of interest, applicable to all OCOG officials, employees, and volunteers. This model calls such reforms "internal reforms." These internal reforms can of course produce a human rights and anti-corruption legacy where the actor remains in existence after the Games (which a Host City or Country obviously would and OCOG effectively would not). Where the entity continues to exist and operate after the Games, and that law, policy, or practice remains intact, it becomes a legacy.

These same four actors may also adopt reforms that take principal effect beyond the organization itself. This chapter styles these "external reforms," and the model is more complex. External reforms differ from internal reforms in two ways. Most importantly, they take effect outside the entity itself: an OCOG might adopt a reform that changes the way companies with which it does business conduct their affairs. Any possible legacy will therefore exist not in the OCOG itself but within or among those companies. Second, external reforms might reflect the influence of multiple actors. For example, a reform targeting the companies with which an OCOG does business may result from the OCOG working in conjunction with the Host City or with an enforcement agency of the national government. Here, the value's model lies in recognizing how and where the same four actors might adopt reforms that take effect outside the actors themselves, and how those reforms might eventually result in various kinds of human rights and anti-corruption legacies.

This chapter will first describe the relatively simple dynamics of internal legacies, and then capture the more complex dynamic of external legacies.

Internal Legacies

The model for internal human rights and anti-corruption legacies and the following charts illustrating that model are quite straightforward. The value of the internal model is simply in recognizing that the Olympics can and do in fact produce reforms which, should they remain in place four years after the Games, would constitute a legacy.

The charts in Figure 9.1 represent the four actors with simple rectangular boxes. Arrows represent reforms the actor might adopt. The boxes following the arrows identify those substantive reforms.

OCOGs can, and certainly should, adopt internal policies or codes concerning corruption and human rights. These policies or codes are the starting point for any compliance program. Indeed, as described in Chapter 6, the Paris OCOG has adopted several key documents related to internal governance.

The first is the Code of Ethics.[1] This code applies to OCOG members, employees, and volunteers; as the Games approach, the sum total of these persons will approach seventy thousand. The Code includes both human

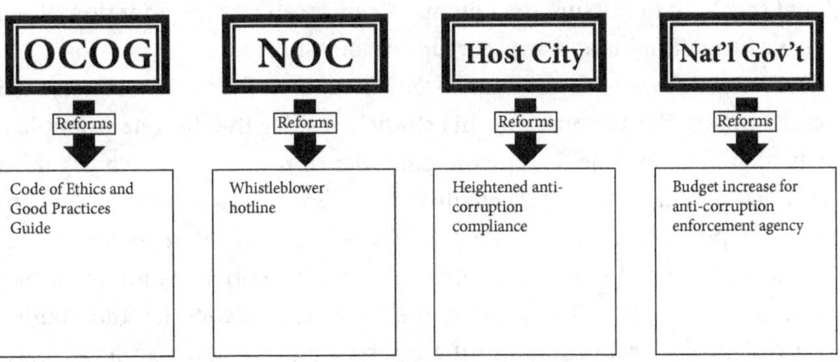

Figure 9.1 Key Olympic Actors and Their Internal Reforms

rights and anti-corruption provisions. It protects individual rights and forbids harassment abuse and discrimination, as well as corruption, bribery, and conflicts of interest. It mandates setting up a whistleblower alert system. It also includes provisions on sport manipulation, doping, gambling, and fraud.

Another illustrative example is the Paris COJO's Good Practices Guide.[2] This document is designed to be an educational tool. It applies to all persons involved with the COJO and is particularly focused on COJO's interaction with third parties. It contains provisions governing conflicts of interest, gifts and hospitality, and partner and supplier relations. It also covers human rights, prohibiting discrimination and harassment based on a number of protected categories.

These two documents both govern the behavior of persons working or volunteering for the OCOG. Because the OCOG will eventually cease to operate following the Games, the organization could not be said to have an internal legacy at the organizational level. However, while the organization will cease to function, its officers, employees, and volunteers obviously will not. Rather, they will move into various jobs in the public or private sectors, in France and beyond. The impact of their time with the OCOG, should it endure, can become a legacy of the Games.

An NOC, like an OCOG, can and should adopt various anti-corruption and human rights policies and practices. Of course, an NOC should not need a successful host bid to bring its governance up to reasonable standards; these policies and procedures would ideally be in place before the country wins the bid to host the Games. More realistically, such an organization will likely be in the earliest stages of adopting reasonable policies and procedures. The sudden awareness that its internal governance may soon come under the global spotlight of hosting the Olympics can accelerate the adoption of reasonable human rights and anti-corruption measures.

Early interviews with the French NOC suggested a variety of ways this could happen. For purposes of this study, consider the discrete example of a whistleblower hotline. It is a core compliance principle that an organization must have a reporting mechanism that allows persons within the company to report potential wrongdoing. The identity of the reporting person should be protected to prevent retaliation, and the organization must have procedures in place to fairly assess the reported misconduct and conduct an investigation proportional to the assessed risk. Imagine an NOC had a code of conduct in place, was fully aware that it needed a reporting hotline to implement the code, and had failed to do so. Further imagine that learning of the country's successful bid to host the Games motivates the NOC to finally implement the hotline. Should that hotline remain in place after the Games, it becomes a legacy.

The Host City has an opportunity to effectuate governance reforms that is even broader than an NOC or OCOG; as a governmental body, a Host City can adopt formal laws. Obviously, laws governing the conduct of their officers and employees in relation to corruption and human rights are commonplace. Still, hosting the Games can again accelerate the adoption of higher standards and more diligent enforcement. Imagine the host city decides to strengthen its internal anti-corruption compliance program. These reforms might bring the city's practices into conformity with applicable local or national laws. So too might the city decide to strengthen its programs beyond legal requirements. Either way, if the reforms remained in place after the event is over, they become a legacy.

Like the Host City, the national government can adopt laws, policies, or practices that can have effect beyond the Olympics preparations and can remain in place after the Games are done. Some, perhaps most, will concern the conduct of all persons under its jurisdiction; these would count as external reforms and are discussed below. However, a national government will of course also adopt laws, policies, or practices related to the operations of its own offices and employees.

Interviews with French anti-corruption officials suggested an interesting internal anti-corruption reform at the national level. As Chapter 6 described, France's Olympics laws granted its new anti-corruption compliance agency, Agence Française Anticorruption (AFA), jurisdiction over the OCOG, thereby tying AFA closely to the Olympic preparation effort. Officials reported that shortly after winning the Paris 2024 Games, AFA submitted a request to expand its operations, to include additional personnel and other funding. They further report that among the arguments they made to justify the budget increase was their role in the Olympic Games. Officials explained that the money AFA requested would not be devoted to Olympic preparations, and for this reason would not become obsolete after the Games were over. That is, AFA used the Olympics to request a permanent expansion of its operations and budget.

The request was granted in large part. Accordingly, France's principal anti-corruption enforcement agency experienced an increase in its capacity to promote anti-corruption practices across France. The precise causal role of the Games, vis-à-vis other influences, is of course impossible to quantify. But precise quantification is not necessary to prove a legacy. To the extent the Games accelerated the implementation of reforms that expand France's anti-corruption enforcement, this can count as a legacy.

All four of the actors are able to adopt internal reforms concerning anti-corruption and human rights governance. These reforms can have effect beyond the Olympics preparations themselves and can remain in place after the Games are over. The reforms will have various kinds of impacts that are already recognized in the legacy scholarship and IOC publications. The chart in Figure 9.2 illustrates reforms becoming legacies. The "legacies" arrow represents the reforms producing lasting impacts. The box beneath the legacy arrows provides a list if the particular kinds, or facets, of legacy those reforms would produce.

First consider the OCOG's adoption of various codes, policies, and procedures concerning corruption and human rights. These policies are internal in the sense that they govern the behavior of the organization's officials and employees. Though the organization will expire soon after the Games, the opportunity for a legacy lies in the lasting effects on those officials and employees. These effects can take two forms, both of which are recognized

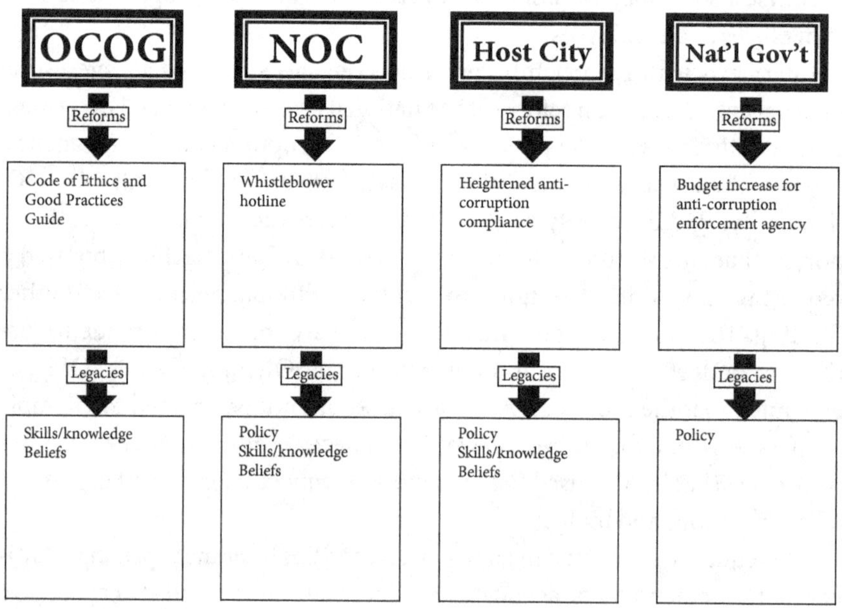

Figure 9.2 Internal Legacies

as facets of legacy. The first is skills and knowledge. OCOG members will, in the course of complying with these internal policies, learn about applicable laws and emerging best practices in reducing corruption and human rights violations. For Paris 2024, they will likely become better acquainted with Sapin II and the Duty of Vigilance Law; for another Games, they would learn of that country's particular legal framework. While they would acquire a working knowledge of these laws, so too would they acquire the skills necessary to comply with these laws. They would learn about codes of conduct and compliance policies and procedures. They would learn how to conduct a tender while reducing corruption risks, or what the permitted and prohibited bases may be for granting or denying a promotion. They would become skillful in identifying human rights red flags in supply chains or corruption red flags in third-party relationships. These skills would, to some degree, almost certainly remain in place years after the Games are over: the former officials and employees would bring these skills to their next jobs and, in at least some instances, utilize and build upon them. The legacy literature has long affirmed that such skills and knowledge constitute a legacy.

So too can beliefs become a legacy, and the internal anti-corruption and human rights policies of an OCOG would quite likely prove highly impactful in molding the normative commitments of its officials and employees. France is, again, an illustrative example. France has historically been a leader, in Europe and beyond, in the area of human rights. From the 1789 Declaration of the Rights of Man, to the 2017 Duty of Vigilance Law that set the standard of imposing human rights responsibilities on corporations, France has been a leader in thought and practice. By contrast, France has until recently been known among anti-corruption experts to lag behind its European peers. Sapin II is designed to remedy this problem. While OCOG lawyers or officials would not make themselves available for interviews in the present research project, one can imagine the rapid evolution of their anti-corruption convictions as they tried to build an operational framework that complied with national law, international standards, and IOC expectations. These new norms about the importance and feasibility of reducing corruption would become gradually internalized and, once set, would not likely evaporate upon completion of the Games.

Consider next the example of an NOC adopting a whistleblower hotline. Unlike the OCOG, the NOC obviously remains in existence and full operation after the Games. The whistleblower hotline, assuming it is not dismantled after the Games, would remain functional. The ongoing existence of a corruption or human rights hotline is probably best classified as a "policy and governance" legacy facet. Provided that the Games accelerated the implementation of this hotline, and it remained in place for one complete Olympic cycle, the hotline would constitute a legacy. In addition to its policy impact, the presence of a hotline would also shape the beliefs of those associated within the organization. Continuing with the example of France, interviews with various French stakeholders repeatedly disclosed an uneasiness with the concept of whistleblowing: some attributed it to the historical French norm of "fraternity," others to the experience of Nazi occupation, and yet others to naked self-interest. Whatever the reason, France has been slow to embrace the concept of anonymously reporting the misconduct of one's peers. Were the NOC to adopt a hotline, its officials and employees, faced with a newly instituted hotline, would likely, over time, tend to see the value of this global best practice and accept it as an appropriate feature of organizational governance. Relatedly, a more limited number of people would acquire skills associated with setting up and operating a hotline. Such skills and beliefs would constitute a legacy.

A similar dynamic would play out where a Host City adopted heightened anti-corruption and human rights compliance for the conduct of its officials and employees. Assuming the various codes of conduct, policies, and procedures remained in place after the Games, they would fall under the policy facet of legacy. Those associated with the design and implementation of the program, as well as those who have to substantially change their conduct to comply with the program, would acquire skills. So too would the operation of these compliance programs tend to inculcate municipal officials and employees with stronger and more refined anti-corruption and human rights norms. These policies, skills, and beliefs would all count as legacies.

The final example of an internal reform is the national government augmenting the resources of an anti-corruption enforcement agency, as seems to have happened in France. Focusing on the impact of this reform within the agency, it would almost by definition leave a policy and governance legacy. Provided these expanded resources were not withdrawn following the Games—and in France, the resources were not earmarked specifically for Olympics work, making them seem more permanent—they too become part of France's human rights and anti-corruption legacy.

As mentioned earlier, the internal reforms are not difficult to conceptualize: the various parties to the contract, plus the national government, implement a number of internal anti-corruption and human rights reforms that remain in place after the Games are over. Perhaps less obvious, but potentially of much broader impact, are the external reforms.

External Reforms

The model for external reforms begins with the same four actors (or variations thereof): the OCOG, the NOC, the Host City, and the national government. However, the reforms, and their impact, take effect outside the organization itself. This chapter names three sectors in which external reforms take effect. The first is the business or private sector. Here, the reforms might take the form of binding statutes or regulations governing corporate conduct, provisions in contracts between the actors and the companies with which they do business, or policies or standards that partners, consumers, enforcement agencies, or other stakeholders expect companies to follow. The second sector is the public sector. These can be laws or policies adopted by any level of government that concern how other government actors conduct their affairs. An example might be a federal anti-discrimination law with application beyond the federal government itself, such as a federal law that applies to municipal bodies. The third sector, which is unique to megasports, is the national sports federations. Though this may not be entirely distinct in any given country from either the public or the private sectors, it warrants identification here as a distinct realm of influence for the obvious reason that the federations are so salient in the megasport space.

External reforms also differ from internal reforms in that multiple actors might work together to effectuate those reforms. This can occur separately or in coordination. The national government might work in conjunction with the OCOG to develop compliance standards for companies doing Olympics business, or, alternatively, each may adopt its own requirements that converge on companies in the Olympics space. The interactions between these actors are potentially far more complex than this study can capture. Still, the chart in Figure 9.3 depicts examples of actors producing reforms in each of the sectors. Here, the small arrows represent the influence of the actor in the sector. These arrows are representative and not exhaustive.

As a result of this influence, reforms will occur in each of the sectors. Of course, the sectors are not themselves adopting the reforms; these sectors are not cohesive entities adopting uniform policies or practices. Rather, the four entities adopt the reforms which take effect in the sectors. As with internal

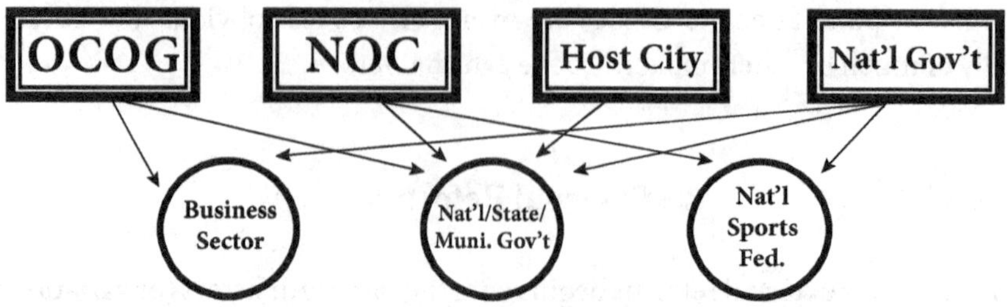

Figure 9.3 The Olympic Actors' External Influence: A Representative Sample

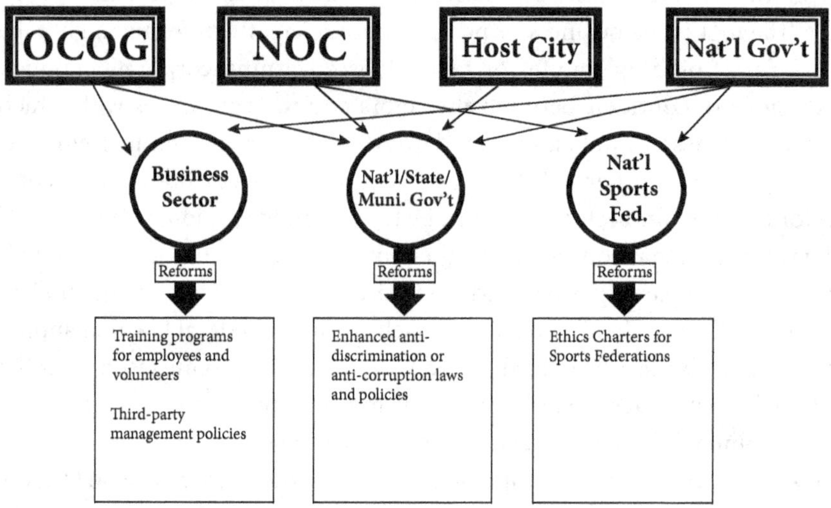

Figure 9.4 External Reforms

reforms mentioned earlier, the chart in Figure 9.4 shows the reforms with larger arrows and the substantive reforms in the boxes below.

To begin, consider two external reforms that would take principal effect in the business sector. The first is a training program for employees and volunteers. As the OCOG strengthens its compliance program, and as the date of the Games approaches, the OCOG will need to conduct training of some kind for all such personnel in applicable anti-corruption and human rights policies and procedures. While the OCOG would implement the training, that training may not be the product of the OCOG's influence alone. The national government may concurrently drive this reform through its expectation that the OCOG adopt a meaningful compliance program that includes an effective training component.

This training can be pro forma, insipid, and ineffective or, with a modest investment of creativity, time, and resources, can become quite impactful. That impact can be measured by not just its quality but the quantity of persons who would receive it: in Paris that number is estimated to approach seventy thousand. While such a training program would, at first glance, seem to be an internal reform, remember that nearly all of the volunteers, and likely a substantial number of the employees, are working for the Games short term. When the Games are over, those persons will end their affiliation with the OCOG and will go on to work in other areas of society. They will bring their new familiarity with applicable anti-corruption laws, policies, practices, and norms with them. Because the recipients of this training are affiliated with the OCOG only for a short while, this training is best understood as an external reform—the reform begins internally, but its lasting effect lies externally. It presents a significant opportunity to shape the beliefs and skills of persons who will very shortly be outside the OCOG.

A more obvious external reform that might occur within the business sector is a third-party management policy in which the OCOG imposed certain requirements on all companies with which it does business. As the previous discussion of the host country contract explains, these requirements would need to be reasonable. Excessively expensive, burdensome, or unfamiliar requirements would deter companies from working in the Olympics space. The extent and nature of the requirements would need to depend on local laws, practices, and customs. The requirements would also need to be tailored to the size of the company: large companies have more resources available to invest in anti-corruption and human rights compliance than do small ones. Still, it is plainly an international best practice that private entities (which the IOC considers the OCOG to be) have such third-party management policies in place. These policies would first involve conducting due diligence in selecting third parties. It might further involve a requirement that the third party has a code of conduct in place, and policies and procedures to implement that code. So too would the OCOG need to periodically review the third-party's policies and practices. But whatever the content and scope of these requirements, they would necessarily have the effect of raising the standards and behavior of those companies working in the Olympics space. In the potentially lasting impact of these heightened norms and practices lies a significant legacy opportunity.

An external reform that might occur across the public sector would be a national law or policy statement requiring all government agencies to improve their anti-discrimination or anti-corruption protections. A legislature might pass a statute, or an enforcement agency might issue new interpretive guidance, concerning the standards applicable to all government bodies. Such a reform might be motivated by a concern among officials that the Olympic spotlight will expose governance lapses within the host government that could prove embarrassing. Though not the topic of the present chapter, Qatar has adopted systemic labor protections (applicable in both the public and private sectors) in anticipation of hosting the 2022 FIFA World Cup for exactly this reason. In France, its anti-corruption enforcement agency has been actively engaged in using the Olympics to help lift France's anti-corruption practices and to implement both the letter and the spirit of the new anti-corruption law, Sapin II. For future Games, it is entirely conceivable that a Host Country would take the Olympic Games as a catalyst to clean up its human rights and anti-corruption legal framework.

For an NOC, its principal sphere of external influence will be the national sports federations. Potentially with the support of other actors, especially within the national government, reforms can be effectuated within the sports federations that will advance human rights and anti-corruption reforms. This process appears to be occurring now in France. For example, an NOC can impose a requirement that all athletes and coaches enter into an ethics charter as a condition of participating in the sports federation. These charters—apparently called a *charte deontologique* in France—can include premises that the athlete or coach will not engage in discriminatory or harassing practices and will not engage in various corrupt practices that will compromise the integrity of the sport. Hosting the Olympic Games could induce a country to strengthen its charters and more rigorously monitor their implementation, with the hopes of avoiding embarrassing scandals connected to the Olympics. Again, where those charters and associated practices remain in place beyond the Games, they too create a significant legacy opportunity.

In sum, hosting the Olympics can induce the above-mentioned actors to adopt reforms that will take effect in various sectors. In some cases, the Olympics will be the original cause of the reforms, but more frequently the Olympics will accelerate an organic governance movement. Either way, those impacts can become legacies.

The chart in Figure 9.5 illustrates the kinds of legacies these external reforms can produce. As with internal reforms, the external reforms produce legacies in the form of policies, skills, knowledge, and beliefs.

Within the business sector, as the OCOG employees and volunteers integrate into the broader economy, they will bring with them a new knowledge

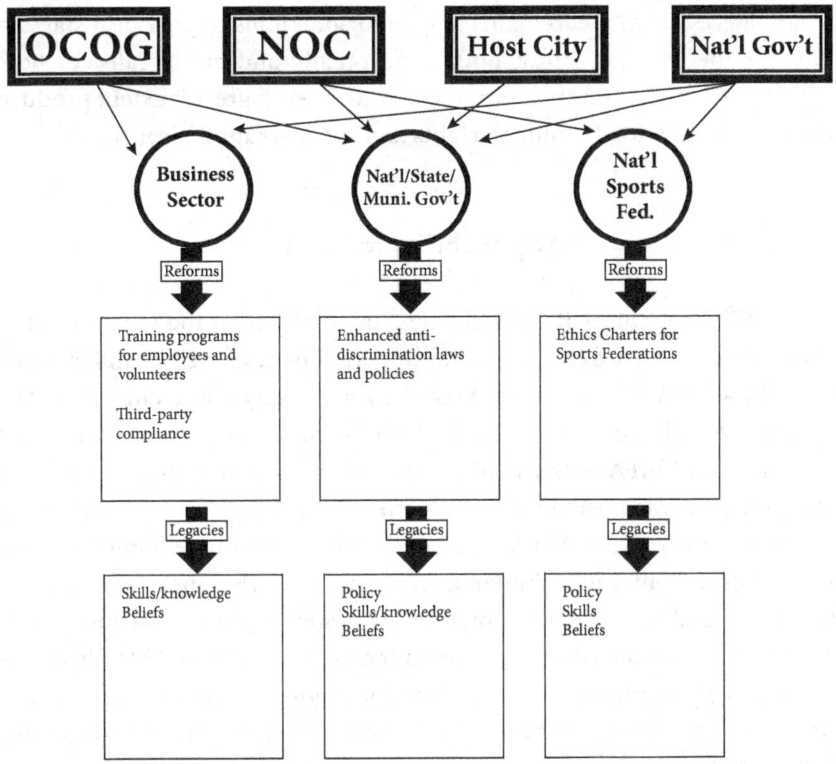

Figure 9.5 External Legacies

of anti-corruption and human rights laws and procedures. So too will they likely bring stronger norms concerning the importance and appropriateness of reducing anti-corruption and human rights risks. This knowledge, and the skills and norms, are all cognizable in the legacy literature and susceptible to measurement.

Within the public sector, enhanced anti-corruption or human rights laws and policies will, of course, fall under the policy legacy facet. The governmental employees will acquire a knowledge of these laws and policies, as well as skills in implementing and complying with them. As with the business sector, they too will likely internalize anti-corruption and human rights norms over time.

This same dynamic would occur in the sports federations and is likely now occurring in France. Implementing an enhanced ethics charter would again constitute a policy for legacy classification purposes. Athletes and coaches who sign and then abide by the charter will acquire knowledge of the new federation policies, skills in complying with them, and hopefully, an internalized norm that corruption and harassment have no place in sport.

Ultimately, this model remains in beta form. It aims to provide a starting point for the ongoing study, both conceptually and empirically, of how megasports are now producing, and could to an even greater extent produce in the future, meaningful human rights and anti-corruption legacies.

Applicability to FIFA

Though FIFA organizes its World Cups differently than the Olympics, the previously discussed dynamics would operate in essentially similar ways. Formally, a FIFA World Cup is hosted by a country while cities host the Olympics: Rio de Janeiro hosted the 2016 Summer Olympics while Brazil hosted the 2014 FIFA Men's World Cup, and Sochi hosted the 2014 Winter Olympics as Russia hosted the 2018 Men's World Cup. However, within the countries hosting FIFA World Cups, matches are distributed among cities. These cities will enter into similar agreements with FIFA, incur similar legal obligations, and be subject to similar human rights and anti-corruption policies. On the flip side, while a city hosts the Olympics, Paris 2024 illustrates the potentially significant role of the national government in adopting and implementing anti-corruption and human rights policies. Accordingly, for both events, both the city and national governments are important actors. Similarly, while the FIFA events would not involve the host country's National Olympic Committee, it would involve the national football federation, which could, and should, consider human rights and anti-corruption reforms similar to those described earlier. These two obvious differences between FIFA and IOC events turn out to be rather inconsequential in thinking about the dynamics by which reforms produce legacies.

However, FIFA's analogue to the IOC's OCOG is, at the moment, somewhat indeterminate. The model is presently evolving. Russia's 2018 Men's World Cup used a local organizing committee not unlike an OCOG. An assortment of issues arising in connection with that event led FIFA to consider alternative approaches. Qatar thus presented an entirely new model of two organizations: the Supreme Committee for Committee and Legacy, discussed at length in Chapter 5, which is a national government agency set up specifically to manage the host-country's obligations; and Qatar22, a FIFA subsidiary on the ground in Doha handling FIFA's Qatar-specific responsibilities. That model may or may not ever be replicated. The following two FIFA World Cups—the 2023 FIFA Women's World Cup in Australia and

New Zealand, and the 2026 United Bid—present unique co-hosting organizational challenges that are not yet fully resolved and may or may not produce replicable models. In short, we do not presently know how future World Cups will be organizationally structured at the local level. Still, we can assume there will be host-country organizing committees of some sort and that they will be tasked with implementing anti-corruption and human rights measures.

The models presented in this chapter thus illustrate what megasports could do. But if they are to do it—if we are to realize megasports' full potential to accelerate the implementation of lasting, positive human rights and anti-corruption norms, practices, policies, and laws—then a number of reforms are in order. Those reforms are the topic of the next and final chapter.

Notes

1. *Code of Ethics of the 2024 Paris Olympic and Paralympic Games*, Paris 2024 Ethics Committee, 5 (2019), https://medias.paris2024.org/uploads/2019/12/Paris2024-191217-Charte-ethique-DIGITAL-EN.pdf.
2. *A Guide of Best Practice*, Paris 2024, https://www.paris2024.org/en/a-guide-of-best-practice/.

10
A How-To Guide

Introduction

The previous chapters look in sometimes excruciating detail at the history, law, and policy of megasports. But if in the end we do not know how to actually build legacies, it is all for naught. Qatar becomes an aberration, the United Bid a set of forgotten promises, and the amendments to the International Olympic Committee (IOC) host-city contract just more useless legalese. Worse than that, this book becomes just one more voice in an already deafening chorus of commentators who insist on change but have little to say about achieving it.

A prominent megasport critic lectured at my university years ago. Over coffee I attempted to share the embryonic form of this book's thesis. But for each of my statements conveying even a faintly optimistic view on possible change, the visitor retorted with unyielding pessimism and despondency. I finally asked, "What do you think needs to happen?" The speaker replied, "The IOC and FIFA need to be disbanded." Well, that would be one approach.

This book takes an entirely different tact. Its argument is essentially twofold. First, megasports are already becoming a catalyst to host-country human rights and anti-corruption reform, though few know of the specific examples, and no one seems to notice the pattern. Second, if we can recognize this pattern, imagine the possibilities, and generate practical tips for supporting them, we can alter the relationship between megasports, human rights, and corruption.

This last chapter thus aims to be practical. It is neither an abstract academic exercise nor a strident call to revolution. It's a how-to guide. It starts from the simple premises that lasting positive anti-corruption and human rights impacts would be good and that time and money are scarce. It then builds from there.

A New Megasport Legacy. Andrew Brady Spalding, Oxford University Press. © Oxford University Press 2022.
DOI: 10.1093/oso/9780197503614.003.0010

This chapter deals with a broader set of actors than Chapter 9's modeling. Relevant stakeholders here include the IOC and FIFA; the hosts, to include organizing committees, national Olympic committees or football federations, city governments, and national governments; and additionally, the broader commentariat, primarily civil society and the academy. It then considers four stages of the megasport cycle: the bidding process; the awarding of the bid and formation of the host-city/country contract; the years in which the host is preparing for the event; and finally, the event and its aftermath. For each, it provides simple, straightforward, practical suggestions, none of which should be particularly resource intensive or politically delicate.

Bidding Stage

IOC and FIFA both have bidding processes that can easily incorporate human rights and anti-corruption legacy content. The IOC revised its bidding processes beginning in 2014 with Olympic Agenda 2020, and then in 2018 with the New Norm.[1] The new approach involves a continuous and more fluid dialogue with interested parties, followed by a targeted dialogue with preferred host candidates. On the FIFA side, the bidding process is perhaps less in transition now and is captured in a document entitled, "Guide to the Bidding Process for the 2026 FIFA World Cup."[2] That document lays out a series of steps by which FIFA approves principles to govern an upcoming bid, including the requirements that each bid must satisfy, and a timeline for approval. The promise of a human rights and anti-corruption legacy can be incorporated into these processes in four ways.

First, the IOC and FIFA should impress upon prospective hosts that a positive human rights and anti-corruption impact is expected, just as it is with infrastructure or environmental sustainability. Require the candidates to address legacy opportunities early on. Legacy considerations already figure prominently in the megasport bidding process; it would be but an incremental step to ask each candidate to specifically address a human rights and anti-corruption legacy. How will compliance with IOC or FIFA host requirements elevate standards in the country? What kinds of new practices may be introduced? How will these new concepts be transmitted to employees, volunteers, athletes, and fans? How might they ripple throughout the host country's corporate sector, as they did in Qatar? What lasting imprint will the event leave on the country? Is that imprint consistent with the IOC and FIFA brand? Present specific, practical examples of reforms the hosts can adopt that will leave such impacts. Share with the bidders the facets of legacy, and the myriad ways human rights and anti-corruption measures can create legacies. Share with them the best practices of recent hosts.

Second, after identifying legacy opportunities, the IOC and FIFA should require the candidates to conduct rigorous risk assessments. This has already occurred with Australia and New Zealand in human rights and the United Bid on both human rights and anti-corruption. Engage independent academics or firms to assist. The assessment should identify risks that arise at the intersection of the event with the host country's unique culture, laws, and practices. Require those assessments to identify legacy opportunities.

Both the benefits and the limitations of FIFA's current risk assessments are apparent in the Women's 2023 World Cup "Sustainability concept and human rights strategy,"[3] which FIFA made available to this author. It is effectively a questionnaire that Australia and New Zealand were required to complete as part of their bid. A close look at that document can help illustrate a couple simple, practical reforms that can substantially advance the legacy effort. The questionnaire is divided into topical sections: sustainable event management, human rights strategy, diversity and anti-discrimination, tobacco-free event, accessibility, and environmental protection. Each section begins with references to applicable international standards and to sections of previously submitted FIFA bids. Each section asks about the country's unique issues, and any applicable national laws. It then asks the bidding country to identify risk mitigation strategies. The document is essentially a multi-faceted risk assessment. In the context of this book's argument, a few growth areas rise into relief.

Notice that anti-corruption receives no express mention. While the concept might be implied in "sustainability," that term is nowhere defined. As Chapter 8 explained, "sustainability" is a highly ambiguous and unreliable word that is used inconsistently even within single documents. So too do the references to international laws and standards fail to mention any anti-corruption document. They instead refer to ISO 20121 and AA1000SES; as Chapter 8 further explained, neither of these standards concerns corruption. This underscores the odd absence of an explicit anti-corruption assessment, a problem that is easily solved.

The human rights section—the most substantial in the document—goes further, but could go further yet. It does indeed require the bidding country to identify a risk mitigation strategy. The document then asks about remediation of harm, and stakeholder engagement. However, nowhere does it ask about legacy. By contrast, the subsequent sections on Accessibility and Environmental Protection do take an additional step, inching toward legacy without actually mentioning it. Both of those sections conclude with a prompt to discuss how the Women's World Cup could "be used to improve and promote" the relevant norm—accessibility and environmental protection, respectively—in the host country. This would seem to be legacy by another name. Any measures that successfully improve and promote accessibility or environmental protection, were they to remain after the event, would constitute a legacy.

To bring both human rights and anti-corruption into conformity with FIFA's standards on accessibility and environmental protection, two specific substantive amendments to the "Sustainability concept and human rights strategy" template are here proposed. FIFA should add a single additional prompt to the human rights section, such as: "How can the World Cup improve and promote the protection of human rights in the host country?" Additionally, FIFA should add an anti-corruption section. It might include four prompts: (1) "Describe the risks associated with hosting this event in relation to various forms of corruption such as bribery, embezzlement, etc. Include specific references to the independent anti-corruption assessment." (2) "What are the applicable national laws or policy guidelines related to anti-corruption compliance?" (3) "Describe the proposed compliance program and other strategies to mitigate these corruption risks." (4) "How can the World Cup improve and promote anti-corruption compliance in the host country?" While FIFA is here used as an example, similar requirements should exist in the IOC bidding process. With these amendments, the risk assessment can become a powerful anti-corruption and human rights legacy tool.

Third, having identified legacy opportunities and conducted a meaningful human rights and anti-corruption risk assessment, candidates should then develop a concrete, practical, and specific human rights and anti-corruption legacy strategy. Based on the above-mentioned legacy presentations and risk assessments, ask the candidates to propose a series of realistic proposals that can leave a lasting impact on norms, practices, policies, or even laws in human rights and anti-corruption. Engage nongovernmental organizations, academics, or other stakeholders to assist. Such recommendations could draw heavily on Chapter 9's model. This would not be a resource-intensive process.

Fourth and finally, expect the host's national government to dedicate modest but meaningful resources toward supporting and monitoring megasport preparations. As Chapters 5 and 6 explained, both Qatar and France have seen very significant engagement from their national governments in human rights and/or anti-corruption. Expect national anti-corruption enforcement agencies, labor ministries, or human rights commissions to actively support and monitor megasport initiatives. Allow the mega sporting event to serve as a laboratory, as it did in Qatar, for new initiatives the national government may eventually seek to adopt. Given the heightened risks of hosting megasports, especially reputational risks, it is in a nation's interests to allocate heightened enforcement resources to this goal.

Awarding Stage

The awarding stage, as the phrase is used here, encompasses both the selection of a host and the formation of a contract with that host. For the former, the recommendation is simple: the IOC and FIFA should consider potential human rights and anti-corruption legacies when selecting a host. One ought not to be naïve: those decisions are likely driven chiefly by financial considerations. But just as human rights and anti-corruption scandals have negative economic consequences, so can human rights and anti-corruption legacies strengthen the IOC and FIFA brand, thus increasing both the event's appeal and its monetary value.

Second, ensure the resulting contract contains rigorous anti-corruption and human rights provisions that are likely to elevate norms, practices, policies, or laws in enduring ways. This recommendation requires the most explication. As Chapter 8 described, the IOC's published model host city contract contains clear and rigorous human rights provisions, but its anti-corruption provisions need further clarification and elaboration. Proposed recommendations to those contractual provisions follow. Designed through collaboration with the Olympics Compliance Task Force (see Chapter 8), the recommendations are legally sound and practical, representing the consensus view of an independent group of practitioners and academics. Similar reforms could likely apply to the FIFA host-country contract.

Recommendation 1: Replace the Phrase "Internationally-Recognized Anti-Corruption Standards"

As Chapter 8 explained, this phrase in the anti-corruption clause of the host-city contract mirrors the human rights clause, but does not do the same work. "Internationally-recognized anti-corruption standards" simply fails to provide meaningfully specific guidance. The replacement phrase must accurately and specifically reference a specific set of standards that equip compliance officers to build meaningful compliance programs. The easiest and best option, both practically and politically, is to explicitly incorporate the IOC's own Basic Principles of Governance. These principles approximate global best practices fairly closely and are already integral to the Olympic Movement. Obligating the counterparties to abide by the Basic Principles is a small step conceptually, but a significant step practically.

Endorsing any other specific standard would prove problematic. Politically, the IOC obviously cannot choose a single country—whether the United States, the United Kingdom, France, or any other country—as the exemplar of leading standards. No international organization has promulgated standards with sufficient rigor. Standards promulgated by private-sector organizations create their own controversies. A vague reference to leading standards would lack the specificity that compliance officers need. Ultimately, a specific reference to the Basic Principles of Governance would be politically viable and would provide compliance officers with a specific set of standards that are both rigorous and reasonable.

Recommendation 2: Establish a Meaningful Third-Party Management Policy

The anti-corruption clause as now written does not establish a requirement that OCOG suppliers, sponsors, and other third parties adopt anti-corruption compliance measures. This stands in contrast to the Human Rights Clause and the IOC Supplier Code, as discussed in Chapter 8. The Anti-Corruption Clause's Operational Requirements should impose compliance requirements on suppliers, following the template of the Human Rights Clause's Operational Requirements. The draft anti-corruption Operational Requirements below thus include a third-party management policy.

Recommendation 3: Create a Fulsome Set of Operational Requirements

The Anti-Corruption Clause deserves a set of Operational Requirements comparable in detail, and impact, to those of the Human Rights Clause. More fulsome Operational Requirements can have a tremendous impact in helping the Organizing Committee for the Olympic Games (OCOG) to reduce corruption in its operations, minimize corruption scandals, and become a catalyst to the adoption of improved governance standards in the Host Country.

Practical operational requirements must balance the need to deter a broad swath of conduct against the reality that OCOGs in particular are often already overburdened. While any anti-corruption operational requirements cannot exceed the OCOGs' capacities, honoring the contractual provisions nevertheless necessitates a meaningful set of new requirements.

Thus amended, the Anti-Corruption Clause should be followed by meaningful operational requirements. The Anti-Corruption Clause's Operational Requirements could require the OCOG, National Olympic Committee (NOC), and Host City to do each of the following.

Requirement 1: Create a Code of Conduct Prohibiting Corruption

Each entity should draft a Code of Conduct that lays out the organization's core commitments on all relevant forms of corruption and fraud, to include:

i. Bribery: the promising, offering, giving, as well as the solicitation or receipt of bribes; what constitutes acceptable and unacceptable forms of gifts, hospitality, and charitable donations; and a prohibition on facilitation payments.
ii. Accounting Fraud: a commitment to accuracy in all books and records, transparency, and effective controls in all accounting matters.
iii. Embezzlement: the prohibition on stealing or misappropriating funds entrusted to the organization or employee.
iv. Illegal Bidding Practices: all forms of bid-rigging, collusion, and other illegal or improper bidding practices.
v. Money Laundering: the conversion, concealment, or possession of money derived from criminal activity.

vi. Conflicts of Interest: exercising entrusted authority for personal gain rather than for the public interest.

Requirement 2: Establish an Effective Compliance Program

The OCOG in particular should build and implement a compliance program designed to prevent the above-mentioned misconduct. The compliance program should include the following components:

i. Risk Assessment: the OCOG must initially, and then periodically, conduct a risk assessment that evaluates the risks of the above-mentioned misconduct in relation to the company's operations and legal environment, with an aim toward allocating compliance resources in proportion to risk.
ii. Policies and Procedures: the OCOG should adopt rules or procedures that the organization will implement to ensure employees and volunteers adhere to the code of conduct in their day-to-day operations.
iii. Training: all officers, employees, volunteers, and third parties should be trained in the applicable anti-corruption and anti-fraud laws and policies. The training should be tailored to the unique business, legal, and cultural environment to identify location-specific risks, and should occur with appropriate methods and frequency.
iv. Monitoring and Auditing: There should be ongoing oversight of the compliance program through both monitoring and auditing. Any deficiencies should be remedied.
v. Reporting: establish a hotline, whether internal or through a third party, for reporting misconduct which ensures the confidentiality of the reporting employee or volunteer as well as procedures for appropriately responding to allegations.

Requirement 3: Ensure Ongoing Compliance among Third Parties

The OCOG should require that all suppliers, service providers, consultants, sponsors, contractors, and other third parties also adhere to the preceding principles. Accordingly, the OCOG should require all such third parties to adopt a code of conduct and a compliance program, commensurate with the third party's size and resources. The OCOG should be required to insert in all contracts formed with third parties a provision obligating the third party to adopt these Operational Requirements, with full rights to audit to ensure fulfillment with both principles.

These draft Operational Requirements are uncontroversial, practical, and closely pegged to the IOC's Human Rights Operational Requirements. Similar requirements could be adopted on the FIFA side (though again, FIFA has not made its host-country anti-corruption requirements known to the public or to this author). If adopted and implemented, they would not only be effective preventative measures but would leave a legacy across the corporate sector and beyond.

Preparations Stage

Once the host is selected and preparations are underway, the hosts can adopt a number of discrete policies that can each produce a significant human rights and anti-corruption legacy. Each is generally legal, affordable, and practical.

First, pursuant to a rigorous host contract of the sort described above, future organizing committees should follow the expected example of Milan/Cortina 2026 and require all third parties to adopt human rights and anti-corruption compliance programs. These programs can be tailored to the size and operations of the third-party company. They might be designed and monitored by a retained independent firm.

Second, the organizing committee should conduct meaningful human rights and anti-corruption training for all officers, employees, and volunteers. This is less expensive and cumbersome than it may sound. The burdens associated with building a human rights and anti-corruption legacy primarily consist of designing policies and monitoring their implementation. However, anti-corruption and human rights reforms generally, and in the realm of megasports specifically, is a topic of tremendous interest among academics and civil society organizations. The IOC and FIFA should explore tapping into this very substantial resource to aid the host city/country organizations in designing and implementing these reforms.

Third, support and monitor the NOC or national football federation as it reviews and strengthens its own human rights and anti-corruption policies.

These might concern internal compliance, training for coaches and athletes under their purview, and so forth. Expect them to meaningfully operationalize their contractual obligations.

Fourth, the host city or country should do the same.

Fifth, engage bloggers to help publicize these and other successes. The worldwide audience for issues related to corruption, human rights, sports, and business is vast and easily reached. Posts on this topic would be very widely read.

Sixth, conduct a workshop on the host's lasting anti-corruption and human rights reforms in the host country. Invite megasports officials, civil society, academics, and the media. The months leading up to a mega sporting event will always see a surge in interest in these topics and create a natural window for generating academic interest.

During and Following the Games

Finally, there is work to be done during and following the event. First, we should catalog all human rights and anti-corruption measures that were adopted and that will likely produce legacies. This would not be as difficult as it sounds. Ask the four key actors—the national government, the city government, the national Olympic committee or soccer federation, and the organizing committee—to draft a memo identifying all ways in which hosting the Games has accelerated the implementation of anti-corruption and human rights norms, practices, policies, or laws. Ask those actors to specifically flag the reforms they are comfortable publicizing.

Secondly, get academics involved in studying and brainstorming legacy initiatives. Carefully analyze past measures and propose ways to expand upon them. Develop reliable methods for measuring norms, skills, and beliefs. Learn how to prove acceleration. Social scientists can do valuable work in this space.

Third, during the games, use social media to broadcast the many successful legacy initiatives the organizers will by this time have adopted. People will want to know about it. Change the public perception of the event's anti-corruption and human rights impacts.

But ultimately, and most fundamentally, a change is needed which transcends, or underlies, all of these specific proposals. To tap megasports' capacity to catalyze positive reforms, we need a change in tone. This author's efforts to interview key megasport stakeholders revealed, far too often, an impediment to effective research that can only be described as an impenetrable wall of mistrust. This was by no means universally true; a great many stakeholders were deeply generous with their time and insights. However, in many other cases, good-faith inquiries were met with radio silence. The reason is no mystery. The stakeholders most responsible for implementing the reforms have the most reason to fear the commentariat's name-and-shame strategy. The hostile quality of much existing commentary on Olympic corruption and human rights challenges thus becomes a significant obstacle to effective empirical human rights and anti-corruption legacy research. If academics and civil society experts are to gather information and robustly exchange the best ideas with those persons who formulate and implement these reforms—the organizing committees, host cities and countries, and national Olympic committees and soccer federations—the tenor of the conversation will have to change.

Perhaps the pivot point can be Qatar. Though it continues to elicit acerbic journalistic criticism, it is now becoming the most powerful example of the dynamic this book documents. The spotlight shone as intensely on that country as any and catalyzed an unprecedented spate of reforms. The notion of a positive human rights and anti-corruption legacy may run contrary to past experience and the current zeitgeist, but as this book demonstrates, it now has substantial factual support. While we should not be naïve about the remaining challenges in Qatar or any other country, we should not be so cynical that we cannot acknowledge a plainly good thing. Neither should we miss the opportunity to lend our support to it, that future hosts might leave ever more deliberate and impactful human rights and anti-corruption legacies.

I am reminded of a roundtable conversation that occurred in the course of this book's research. As I presented to the group an earlier version of this book's argument, none objected normatively, but many expressed practical concerns: it's too novel, organizing committees are already overtaxed, getting buy-in will just be too difficult, and so on. After many minutes of such comments, a more senior participant made a powerful observation. She said that twenty years ago, these same arguments were made about the notion that megasports could, or should, leave an environmental legacy. And yet today it has become a standard component of a megasport hosting bid. There may be no reason why a human rights and anti-corruption legacy could not follow this same trajectory.

This book is written in the hopes that it can.

Notes

1. *IOC Executive Board Puts Forward Brisbane 2032 for Election by IOC Session*, International Olympic Committee (June 10, 2021), https://olympics.com/ioc/future-host-election.
2. *Guide to the Bidding Process for the 2026 FIFA World Cup*, FIFA, https://digitalhub.fifa.com/m/5730ee56c15eeddb/original/hgopypqftviladnm7q90-pdf.pdf.
3. *Sustainability Concept and Human Rights Strategy*, document available with the author.

Index

For the benefit of digital users, indexed terms that span two pages (e.g., 52–53) may, on occasion, appear on only one of those pages.

Figures are indicated by *f* following the page number

231 Model, 258, 260–61
  and Decree 231, 260–61
1690 *Two Treatises of Civil Government*, 46
1776 United States Declaration of Independence, 46–47, 65–66
1789 Bill of Rights, 46–48, 231
1789 Declaration of the Rights of Man, 46–47, 231–32, 321
1789 French Revolution, 44
1844 Montreal Summer Olympic Games, 7
1908 London Summer Olympic Games, 9, 27
1916 Sixth Olympic Games, 10
1936 Berlin Summer Olympic Games, 10, 30
1940 Summer Olympic Games, 11
1942 FIFA World Cup, 11
1944 Summer Olympic Games, 11
1946 FIFA World Cup, 11
1948 London Summer Olympic Games, 11
1948 Universal Declaration of Human Rights, 47–48, 64, 276
1950 FIFA World Cup, 11
1954 FIFA World Cup, 11–12
1956 Melbourne Summer Olympic Games, 18–19
1964 Tokyo Summer Olympic Games, 11–12, 130
1966 International Covenant on Civil and Political Rights, 276
1966 International Covenant on Economic, Social, and Cultural Rights, 276
1968 Mexico City Summer Olympic Games, 12, 21
1972 Munich Summer Olympic Games, 11–12
1974 FIFA World Cup, 11–12
1978 FIFA World Cup, 21
1980 Moscow Summer Olympic Games, 12–13
1984 Los Angeles Summer Olympic Games, 12–13, 30
1988 Calgary Winter Olympic Games, 18–19, 130–31
1988 Seoul Summer Olympic Games, 130
1989 Tiananmen Square Massacre, 21
1995 World Summit, 50–51
1996 Atlanta Summer Olympic Games, 19, 22–23, 30
1998 Nagano Winter Olympic Games, 21–23, 130–31
1998 Salt Lake City Bid Scandal, 19, 20–21, 23–24, 30
2000 Sydney Summer Olympic Games, 21, 22–23, 30
2002 Salt Lake City Winter Olympic Games, 19, 20–21, 22, 23–24, 30
2002 Sarbanes-Oxley Act, 72
2004 Athens Summer Olympic Games, 19
2005 United Nations Commission on Human Rights (HRC), 52–54, 68–69
2006 Asian Games, 178
2006 Germany FIFA Men's World Cup, 29
2008 Beijing Summer Olympic Games, 24, 29
2008 Global Financial Crisis, 85
2010 Bribery Act, 68–69, 73
2010 South Africa FIFA Men's World Cup, 24–25

2010 Vancouver Winter Olympic Games, 29, 130–31
2011 Asian Cup, 178
2011 Information Access Law (Freedom of Information Law–FOI), 91, 96–97
  and eternal classification, 96
  and transparency, 96–97
2011 procurement reforms (Regime Diferenciado de Contratações–RDC), 91–96
  and bidding, 93–94, 95
  and transparency, 91, 94, 95
2012 London Summer Olympic Games, 19, 29, 30–31
2013 Clean Companies Act (CCA), 91, 97–103
  and Chapter III, Article 7, 102–3
  and compliance programs, 102
  and cooperation credit, 101, 102–3
  and corporate criminal liability, 99
  and deterrence, 99–102
  and leniency agreement, 103
  and non-trial resolutions (NTRs), 101–2
2013 organized crime bill, 91, 103–9
  and construction, 105–6
  and expanded plea bargain, 104–5
  and obstruction of justice, 104–5
  and Operation Car Wash, 95, 105, 109
  and Petrobras scandal, 91, 103, 104–5, 108–9
  and Port Maravilha, 106
  and Turquesa 2, 106
2014 Brazil Sustainability Strategy, 33, 37
2014 FIFA Men's World Cup, 25–26, 85–110, 171, 328
  and Mensalão, 89–90, 97–98
2014 Sochi Winter Olympic Games, 25–26, 29, 30, 131, 328
2016 Law Sapin II, 69, 320–21, 325–26
2016 Rio de Janeiro Summer Olympic Games, 4–5, 25–26, 37, 57, 85–110, 130, 328
  and human rights legacy, 88–89
  and infrastructure, 88–89
2018 FIFA Men's World Cup, 25, 33, 177–78, 192, 200, 201–2, 328–29
2018 PyeongChang Winter Olympic Games, 4–5, 25–26, 37, 119–20, 130–31, 132–33, 150–52
2019 France FIFA Women's World Cup, 17, 34
2022 Beijing Winter Olympic Games, 4–5, 6–7
2022 Qatar FIFA Men's World Cup, 5–6, 25–26, 34, 167–69, 175–76, 204, 209, 210, 214, 298
2023 FIFA Women's World Cup, 37, 249–58, 328–29, 333
  and anti-corruption legacy, 254, 262, 264
  and equal pay, 251–52, 254–57
  and ethical sourcing principles, 252–53
  and human rights legacy, 253–54, 257–58, 262
  and Spectator Code of Behavior and Disciplinary Code, 252–53
  and sustainability, 254
  and *Sustainability Concept and Human Rights Strategy*, 252–53, 333
2024 Paris Summer Olympic Games, 4–5, 37, 229, 230–31, 238–40, 271, 272–73, 274, 275, 315, 316, 319, 320–21, 328
2026 FIFA Men's World Cup, 37, 50, 249–51, 261–64
  and anti-corruption legacy, 262, 264
  and compliance and ethic program, 263
  and Ethical Sourcing Principles, 251
  and Guide to the Bidding Process, 298, 299–300, 303, 304, 307–8, 332
  and human rights legacy, 253–54, 257–58, 262
  and Proposed United Human Rights Strategy, 262–63
  and regulations for the selection of venue for the final competition, 298, 299–300
  and Stakeholder Engagement Plan, 263
  and sustainability, 262
2026 Milan Cortina Winter Olympic Games, 37, 249–51, 258–61, 316
  and anti-corruption legacy, 261
  and human rights legacy, 261

2028 Los Angeles Summer Olympics, 50, 69, 316
3–5–10 Rule, 142–43

AA1000SES, 308, 333
Abu Dhabi, 177–78
accessibility, 211–12
Act on Aggravated Punishment of Specific Crimes, 136
Act on Anti-Corruption and Civil Rights Commission, 136
Act on Preventing Bribery of Foreign Public Officials in International Business Transactions (FBPA), 128–29
Adamu, Amos, 209–10
Adamu, Samson, 209–10
Afghanistan, 12–13, 176
Africa, 17–18, 178–79
  and African Charter of Human and Peoples' Rights, 64
  and African Football Legends Dinner, 209–10
  and African Union, 17–18
Agence Française Anticorruption (AFA), 68–69, 73, 229–40, 319
  and guidance, 68–69
Airbus, 238
Alatas, Sayed, 59–60
Alcatel–Lucent, 235
Algeria, 173–74
Alsace, 7–8
Alstom, 235
Al Bayt Stadium, 206
Al Jazeera, 174–77, 178, 179
  and channel, 176–77
  and Media Network, 176
  and news network, 174
  and Satellite Channel, 176
Al Thani, Hamad bin Jassim, 174, 179
Al Thawadi, Hasan, 181–82
American, 122, 123–24
  and Convention on Human Rights, 64
  and Declaration of the Rights and Duties of Man, 64
  and University, 22
  and zones of occupation, 122
Amnesty International, 193–94, 195–96, 216–17
  and Qatar: The Dark Side of Migration, 193–94
  and Reality Check 2020: Countdown to the 2020 World Cup, 216–17
Anglo-American, 47, 66
  and liberalism, 67
anti-bribery
  and Convention, 72, 98, 99
  and enforcement, 72–73
  and law, 8–9, 62, 72–73
  and provisions, 145
anti-corruption
  and abuses, 6
  and Anti-Corruption Clause, 274, 276, 282, 283–84, 287, 288–89, 295–96, 304, 307–8, 309–10
  and anti-fraud laws and policies, 338
  and assessment, 333, 334
  and Civil Rights Commission (ACRC), 136
  and Civil Rights Commission's 2015 Perceptions Survey, 129–30
  and Civil Rights Commission's Anti–Corruption Guideline for Companies, 141
  and Civil Rights Commission's Handbook, 136–37
  and compliance, 3, 43, 68–69, 75, 102, 319, 322, 325, 334, 336, 339
  and conventions, 13, 62, 64, 67
  and enforcement, 64, 73, 120, 135, 149–50, 319–20, 322, 325–26, 335
  and Global Organizations, 129
  and law, 33, 35, 56–57, 60, 64, 119–20, 128–29, 136–37, 139, 141, 143–44, 145, 325–27
  and legislation, 128, 149–50
  and movement, 60, 64–65, 66
  and policies, 34, 35, 37, 141, 318, 321, 324, 328, 339–40
  and practices, 33, 34, 35, 37, 120
  and prosecution, 140
  and reform, 3, 4–5, 25–26, 32–33, 35–36, 37, 60, 135, 322–23, 326, 328, 331
  and regulation, 129
  and riots, 90–91

anti-corruption (*cont.*)
and standards, 13
and values, 33
Anti-Corruption Ethics and Compliance Progamme for Business, 68–69
anti-discrimination, 325–26
and clause, 275–77, 294, 300, 305, 307
and law, 316, 323
apartheid, 21
Arab Spring, 174–75, 176–77
Argentina, 9, 14, 21, 177–78
Asia, 130, 133
and Asian Football Confederation, 210
and Asian Football Confederation Asian Cup, 256–57
and Asian Tigers, 130
and countries, 130
and East Asia, 15
and South Asia, 66–67
Asia Pacific Economic Cooperation (APEC), 63–64, 68–69
and Anti-Corruption Code of Conduct for Business, 68–69
and Course of Action on Fighting Corruption and Ensuring Transparency (2004), 63–64
Auditing, 75
Australia, 11, 14, 30, 37, 249–58, 328–29, 333
and Australian Human Rights Commission, 257–58
and Australian Men's National Team (The Caltex Socceroos), 255–56
and Australian Women's National Team (The Westfield Matildas), 251–58
and Sydney, 21
authoritarian, 15, 120–21, 124
Axis Powers, 11

Babylon, 46, 71–72
Bahrain, 170–71, 173–75
Bailyn, Bernard, 65–66
Bangladesh, 168–69, 232
Baron de Montesquieu, 46
Belgium, 9, 210
bereavement pay, 126
Bhopal, 52
Bhutan, 49–50
bid, 93–94, 95, 130–33, 150, 331, 332–33, 334–35, 337, 341
and bidders, 167
and bidding competition, 131
and bidding process, 30–31, 93–96
and bid committees, 19, 35–36
and bid for the 2010 Games, 130–31
and bid for the 2012 Games, 30–31
and bid for the 2014 Games, 132
and bid for the 2018 Games, 132–33
and bid for the 2022 World Cup, 174–75
and Bid Book and Qatar, 179, 181, 182, 187–88, 202, 214
and Illegal Bidding Practices, 337
and megasport bidding process, 332
and Resolution for the 2018 Winter Olympic Bidding, 132
and United Bid, 37, 249–51, 261–64, 328–29, 333
Bilchitz, David, 56
Bin Hammam, Mohammed, 210
Blatter, Jack, 210
Blikkiesdorp, 24–25
blockade, 174–75
Blue House, 146, 149
Blue K, 146–47, 151–52
BMW, 141–42
Bohemia, 9
Bolsonaro, Jair, 96–97, 107–8
Brazil, 4–6, 13–14, 15–16, 25–26, 27, 31, 32, 33, 34, 35, 37, 60–61, 72–73, 85–110, 119, 120, 130, 152–53, 171, 230, 271, 328
and Brazilian Leniency Agreement, 237–38
and Rio de Janeiro, 328
Breen, Michael, 133
bribery, 59, 60, 61, 62, 63–64, 68–69, 72–73, 125, 126–29, 136, 139, 141–42–, 143, 144, 145, 146, 147–48, 149–50, 152, 208, 209–11, 237, 238, 240, 282, 288, 289, 292, 293, 303–4, 306, 309, 317–18, 334, 337
and legislation, 128–29
BRIC Nations (Brazil, Russia, India, China), 15–16, 90

Brunei Darussalam, 50
Building and Wood Workers International (BWI), 169, 183–84, 197–98, 200–2, 205, 215

California Transparency in Supply Chains Act, 234
Canada, 14, 37, 249–51, 261–64
and Vancouver, 131
candidate
and Athens, 1997, 19
and Calgary, 1981, 18–19
and candidature file, 18–19
and city, 24
Caribbean, 17–18, 210
Carter, Jimmy, 12–13
Cashman, Richard, 27
central administrative agencies, 137–38
chaebol, 119–20, 121–22, 124–25, 139, 140, 146, 147–48
Chalip, Laurence, 27
Chappelet, Jean-Loup, 27
charte déontologique, 326
Charter of the Environment of 2004, 231–32
Cheil Industries, Inc., 147–48
cheongtak, 142–43
Chile, 9
China, 4–5, 6–7, 11, 12, 13–14, 15–16, 26, 44, 45–46, 49, 66, 119–20, 130
and Beijing, 21
and China Eastern Airlines, 129
and Manchuria, 11
and Singapore, 172, 178–79
and Tibet, 24
and Xinjiang, 24
Chirac, Jacques, 235
Choi-gate, 146
Chonghaejin Marine, 134–35
Chong-Bum, An, 151–52
Chong, Kim, 151
chonji, 127
Chung-hee, Park, 122–23
Chusok, 121
and the Lunar New Year, 121
Civil Law Convention (2003), 63–64
civil servant, 127, 136–37, 138
civil society, 65, 167, 183, 184, 194, 214, 332, 339, 340–41
Clean Companies Act, 73
Clean Record Law (Lei de Ficha Limpa), 107
Clinton, Bill, 30
Code of Conduct, 135–36, 137–38, 141–42, 143–44, 145, 337, 338
Code of Conduct for Public Officials, 128–29
code of ethics, 317–18
Cohen, Daniel, 47
COJO, 317–18
and Good Practices Guide, 318
and Paris, 240, 241, 318
Cold War, 6–7, 9, 12–13, 16, 18–19, 48, 56–57, 61
Collective Bargaining Agreement (CBA), 255–57
Collor de Mello, Fernando, 60–61
commercialism, 12
Committee of Sponsoring Organizations of the Treadway Commission, 68–69, 294–95
communist, 122–23, 130
and communism, 61
Comoros, 174–75
compliance, 43–44, 51, 62, 63, 68–75, 317, 318–19, 320–21, 322, 323, 324, 325
and Corporate, 69, 71–72
Confédération Africaine de Football (CAF), 17–18
Confucian, 66–67, 119–22, 123, 124, 126, 127–28, 139
and Confucius, 66
and dynasty, 124
and neo-Confucianism, 120–22, 126
conglomerates, 119–20, 121–22, 124–25, 146, 147–48
constitution
and 1787 US Constitution, 46–48, 65–66, 71–72
and Constitutional Convention, 65–66
and Qatar, 179
constitutional institution, 137–38
Convention Against Torture and other Cruel, Inhuma, or Degrading Treatment or Punishment (1984), 62

Convention on Combating Bribery of Foreign Officials in International Business Transactions (1997), 62
Convention on the Elimination of All Forms of Discrimination Against Women (1979), 50
Convention on the Prevention and Punishment of the Crime of Genocide (1948), 49–50
Convention on the Rights of the Child (1989), 50
Convention on the Right of Migrant Workers, 231–32
Convention Relating to the Status of Refugees, 231–32
Convention Relating to the Status of Stateless Persons, 231–32
Corporate Social Responsibility programs (CSR), 53–54, 55
corruption
  and defensive, 59–60
  and extortive, 59–60
  and incidental, 60
  and institutional, 57, 60
  and International Corruption Perception Index, 129
  and investive, 59–60
  and Olympic, 340–41
  and Republic of Total, 128
  and scandal, 119, 128, 136, 146, 147, 151, 152–53, 335, 337
  and systemic, 60
  and transactive, 59–60
corruption eruption, 4, 24, 56–57, 60–61
Coubertin, Pierre de Fredy, Baron de, 7–9, 12–13
Council of Europe, 17–18, 63–64
Court for Arbitration in Sport, 210, 284
Criminal
  and Act, 128–29, 139
  and Convention, 63–64
Cuervo-Cazurra, Álvaro, 60
cultural imperialism, 45–46, 66
cultural self-examination, 130
Culture Minister Jong-deok, 151–52
Cyrus Cylinder of 593 BCE, 46
Cyrus the Great, 46
Darfur
  and Peace Agreement, 176
  and rebel group, 176
Declaration on Fundamental Principles and Rights at Work, 54–55, 287
declination, 70–71
Denmark, 9
diplomatic engagement, 175
Dirty War, 21
DLA Piper, 194, 195–96, 197
Doha, 176, 177–78, 197–99, 201–2, 217, 328–29
  and 2008 Agreement, 176
  and Brookings Center, 177
  and Debates, 177
  and film festival, 175–76
  and round, 176
  and Tribeca film festival, 177
Domestic Workers Law, 167–68, 216–17
Dominican Republic, 49–50
Dong-bin, Shin, 148, 152
Donga University, 132–33
Doosan Engineering, 151
Dubai, 177–78
due diligence standards, 282, 287, 295, 296
due process, 8–9
Dutch Senate and the Child Labour Due Diligence Bill, 234
Duty of Vigilance Law, 229–30, 232, 234, 286, 320–21

Eagin, Hugh, 173
Eckert, Hans, 209–10
economic, 121–22, 123–24, 125, 130, 132, 168–69, 175, 179–81
  and development, 179–81
  and growth, 121–22, 123, 125, 130, 132, 168–69
  and legacy, 18–19, 27, 31
  and openness, 175
  and Planning Board, 123–24
  and Planning Council, 123–24
educational corporations, 137–38
Egypt, 172–75, 208
elections, 189
  and Qatari, 179
embezzlement, 59, 64, 67, 125, 147–48, 334, 337

emir, 170, 192
and His Highness Sheikh Tamim Bin Hamad Al Thani, 172
and His Highness Sheikh Hamad Bin Khalifa Al Thani, 170–71, 172, 174, 187
Emirates Air, 177–78
employment contract, 169, 189, 190–91
enforcement challenges, 168
Enforcement Decree, 142–43
England, 7, 46
and London, 30–31
Enron, 72
environmental
and development, 179–81
and legacy, 18, 31
and Programme, 17
Espy, Richard, 21
Essomba, Sonia, 22
ethnocentrism, 45–46
Etihad, 177–78
European Commission, 234
European Convention on Human Rights, 231–32, 286
European Convention for the Protection of Human Rights and Fundamental Freedoms, 64, 233
Europe's Group of States Against Corruption (GRECO), 293
European Parliament of the Council on Public Procurement, 241
European Union, 14, 17–18, 234, 240–41
and anti-corruption compliance, 241
and human rights due diligence, 241
expatriate, 179–81
external legacies, 317, 327*f*
external reforms, 316–17, 319, 322–23, 324–26, 324*f*
extortion, 59

favor, 87–88
FC Barcelona, 175–76, 178
Federal Bureau of Investigation (FBI), 210–11
Federation International de Football Association (FIFA)
and Anti-Corruption Directives, 292, 303, 306
and anti-corruption requirements, 272–73, 297–98, 306, 308–9
and Bidding Regulations, 303, 304, 305, 307, 308–9
and bidding requirements, 202, 214
and bribery, 25–26
and code of conduct, 16, 298, 306
and Code of Conduct for Third Parties, 298, 299, 303, 305, 306
and Code of Ethics, 298, 303, 306, 309–10
and Compliance Handbook, 304–5, 306–7
and Congress, 10
and Corporate Social Responsibility, 180–81
and Executive Committee, 172–73, 208, 210
and General Secretary, 183–84
and governance documents, 298, 299–300, 303, 304, 305, 306
and host agreement, 271, 273
and Human Rights Overview, 298
and Human Rights Policy, 298–99, 302–3, 305, 308–9
and Men's World Cup, 3, 15–16, 85–110, 170, 172, 249–51, 261–64, 315, 328
and Organizing Committee, 297
and Qatar literature, 34
and reforms, 211
and Structure, Content, Presentation, Format and Delivery of Bid Book, 298, 299–300, 301, 303, 304, 308–9
and Statutes, 16, 298, 303
and Sustainable Event Management and Human Rights, 300, 307, 308–9
and sustainability strategy, 33, 34, 304–5, 306, 307–9
and Under-20 Football World Championships, 178
and Women's World Cup, 17, 34, 249–58, 315, 328–29, 334–31
Fillon, Francis, 235, 238
Finland, 11
First Charter of Human Rights, 46

Flagship Corporations, 72–73
and Airbus, 72–73
and Petrobras, 72–73
and Samsung, 72–73
and Siemens, 72–73
Football Federations, 332, 339–40
Football Federation Australia (FFA), 255–56
Foreign Corrupt Practices Act (FCPA), 57–58, 72–73, 99, 141–42, 145, 235
and anti-bribery provisions, 145
foreign policy, 173, 174, 177,
foreign public official, 62, 63–64
fossil fuels, 172–73
four pillars, 90–109
France, 4–5, 6, 9, 14, 20, 27, 31, 34, 35–36, 37, 44, 46–47, 60–61, 69, 72–73, 208, 274, 287, 316, 318, 319–20, 321–22, 325–26, 327, 335, 336
and 1789 Revolution, 231
and Agence Française, 294–95
and anti-corruption compliance programs, 229, 236
and Auchan, 232
and Carrefour, 232
and CJIP, 237–38
and Compliance 2024, 286
and Convention on the Elimination of All Forms of Discrimination against Women, 231–32
and Convention on the Rights of the Child, 231–32
and Convention on the Rights of Persons with Disabilities, 231–32
and Corporate Accountability, 238
and French Constitutional Council, 231–33
and French Constitution of 1946, 231–32, 233
and French Development Agency, 17
and French Ministry of Justice, 236–37
and French Youth, 7–8
and GAN French Corruption Report, 234–35
and Human Rights Reforms, 229–32, 233, 234–35, 238–39, 241–42
and International Convention on the Elimination of All Forms of Racial Discrimination, 231–32
and Minister for the Budget, 236–37
and National Action Plan, 286
and OCOG, 297
and supply chain management, 232–33, 234, 235, 236
and vigilance plans, 233–34
fraud, 210–11, 238, 240, 292–93, 296
free enterprise, 123–24
Friedman, Thomas, 15, 18–19

Gak-gyu, Choi, 130–31
Gangneung, 151
Gangwon, 130–31, 132–33, 151
and governor, 132
and Province, 130–31, 132–33
Garcia, Michael, 209–10
Garcia Report, 207, 208, 209–11
GDP, 124–25
and real GDP, 172
gender equality, 45–46, 257
Gender Equality Action Plan, 253–54
General Assembly Declaration, 48
General Comment 18 of the UN Human Rights Committee, 278
genocide, 49–50
geopolitics, 4
Germany, 7, 10, 11–12, 14, 130, 146–47, 208, 229
and Berlin, 10
and Berlin Wall, 13
and East Germany, 12, 130
and German educational system, 7–8
and Hamburg, 19–20
and Munich, 11–12, 19–20
and Munich organizers, 11–12
and West Germany, 11–13
and West German Flag, 11–12
Geun-hye, Park, 146
gift-giving, 121, 125, 126–28, 142–43
and holidays, 143
gigantism, 19
Global Reporting Initiative (GRI Standards), 254, 263–64
globalization, 9, 13–16, 17–19, 20–21, 24–25, 44, 71–72, 153
Globalization and Its Discontents, 14
Good Practices Guide, 240, 241–42
governance, 13, 14, 17–19, 20, 21, 29, 31, 34, 36
and abuses, 5–6

and global standards, 8–9, 13–14
and legacy, 26, 27, 287
and reform, 4–5, 25–26, 31, 32
government declaration, 308–9
Great Britain, 9, 10, 11, 12–13, 60–61, 170–71
Great Depression, 170–71
Greece
and Athens, 9
and Greeks, 7
and Greek City-States, 7
and Greek Games, 7
Grondona, Julio, 210–11
Group of States Against Corruption (GRECO), 63–64
and Evaluation Team, 63–64
Group of 8 (G8), 14
Group of 20 (G20), 14
Guardian, The, 193
guided capitalism, 123–24
guiding principle 13, 253
Gulf Cooperation Council, 174
Guttmann, Allen, 8

Haiti, 50
Halphen, Eric, 235
Hamad Port and International Airport, 174–75, 211–12
Hammam, Mohammed Bin, 207
Hammurabi, 71–72
and Code of Hammurabi, 71–72
Hanjin Heavy Industries, 151–52
Harvard, 57–58
Hayes, Graeme, 29–30
Hee-jun, Chung, 132–33
Henkin, Louis, 47
high-speed railway, 151
Hitler, Adolf, 10–11, 30
Hodler, Marc, 22, 23–24
Holland, 210
Holocaust, 47
Holt, Richard, 27
Horne, John, 30
host city, 316–17, 319, 322, 323, 335, 337, 339, 340
and Anti-Corruption Clause of the Host City Contract, 296, 303–4, 306–7
and contract, 271, 272–74, 277–78, 279, 282, 285, 288–89, 291, 292, 295, 296, 297, 302–3
and contract compliance, 286, 292, 296, 298–99, 302–4
and Contract Operational Requirements, 279, 285, 288, 300–1
and declaration, 308–9
and discrimination, 278, 307–8
and human rights legacy, 297, 298–300
and intergovernmental organizations, 287, 294–95
and National Olympic Committee (NOC), 274, 276
and Paris, France, 271, 286
host country, 3, 13–14, 19, 25–26, 30–31, 33–34, 119, 316, 325–26, 328, 332–33, 334, 337, 340
and corruption, 3–4, 21
and governance, 168
and organizers, 25–26
and reforms, 25–26
human development, 179–81
human rights
and abuses, 6, 21
and clause, 337–36
and compliance, 68–69, 322, 325
and controversies, 6–7
and conventions, 13
and laws, 33, 35, 45, 55, 64, 319, 326–27
and movement, 44, 56, 64–65
and policies, 34, 35, 37, 318, 321, 324, 328
and practices, 33, 34, 35, 37
and standards, 13
and violations, 24, 35
Human Rights Commission, 47–48
Human Rights Council, 272, 287, 296, 300
Human Rights Watch, 183, 184, 186–87, 195–96
and Building a Better World Cup, 184
and Report, 192, 194
human trafficking, 234
Hungary, 9
Huntington, Samuel, 44
Hyundai, 124–25, 151
and Engineering, 151

illicit enrichment, 59
Il-sung, Kim, 122–23
impeach, 60–61, 146, 148–49

Improper Solicitation and Graft Act, 135, 136
Incheon International Airport, 151
India, 14, 15–16, 50, 168–69
Indonesia, 14
industrialization, 122–23, 124, 125
infrastructure, 88–89, 170–71, 178–79, 191, 200, 211
Inter-American Convention Against Corruption (1996), 63–64
intergovernmental organizations, 16, 17–18
internal legacies, 317, 318, 320*f*
internal reforms, 316–17, 320, 322–24, 325, 326
International
  and Chamber of Commerce Rules on Combating Corruption, 68–69
  and Federation, 24
  and Football, 170
  and Government Agencies, 169–70
  and Human Rights Agreements, 285
  and Human Rights Conventions, 167–68
  and Human Rights Laws, 285, 288
  and Human Rights Regulations, 285
  and Investment, 175
  and Organization for Standardization, 68–69
  and Skating Federation, 150
  and Sports Federations, 19
  and Trade Union Confederation (ITUC), 169, 197–98
International anti-corruption agreements, 293–94
International Bill of Human Rights, 54–55, 233, 276, 277, 279
International Code of Conduct for Private Security Service Providers, 301–2
International Convention on the Elimination of All Forms of Racial Discrimination (1965), 49–50
International Covenant on Civil and Political Rights (ICCPR), 48, 51, 64, 216–17, 298–99
International Covenant on Economic, Social, and Cultural Rights (ICESCR), 48, 49, 51, 64, 216–17, 298–99
International Federation of Consulting Engineers, 301–2
International Labour Organization (ILO), 5–6, 17–18, 50–51, 54–55, 168, 169, 181, 183, 193, 195, 197–99, 200, 202, 203–4, 205, 206–7, 214, 216–17, 287
  and Code of Practice on Safety and Health in Construction, 301–2
  and Declaration on Fundamental Principles and Rights at Work (FPRW) (1998), 50–51, 54–55, 231–32, 298–99
International Olympic Committee (IOC), 3, 9, 10, 11–12, 13, 16–18, 19, 21–24, 25–26, 30–32, 35, 36, 37, 43, 131, 132, 150, 229–30, 238–39, 258–59, 315, 320, 321, 325, 328–29, 331, 332, 335–36, 339
  and 2000 Commission, 24
  and 2002 Legacy Convention, 7, 19–20, 30–31
  and anti-corruption framework, 289, 310
  and Basic Principles of Governance, 336
  and Basic Universal Principles of Good Governance of the Olympic and Sports Movement, 288–89, 291, 296
  and bribery, 21–22
  and by-laws, 19
  and Chief Ethics and Compliance Officer, 290
  and Chief Ethics and Compliance Hotline, 290
  and Code of Ethics, 288–89, 291, 296
  and Contractual Clause, 292
  and Ethics Commission, 290
  and Host Agreement, 273, 286
  and Host-Country-Anti-Corruption Requirements, 271–73, 289, 302–3
  and Human Rights Reforms, 271–72, 310
  and International Symposium, 19
  and Legacy, 33
  and legal obligations, 273–74
  and model Host City Contract, 53–54, 68–69, 315–16, 337, 338–39

and Model Host-City Human Rights Clause, 274, 275, 276, 278, 279–80, 282, 285, 287, 288, 291, 293–94, 295, 297
and Olympic Games Study Commission, 19
and rules, 19
and sexual orientation, 277
and supplier code, 283, 295, 296
and third parties, 283
International Olympic Truce Centre, 7
and Director, 7
International Organization for Standardization (ISO) 20121, 254, 294–95, 308, 309, 333
International Trade Union Confederation (ITUC), 183–84
Iran, 45–46, 172–74
Iraq, 71–72, 208
Islam
and culture, 15
and law, 66–67
and militant, 15
Islamic Museum of Art, 177
Israel, 173–74
and Israeli Olympic Athletes, 11–12
and trade office, 176
Italian National Action Plan, 259, 261
Italy, 14, 37, 177–78, 249–51, 258–61, 287
and Rome, 14

Jae-in, Moon, 150
Jae-soo, Yoo, 149–50
Jae-yong, Lee, 152
Japan, 11–12, 13–14, 15–16, 122–23, 124, 130–31, 208
and colonial rule, 122
and military, 123
and Nagano, 21–22, 130–31
and occupation, 122–23
and Tokyo, 11–12
Jefferson, Thomas, 45
jeitinho brasileiro, 85, 86–88
jeopdae, 127, 142–43
Jeux Olimpiques Scandinaves, 7
Jin-sun, Kim, 130–31, 132
Johnson, David, 22–23, 24
Jordan, 173–74
Joseon, 120–22
and Dynasty, 120–22
and Society, 121
journalist, 127, 136–38, 143, 176–77, 341
Journalists Association of Korea, 138
JTBC cable TV Network, 147
Judicial Agreement in the Public Interest (CJIPs), 237–38
Justice, 167–68, 194, 197, 198–99
Justice Ministry, 147
Justice Party, 149

kafala, 5–6
and sponsorship system, 167–68, 185–86, 193, 194, 195, 197–99
Kamrava, Mehran, 173–74
Kang, Sungyong, 104–5
Karamichas, John, 29–30
KCC Engineering, 151
Keon-hee, Lee, 132
Key Olympic Actors and Their Internal Reforms, 317*f*
kickback, 59
Kim, John, 22–23
Kim Young-ran Act, 73, 120, 135–38, 139, 140–42, 143–44, 145, 149–50
and joint penal provision of the Kim Young-ran Act, 140
Klitgaard, Robert, 60–61
Konecke, Thomas, 28
Korea
and Assistant Foreign Minister, 133
and Bar Association, 138, 139
and Congress, 136, 137–38, 139, 140
and Constitutional Court, 138, 139, 140, 146–47, 148–49
and Customs Service, 152
and Korean Air, 150
and Korean Disease, 128
and Korean Peninsula, 122–23, 130, 131, 132
and Korean Sport & Olympic Committee (KOC), 130–31, 132
and Korean War, 119–20, 121–22, 125, 148
and Korean Won (KRW), 127–28, 134–35, 142–43, 145, 148, 151–52
Krakow, Poland, 19–20

K-Sports, 146–47, 151
Kuala Lumpur, 178–79
Kuk, Cho, 149–50
Kun-hee, Lee, 150

labor, 167–69, 179, 192, 199–200, 208–9, 215–16
  and abuses, 5, 25–26
  and reform, 5–6, 25–26
  and rights, 5–6, 8–9, 25–26, 37
La Mont, Alfredo, 22–23
law of nature, 46, 64–65
Le Cercle de la Compliance, 274
Lebanon, 176
Lee, Jay Y., 147
legacy
  and accidental, 27, 35, 37
  and beliefs and behavior, 28, 36
  and cube, 28
  and facets, 28–29, 33, 36
  and intentional, 37
  and literature, 26, 27–28, 32–33, 34–35, 36
  and one-dimensional, 36–37
  and planned, 25–26, 27, 28, 32, 35, 36
  and policy and governance, 28, 29, 36
  and proactive, 26, 36–37
  and reactive, 26, 36–37
  and scholarship, 19–20, 26–27, 28, 29, 31–32
  and skills, knowledge, and network, 28, 29, 33, 36
  and two-dimensional, 36, 37
Legacy Strategic Approach: Moving Forward, 31–32, 33
Leopkey, Becca, 29
Leoz, Nicholas, 210–11
LG, 124–25
liberalism, 15
Libya, 174–75, 176, 235
local organizing committee (LOC), 33–34
Locke, John, 46–47, 64–66
Lorraine, 7–8
Lotte, 146, 148, 152
  and Corporate Social Responsibility Team, 152
  and Group, 148
Lula da Silva, Luiz Inacio, 89–90, 108
Lviv, Ukraine, 19–20

MacAloon, J.J., 26–27
Macao, 172
Madison, James, 65–66, 71–72
Magna Carta of 1215, 46, 47–48
Making Globalization Work, 14
Maldives, 174–75
Map to Success Strategy, 253–54
Marxism, 66
Mauritania, 174–75
media, 127, 132–33, 136–38, 143–44, 145, 146, 151–52, 174–75, 176, 177, 179, 183, 197, 209, 210, 340
  and company, 136–37
  and education, 137
  and internet, 62, 138
  and mass, 127
medical insurance, 169, 190
megasports
  and bribery, 208, 209, 211
  and corruption, 151, 152
  and globalization, 9, 13–14, 15–16
  and governance, 4, 9, 13, 20–21, 172–73, 207
  and human rights legacy, 3, 170, 171, 183, 188, 206–7
  and ideals, 9
  and legacy, 5–6, 13, 20–21
  and movement, 24–25, 26
  and police, 212–13
  and reform, 167
  and stakeholders, 13, 18, 37
  and West's domination of standards, 168
mega sporting events (MSEs), 3, 5–6, 13–14, 18–19, 24, 32–33, 35–36, 44, 50, 51–52, 55, 56, 68–69, 167, 169–70, 178, 182, 212–13, 214, 217
  and governance, 9, 16, 18–19
Mesopotamia, 71–72
Mexico, 14, 37, 249–51, 261–64
Middle Age, 71–72
Middle East, 13–14, 66–67, 167, 173–74, 176–77, 178–79
  and Middle Eastern, 168, 178
migrant workers, 3, 5, 25, 167, 168–69, 179–81, 182, 184, 189, 193–98, 200, 201–2, 204, 215, 216–17
  and accommodations, 169, 185, 186, 187, 189, 190–91, 193, 194, 196, 197–98, 201, 203–5, 215

and air ticket, 206, 215
and collective bargaining, 185, 194, 197
and contractors, 188–89, 190–91, 196, 203, 215–16
and debts, 184–85, 193, 194–95, 197–98
and deportation, 216–17
and employment conditions, 190
and employment contracts, 169, 189, 190–91
and exploitation, 184–85, 197–98
and fees, 188–89, 194–95, 197–98, 203, 206
and freedom of movement, 190
and grievance, 189, 191, 197–98, 201–2, 213–14, 216–17
and health, 180–81, 185, 188, 190–91, 192, 194, 196, 200, 204, 214, 215–16
and illiteracy, 195–96
and inspections, 186, 188, 194, 196, 197–99, 200, 201–2, 205, 215
and language, 186, 188–89, 195–96, 197, 215
and leave, 185, 190
and living conditions, 188, 195, 205, 213–14
and medical care, 189, 190–91, 196, 204, 215–16
and minimum wage, 185, 192, 203–4, 215–17
and occupational deaths, 185
and occupational injuries, 185, 190
and passports, 185–86, 190, 193, 195, 196, 197–98, 216–17
and recruitment, 184–85, 188–89, 194–96, 213–14, 215
and representation, 213–14
and retaliation, 189, 195, 216–17
and safety, 190–91, 192, 194, 196, 198–99, 200, 204, 213–14, 215–16
and termination, 185
and transportation, 190, 191
and unionization, 185, 197
and wages, 176, 185, 186, 188, 189, 190–91, 194, 195, 196, 197–98, 203–4, 213–14, 216–17
militarism, 11
minimum wage, 167–68, 185, 192, 203–4, 215–17
Ministry of Culture, Sports, and Tourism, 151
Mir, 146–47
modernization, 123, 124, 125
money laundering, 63–64, 72, 210–11
Moro, Sergio, 107–8
Morocco, 173–74
Muhammad (sunnah), 67
Muju, 130–31
multinational corporations (MNCs), 141–42
multi-sport Arab Games, 178
Muslim, 242
Myung-bak, Lee, 150

Naim, Moises, 56–57, 61
Nakheel Landscape Company, 206
nationalism, 12
National Contact Point (NCP), 200, 201
National Multi-Year Plan to Fight Corruption, 239–40
National Olympic Committee (NOC), 19, 24, 239, 258, 275, 276, 278, 284, 286, 287, 291, 292, 293–94, 315–16, 318–19, 321–22, 323, 326, 328, 337, 339–40
National Police Agency, 143–44
National Public Radio, 22
national sports federation, 323, 326
natural gas, 172
natural minerals, 172–73
Nauru, 49–50
Nazis, 10
and Aryan supremacy, 10–11
and Germany, 10
and government, 10
and propaganda, 10–11
negligence, 134, 139–40
Nepal, 168–69, 185, 193
nepotism, 59
Netherlands, 9
new norm, 332
New York Times, The, 22, 23
New Zealand, 37, 249–58, 328–29, 333
and human rights commission, 257–58
NGO, 37, 47–48, 52, 57–58, 129
Nike, 52
Nolan, Justine, 56
non-aligned nations, 130

nondiscrimination, 276, 277–78
non-public officials, 136
no-objection certificates, 167–68
North America, 13–14
North Atlantic Treaty Organization (NATO), 176
North Korea, 12, 15, 122, 131
nulla peona sine lege, 140
Nussli, 151–52
Nye, Joseph, 28, 57–58, 60–61, 173

oil, 170–71
Olympia, 7
Olympic Actors' External Influence, 324*f*
Olympic Charter, 258–59
Olympic Games
 and Agenda 2020, 332
 and anti-corruption compliance system, 239–40
 and anti-corruption policies, 288, 291, 295
 and Athletes' Village, 178
 and Basic Universal Principles of Good Governance of the Olympic and Sports Movement, 289, 296
 and bribery, 4
 and charter, 16, 19
 and code of ethics, 289, 296
 and Compliance Task Force, 274, 279–80, 292, 293–94, 335
 and corruption, 23–24
 and Delivery Authority (SOLIDEO), 316
 and governance, 24, 31
 and history, 277
 and human rights reforms, 230, 239–40
 and ideals, 12
 and inadequate third-party management, 297
 and legacy, 3, 19, 28, 31, 32
 and movement, 10, 11, 32–33, 55
 and movement for anti-corruption, 287
 and nondiscrimination, 276
 and stakeholders, 29–30
 and Study Centre, 315
 and Summer Games, 11
 and values, 33
 and Winter Games, 11, 21–22
Olympism, 19
 and the Fundamental Principles, 19, 274
Oman, 173–74
ombudsperson offices, 55
Oracle of Delphi, 7
Organisation for Economic Co-operation and Development (OECD), 55, 62–64, 68–69, 72, 92, 128–29, 135, 143–44, 149–50, 197, 199, 201, 214, 234–35, 260, 287
 and Anti-Bribery Convention, 128–29, 135, 143–44, 149–50, 293–94
 and convention, 62–64
 and Good Practice Guidance on Internal Controls, Ethics, and Compliance, 68–69
 and Guidelines for Multinational Enterprises (Guidelines), 199–201
 and National Contact Points, 284
Organizing Committee for the Olympic Games (OCOG), 19, 35, 68, 69, 151–52, 239, 250, 258, 259, 261, 273, 274, 275, 276, 278, 279–80, 281, 284, 286, 287, 288, 289, 291, 292, 293–94, 295, 296, 297, 315–17, 318, 319, 320–22, 323, 324–25, 326–27, 328–29, 337, 338–39
 and Sustainable Sourcing Code, 296
Osario, Carlos Roberto, 88
Oslo, Norway, 19–20
Owens, Jesse, 10–11

Pacific, 17–18
paid annual leave, 169
Palau, 49–50
Palestine, 176
 and Palestinian terrorist group, 11–12
Parent, Milena, 29
Paris, France, 315, 325
 and 2024 Code of Ethics, 240, 241–42
 and 2024 Organizing Committee, 240, 241–42, 317
 and domestic anti-corruption, 239–40
 and environmental legacy, 239
 and human rights reforms, 230
 and social inclusion, 239
Paris St. Germain, 175–76, 178
Parquet National Financier (PNF), 237–38
passport confiscation, 167–68, 169, 185–86, 196, 197–98, 216–17

Performance Standards of the International Finance Corporation, 301–2
Persian Gulf, 173
petroleum, 170–71, 172
Philippines, 168–69
Pigeon Engineering, 206
political, 122, 123, 125, 126–27, 132–33, 146, 147–49, 150, 152–53, 332, 336
 and corruption, 146, 150
 and legacy, 10–11, 28, 29–31
 and opposition groups, 147
 and parties, 126–27
 and refugee, 17
Polley, Martin, 27
polycentric governance model, 53–54
poomasi, 126
populist movements, 13–14
Portugal, 210
postwar era, 47–48, 62, 71–72
Preuss, Holger, 27–28
Professional Footballers Australia (PFA), 255–56
Progress Report on the Enforcement of the OECD Convention, 129
protect, respect, and remedy framework, 52
provincial education offices, 137–38
Prussians, 7–8
public
 and institution, 137–38, 146
 and official, 127, 128–29, 135–37, 138–39, 140, 141–44, 145
Public Service Ethics Act, 128–29, 136
Putin, Vladimir, 25, 30
Pyeongchang, 18, 119–20, 130–31, 132–33, 150–51, 152
 and organizing committee (POCOG), 150–52

Qaddafi, 176
Qatar, 5–6, 13–14, 15–16, 20, 25–26, 27, 31, 34, 35–36, 37, 44, 167–82, 183–88, 189–90, 191–96, 197–99, 200–7, 208, 209–14, 216–17, 230–31, 241, 242, 271, 300–1, 303–4, 306, 325–26, 328–29, 331, 332, 335, 341
 and 2022 Strategic Plan, 169, 179, 181–82
 and Accessibility Forum, 211–12
 and Airway, 175–76, 177–78
 and branding strategy, 175
 and corruption, 207
 and Culture Ministry, 176–77
 and domestic currency reserve, 174–75
 and Domestic Workers' Law, 216–17
 and economy, 174–75
 and Education City, 175–76, 177, 187, 206, 215
 and emir, 174–75
 and Foundations Worker Standards, 183
 and government, 176–77, 192, 194, 198–99, 200–1, 202, 207
 and independence, 170–71
 and Investment Authority, 175–76, 178
 and labor, 197–99
 and labor inspection, 196, 197–98
 and Labor Law, 184–85, 190, 196, 211
 and labor standards, 181–82, 187
 and Law No. 15 of 2010, 196
 and Laws, 188, 189, 191–92, 196, 197–98, 203, 204–6
 and liquidity, 174–75
 and Masters golf tournament, 178
 and migrant workers, 184
 and Ministry of Culture and Sport, 211–12
 and Ministry of Information, 176
 and Ministry of Labor, 167–68, 185, 186, 191–92, 198–99, 202, 203–4, 205
 and National Development Strategy, 179, 181–82, 187
 and national government, 169, 183
 and National Vision 2030, 171, 179–82, 187
 and News Agency, 174–75
 and open, 178
 and population, 171
 and public education system, 177
 and public health, 180–81
 and reforms, 211, 214
 and sheikhdom, 170–71
 and Strategic Plan, 187–88
 and Tourism Agency, 211–12
 and universities, 177
 and Vision 2030, 174
Qur'an, 67

Racial Discrimination, 49–50
racial equality, 45–46
racketeering, 210–11
Ramasastry, Anita, 56
RAND–Qatar Policy Institute, 177
recruitment procedures, 169
remediation, 54–55, 70–71, 75
reporter, 127, 137–38, 141, 146, 147
Republic of Korea, 122–23, 138–39
respondeat superior, 98
Rhee, Syngman, 122–23
Robinson, Mark, 60
Roman Empire, 7
Roosevelt, Eleanor, 47–48
Roosevelt, Franklin Delano, 10–11
Roosevelt, Theodore, 7–8
Rose, Cecily, 63
Rose–Ackerman, Susan, 60–61
Rouseff, Dilma, 90, 106
Ruggie, John, 52–54, 55, 214
Russia, 9, 13–14, 15–16, 20–21, 25–26, 30, 44, 57, 167, 171, 271, 328–29
  and Russian oligarchs, 25
Ruta, Dina, 27

Salt Lake City, 20–24
  and bid committee, 21–23
  and organizing committee, 22, 30
Sam, David, 23
Samsung, 124–25, 132, 146, 147–48, 150, 152
  and C&T Corporation, 147–48
  and Group, 132
Sanctions Committee, 236–37
Sapin II, 229–30, 234–38, 239, 240, 294
Sarkozy, Nicolas, 235
Saudi Arabia, 14, 44, 47–48, 49, 173–75
Scheu, Anja, 28
security training, 211
Sewol Ferry, 119–20, 134–35, 136
sexual orientation, 277
sharia, 67
Simmons, David, 22–23
SK Group, 148
slush funds, 146–47
Sochi, 132, 328
social
  and contract, 46, 65
  and development, 179–81
  and legacy, 18, 31
Social Charter, 241–42
soft law, 45, 56–57
solicitation, 125, 135–36, 138–39, 140, 141–43
  and of a public official, 135, 138–39, 140
SOLIDEO, 240
Soon-sil, Choi, 146–48, 151
South Africa, 9, 13–14, 21, 47–48, 171
South America, 73, 178–79
South Korea, 4–6, 12, 13–14, 15–16, 25–26, 27, 31, 32, 35, 37, 72–73, 119–21, 122–25, 126–29, 130–32, 133–34, 139, 140, 146–50, 151, 152, 153, 208
  and Ambassador to Vietnam, 149–50
  and bid for the 2018 Olympics, 150
  and Coast Guard, 134
  and constitution, 140, 148–49
  and economy, 123–24
  and government, 122–23, 133
  and Jeju Island, 134
  and Jeonbuk Province, 130–31
  and judiciary, 150
  and members of the International Olympic Committee, 132
  and members of the Korean Sport & Olympic Committee, 132
  and Olympic Bidding Committee, 130–31
  and parliament, 147
  and provinces, 132
  and Seoul, 122, 129, 132, 151, 152
  and Seoul Central District Prosecutor's Office, 129
  and society, 127
  and Southern Island of Jindo, 134
  and sports teams, 124–25
  and Wonju, 151
South/North Korea Joint Winter Olympics, 131
South Korea, 230
Soviet Union, 11, 12–13, 15, 47–48, 71–72, 122, 130
  and collapse, 61
Spain, 9, 177–78, 210
Spirit of the Laws, 46

sponsor, 144, 147–48, 150–51, 152, 336, 338–39
and sponsorship, 144
sporting legacy, 18, 31
sports tourism, 132
Sri Lanka, 168–69
stadiums, 212
state
and capitalism, 15
and capture, 60
state of nature, 64–65
state-owned enterprises, 98–99
Stewart, Potter, 57
Stiglitz, Joseph, 14
strange power of Qatar, 173
Strategic Council, 236–37
subtle power, 173
Sudan, 50, 176
Suez, 170–71
Sunday Times, The, 209–10
Supreme Committee (SC) for Delivery and Legacy, 168, 170, 171, 172, 179, 180–82, 183, 187–89, 191–92, 193, 194, 201–3, 205–7, 208–9, 211–12, 213–14, 215–16, 217, 298, 306, 328–29
and Legacy Framework, 179, 182
Supreme Federal Tribunal of Brazil, 89–90
sustainability, 30–31, 252–53, 254, 262
and Sustainability and Legacy Commission, 19
Sweden, 7, 9
and Stockholm, 19–20
Switzerland, 9, 151–52, 197, 234

Taiwan, 12
tax evasion, 125, 148, 150
Teachout, Zephyr, 65–66
Technical Cooperation Programme, 183, 197, 198–99, 203–4, 205
Technip, 235
Teixiera, Ricardo, 210–11
Temer, Michel, 107
Termarii, Reynard, 210
terrorism, 72
Teyseer Security Services, 206
The World Is Flat, 15
Third Reich, 10, 11, 30
Tin Can Town, 24–25
tokkap, 127, 128
Toohey, Kristine, 30
TOTAL, 235
Transparency International, 57–58, 68–69, 129, 172–73, 235
and Corruption Perception Index, 129
transportation, 169, 190, 191, 211–12
Tunisia, 173–74
Turkey, 14, 170–71, 173–74

UNICEF's Children's Rights and Business Principles, 301–2
Union Carbide Chemical Leak, 52
United Arab Emirates, 170–71, 173–75
United Kingdom (UK), 14, 69, 73, 170–71, 229, 336
and anti-corruption compliance movement, 236–37, 238
and Bribery Act, 141, 145, 294, 306
and Ministry of Justice, 68–69, 294–95
and the Modern Slavery Act, 234
United Nations (UN), 5–6, 16, 17, 47–48, 49–50, 51–52, 55, 57, 68–69, 176, 197, 287
and Convention Against Corruption (UNCAC), 57, 59, 62–64, 292, 293
and General Assembly, 49–50
and Global Compact, 294–95
and Global Development, 180–81
and Guiding Principles on Business and Human Rights (UNGPS), 8–9, 51–52, 53–56, 68–69, 199–201, 232–33, 251, 262, 272, 273, 274–75, 278–79, 280–85, 287, 294, 295, 297–99, 300–1, 302–3, 304, 305
and Human Rights Council, 193–94, 294–95
and Millennium Goals, 180–81
and Office of Drugs and Crime (UNODC), 68–69, 304, 309–10
and Office on Drugs and Crime Strategy for Safeguarding Against Corruption Handbook, 263–64
and Security Council, 176
and Special Rapporteur on Human Rights, 194
and Special Representative of the Secretary-General (SRSG), 55–56

United Nations (UN) (*cont.*)
and UNGPs Compliance, 272, 279, 281–82, 296, 302–3
and Women's Empowerment Principles, 301–2
and Working Group on Business and Human Rights, 287
United States (US), 7–8, 9, 12–13, 14, 23–24, 37, 44, 48, 49, 50, 60–61, 69, 71–72, 122, 124–25, 176, 207, 208, 249–51, 261–64, 316
and Agency for International Development, 57–58
and anti-corruption compliance movement, 236–37, 238
and Attorney's Office, 22–24
and Boston, 19–20
and Declaration, 231
and Department of Justice (DOJ), 68–69, 72–73, 109, 210–11, 235, 294–95
and Department of State, 192
and Foreign Corrupt Practices Act, 294, 306
and government, 122
and government agencies, 23–24
and military, 124
and Olympic Committee, 22–23
and Sentencing Guidelines, 72–73
and Supreme Court, 57, 61
and Washington, DC, 22
United States Soccer Federation (USSF), 256–57
United States Women's National Soccer Team (USWNT), 255–57
Universal Declaration of Human Rights, 298–99
Universal Exposition (Expo), 258
Urban Legacy, 18, 31

Vanocur, Chris, 22
Vanocur, Sander, 22
Venezuela, 60–61
Vienna, Austria, 19–20
Vietnam, 149–50
visually impaired, 212
voluntary disclosure, 70–71

wage protection system (WPS), 167–68, 203–4, 205, 216–17
Warner, Jack, 210
Welch, Thomas, 22–23, 24
Western Europe, 13–14
wheelchair, 212
whistleblower, 146, 149–50
Widec Sports, 146–47
Workers' Party, 89–90
workers support and insurance fund, 167–68, 203–4, 216–17
Workers' Welfare Charter, 187–88
Workers' Welfare Forums (WWF), 169, 188–89, 190–91, 203, 205, 216–17
Workers' Welfare Office (WWO), 191
Workers' Welfare Standards (WWS), 169, 181, 183, 187–92, 202, 203–6, 213–14
World Bank, 57–58, 60, 68–69, 172
and Group Integrity Compliance Guidelines, 68–69
World Com, 72
World Cup
and host, 174–75
and hosting rights, 173, 202
and Human Rights Advisory Board, 200, 201–2
and organizing body, 168
and preparations, 172
and projects, 169
and security, 212–13
and stadiums, 24–25, 178–79
World Economic Forum Partnering Against Corruption Initiative Principles for Countering Bribery, 68–69
World Health Organization, 17
World Trade Center, 72
and Terrorist Attack, 72
World Trade Organization, 175–76
World War Era, 11–12, 13
World War I, 6–7, 9–10, 11–12
World War II, 4, 6–7, 9, 11, 12, 15–16, 47–48, 49–50, 52, 56–57, 62, 71–72, 170–71

Worldwide Governance Indicators (WGI), 172–73

Yahoo!, 52
Yale Law School, 60
Yang-ho, Cho, 151–52
Yemen, 174–75, 208
  and Government, 176
Yoo-su, Cho, 151
Young-ran, Kim, 136
  and Former Supreme Court Justice, 136
Young-sam, Kim, 128
Young-sun, Park, 132
Young-tae, Ko, 146–47

Zakaria, Fareed, 14
Zeus Olympios, 7
Zika virus, 57